PSY CHO LOG Y FOR YOU

SOL GORDON
Professor of
Child and Family Studies
Syracuse University
New York

OXFORD BOOK COMPANY

A Division of William H. Sadlier, Inc.
New York   Chicago   Los Angeles

To the Teacher

When I discuss psychology with a high school or college student, one question that is bound to come up is, "Why are introductory psychology courses so boring?"

Over the years, this question has made quite an impression on me. Also, I began to think back on my own absurd experiences many years ago with the course known as "Psych I." The idea entered my mind of how much fun it would be to write my own book — a book that would be "right" for today's young people in secondary schools and colleges. It would be "right" because it would focus on the things that really interest and concern them. It would go light on rats, pigeons, and reflexes; it would go heavy on the processes and problems of personality and interpersonal relations that are the very texture of living in the modern world.

This book is the outcome of that longstanding sense of dissatisfaction with conventional texts, and of my hope that I might be able to do something about it. The selection of topics, the method of exposition, the documentation, the language all represent what I feel, on the basis of long experience, are most suitable for students taking an introductory psychology course, whether in the 11th or 12th year of a secondary school, in junior college, or in the first year of a four-year college. It will be noted that not everything in the book is "contemporary" or "up to the minute." There is much that is rooted in past experience and in the accumulated knowledge and insights of great thinkers of earlier generations. But the main thrust is toward the developments, needs, and concerns of the 1970's — whether it be sex and morality, youth alienation, Women's Lib, population pressures, encounter groups, street crime, drug abuse, the counter-culture, and many, many others. (The table of contents and the index will provide a better idea of the range of content.)

When I thought of writing "my own book," many years ago, I made up my mind that I would emblazon the preface with a "warning" something like the following:

Please, don't "force" every student to read every chapter, or to memorize anything in any chapter.

I think that is still pertinent. Not everything is important or interesting to every student. A few chapters may be pretty heavy going

III

for some. But I honestly believe that *every* young person can find much here that *is* meaningful and valuable for him at this stage of his life.

The real joy of this course is realized when the teacher can stimulate the student to do, think, feel, and experience the idea that life is not just a single meaning. It is above all an *opportunity* to have many meaningful experiences. And when this is made clear, the courageous teacher may be able to communicate the further idea that all really meaningful experiences in life involve controversy and risk-taking.

ACKNOWLEDGMENTS

Many people helped me to write this book. I'm glad to say that most of them were either students or young friends. They helped with research, with the preparation of the manuscript, with tough criticism, and with fruitful ideas. I am grateful to all of them. In the final analysis, however, I hold myself responsible for everything in this book — including the mistakes, inadequacies, and other weaknesses that are bound to be uncovered. I hope that teachers and students will write me about them. I hope they will also write me about areas of disagreement and will offer suggestions for improving later editions.

The people who were the most helpful to me were Roger Conant and Kathleen Everly. Other important contributors included Rodger Kamenitz, Brian Gardam, Peggy Johnson, Paula Eigenfeld, Eugenia Abrams, and Nina Plescia. Others are acknowledged in the text. One person of my generation was also enormously helpful: the creative mind of Milton Elson, Senior Editor of the Oxford Book Company, is in ample evidence throughout the body of this book.

But most of all, this book is for my wife, Judith.

S. G.

Contents

● ●

Youth in a Changing World

Psychology and Social Problems

Psychology and Education

PSYCHOLOGY FOR YOU

PSYCHOLOGY
What Is It?
What's in It for You?

● ●

"The proper study of mankind is man."
— ALEXANDER POPE

What Is Psychology?

Psychology is the study of the mind.

The word psychology comes from two Greek words: *psyche,* meaning "mind" or "soul"; and *logos,* meaning "theory" or "science."

Presumably any conscious person is aware that he has a mind, but the concept is not as simple as one might think. Indeed, there is little general agreement among authorities as to just what it means. To avoid this ambiguity, the following definition is sometimes used:

Psychology is the study of behavior.

Both definitions are acceptable, but unfortunately neither tells us very much. As a matter of fact, once we go beyond the simple terms of these definitions, psychologists are far from fully agreed on just what their field of inquiry is. We can, however, recognize two basic orientations among psychologists, which may be designated as "scientific" and "philosophical."

Applying the Scientific Method to Psychology

Many psychologists feel that the study of psychology need not be essentially different from the study of the "hard" sciences, such as chemistry and physics. These psychologists, many of whom are called

1

behaviorists, believe that it is possible to pursue psychology as an exact scientific discipline. They do their best to apply the scientific method to the study of human behavior. This usually means in practice that they carry out scientifically controlled experiments to get exact information about behavior. They frequently use laboratory animals, including rats, monkeys, and dogs, as well as human subjects, in their investigations. They place emphasis on precise measurement, often employing sophisticated apparatus for this purpose. They devote much attention to *physiology* — the study of the physical functioning of the body. Obviously, this aspect of psychology is closely related to biology.

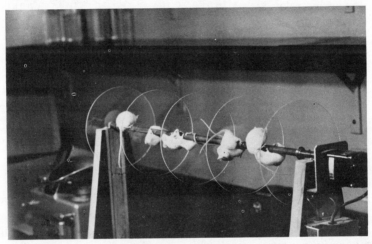

The white mice shown here are balancing on a turning rod in a medical laboratory. Scientists in this laboratory study the effects of drugs used for mental and emotional illnesses. The influence of the drugs on the behavior of mice may be an important clue to their possible value for humans.

Philosophically Oriented Psychology

Other psychologists believe that in order to get a fuller understanding of the scope of the human mind and the possibilities of human behavior, it is essential to become involved with the ideas of philosophy and especially ethics. By *ethics,* we mean the consideration of what is good or bad, right or wrong, useful (in human terms) or destructive. These distinctions and standards are not just theoretical. After all, it is argued, the way a person looks at the world and his concepts of right and wrong inevitably have a far-reaching effect on the way he *thinks* and *behaves.* But it must be acknowledged that these factors cannot be analyzed or measured by the tools and methods used, for example, to determine how long it takes a subject to react to a stimulus under certain conditions.

Philosophically oriented psychologists generally acknowledge the importance of the experimental approach to psychology, but they emphasize that *ideas* — which cannot be measured with a caliper, weighed on a scale, or analyzed in a test tube — are also valid areas of psychological study. This is *not* a rejection of the scientific method. Concepts such as imagination, creativity, and love are seemingly intangible, but they can still be investigated scientifically — that is, rationally and intelligently. Indeed, many psychologists feel that it is just such intangible and "unmeasurable" ideas that are most immediately and deeply useful to a person who is interested in understanding himself and his relationship to others.

At any rate, most psychologists believe that science, philosophy, and ethics *all* contribute to psychology — but which of these receives the greatest attention depends on the individual thinker. A few of the pioneers in psychology, notably Sigmund Freud and John B. Watson, have attempted to bridge the gap between physiology and philosophy, as applied to human behavior, but such attempts can never be satisfactory to everyone.

Psychology and Sociology

Psychology also interlocks closely with *sociology* — the study of *human group life* or *group relations*. It is easy to see why this is so. The individual does not function in a vacuum. What he does or does not do inevitably affects the behavior of many other people, and his own behavior in turn is influenced by that of many other people. Thus, we cannot hope to understand the psychology of a person unless we have some awareness of the social conditions within which he is living, and of the social problems that concern him and the other members of his group. Conversely, if you hope to deal intelligently with social problems, you must know something of individual human motivation and behavior patterns.

Psychology can help us to clarify and interpret such basic social issues of our times as war, crime, economic exploitation, prejudices against minority groups, sexual conflicts, drug abuse, the "generation gap," and many others. These matters will be discussed in the various chapters of this book. Perhaps you have already studied many of them elsewhere, but the point of view here will be distinctively that of the psychologist. For example, the chapter on the Women's Liberation movement will focus on twin concepts central to any study of psychology — *masculinity* and *femininity*. In fact, a large part of this book places psychology in the context of current social issues and trends.

The Idea of Growth

In this text, we shall not be primarily concerned with the "scientific" approach to psychology, in the narrow or specialized sense of the term. We shall focus our attention, rather, on *ideas* that will help you develop an understanding of yourself, both as an individual and as a social person relating to other people.

(However, you will also be presented here with a wide range of theory and with specific information relating to aspects of "scientific psychology." If you continue your study in this area, you will certainly want to consider courses and texts that offer what might be called the "behaviorist viewpoint.")

One of the key ideas that is stressed throughout this text because it is an essential aspect of all living is *growth*. This concept lies at the very heart of the study of psychology. We shall see that psychological knowledge and insights can help the individual to guide the development (growth) of his personality in desirable ways.

Since we live among other people, it is essential for each of us to gain an understanding of the feelings, needs, and motives of others. But you cannot hope to do this unless you first become *aware of yourself* — your own feelings, your own needs, your real reasons for doing or not doing things. In fact, an expanding awareness of yourself and of others is an essential part of the often painful process of *growing up*.

Unfortunately, many people stop growing up before they reach maturity, or become lost on the way. These people, as they get older, tend to become less sensitive to others, less willing to look objectively at their own behavior, and less likely to "lower their guard," so as to be open and honest with other people. Their mental defenses have locked them into patterns of thought and behavior that work *against* growth and improvement.

Professional Help for Emotional Problems

Often a person becomes aware that he is having difficulty in achieving a satisfactory understanding of himself and of others. Even if he can't identify the source of the problem, he knows that there *is* a difficulty because he is acutely unhappy. In this case, he may turn to professional therapists for help. Therapists in this field include:

▶ *Clinical psychologists,* normally with the Ph.D. degree.

▶ *Psychiatrists* — doctors of medicine (M.D.'s) specializing in mental or emotional disorders.

▶ *Social workers,* with the degree of M.S.W.

The kind of help these professionals render, which consists primarily of communicating verbally with the patient, is called *psychotherapy*. (Use of drugs and other similar treatments is limited to psychiatrists.)

But how do people get into the mental traps that require such professional attention? How is it that the mental and emotional growth of so many people (most of whom never receive any professional treatment) is snarled and stunted? You may already know the answer, and as a student of psychology, you will come to appreciate it more fully: Problems of perspective, insight, and behavior are almost always closely related to *love*. Love is a crucial force in human relationships, and therefore in emotional difficulties involved in those relationships.

Problems Connected with Love

Many people are confused about love, even though almost everyone thinks that he or she knows what it is. Some people concentrate their energies on finding and cultivating "romantic" love, without stopping to consider the possibilities of other love relationships. They have difficulty understanding how a person can love many individuals of both sexes, instead of maintaining an exclusive "man-woman" partnership.

Some people think that just about everything in life is bound to be "perfect" if they can only find the right individual with whom to be "truly in love." Such a relationship means, they think, that there will be no disagreements, and that each partner will always want to be with the other.

When such people become involved in a love affair, and problems arise, as is inevitable, they are likely to abandon the relationship with the thought (spoken or unspoken): "Love has died." Then they usually start to look for another person with whom to experience "the real thing." As a result, every relationship for them turns out to be disappointing, and they may end up believing that no one else is as sensitive and responsive as they are. Disappointment often arises when reality clashes with the romanticized version of love as a state of sweet, carefree, do-nothing ecstasy. Such a fantasy, sometimes fostered by the mass media, cannot work for real people who have real needs, problems, and feelings.

Sometimes young people who find a love affair "going sour" may feel that they can remedy things by getting married. This too is an illusion. Marriage is not a cure for any difficulties a couple may be having in their relationship. Indeed, it usually *magnifies* the problems because after marriage the man and woman will have to spend more time together, and the original tensions are bound to get worse. A couple must learn to work out their problems, and in order to do this, they must be able to express their feelings in a constructive way. It is foolish (*not* "romantic") to pretend that "nothing is wrong" when it is only too obvious to all concerned that there *are* genuine difficulties to be worked out. A young woman college student expressed this idea as follows:

> Most of the time, it is better to have a real fight and get things out in the open, than just to keep resentment inside of you and let it build up. Having a fight clears the air. This is something different and difficult for me to learn and follow because in my family, I never saw my parents fighting. My father just kept quiet for a week or two, and the whole situation was miserable. It would have been much better if he blew his stack and got things out in the open.

"Fighting" can be done constructively; neither partner need be hurt, and the relationship need not be weakened. As long as each partner cares for the other's feelings, an argument may sometimes be an effective way of resolving a problem. But if resentment is allowed to build up without being given expression, it often explodes into a knock-down, drag-out fight, with each party actively seeking to hurt

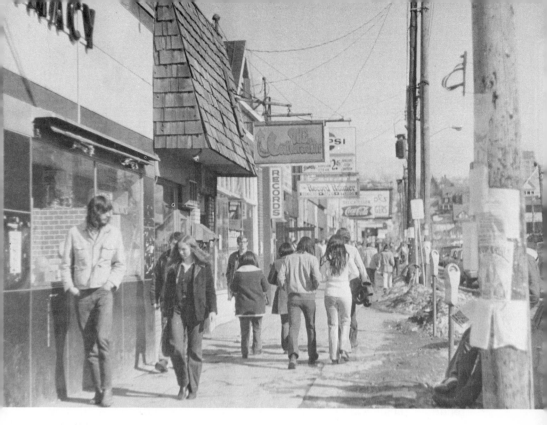

the other. As long as a quarrel remains rational and sticks to the issues, there is no point in trying to avoid it at all costs, as though it were a disaster.

Working for Love

Love doesn't just happen. Like everything else in life, it must be *worked* at. What kind of work is needed? This is the type of question that "psychology" can help you answer.

Here are one college student's thoughts about what a psychology course had done for his understanding of love:

> I had mistakenly assumed that one's role in relationships was *first* to make the partner happy. This attitude, at times a somewhat missionary one which fit well with my general orientation ("Gee, I'm *helping* someone!"), caused many problems because, as I realized only recently, I had begun to live first for others and began to be torn apart by what I ultimately (but not at the time) recognized as intense guilt. For not only was I *not* being true to myself, and not considering making *myself* happy *as well* as others, and thus not learning certain things about myself (for I was afraid to burst the goody-goody image I had constructed), but I also was not allowing that other person to relate to a truly open, honest, and accepting *me*.

7

The student's insight which is expressed here is basic. A key goal in life is to *be true to yourself* — to grasp who you are, why you behave as you do, what you may become. Blindness to your own needs hampers your ability to support and understand (to love) anyone else. Of course, going to the other extreme is equally unsatisfactory. Being concerned *only* for oneself results in isolation. Cut off from the warmth of human relationships, there is no chance for the individual to develop a sense of personal worth. This is another way of saying that there is *no meaning in life*.

The Message of the Unconscious

There is no hard-and-fast formula for gaining such an understanding of yourself, or for developing good relations with other people. However, as you will come to appreciate in your study of psychology, part of the secret lies in paying attention to certain experiences in everyday life that many people ignore. These experiences, which can tell you a great deal about yourself and the people you relate to, include *dreams, habits,* and *fears*.

Types of behavior such as these may be thought of as "signals" from the *unconscious* (sometimes called the "subconscious"). As used in psychology, this term refers to that phase of the mind's functioning of which we are normally unconscious or unaware. Thus, the behavior of every person is deeply influenced by needs, desires, and fears which are normally kept below the level of consciousness. However, the unconscious does express itself to us not only in dreams but also in repetitive thoughts, unrealistic fears, and patterns of behavior that we "can't help."

The study of psychology will reveal to you the fact that various problems and thoughts which you may have believed to be "unique" to you are actually shared by many (if not virtually all) of your contemporaries. For example, thoughts about suicide, or fears of going insane, or concern about what may seem to be homosexual impulses are not at all unusual. Most people have had such thoughts as these at one time or another. If more of us were aware of this, much needless worry and suffering might be avoided.

A college freshman told how a psychology course gave him an insight into the expression of the unconscious:

> Particularly important to me was the class where we discussed the unconscious. I had been having trouble falling asleep for about a month or two before the lecture. Not until I probed into my mind, via the discussion, could I find its root. I had had a head-on car acci-

dent prior to my insomnia. Every so often a flash of the accident would pop into my mind unexpectedly, actually causing me to shiver with fright at times. I had never related the insomnia to the accident before the lecture. After that I had no trouble falling to sleep at all.

No psychology course can promise to work for you the kind of "cure" this student experienced. But the study of psychology can help you see, in general terms, how personal troubles of this nature may be the result of unresolved and often unconscious problems. By bringing these problems into the open (or making them conscious), they may become easier to resolve — as this student found out when he finally accepted the fears caused by the accident.

When we try to bury and ignore our problems they can have a very disruptive effect on our lives. Such disruption is usually expressed in the forms of behavior that are *impulsive* and/or *compulsive*. Behavior is *impulsive* when we do something in response to a sudden, unexamined, and quite possibly irrational urge or impulse. It is *compulsive* when we find ourselves doing things again and again not because we particularly want to but because we "can't help it." In either case, we really don't know why we behave as we do.

An understanding of psychology can reveal reasons for actions which otherwise might seem meaningless. For example, if you forget about an appointment with a teacher, it may be because you have unconscious feelings of hostility toward him, even though on the conscious level you are not aware (or have not admitted to yourself) that you feel this way. If you find yourself continually humming a certain song, it may be that the song has some important association for you. Perhaps you heard it first when you met a person to whom you were strongly attracted; at the time you may not have even been aware that the song was being played. Or perhaps the lyrics of the song say something you are unconsciously feeling.

Communicating with Others

Becoming aware of the things we do unconsciously is very important to improving our relationships with others. Facial expressions, for example, are a significant means of communication between people. But many facial expressions are unconscious. A person who doesn't know that he tends to frown whenever someone speaks to him is likely to have a hard time making friends. For him frowning may be the result of his fears about meeting people; he is unwittingly giving out the warning, "Keep away!" But he really *does* want to make friends, and he doesn't know that he is defeating his own purpose by frowning. Awareness becomes the first step in working through a problem. Often, one must also discover the meaning of the original fear.

Facial expressions, of course, are only one of the ways we communicate with others. People react to us according to the way we talk, the gestures we make, the way we hold our bodies, and the way we dress, among other things. It is necessary to be alert and perceptive if we are to avoid the blocks between people which occur because of misunderstandings of the intent of unconscious communications. Obviously, it is often difficult to know what impressions other people have of us. But if we are to be aware of ourselves, it is necessary to have a useful awareness (*not* aimless suspicions) of what other people are thinking and feeling about us. In this connection, bear in mind one of the most important psychological truths: *We are often most likely to see the faults in others that we ourselves have.*

If a person is sensitive to his own motivations and to the feelings of others, he will realize that it is not always beneficial to be completely "open." There are occasions when saying something which happens to be true is a hostile act. Telling a person the "truth" about himself, even when done to "help" him, may actually be an expression of your anger, a way of getting back at him for not living up to your expectations. On the other hand, in a mature relationship, telling the truth is more often than not an act of love.

"Good" and "Bad"

One of our most basic and sustained activities throughout life is trying to define for ourselves what is meant by "good" and "bad," and to provide standards for distinguishing one from the other. Whether we are aware of it or not, we are constantly involved in this process. Psychology can be of great help to us in this kind of activity.

Whether something is "good," "bad," or somewhere in between depends on the relationship it has to the circumstances of your life. For example, is it a "good" thing for a person to strive for self-improvement — to think constantly in terms of achieving excellence? If a person is generally happy (not necessarily *satisfied*) with himself, the search for excellence may be an effective way of developing his full potential as a human being. But if a person is obsessed with trying to achieve "perfection" because he doesn't like himself, he will rarely be satisfied with his achievements. The harder he works, the more frustrated he will become. In this case, striving for excellence is likely to be counter-productive; it defeats the very purpose at which it is aimed. It is more important to accept ourselves for what we are, with all our faults and virtues, than it is to deny our personalities by striving for unattainable goals.

Guilt can also be good or bad, depending on how it is handled. If feeling guilty keeps a person from repeating past mistakes, then it can be a valuable organizing force in his life pattern. But if a person continues to perform the very acts which make him feel guilty, it is likely that his behavior has become *compulsive*. In this case, guilt feelings *increase* the likelihood that the unwanted behavior will be repeated, possibly as a form of self-punishment.

Sometimes people feel guilty for things which are not their fault. For example, a person who was taught by his parents that sex is "dirty" will probably feel guilty about his sexual thoughts. This form of guilt can be a disorganizing or disruptive influence in the person's life, causing him to blame himself for "sins" because of desires and feelings which are normal for every healthy human being.

The essence of psychological health is to have a *wide range of real choices for behavior*. A healthy person is not driven by compulsions or dominated by a single mood. He is flexible and in control of

Various techniques have been developed to help people express their deeper feelings and discharge their tensions. One of these is called "psychodrama," as shown here.

his actions. Psychology seeks to find ways of helping people to break free from self-defeating, rigid patterns of behavior. By providing insights into the unconscious forces underlying our behavior, psychology can equip us with the resources we need to make our lives more fulfilling and successful — that is, more meaningful.

Looking at ourselves and at the world only in terms of our conscious thoughts and traditional beliefs is like driving a car without a rear-view mirror. For a driver to change lanes safely, for example, he must know what's going on "behind" as well as "in front." Similarly, in making your adaptations to life problems and opportunities, it is necessary to be sensitive to the messages flowing from your unconscious, as well as from your conscious perceptions and beliefs. Only then will you be able to take a really searching look at yourself, and only then will you be able to attain a clear view of other people.

Obviously, your course in psychology will not magically solve any of your problems. It certainly does not guarantee success and happiness. Understanding people and gaining insight into complex and subtle forms of behavior is what this psychology course is all about. And as you learn more about your own motivations and the motivations of other people, you will be better able to appreciate *how your life is happening.*

That's what's in it for you!

THE WORLD IS NOT COMING TO AN END

THEREFORE, YOU MUST SUFFER ALONG AND LEARN TO COPE.

Drawing by Dana Fradin; © 1971 The New Yorker Magazine, Inc.

What is
NORMAL?

●●●●●●●●●●●●●●●●●●●●●●●●●●●●●●●

"I never felt normal, and I guess I walked around like a 'forbis' — which means kind of depressed. I get these letters from kids today telling me I am 'different' just like them. I write back and ask, 'Do you have a buzz in your ears?'"
— BARBRA STREISAND

"I don't have to be what you want me to be."
— MUHAMMAD ALI

Normality and Conformity

Normal is a word used in many different ways by many different people. Like other loaded words, it can be used as a weapon.

Many people use the word *normal* to describe persons and situations they consider "safe" — not likely to be harmful to them. Likewise, many people use the word *abnormal* to describe behavior they find personally distasteful, politically undesirable, or merely different from their own.

It is easy to understand this kind of misuse. In everyday situations, normality is commonly associated with adjustment to existing conditions, and with obedience to rules laid down by the "establishment," as those in positions of authority are sometimes called.

Often normality is confused with *reality*. Someone has defined reality as "anything a group of people are agreed upon." The more agreement there is about something, the more "real" it is. If this definition holds any truth, reality is dependent, to some degree at least, upon the particular group (society or culture) of which the individual is a member.

13

The idea behind this concept of reality is often applied to normality. In other words, *normal behavior* agrees with or conforms to society's accepted pattern of customs, rules, laws, fears, and taboos. If what you are doing does not conform to the type of behavior usually expected by your family and friends, they are likely to say that you are not dealing with "real" things, and that your behavior is not "normal."

But are we justified in assuming that because something is common and familiar, it is "normal"? Even more significantly, should we apply the label of "abnormal" to that which is not common or familiar? These are problems we are going to wrestle with in this chapter.

Are Most People Normal?

The term *normal* is sometimes used to describe a condition which is generally accepted as being ideal for certain purposes. For example, we use the expression "normal body temperature" for the figure 98.6°F. It has been determined that at this temperature the various body processes are carried on most satisfactorily, and the individual feels most fit. And indeed, unless an epidemic of some kind is prevalent, most people at any given time and place do have body temperatures very close to 98.6°. But just because most people have the body temperature which is considered ideal for health, can we assume that most people show a pattern of *behavior* which is also ideal? In other words, are most people normal?

One way of answering this difficult question is to say that *in comparison with each other,* most people are normal — that is, they meet the standards agreed upon by the group, which represent basically the existing characteristics of the group. However, *in comparison with themselves,* most people are abnormal — in the sense that hardly anyone has resolved all his problems so that he can use *all* his energies and capacities constructively.

This is the distinction between normality as a measure of *conformity to accepted standards,* and normality as a measure of the *best possible functioning of the human organism and the human personality.*

Are Normal People "Well-Adjusted"?

Suppose that one person in a given social situation appears to be stable and well-adjusted emotionally, while another shows such symptoms as guilt, depression, anxiety and rage. Would you be inclined to say that the former person is "normal," and the latter "abnormal"?

Perhaps — but don't jump at conclusions. During World War II, the Nazis in Germany carried out a deliberate coordinated plan that resulted in the murder of many millions of persons, mostly Jews. Which Germans were normal in this situation? Those who participated in the murders with a clear and happy conscience? Or those — and there were some — who were torn by feelings of guilt and who exposed themselves to severe punishment by refusing to cooperate in killing innocent people?

Is it normal to accept the fact of war without being disturbed, and to watch military operations on the television news as though it were a sort of show? Or does the normal person rather feel a sense of deep revulsion at this pain and destruction of life?

In short, we cannot assume that whatever is "common" or "average" or "accepted" is also normal, in any meaningful sense of that term. Such a concept of normality might be based on a hideous psychological deformity which is so prevalent that many people no longer notice it.

Use of "Abnormality" as a Social Weapon

If we consider completely normal behavior to be ideal, in the sense of promoting human happiness and efficiency, abnormal behavior would be that which is basically damaging to the self and to other people.

GUERNICA, by Pablo Picasso (1937)

The artist's way of perceiving and interpreting reality may sometimes seem "abnormal" to his contemporaries. Later generations may have a better understanding of his vision.

On the other hand, if we mean by "normal" merely conformity to rules and regulations (which change from culture to culture, and from time to time), we open the door to bigots and reactionaries. They may then use the concept of "abnormality" as a weapon against creative, forward-looking people who favor changes in society. Similarly, we must be wary of uncritically accepting the majority's view as the norm. For example, prejudice against minority groups, such as blacks, Mexican-Americans, Puerto Ricans, and Jews, has long been common in our society. But is it really "normal" to be prejudiced against such groups because many or most members of your own group have come to accept such prejudices? Is it "normal" to follow the latest fashions or fads undeviatingly because the "pace-setters" in society do so, or because the mass media tell us that these things are "in"? (How many young people wear long hair or short skirts not because they especially want to but simply because "everybody is doing it"?)

Rather than try to pinpoint what kind of social behavior is normal, it might be wiser to think about *what is not abnormal.*

For one thing, it is *not abnormal* to refuse to accept and adjust to all existing conditions. Martin Luther King, for example, refused to go along with certain prevailing social patterns resulting from racial segregation that were well-established in both law and custom. By realistic, well-planned protest and opposition, he helped to bring about significant changes. Similarly, it is certainly *not abnormal* for young people to feel a deep sense of dissatisfaction with certain conditions prevailing in our society, such as pollution of the environment, slums in the cities, inadequate educational and health facilities, and mistreatment of minority groups.

Conformity *for its own sake* is not the measure of normality.

A Scale for Measuring Adjustment and Maladjustment

Perhaps, when we are discussing purely personal behavior, it would be better for us to abandon the notion of normality altogether. Terms like "mature" and "adjusted" are probably more suited to describe characteristics in individuals.

Instead of casually branding someone as "normal" or "abnormal," we might classify human beings according to an "adjustment-maladjustment scale," as follows:

▶ *Excellent adjustment* refers to a person who enjoys life, has friends, works close to his maximum abilities, has a good relationship with his family, makes rewarding use of his leisure time, and can generally cope with problems.

▶ *Good adjustment* describes a person whose behavior is excellent in most areas of everyday life and personality development, but is less than excellent in a few areas.

▶ *Adequate adjustment* describes a person who functions reasonably well and who has no problems so serious that they overwhelm him. He does have ups and downs, but he also has friends and satisfying interests.

▶ *Poor adjustment* refers to a person with at least one serious problem (see the list of six given below), but who also does well in at least one area, such as schoolwork or relationships with friends.

▶ *Very poor adjustment* describes a person with one or more problems so severe as to be disabling, or with symptoms that threaten future personality development. Poorly adjusted young people often appear to be on the road to mental illness or delinquency, or give the impression of being grossly inadequate, in terms of what is expected of them.

Symptoms of Poor or Very Poor Adjustment

A young person who has made a poor or very poor adjustment to life shows at least one of the following symptoms or indications:

An inability to learn at a level close to what his intelligence would call for. This gap is not caused by sensory or neurological handicaps, such as those resulting from brain damage or other health problems; or by language barriers resulting from recent immigration; or by a move from an area with a backward educational system; or by temporary conditions, such as grief over the breaking-up of an important relationship.

An inability to build and maintain satisfactory relationships with other people, especially people in the same age group. (This symptom is usually significant only if it persists for a long time.)

Continued inappropriate or immature behavior in everyday circumstances. Such behavior might include "silliness," bizarre mannerisms, or frequent aggressive outbursts, as well as the use of passivity as a common response to frustration.

A persistent mood of unhappiness or depression. This does not refer to a temporary reaction of shock triggered by death of a loved one, for instance. And it does not apply to occasional anxiety, tension, and unhappiness, which are all part of *normal* growth and development.

Fears or physical symptoms (such as stuttering, tics, pains, and phobias) that develop in response to personal and school problems. (When psychological problems result in physical symptoms, the behavior is called *psychosomatic.*)

Compulsive behavior — that is, rigid or ritualistic ways of acting which the individual can't control or stop, such as overeating or excessive concern with cleanliness.

Remember — the maladjusted person does not necessarily exhibit all six of these symptoms. Also, even the most maladjusted individual may sometimes have areas of adequacy, or even demonstrate exceptional talents and accomplishments.

In contrast with the maladjusted person, the individual who shows excellent or good adjustment sees life as filled with opportunities, rather than problems. He is not dominated by compulsions or "have-to's" but sees many alternatives. He chooses his friends from among many acquaintances. He decides to spend his leisure time on one or several of the many activities he finds beneficial, enjoyable, or rewarding.

He likes people and he engages in many group activities — but occasionally he may prefer to be alone to think things out, or even to daydream.

Fantasy, Reality and Normality

All of us have a *fantasy life.*

This is made up of dreams, imaginings, wishes, impulses and the like, which often originate in the unconscious. (See Chapter 5.) At the deeper levels of the mind, these elements represent the raw, primitive, amoral ("don't-care-about-anyone-else") forces in the personality. Thus, from time to time, we become aware of impulses or desires which may be characterized as murderous, sensuous, sadistic, romantic, weird, sexual, heroic, incestuous, and so forth.

If we feel guilty or frightened by these ideas, they are likely to occur again and again. *Guilt provides the energy for the compulsive (involuntary) repetition of images which are unacceptable or even repulsive to us.*

The point to keep in mind is that fantasizing is entirely normal. It is a healthy and indeed a necessary part of life. For example, we may enjoy fantasies of a sexual nature, and we may choose to repeat them again and again, even though we know that we cannot put them into practice. Particularly among young people, this kind of daydreaming may provide preparation for a more stable and creative adulthood. In a sense, fantasy is part of the reality of preparing for life as an adult. Or to put it even more simply, *fantasy is part of the reality of life.*

Thus, you should reject the rather common fears that any kinds of thoughts can in themselves be abnormal, or can drive you "crazy" (mentally ill).

However, it is clear that fantasy can also become an escape, a "cop-out," a way of avoiding real life. Excessive or uncontrolled fantasizing becomes a symptom of internal conflicts, such as feelings of inferiority.

The Generation Gap

Today, parents and other adults sometimes use the word *abnormal* to describe the dress, music, dating patterns, political ideas, and other forms of behavior of many young people. This criticism is often accompanied by such comments as:

"When I was young, we didn't do such things."

"My generation had some sense."

"We had respect for our elders."

"Kids today are a bunch of freaks."

Many adults are quick enough to use the label of "abnormality," but who is willing or qualified to define a "normal" teenager? Adults

"Gee, Dad, just because I have contempt for your politics, social standards, religious beliefs, and moral code doesn't mean I don't *like* you. I really like you a lot!"

Drawing by Whitney Darrow, Jr.; © 1970 The New Yorker Magazine, Inc.

who draw such conclusions have very probably forgotten that when they were young, they were subjected to much the same complaints and criticism by *their* parents. The "generation gap" is a continuing fact of life — it didn't suddenly appear in the 1960's or 1970's.

Sometimes a critical adult may say patronizingly, "You're just going through a phase. You'll grow out of it." Even if this were true, it does not mean that the behavior in question is without meaning or value for the young person *at the time*. He may indeed "grow out of it," but this change will not necessarily represent an improvement or a move toward normality. Indeed, the behavior so lightly dismissed as "abnormal" may prove to be among the most meaningful, satisfying, and developmentally important phases in the person's life. How many middle-aged people today look back on an early love affair as an unforgettably beautiful and rewarding experience?

Normality and Self-Hatred

The next time you think of anyone, including yourself, in terms of "normal" and "abnormal," consider the following questions:

▶ Is the use of this concept of normality the real issue in the situation — or is it really a means of avoiding the issue?

▶ Is it being used as an attack against a non-conformist who may be a creative, healthy person with ideas that you personally don't like?

▶ Is it being used on the basis of an unexamined assumption that anything the majority does, thinks, or likes is thereby good — and "normal"?

▶ Is it being used as a way of debasing or hating yourself?

Sometimes we become our own worst enemies, especially when we accept as "normal" the prejudices, folk myths, maladjustments, and even the moral scruples of other people and use them against ourselves. Technically, this is called *identification with the aggressor*. This kind of behavior has been particularly typical of minority groups in our society. Black Americans, Jews, Orientals, and others have sometimes tended to accept the stereotypes* which the majority culture attached to them, and have sought to "improve" themselves so

---

* These familiar stereotypes may sometimes appear to be complimentary but they almost always involve a judgment that the minority group is inferior or objectionable in some way. Thus it may be said that "Negroes are naturally good in athletics or in music," which carries a thinly veiled implication that they are not "naturally good" in intellectual matters. The traditional picture of the Jews as being "naturally bright" and "good businessmen" ties in with the ancient prejudice that they are greedy, crafty, and opportunistic.

that they would be as indistinguishable as possible from the dominant group. Thus, Negroes used hair-straighteners; Jews adopted Anglo-Saxon names; Orientals have even been known to undergo surgical operations to change their eye structure.

This kind of behavior at its worst reveals a pattern of self-hatred. At the very least, it is indicative of lack of confidence and of a desire (inherently futile and self-defeating) to be fully "normal," as judged by the standards of another group. It is significant that the "black power" and the "black pride" movements in recent years have strongly disapproved of the use of skin lighteners, hair straighteners, and other similar products. It may be said that hair texture is extremely unimportant, but the *attitude* toward hair texture may be highly revealing psychologically for both the "in-group" and the "out-group."

One further point: While self-contempt has not been uncommon among minority groups in the United States, it is also not uncommon among people who express hatred for these groups. In both cases, the concept of "normality" is being misused to produce negative, fallacious, and destructive judgments.

Can a Society Be Abnormal?

We have all heard many times statements such as "Society is sick," or "Government is corrupt." Do such generalizations make any sense?

A society, of course, is a complex entity, and it is highly unlikely that it can ever be characterized adequately or fairly by any one term. However, a society is made up of people, and also of the rules which these people have adopted (consciously or unconsciously) to regulate the relations among them. Most of the people probably seem quite normal to one another, but from another point of view, their behavior may appear to be predominantly self-defeating, ignorant, unconscious, repressive, destructive of life, and generally irresponsible. This might provide some basis for the assertion that the society in question is "abnormal" or "sick."

Very often, the people of one generation will apply their own standards to judge harshly some aspects of the society of an earlier generation. For example, our present-day attitudes about sex are far more open, frank, and outspoken than they were only a few decades ago. We can now discuss quite openly and unashamedly matters whose very existence would not have been acknowledged during Victorian times. By our standards, then, the attitude of Victorian society toward sex was extremely prudish, unnatural, and hypocritical. There was a vast gulf between the way "respectable" people spoke and the way

Is a society "sick" or "abnormal" when it is based on hatred, fear, and persecution? This picture shows storm troopers in Nazi Germany arresting "enemies of the state" (about 1938).

that society actually operated. We might say then that, in regard to sexual matters, Victorian society appears abnormal to us.

However, a society need not be judged only from the vantage point of a later generation. People may be aware of certain characteristics of the society in which they are living, and may on this basis raise questions about its state of health. For example, the United States today is the richest and most powerful nation in the world, but we are aware that prevailing rates of murder, other violent crimes, suicide, alcoholism, and drug addiction are almost incredibly high. On this basis, many observers have questioned whether our society is as healthy or normal as we would like to think it is. For example, Erich Fromm (page 120) has asked why it is that "the middle class life of prosperity, while satisfying our material needs, leaves us with a feeling of intense boredom." He suggests that "suicide and alcoholism are pathological ways of escaping from this boredom." And even on the level of satisfying material needs our society is far from fully satisfactory because, in spite of the tremendous overall wealth and productive resources, many millions of our countrymen depend on public charity and are living below the "poverty level."

Most of the technologically advanced societies throughout the world seem to be deeply immersed in anti-life activities. It is a matter of historical record, for example, that in the last 50 years, "normal" men have killed more than 100 million of their fellow normal men. Certainly, war and mass killing are familiar phenomena, but are they characteristics of a sane and healthy society?

The conclusion seems to be that the world today is, as it has always been — filled with many confused, ignorant, irrational people whose irresponsibility is not exactly counterbalanced by the influence of the aware, humane, and "together" people. All societies past and present, seem to have had, and still have, their share of both kinds of behavior. Whether we characterize a given society as "normal" or "abnormal," "healthy" or "unhealthy," depends on how we evaluate a huge number of pluses and minuses.

Some Questions About Normality

QUESTION: Do normal boys wear their hair long or short?

Comment: Check the pictures in history books. Look at men from the 16th century to the 19th century. For example, how about Thomas Jefferson, Andrew Jackson, and Abraham Lincoln?

Only a generation apart — the Big Man on Campus with coed in the 1950's and the 1970's. How great are the differences, aside from clothing and hair styles?

QUESTION: Why did so many people, only a few years ago, consider it abnormal for girls to want a career of their own? In fact, why do so many people still feel that way?

Comment: "Abnormal" is a word used to condemn a deviation from our idea of the norm, even when our idea may not be able to stand up under rational analysis.

QUESTION: Then, what *is* normal?

Comment: Well, for one thing, it isn't normal for men to use perfume — unless a smart businessman gets an inspiration to call it "after-shave lotion." Moralists tell us it is evil and not normal to kill. Evolutionists tell us that killing is part of "natural selection" by "survival of the fittest," and is therefore normal.

In short, what is normal at a given time, for a given person, or under a given situation may not be normal in a different frame of reference.

QUESTION: Can you think of one idea presented in this chapter that has particularly interested or influenced you?

THINGS TO DISCUSS :: THINGS TO DO :: THINGS TO READ

1. Conduct your own opinion poll on normality. Separately, ask five cooperative people — members of your family, friends, their parents — this question:

Do you think killing is normal?

This is in a sense an ambiguous question. It could be interpreted to mean: "Is there a lot of killing going on today, and has there always been killing in the history of the human race?" *or* "Is killing socially, psychologically, or morally an acceptable form of behavior?"

Considering that a person's ideas about normality have a strong effect on his behavior, you may find it interesting to determine how much thought each of the persons questioned has given to this question. Accordingly, score each answer according to the following scale. (However, don't make your "subject" uneasy; remember his answer, and record the score later.)

▶ *Little thought*. He gives either a "Yes" or "No" answer, with little supporting argument. Or he may say something like, "Well, people have been killing each other for thousands of years" or "Anyone who kills another person must have something wrong with him."

▶ *Some awareness*. He qualifies his answer with phrases such as "It all depends . . ." or "Under certain conditions. . . ." He may raise the question "What *is* normal?" but without supplying much of an answer. He may say something like, "Murder is abnormal, but killing in self-defense is normal." He may advance the idea uncritically that "It is normal for soldiers to kill, but not for civilians."

▶ *Good understanding.* This type of person will reveal the essential ambiguity of the question by saying something like, "That depends on what you mean by *normal.* Are you asking if killing happens commonly, or if killing is bad for the killer, as well as the victim?" A sensitive person may ask, "Are you implying that just because something happens often, it can't be too bad?"

In some cases, you may not be too sure how to rate an answer. Get someone else's opinion. Bring the results to class, and discuss them.

2. Select a character in American history whom you particularly admire. Was he generally considered normal by most people in his day? Is he considered normal today? If there has been a change in the view of his normality, how do you explain it?

3. What would you consider a normal reaction to each of the following situations?
    (*a*) You find out that your girl friend (or boy friend) has been dating someone else.
    (*b*) The doctor tells you that you have only six months to live.
    (*c*) A student about to graduate from high school learns that because of family finances, it will be impossible for him to attend college, as he had planned to do.

4. Are there any ideas in this chapter which gave you some uncomfortable moments? What were they? Why do you think they had this effect on you?

READINGS

The following books are not about "normality" or "abnormality" as such, but they offer some interesting insights into the ideas and standards that lie behind evaluations of this matter. (The first three are works of fiction.)

The Once and Future King, by T. H. White (Medallion, 1962).
The Lord of the Rings Trilogy, by J. R. R. Tolkien (Ballantine Books, 1965).
Stranger in a Strange Land, by Robert A. Heinlein (Medallion, 1968).
Future Shock, by Alvin Toffler (Bantam, 1970).

NOTE: The great majority of the readings listed here and in later chapters are available in inexpensive paperback editions.

Problems of the Self

Problems of Society

● ●

From ghoulies and ghosties
And long-leggety beasties
And things that go "bump" in the night
Oh Lord, deliver us
— OLD ENGLISH PRAYER

Fears and Neuroses

Emotional Problems and Mental Illness

▶ Fear is one of the most powerful forces in the human mind.

▶ It is one of the main factors in emotional disturbances and neurotic behavior.

▶ Almost all people have fears, many of which are not on the conscious level.

But, if you have emotional problems, that does not automatically mean you are mentally ill. On the other hand, we would be foolish to deny that emotional problems are serious.

Some observers believe that almost all people at times display behavior which is neurotic — that is, directed by unconscious emotional problems or conflicts. Virtually all people (except possibly a few extraordinary personalities) are driven in part by unconscious fears and desires which can lead to inner conflicts. In short, the great majority of us experience real difficulties in coping with life, but only those people whose inner conflicts are so severe that they are virtually

26

unable to deal with life in a significantly constructive, self-fulfilling, and healthy way should be regarded as mentally ill.

The difference between someone who is *emotionally disturbed* or *neurotic* and someone who is *mentally ill* is more than just a matter of degree. *Mental illness* implies that most of the personality is directed toward self-defeat and self-destruction. The behavior is characteristically inappropriate, unconsciously motivated, and determined as a mechanical *re*-action to situations that produce fear and anxiety. *Emotional disturbance* implies that there is some behavior which is self-defeating in the sense indicated above, but that in at least a substantial sector, the person's actions are rational and are calculated to produce the desired results and to bring about good relations with other people.

Adjustment

In general, the less emotionally disturbed a person is, the less numerous and less severe are his inner conflicts, and the more harmonious is his personality — the more "together" he is. Also, the more willingness and ability a person has to recognize and overcome his emotional problems, the more he is pro-life and the more healthy is his outlook.

A reasonably high degree of inner harmony is what we mean by *adjustment*. In this context, we are not referring to adjustment to "society," but rather adjustment to *oneself*. However, one outcome of such self-adjustment is the ability to adjust maturely to other people, including new acquaintances; also, an ability to meet the basic challenges of life with a measure of success and happiness.

In large part, this adjustment means a recognition and overcoming of unconscious fears which can lead to compulsive, repetitive behavior. In fact, *neurosis* may be defined as *repeated involuntary or mechanical reaction to fear- or anxiety-provoking situations*.

A Basic Health Problem

Neurosis is one of the world's most common health problems. Almost everyone knows someone with a harmful neurosis, just as almost everyone knows someone who is or has been mentally ill. It has been estimated that damaging emotional disturbances afflict more than 30% of all the people in the United States.

Dismissing these people as "creeps" or "weirdos" is only a sign of ignorance on the part of the name-caller. As a matter of fact we often have a tendency to be intolerant of precisely those problems in other people that are of most direct concern to ourselves. For example, people who "talk too much" usually can't stand other people who "talk too much." If you want a good indication of the kind of emotional problems you are harboring but may not be aware of, try drawing up a list of the people whom you find most difficult to get along with, and of the specific characteristics they have that you find most objectionable. Such a list almost certainly will point up the "problem" phases of your own personality and behavior.

The implication of this is that someone who shows a scornful and intolerant attitude toward people with emotional disturbances probably is suffering from disturbances of his own. A person with generally sound emotional health is much more likely to react with sympathy and understanding. The emotionally disturbed person needs above all the assurance that he is recognized as a troubled but worthy human being — one who is capable of much responsible behavior, if he is given a fair chance.

What an emotionally disturbed person frequently needs more than anything else is respectful attention from an understanding person.

Basic Emotional Needs

Emotional disturbance is always the result of the disruption or the denial of certain emotional needs basic to all of us. Many psychologists would agree that these needs include the following: a sense of belonging, achievement, economic security, freedom from fear, love and affection, freedom from intense guilt feelings, understanding, and self-respect.*

Obviously, all these needs are closely intertwined in actual social situations and in the individual human personality, but it will be convenient for us to consider them one by one.

The Need to Belong

The individual's self-image or sense of identity is closely tied to his need to belong to one or more groups in which he has an important role to play. The most common and universal of such groups is the family, but there are many others involving friends, co-workers, religious activities, school, athletics, politics, hobbies, etc. Some of these groups may not be "organized" in a formal sense but they are an essential part of the structure of the individual's life.

A person whose participation in such groups is weak or limited is likely to suffer from a sense of rejection, of "not belonging." He may well have the type of personality that strongly needs reassurance. If you know such a person, you will do well to let him know that he has your interest and respect. If he is away from home, keep in touch with him. When he returns, greet him and let him know that you missed him. Such attentions will be greatly appreciated for the very reason that this person has grave doubts about how much he "means" to other people.

The Need for Achievement

We all have goals in life — things that we hope to achieve. Some of these goals are major and may extend years into the future — for example, becoming a doctor, writing a book, contributing to some program of public service. Others may be small and immediate, such as getting to work or to school on time tomorrow. *A person who fails continually at achieving his small goals is likely to have a great deal of trouble in achieving his long-term objectives.*

People who have a nagging sense that they are not accomplishing all that they "should" in life often think of themselves as "failures."

---

* This listing of emotional needs is presented in the book *Understanding the Problem Child,* by Louis Raths and Anna Burrell (Economics Press, 1962).

This may lead to severe emotional disturbances. Some individuals express such a disturbance by continual "whining and moaning." At one moment, they may be deploring their "bad luck"; at another they may blame the failure on their own inadequacies. Still another type of reaction is to brag unrealistically by inflating minor accomplishments, or perhaps by "dreaming up" accomplishments that never occurred.

A person of this type badly needs approval, and you may be helpful to him by offering considered praise, even for minor successes. If he is involved in some undertaking or situation with you and "falls down on the job," try not to condemn him; he is probably already condemning himself.

The Need for Economic Security

In one sense, this is a biological need, for we must all have food, shelter, and other necessities in order to survive. However, in a country such as the United States, few people literally starve to death or die because of exposure. The problem is far more a social one, in the sense that some people suffer from poverty — from living standards that may be biologically tolerable but are considerably below those of the rest of the population. And there is ample evidence that being poor, especially in a society marked by great emphasis on material wealth, can lead to serious personality conflicts.

One symptom is that a person who has experienced severe poverty, especially in childhood, may be obsessed with a fear of poverty for the rest of his life. He may show this by obsessive efforts

to gain wealth. For example, he may be an extremely hard worker, or he may be utterly ruthless in his economic dealings with other people. Another symptom is the "miser syndrome" — irrational emphasis on saving, even to the point of doing without the simplest comforts. Such a person can literally never have "enough" money in the bank or in other forms of property.

The opposite reaction is that people who have been poor in childhood and youth, and who later make money, become compulsive spenders. By "conspicuous consumption" they seek continually to prove to the outside world (and perhaps to themselves) that they now have plenty of the material goods that were denied to them when they were young and poor. They delight in such "status symbols" as big, expensive automobiles.

People who place an exaggerated emphasis on acquiring wealth, and who are willing to ride roughshod over the needs and interests of other people, naturally often evoke fear and resentment. The best way to cope with this type of personality is to make it clear by your behavior that you value him as a human being, and that he doesn't have to demonstrate his wealth and power to relate to you on a friendly and equal basis.

Frequently, people who seem to have an insatiable greed for material things are motivated by repressed but intense needs for love and affection. Also, they may have an unconscious need to be reassured regarding their sexual adequacy. Many psychologists feel that a craving for food (beyond what is required for sustenance) is a largely unconscious symbol for motherly love, remembered from childhood and still deeply desired. Also, money and the power that goes with it are frequently accepted by the unconscious as a guarantee of sexual potency. This last in our society is much more likely to be true of men than of women.

Freedom from Fear

This is freedom in the truest sense of the term. To gain relief from the fears projected by the unconscious is perhaps the most difficult single task facing every human being. Fears are the great cripplers of the human personality. They distort reality, create illusions, destroy our capacity to deal with the outside world. On the most simple and literal level, it has been demonstrated that a person who is intensely afraid can't even recognize a straight line as being straight.

We are not suggesting, of course, that all fear is irrational and destructive of mental health. There are many situations in which we *should* feel fear, because only in this way are we likely to do what is necessary to protect ourselves and others. A good example from everyday life is fear of automobile accidents resulting from reckless driving. In this case, the individual knows exactly what he is afraid of and can take reasonable precautions to avoid the danger. But irrational, often unadmitted, fears make life miserable and cause neurotic behavior.

There are people who show an exaggerated, unmotivated sense of apprehension in regard to most of the experiences of life. They seem almost literally to "be afraid of everything." Such people are unsure of their own abilities or worth. However irrational their timidity may seem, they should never be laughed at. Mockery will only add to their distrust of themselves, and what they need above all is more self-confidence.

The Need for Love and Affection

The need for love and affection is universal among human beings — men, women, and children. People who deny that they have such a need are deceiving themselves and probably laying the groundwork for severe emotional troubles.

On the other hand, it is childish to *demand* love, or even to *expect* it, without taking into account the conditions and the needs of the other person in the equation. Love cannot be a one-way street. You cannot get without giving. As a matter of fact, it is a good general rule (although a very difficult one to follow) to give love freely and unselfishly without expecting any "reward." In this way, paradoxically, you are most likely to receive an honest, satisfying reciprocal emotion. The person who always thinks in terms of what he is going to *get* is most likely to become sidetracked and entangled in complex webs of unhappy relationships. Another way of saying this is that to have a satisfactory emotional relationship with another person you must regard him (or her) as a personality equal to yourself — not an object to be used for your own wants.

Freedom from Feelings of Guilt

The need to be free from intense or obsessive feelings of guilt is another aspect of the need to be free from irrational fears. We all have at times a sense of regret for things that we have done, or failed to do, but an emotionally healthy person does not allow such reactions to dominate his personality. He is aware that as time passes, his present feelings regarding certain events will change. He knows, too, that to be constantly preoccupied, consciously or unconsciously, with things that were done in the past is a waste of time and energy. The future lies before us, and to some degree can be controlled. We should, therefore, concentrate on what we can do in the period ahead to counteract the effects of mistakes that may have been made in the past.

On the other hand, there is a reasonable place for a sense of guilt, just as there is for fear. Regret for improper or misguided actions can be used as a prod and a reminder to avoid similar mistakes in the future. The personal background of feelings and ideas against which the individual judges his actions and decides whether or not guilt feelings are appropriate is called his *conscience*.

If someone has been guilty of wrong action toward you, it is not constructive to try to shame or humiliate him. Let him know, if necessary, what you believe has been done improperly, and give him a chance to rectify matters. Show by your behavior that you are not being vindictive or brooding over the injury received. There is a familiar type of personality (sometimes called the "grievance collector") that actually enjoys "collecting" injuries from others and then reproaching them bitterly for their misdeeds.

The Need to Understand and to Be Understood

There are two aspects to *understanding* as a basis for sound emotional development. The individual must feel that other people understand him; and he must have a sound understanding both of other people and of himself.

The ability to understand other people arises out of an understanding of one's own qualities and problems. If a man has, for example, an accurate conception of his own emotional needs, he will appreciate the emotional needs of others. If he has a mature insight into his own strengths and weaknesses, he will be able to value the strong points in the personalities of his associates, and also to see their weaknesses in the overall context of human frailties, not necessarily as crushing disabilities.

By the same token, we all need recognition and understanding of ourselves by other people. This doesn't suggest that we should receive a constant diet of commendation and approval. What is needed, rather, is *in-depth communication,* so that the true aspects of the personality are brought out from behind the screen of conventional concealments and "defense mechanisms." Being "understood" in this sense by at least a few people is essential to healthy personality development.

The Need for Self-Respect

In order for a person to build self-respect and self-confidence, he needs to take actions for which he can assume and feel responsibility.

If he has been continually deprived, by others and by himself, of the right to undertake tasks which require his judgment, his ability, his action, his direction, and his responsibility, he will have an image of himself as being incapable of carrying his part of the burden of life. In consequence, he will be overly-dependent on other people to live his life for him.

Symptoms of Emotional Maladjustment

Frustration and Aggression

A very large part of the emotional disturbances which people experience can be traced to *frustration*. Frustration may be defined as the *blocking or "turning aside" of behavior to which the individual is motivated but which he is unable, for some reason, to carry out in practice*. Thus, a person is frustrated when he wants to do creative work but is kept at some humdrum, routine occupation; when he wants to make a living for himself and his family but can't find a job; when he wants to love but is unable to find a suitable love object; when he has an urge to dominate or control other people but is kept in a subordinate position. The more intense the frustration, the more intense the reaction. As we shall see, this reaction is often negative — either passively or actively hostile, sometimes to the point of physical violence.

Most unconscious motivation is inherently aggressive — that is, it puts the felt or the imagined needs of the self before those of others. However, the neurotic activity proceeding from frustration is not regarded as aggressive in popular usage unless it involves obvious interference with other people, particularly in the form of physical force or violence.

From the standpoint of the psychologist, however, passive withdrawal as a response to frustration may also be a form of aggression and hostility. By obstinately refusing to cooperate with others, even in the "little" details of social interaction, an individual in effect "interferes" with other people. The withdrawal may make these people feel uncomfortable, or it may force them to assume greater responsibility for getting things done.

Children often suffer frustration and may react aggressively. However, aggression in children (even violent aggression) is not necessarily a sign of severe emotional disturbance. Many children have been known to fight and to destroy property, although in most respects they apparently have a good overall emotional adjustment.

Aggressive, well-considered, constructive action to combat and correct social evils is psychologically healthful. Here we see Martin Luther King, Jr. leading a peaceful civil rights demonstration.

It should be pointed out that aggressive resistance to an intolerable situation causing severe frustration is not necessarily neurotic. Indeed, it may be the only way of *overcoming* the frustration and thus making possible more satisfying behavior. On a mass basis, revolutionary movements, such as the American Revolution, may be considered in this category. In the 20th century, we have seen social frustrations overcome by means of passive or peaceful resistance, led by such great figures as Mohandas K. Gandhi and Martin Luther King.

NOTE: We should distinguish between *aggression* and *aggressiveness*. Unconsciously motivated *aggression* is usually directed against other people and acts as a life-damaging force. *Aggressiveness* suggests strength, determination, and energy consciously directed. This is normally a pro-life force.

Depression

Another response to frustration is depression. This suggests a mood of sadness and pessimism. The depressed person is aware of a problem, but he feels powerless to do much about it, and he lacks normal energy and aggressiveness.

At one time or another, we all suffer mild bouts of depression, which we call familiarly "being in the dumps" or "having the blues." Such "normal" depression may follow an emotionally unsettling experience, such as the death of a loved one, losing a job, or failing a course in school.

On the other hand, a deep, long-sustained, or repeated mood of depression is symptomatic of neurosis. Often, the intensity of the depression seems out of proportion to the seriousness of the problem that caused it. On the other hand, the matter on which the depressed person is apparently focusing his attention may be no more than a substitute for the problem that is really bothering him. A girl may appear to be deeply depressed because she has not been invited to the Junior Prom. In the "back of her mind," however, she may be worried because she has grave doubts about her feminine charms, her womanliness, and her prospects for marriage.

Depression is particularly futile and self-defeating when it is based on a condition that one cannot possibly do anything about. An example is people who "worry" about their age and actually seem to resent growing older.

"Where's my lost youth? Someone will have to answer for this!"

Copyright 1970 Saturday Review, Inc. Cartoon by J. B. Handelsman.

Depression involves feelings of guilt. Frequently a depressed person is unconsciously (and perhaps even consciously) accepting blame for something that is not his fault. Suppose, for example, that while a girl is away at college, her mother dies. This girl may reproach herself by saying (perhaps without expressing it openly), "If only I had stayed home, maybe Mother wouldn't have died!" Consciously, the girl may know that this sense of guilt doesn't make sense, but unconsciously she accepts it, and it may well contribute to a mood of deep depression.

The deeper the depression, the more inclined the person is to withdraw from involvement in the affairs of everyday life. If he does participate, he does so halfheartedly, and he usually accomplishes little. Frequently he will go out of his way to avoid activities that he ordinarily enjoys. The more extreme the depression, the more it becomes a form of calculated self-punishment.

Depression is not always unhealthy or negative. It may be a sign that a person has become aware of an emotional problem about which he can do something constructive. It may be a prelude to effective action. But chronic depression is anti-life, sapping the very energies which are needed to work out the problem successfully in everyday living.

Hyperactivity

Another sign of frustration and emotional maladjustment is *hyperactivity*.

Typical compulsive, hyperactive behavior is shown by people who "can't sit still," "can't stop talking," or "can't stop reading" (to the point that they do almost nothing else). Similar symptoms are shown by people who "can't stand it" unless the television set, radio, or record player is on all the time.

To be hyperactive certainly doesn't mean to be able to accomplish more than the average person, or to have a surplus of energy, as the term might imply. It suggests, rather, that energy which could be directed into planned activities and used with some continuity and purpose is wasted by being fragmented.

A person who "can't sit still," for instance, jumps about from one thing to another. He starts something and then before he has really "gotten into it," abandons it and turns to something else. He seems to be always in motion, but rarely uses that motion for any attainable goal.

Hyperactivity is an unconscious way of keeping oneself so "busy" and distracted that there is no time to examine problems objectively and to try to do something about them. A person showing this type of emotional disorder is actually afraid of his problems — apprehensive that he won't be able to handle them. In the long run, however, the strain involved in this conflict and evasion is greater than the pain the person might experience if he "slowed down" and faced his problems head-on.

Societal and Emotional Disorders

Societal disorders and emotional disorders feed on each other. Both are causes, and both are results. They manifest themselves in the major problems that beset our troubled society.

Crime in the United States

Certainly crime is a major symptom of social malfunctioning in the United States today. It is also a problem in virtually all other countries, but our crime rates are among the worst in the world.

In analyzing this situation one of the first things we notice is that there is a striking parallel between the incidence of crime and the incidence of poverty. Where poverty rates are high crime rates are high, and vice versa.

This, of course, does not mean that to be poor leads directly and inevitably to crime. Most poor people are generally law-abiding. And more often than not, poor people are the *victims* of serious crimes. Also, being well-off financially by no means guarantees respect for the law. A rich man is not likely to commit a "mugging" or to "stick up" a gas station, but there are other types of "white-collar crime" that are by no means uncommon in our upper-income groups, such as embezzlement, income tax evasion, price fixing, and various forms of fraud.

Crime rates are reflected to some degree in the ebb and flow of economic conditions. For example, the murder rate in the United States in 1933, at the depth of the great depression, was 14% higher than in the prosperous year of 1967. This can probably be attributed to two factors. Widespread economic distress led to more crimes against property — such as holdups and burglaries during which killings occurred. Also, the prevailing conditions of mass unemployment, insecurity, and deprivation created emotional tensions that sometimes erupted in violence. It has been observed, for example, that an unemployed man who is home most of the day is far more likely to quarrel with his wife than if he is occupied at a regular job. And prolonged, bitter husband-wife quarrels can lead to violence.

However, even during the generally prosperous 1960's, crime rates in the United States showed alarming rises. Here are some facts:

▶ A 1970 FBI report on serious crimes (a category including murder, rape, assault, burglary, larceny, and car theft) noted that while the population of the United States increased by 13% in the 1960's, the crime rate increased by 148%.

▶ Studies have shown that much of the increase in arrests for serious crime is accounted for by minors ("juvenile delinquents").

▶ The FBI's "crime clock" ticks off one serious crime in the United States every minute of the day. A murder occurs on an average of every 39 minutes, a forcible rape every 17 minutes, a robbery every two minutes.

These figures are shocking. However, they are more understandable if we go back to a phrase used above — "the generally prosperous 1960's." This prosperity did *not* extend to important sectors of our population. According to figures released by the U. S. Census Bureau in 1971 —

▶ In 1970, there were more than 25.5 million Americans living below the level which the Federal government designated as the "poverty line." Although this was considerably less than the 40 million poor in 1959, it represented an increase of 1.2 million over 1969.

▶ There were 17.5 million poor whites in 1970, and 7.7 million poor blacks. This meant, however, that one out of every three blacks was living in poverty, as compared with one out of every ten whites. Moreover, there are gradations even within the "poverty" classification. The average income for a poor black family in 1970 was $1300 less than the Federal standard of minimum adequacy (based on $3968 for a family of four). The average deficiency for a poor white family was about $1000.

▶ For all races, families headed by women accounted for only 14% of the total population but for 44% of the poverty population.

Other revealing figures were issued by the 1970 White House Conference on Children:

▶ In 1969, 15% of all American children 5 years old and younger were in families classified as "living in poverty." (This comprised about 3 million children.) About 14% of all young people between the ages of 6 and 17 were living in poverty.

▶ In 1970, between 20% and 25% of all black families in American cities lived in poverty. Of black families living in rural areas, between 45% and 60% lived in poverty.

▶ In 1970, 80% of Indians on government reservations were living under conditions of poverty.

As a further example of the relationship between poverty, crime and emotional disturbance, we quote from a report by the South Dakota Public Welfare Department (1970):

> While poverty and hunger affect only a minority of South Dakota's white children, for the Indian child it is a way of life. Indians account for only six percent of South Dakota's population, but they constitute *46% of the state's welfare recipients and 40% of the state training school inmates.* Other problems confronting Indian youngsters are a tragic breakdown and disorganization of family and community life, learning disabilities, a certain amount of discrimination by whites, and a corresponding tendency of many Indians to reject whites.

Social Causes of Emotional Disorders

In the general context of poverty, we find a number of specific conditions in American life today that social scientists believe contribute significantly to emotional disorders and to anti-social behavior.

The Welfare System. Our prevailing welfare system — a carry-over in its essentials from the 1930's — has been widely condemned for its effects on family life. In many cases, a father may leave his family because he finds that he is unable to make a living, and he has reason to believe that his wife and children will be eligible for greater welfare benefits if there is not an "able-bodied man" in the house. Thus, poverty results in a "broken home," and the broken home in turn creates emotional disturbances and other disadvantages for the children that tend to perpetuate poverty — and to breed crime. A recent survey showed that almost one-fourth of all children in welfare families are emotionally disturbed, as compared with only about 12% of non-welfare children.*

Effects of Racism. Some psychologists have cited the factor of racism as disrupting the emotional life of a great many minority group children, especially in black families. Even where there are no overwhelming economic problems, the prevailing atmosphere of discrimination — the child's sense that he is "different" and "doesn't belong" in the social mainstream — may lead to a negative self-image and to severe personality disturbances. This applies particularly to welfare

---

* Some authorities feel that these figures may be somewhat misleading. The study is vulnerable to the criticism that children from poor families are more likely to be classified as "emotionally disturbed" for behavior which, in middle class families, would be considered only "different" or atypical. However, the study does provide an indication of general trends.

families, but there is also evidence that it affects self-supporting families. Of course, other minority groups, such as Mexican-Americans
(Chicanos), Puerto Ricans, and American Indians may suffer from
similar disadvantages.

Illiteracy. Another reinforcing factor for poverty, emotional disturbances, and crime is the incredibly high incidence of illiteracy in
this economically developed country. According to figures of the U. S.
Office of Education, there are now about 24 million Americans 18
years of age and older who cannot read at all, or who can't read more
than a few simple words. Most of these people are from poor families,
but almost all of them did attend school. Clearly, our educational system failed these people.

An illiterate person in our society will almost inevitably be jobless or will be limited to the most menial, lowest-paying jobs. Aside
from this, his self-esteem is bound to suffer because he lacks the most
basic of all educational skills; he is inferior in this respect even to small
children. Very few people can suffer such handicaps without more or
less serious personality disruption.

Powerlessness and Frustration. Thus, there are millions of persons in our society who are caught in a vicious cycle — poverty, leading to degrading social conditions, leading to personality disorders
(including alcoholism and drug addiction), leading to anti-social behavior (including crime), leading to punishment, leading to more
misery and poverty. The people trapped in this process may realize
what is happening to them and may aspire to break out of the cycle
and to build a better life, if not for themselves then for their children.
But in too many cases they find themselves powerless to do anything
about it. From one point of view, it may be said that they are purely
victims — that "society doesn't give them a chance." Another analysis
might emphasize their own lack of discipline and personal resources
— although these weaknesses too are a product of social experience.
In any case, the people involved in this situation are likely to suffer a
crushing loss of self-respect and self-confidence. Their reactions and
their behavior then add up to the emotional pattern that we have
characterized by the word *frustration*.

The "Crime of Punishment"

Problems of poverty, emotional disturbance, and antisocial behavior are made worse in many cases when people run afoul of the law
and are sent to jail. Then begins what psychiatrist Karl Menninger
has called the "crime of punishment."

Recent years have witnessed violent uprisings in many American prisons, some of them marked by killings of both inmates and prison personnel. Psychological pressures of various types have produced a "time bomb" that is ticking away in virtually every prison in the United States.

Bruce Shanks in the *Buffalo Evening News*

The nation's penal institutions (jails, prisons, reform schools, etc.) are by and large a horror and a disgrace. With relatively few exceptions, they do little or nothing to rehabilitate anyone. They are rather schools for crime, for sexual abnormality, and for other forms of deviant behavior. In too many cases, men come out of these institutions more brutalized, more embittered, more committed to a life of crime than they were when they went in.

Part of the trouble lies in the sheer inadequacy of the physical facilities. A great many of our prisons and jails are antiquated and dilapidated. Most of them are badly overcrowded. A report made in 1971 by a United States agency remarked that many inmates, whether convicted or not,* were living under "less than human conditions." Another fault lies in inadequate personnel. There have been devoted, humane, and creative wardens in American prisons, but by and large custodial jobs such as those of prison guards are not highly prized and

---

* It should be noted that many men are arrested and are held in city and county jails for considerable periods of time without having been convicted of anything. The basic reason for this is the overburdened court system in most localities. Among all the reforms needed in our court and penal system, one of the most urgent is greater promptness in administering justice — either in meting out a definite punishment or in releasing the suspect if he cannot be proved guilty.

are not likely to attract men of superior capabilities. And the shortage of professional staff — doctors, psychologists, teachers, and the like — is notorious.

But more and more observers are beginning to suspect that the greatest and most irremediable weakness of all may lie in the *very concept of a prison* as it exists in this country. To cage men like animals, to subject them to a grim, dehumanizing routine, to cut them off for extended periods from all the satisfactions of life, including normal expression of sexual impulses — this is regarded by many as an act of outrageous violence against the human personality; and in a high proportion of cases, it is bound to yield bad results. The question is not whether the convicted criminals *deserve* such punishment, but whether we are accomplishing any good purpose by maintaining these "human zoos." It may be granted that in our society some facilities or measures must be provided to punish lawbreakers, but there is nothing "natural" or "inevitable" about prisons as a means for this. Apparently, prisons as we know them have been developed only within the last few centuries. In the years ahead we may have to rethink and reshape our entire institutional machinery for punishing crime and (just as important) for doing something to turn the errant individual away from crime and toward a normal, productive human life. (Of course, *prevention* of crime should be our number-one priority. To accomplish this, we need above all economic arrangements that will make it possible for everyone capable of working to earn a decent living, and that will provide adequate aid to those incapable of working.)

Why has it been so difficult to bring about much-needed changes in our handling of crime and the penal system? Perhaps part of the answer lies in our own dominant attitudes toward crime and punishment. Karl Menninger has suggested that "normal" people, who are to some extent repressed and frustrated, may take secret pleasure in watching criminals do the things that they would like to do. For example, we have all had fantasies of unlimited wealth. Thus, there is perhaps some element of vicarious satisfaction when we learn that holdup men have had the audacity to seize large sums of money in a bank at gun point. May it not be that this is one reason for the great and undiminished popularity of "crime stories" not only in fiction (books, moving pictures, television) but also in "real life" as reflected in news reports?

Menninger also suggests that the emphasis on "crackdowns" and on "getting tough" in treating criminals, rather than on real rehabilitation, may be evidence of a secret sadism — giving "law-abiding" citizens a stimulating sense of power over others by subjecting them to cruel but *usual* punishment.

Youthful Offenders

The faults of our penal system today are probably most flagrant as it applies to youthful offenders (juvenile delinquents). This means people accused of violating the law who are under a certain age (16, to 18, depending on the state).

U. S. Senator Birch Bayh, chairman of the Senate Juvenile Delinquency Subcommittee, has evaluated the present system of dealing with juvenile offenders in the following terms (1971): "It does not deter, it does not correct. At best it furnishes a means of warehousing human beings. At worst it provides a tuition-free school for crime."

To be young, poor, and in trouble with the law is not an encouraging prospect in the United States today. In some respects, the outlook for the juvenile accused of wrongdoing is even worse than that for an accused adult. Adults at least are entitled to certain constitutional rights, which in most jurisdictions have usually been reasonably well protected. However, as one student of this problem, Lois G. Forer,* pointed out, there has been a tendency to make the laws dealing with juveniles extremely flexible, so that judges can use their personal discretion to protect or help the child in individual cases. The intent of this is undoubtedly good, but the effect has often been to give the judge such a wide range of authority that the accused juvenile is, for all practical purposes, deprived of his constitutional rights as a United States citizen. Miss Forer writes: "An adult must be accused of a specific crime, a violation of a criminal statute" . . . but "a juvenile can be brought to court on a charge of being wayward, incorrigible, truant, in need of guidance or care, or likely to lead an idle and dissolute life."

Another commentator, Jean Strouse†, notes that young people can be punished severely for modes of conduct that in the case of an adult would be merely a matter of individual judgment or taste — for example, wearing long hair, dressing unconventionally, or expressing opinions critical of a school principal.

In a recent decision, the U. S. Supreme Court ruled that minors are entitled to all the traditional protections of due process of law, including the right to a fair trial and to be represented by a qualified attorney. Unfortunately, this has not yet halted widespread abuse of juvenile rights by authorities in some jurisdictions.

---

* Lois G. Forer, *No One Will Listen* (John Day, 1970).

† Jean Strouse, *Up Against the Law: The Legal Rights of People Under 21* (New American Library, 1970).

Suicide

Factors Involved in Suicide

Suicide (actual or attempted) is regarded in most cases as a sign of severe emotional disorder. By the same token, the *suicide rate* is often interpreted as a sign of the level of *social* turbulence in a nation or community.

The suicide rate seems to show a correlation with prevailing economic conditions. For example, the suicide rate in the United States soared in the period following the stock market crash and general economic collapse of 1929. In this situation, apparently, some people concluded that "life is no longer worth living" — not so much because they were faced with actual poverty as because of a feeling that fortunes had been lost and that expectations of lifelong affluence had been cruelly disappointed. But economic setbacks (as a cause of suicide) are only one factor in what is actually a complex psychological pattern.

In general, suicide rates appear to be much higher in economically developed (industrialized) countries than in countries with a predominantly agricultural or pastoral economy. According to the latest available figures* from the UN World Health Organization, the countries with the highest suicide rates are: Hungary, Austria, Czechoslovakia, Sweden, West Germany, Finland, Switzerland, Denmark, Iceland, Australia, Belgium, Japan, Nationalist China, the United States, Bulgaria, Poland, New Zealand, and Great Britain.

Most of these countries are economically advanced. Note, also, that most of the leading industrial powers are included. The actual suicide rates range from 31.3 (per 100,000 people) for Hungary to 10.8 for the United States and 9.7 for Great Britain. In sharp contrast are such rates as 1.9 for Mexico, 2.3 for Chile, and 3.2 for Costa Rica.

Undoubtedly, *all* the suicide rates cited here are too low since many suicides go unreported. For one thing, family doctors are often reluctant to report deaths as suicides. Also, it may be difficult to distinguish an accidental death from a suicide — for example, in highway crashes. Still another complicating factor is that some governments, eager to make favorable propaganda for their social and economic systems, either refuse to release suicide statistics at all, or issue figures which are far too low to be taken seriously. The Soviet Union and the People's Republic of China are cases in point. (Note that neither of these two giant countries appears in the list above.)

---

* The figures in question are for 1966 and for 1967.

While allowing for the incompleteness and undependability of the statistics, we are probably justified in recognizing a general trend: *suicide rates are highest in highly industrialized societies.* Stated otherwise: the complex, sophisticated society typical of our industrial civilization produces a high degree of psychological strain that sometimes leads to suicide.

It is in industrialized societies, such as those of the United States and Western Europe, that competition between individuals is keenest. Under such conditions, there is an intense fear of "failure" — which is commonly interpreted as not making enough money or attaining sufficiently high status. There is general acceptance of an ethic based on hard work, "respectability," and "getting ahead" on the basis of one's own efforts. This scheme of values virtually guarantees a high degree of frustration for a substantial part of the population. As we have noted, when frustration builds up, it frequently leads to aggression — and with some people this aggression may be turned against the self.

In particular, people coming from relatively prosperous, well-established families are usually expected to "make it" — to show some degree of success. Under these circumstances, "failure" can be a crushing experience, leading to depression and in extreme cases to suicide. And the "failure" in question may be an event which a person from another social background would probably take rather lightly — such as losing a job, a poor record in school, having to apply for relief, etc.

A "Cry for Help"

Very often an attempted suicide is in effect a *cry for help*. The individual doesn't want to die. What he does want is *attention,* and unconsciously he feels that the best way to get it is to place his own life in jeopardy. "Then they'll be sorry!"

A person in this frame of mind doesn't really expect to die. If he drives a car into a tree, or leaps overboard from a ship, he expects, again perhaps unconsciously, that he will be saved by "someone's" last-minute intervention. Illogical? Yes — but a person who has reached this level of emotional disturbance is not likely to concern himself with considerations of logic. If the plea goes unheeded, it may be too late to withdraw, and death results.

Is this a suicide or an accident? Does it really make much difference which it is called?

Teen-Age Suicides

Many adults do not remember the intensity of childhood and adolescent experiences. Accordingly, they find it all but impossible to

understand how a young person "with his whole life before him" can have problems so severe and disappointments so painful that they will lead him to attempt suicide. But adolescence is an extremely difficult period in life, and it is a time when emotional stress can take particularly damaging outlets.

It is typical of many suicidal teen-agers that they were involved in a highly possessive and exclusive romantic relationship — one so demanding that it practically isolated them from people other than the loved one. Being caught up in such a relationship at an early age is often a sign that the boy or the girl involved (or both of them) feel unloved and neglected by their families. If such a romance breaks up, as early romances so often do, the teen-ager is likely to feel alone in the world, with no one to turn to. This experience may well be a crushing one, especially for girls, and especially when they know or fear that they are pregnant.

Psychologists who have had experience with large numbers of suicidal children and adolescents have recognized the following patterns:

▶ The young people often come from disrupted or unhappy homes.

▶ They have a background of having changed residences and schools frequently.

▸ In a large number of cases, they have a parent, relative, or close friend who has attempted suicide.

▸ Finally, an astonishingly high proportion of young people who succeed in killing themselves have actually attempted suicide before.

How to Deal with Suicidal Persons

There is a reasonably good chance that at some stage in your life you will come into close contact with a person who is threatening to commit suicide, or is actually attempting to do so. You may be alone in a room with this person. What should you do?

The one thing you should most decidedly *not* do is shrink away from him in horror or disgust. Nor should you try to pass it off as a joke — even if the potential suicide seems to be making fun of himself and of his situation in life. The person who attempts or threatens suicide, as we have noted, is sending out a "cry for help," and what he wants above all is serious and sympathetic attention.

On the other hand, you will probably not do much good by smiling and mumbling a few optimistic words. Try to give the impression that you are truly interested in the person's problems, and encourage him to sit down and talk about them. When he does talk, listen! Make responses that you have reason to think will be relevant and encouraging. As soon as possible, of course, you should summon the professional people who will be able to furnish the controls and the therapeutic help he so obviously needs.

If you are close to the potential suicide — for example, if he (or she) is a member of your immediate family — your job is not ended when the immediate danger has been overcome. It is now your responsibility to relate to him as a human being in trouble — to make it clear to him that you care about him, that you have some insight into his problems, and that you are ready to help him to the very best of your ability whenever he feels that he needs help.

Fallacies About Suicide

A number of myths or fallacies have grown up about the subject of suicide. Although these beliefs are widely held, they have no basis in actual fact. Here are some of them.

▸ "Monday is the favorite day for suicides." This idea probably stems from the fact that most people return to work on Monday after a free weekend. It is, therefore (according to this theory), a day on which depressed people may feel worse than ever. However, the fact is that the type of emotional disturbance that may lead to suicide is far more likely to result from family conditions than from work conditions. All of us have probably experienced a "blue Monday," but the fact is that there is no "favorite day" for suicide.

▶ "More women than men commit suicide." The reverse is true. Roughly twice as many men as women actually kill themselves in the United States each year. This would not necessarily apply, however, to *attempts* at suicide.

▶ "College students have an unusually high suicide rate." The highest suicide rate of any age segment of the population occurs in the 45-to-60 range. However, it is true that college students have the highest *attempt* rate.

▶ "People who talk about suicide are not the ones who will actually do it." The evidence shows that almost everyone who attempts suicide gives some indication of his intentions, and often this is in plain language. Threats to commit suicide (even when they are made "casually") should always be given serious attention, especially in the case of a depressed person. Such remarks, as we have noted, are a "cry for help," and the person who makes them needs desperately the attention of a psychiatrist, a psychologist, or a mental health clinic. Sometimes the most appropriate person to help is a clergyman or counselor.

▶ "Once a person has been saved from suicide, the worst is over." The fact is that of all the people in the United States who attempt suicide and fail, more than half try again within a year.

▶ "Well-adjusted people don't even think about suicide." Almost everyone thinks about suicide at some stage in his life. In the case of a reasonably well-adjusted person, however, the pro-life force is much stronger than the impulse to self-destruction.

Types of Emotional Disturbances

Every emotional disturbance is unique. None is the exact duplicate of another because no two human beings are exactly alike, and life circumstances are never identical. However, neurotic behavior does tend to follow some recognizable patterns. These are referred to by terms which are used frequently, but rather loosely, in everyday life. We shall now consider some of these.

Perfectionism

A *perfectionist,* as we commonly apply the term, is one who wants to do something "better than he possibly can." Whether the job is cleaning a room, preparing an assignment, painting a picture, or administering a business, the perfectionist will go to great pains to try to do everything exactly as he thinks it should be. And he seems never to be fully satisfied.

Some forms of perfectionism are considered neurotic because they are compulsively rooted. The person has an underlying (unconscious) fear of criticism, or a sense of self-doubt, and he "overdoes" in an effort to compensate for this. Thus, a woman whose house or apartment has been thoroughly cleaned may continue to "fuss," straightening out things that are already straight, removing invisible specks of dust, and generally tiring herself and making everyone else uncomfortable.

It must not be assumed, however, that all perfectionism is primarily compulsive in a self-damaging way, and that it is unconsciously motivated. It is probably true that most, if not all, of the great accomplishments of man (in art, science, scholarship, public affairs, etc.) have been the work of perfectionists — people who were "never satisfied," who constantly sought improvement, and who insisted always on attaining the very highest standards that their abilities made possible. Michelangelo was certainly a perfectionist. So in their own ways were such diverse figures as Beethoven, Sigmund Freud, St. Francis, and Ted Williams. A perfectionist, in this (non-neurotic) sense of the term is fully aware of his motivation and is consciously directing his efforts to attain greater self-realization. It may be said that anyone who is exceptionally good at his work has an element of perfectionism in his "makeup."

Kleptomania

The most self-damaging compulsions or neuroses are those that invite punishment. (All compulsive behavior invites punishment in some degree, but there are those which call for a well-defined penalty prescribed by law or custom.)

A good example of such self-damaging behavior is *kleptomania,* or compulsive stealing. Kleptomaniacs are aware that they are stealing, but they don't know why. They may not particularly need or want the things they take, but they literally cannot help themselves, and they continue until they are caught.

The most common basis of kleptomania is believed to be sexual in nature. The person unconsciously connects sexual arousal and gratification with what is forbidden. Thus a "forbidden" activity, such as stealing, acquires a sexual overtone. This interpretation is supported by the fact that many compulsive thieves report that they feel erotic stimulation while engaged in stealing.

Frequently, also, the kleptomaniac feels a need to be punished for his transgression. This is why kleptomaniacs so often are caught as a result of making "stupid" and even childish mistakes that lead to their being found out. These blunders, it is believed, are "planned" in an unconscious way.

Hypochondria and Psychosomatic Illness

Hypochondriacs are people who worry excessively and compulsively about their health and make a great show of complaining to others. This type of neurotic behavior is closely related to psychosomatic illness — that is, physical disorders which are greatly influenced or caused by the emotional state of the patient.

Hypochondria can usually be traced to feelings of insecurity and to an immature need to be dependent on others. Psychosomatic illnesses, which Freud first systematically analyzed in his *Studies in Hysteria,* can be just as real to the patient as any other. As Freud pointed out, however, psychosomatic ailments do not have an identifiable physiological cause, such as bacterial infections or degeneration of the heart tissue. Rather, they are the result of psychological pressures which, because of unconscious blocks, can find no other means of expression than the physical symptoms.

For example, impairment of vision may be the result of a severe psychosomatic reaction. This may result in complete blindness, or it may be expressed in a progressive limiting of peripheral (side) vision, so that the person can see only straight ahead ("tunnel vision"). It is believed that this may be a reaction to avoid "seeing things as they are" when full observation of what is happening might cause great pain. It is actually putting blinders on life.

Paranoia

The term *paranoia* in its popular usage applies to quite a variety of symptoms. In the language of the youth culture, it usually indicates someone who is exceptionally apprehensive or fearful, regardless of whether or not there appears to be adequate "justification" for these fears. In some cases, paranoia is used to mean simply the state of being extremely self-conscious, timid, and sensitive to criticism, but there are certainly many people showing such patterns of behavior who cannot be considered truly paranoid.

As the psychologist uses the term, paranoia refers to fear which has accumulated as a result of inner tensions and *which is not grounded in reality*. The term does not refer to any manifestation of fear which has a reasonable basis. For example, if a drug dealer is constantly afraid of being "busted" by the police, he is not being paranoid because the danger certainly exists. However, even fear which is "justified" or "rational," in this sense, when combined with deepseated guilt feelings can contribute to paranoid delusions.

Severe cases of paranoia constitute a form of mental illness. This will be discussed in some detail in the next chapter (pages 74-75).

Phobias

A great many people in the modern world suffer from phobias, or irrational fears directed to specific things or circumstances. A very common, and in itself relatively harmless, phobia, for example, would be a morbid fear or dislike for spiders or snakes.

People who have phobias typically realize that their fears are unrealistic but are unable or unwilling to do anything about them. The reason is that the phobia has deep psychological roots. Usually it is a projection onto the outer world of an inner conflict. The feared thing or condition becomes a substitute for another fear which is so strong that it must be expressed, but so unacceptable that it must be repressed. This may occur even in small children. Freud reported the case of a five-year-old boy who showed a fear of horses but who actually was afraid of his own father. Similarly, an irrational fear of thunder may be the result of a sense of guilt over some form of personal behavior. The "conscience" associates the loud, dominating sound of the thunder with the reprimands expected from the father for misconduct.

Claustrophobia. This refers to a morbid fear of confined spaces. It is perhaps the most common of all phobias. All people fear in some degree confinement in close quarters, but claustrophobics tend to panic. They associate any confinement with the fear that they "won't be able to get out," or that they will somehow run amuck and hurt themselves.

Claustrophobics apparently unconsciously associate confined spaces with being alone, and with having to face their own impulses and needs. The panic may be based specifically on a fear of letting sexual impulses run wild.

Some claustrophobia can be traced to repressed childhood incidents — the most common being getting locked up in a closet or basement.

Agoraphobia. This is a morbid fear of open spaces. It may be expressed as an unwillingness to leave a familiar room or house. The idea of "going out" — of venturing into unfamiliar and unrestricted environments — fills the agoraphobic with acute fear.

The agoraphobic is typically an extremely fearful and dependent person. Unconsciously, he associates an open space with emancipation and independence, and this causes a sense of panic. The world in his eyes is filled with threats — not with opportunities and possible rewards. If he remains in a closed room, he is protected against these nameless menaces.

Agoraphobia may also be a form of counter-behavior (technically, a "reaction-formation") against a fear of strong exhibitionist tendencies. In the case of a woman, it may be a symptom of a repressed urge toward sexual promiscuity. So long as she remains in her closed environment, she cannot be guilty of shameful misconduct.

Acrophobia. This is a morbid fear of high places. People who chronically suffer from this phobia may be repressing strong urges toward self-destruction. These in turn may be the result of unresolved guilt feelings.

Alcoholism

An alcoholic is a compulsive drinker of alcoholic beverages. He can't control his drinking, even though he knows that he is doing great harm to himself and others.

Alcoholism is an emotional disorder affecting large numbers of people throughout the world. Estimates of the numbers of alcoholics (persons actually addicted to alcohol) in the United States run from about 4 million to more than 9 million. And there are many others who from time to time are "problem drinkers," in the sense that they drink more than they should and react in some unfavorable way. The total number of "problem drinkers" (including alcohol addicts) in the United States is estimated by some authorities to be as high as 28 million.

The typical picture of an alcoholic is of a homeless, jobless derelict, "sleeping off a drunk" in an alley. And indeed there are many alcoholics of this type. But there are other alcoholics who hold responsible positions and who may fill these jobs with a high level of competence — when they are not drinking. When they do drink, however, they cannot do so in moderation. They often continue until they become unconscious. Or they may become involved in a senseless fight, or may attempt to drive a car and cause an accident. (Drinking drivers account for about half of the roughly 50,000 traffic fatalities in the United States each year.)

Here is one manifestation of the disease called alcoholism. On different socio-economic levels, the behavior may be less flagrant, although perhaps just as destructive.

The most tragic aspect of alcoholism is not so much what the alcoholic does to himself as what he does to those who love him and depend on him. In particular, some of the worst cases of neurosis and mental illness among children occur when one or both parents are alcoholics.

Alcoholism has come to be widely recognized as an illness. It is a form of drug abuse and addiction, since alcohol must be considered a drug. Like other drugs, it causes metabolic changes and alters perception. (See pages 242-253.)

There is much uncertainty about the conditions that lead people to become alcoholics. A few experts in the field think that alcoholics, in some cases at least, have an inherited or congenital biological defect which lowers their tolerance to alcohol, makes them become intoxicated easily, and leads to addiction, or compulsive and excessive drinking. But this certainly does not apply to all of the millions of alcoholics and other "problem drinkers." To explain their difficulties, we must turn to emotional or personality factors. Research done on alcoholics shows that most of them suffer from emotional disturbances and personality disorders that often date back to childhood. Freud thought that some men drink to excess to prove their masculinity. This relates to the popular stereotype of the "hard-drinking, two-fisted he-man." Other researchers have attributed excessive drinking to a desire to escape from tension produced by feelings of guilt, inadequacy, or insecurity. There is probably some element of truth in all these explanations, varying with individual cases.

There are evidently cultural influences that produce higher rates of alcoholism in some groups than in others, even within the same larger society. For example, many studies have revealed that Irish-Americans show a fairly high rate of alcoholism; the rate among Jewish-Americans is notably low. It certainly is not claimed that American Jews are less prone to neurosis than Americans of Irish origin, but only that they show less tendency to express this in the form of alcoholism. In some groups, cultural conditions may be such that there are very few ways of relieving emotional tension. For example, an open display of emotion may be condemned as "weak" and "childish." Then getting drunk may be the "best" available outlet.

What makes alcoholism particularly dangerous is that intensive and long-continued use may lead to addiction, not much different from addiction to heroin and other similar drugs. This addiction is not merely psychological but physiological or metabolic. The individual's system becomes accustomed to heavy intakes of alcohol, and "demands" regular doses. Sudden and complete deprivation can cause severe withdrawal symptoms. One reaction after prolonged heavy drinking may be the "DT's" (delirium tremens), which sometimes results in self-inflicted injuries.

Conclusion: Emotional Problems and Social Problems

From your own experience, you probably know that emotional problems can lead to disturbing behavior. People who behave in this way may "bug" you, but you can make a positive contribution to the situation by understanding what is "bugging" the other fellow, and then acting accordingly.

Some emotional problems lead to social problems. We have described a few of them: crime, juvenile delinquency, alcoholism. But it is also important to realize that the reverse is true — that social problems produce emotional problems. For example, the strong emphasis on competition in our society is a factor in producing emotional disturbances that lead to irrational fears (paranoia and phobias) and to such deviant behavior as attempts at suicide. Grinding poverty, inadequate education, racial discrimination, and generally poor social conditions have a marked effect on children, who may grow up into adults struggling with emotional disorders of various types.

Emotionally healthy people are the products of a sound and wholesome social environment. But the social environment is in large measure a reflection of the people constituting the group, community, or nation. You may ask then: If we wish to achieve higher standards of emotional health, do we concentrate on improving our overall social order, or rather on providing specific help for those with emotional problems or weaknesses?

The best answer is that we must attack *both* phases of the situation at once. We must certainly work to rid our society of slums, racial discrimination, unemployment, and poverty. We must also seek for greater knowledge and better facilities to guard people against emotional disturbances and to help those who are afflicted.

On the other hand, it is futile for the troubled person to follow the pattern of *blaming others* for his emotional disturbances. The "others" in question may be parents, teachers, clergymen, the police, the courts, employers, and the "establishment," or society as a whole. Admittedly all of these individuals and organizations are imperfect, and in the course of your experience, you may have legitimate grievances against any or all of them. But don't use them as an "out" to excuse your own disturbed behavior. In the last analysis, *you* are the only person who can be fully responsible for correcting your own weaknesses and "getting yourself together."

THINGS TO DISCUSS :: THINGS TO DO :: THINGS TO READ

1. Why do some people like to get drunk?

2. On Halloween night in the depression year of 1938, Orson Welles did a broadcast based on H. G. Wells' novel *The War of the Worlds*. The program was done as a series of simulated newscasts describing a Martian invasion of earth. Of 6 million listeners, possibly 1 million panicked. One woman ran into a church gathering and shouted, "It's the end of the world! I just heard it on the radio!" The rest of the people evidently kept their cool and soon figured out that it was a radio play. How would you explain the behavior of the people who panicked? Is it plausible to say that there was a connection between the poverty and misery so widespread during the great depression and an individual tendency to expect catastrophe?

3. Psychologist Avery Weisman has called suicide "the decision to end all indecisions." Do you think this is a good characterization? Explain.

4. In this chapter we have described only a few of the forms that neurotic behavior may take. Bearing in mind that neurotic behavior is *repetitive, compulsive,* largely *unconscious,* and usually *inappropriate,* describe some forms of neurosis that you have seen at first hand or have heard about. What can be done to modify such behavior?

5. Former Supreme Court Justice Abe Fortas once said: "Under our Constitution, the condition of being a boy does not justify a kangaroo court." Give some examples of the types of abuses you think he had in mind. What changes should be made to correct these abuses and protect young people?

6. Are there any places in this chapter that gave you some uncomfortable moments? What are they? Why do you think you reacted in this way?

7. There is some disagreement among experts as to whether heavy smoking is a neurotic symptom ("compulsive oral gratification"). Make your own assessment. Talk to people who represent the following patterns: (*a*) smokes heavily and has made no attempt to stop; (*b*) smokes heavily and has been unsuccessful in attempts to stop; (*c*) formerly smoked heavily but quit and has not smoked for at least the last six months. Ask the first smoker why he doesn't at least *try* to stop, in view of the fact that he knows he may be doing himself serious physical harm. Ask the second smoker what prevents him from controlling his urge to smoke when he makes an effort to stop. Ask the "reformed" smoker how he did it and what difference it has made in his life.

8. Help an emotionally disturbed kid. Invite him out to a movie, to play ball, to go hiking, to church. Teach him to do something interesting and amusing, such as playing a musical instrument.

9. Become a pen pal with a child confined in an institution.

10. If you can afford it, subscribe to a magazine or newspaper for a child who cannot afford it.

11. Offer your services as a repairman. Fix toys and do other jobs at a day-care center.

READINGS

NOTE: All of these books are available in paperback editions.

Tender is the Night, by F. Scott Fitzgerald (Scribner's, 1933). A compelling novel about the onset, symptoms and effects of emotional disorder. (Fitzgerald himself became an alcoholic.)

The Catcher in the Rye, by J. D. Salinger (Little Brown, 1951). Not as popular today as it once was, but still a brilliant and enjoyable description of a teen-aged boy and his emotional difficulties.

Children in Trouble by Howard James (David McKay, 1970). A shocking, but thoroughly researched account of a "national scandal."

Who is Sane?
Who is Not?
Who is to Judge?

● ●

"Being crazy is like one of those nightmares where you try to call for help and no sound comes out. Or if you can call, no one hears or understands. You can't wake up from the nightmare unless someone does hear you and helps you to wake up."

— A Former Mental Patient

Nature of Mental Illness

What Is Mental Illness?

Mental illness frightens many people. Probably no one goes through a lifetime without some concern about his mental health. A person may have weird dreams . . . or a bitter quarrel with a loved one . . . or a temporary fit of depression . . . or a sense of confusion and inadequacy while trying to cope with a new situation. Before long he may be asking himself, "Am I mentally ill?"

As long as the disturbance affects only *part* of his life (that is, only *partially* limits his ability to handle life situations), the answer is probably *no*. More than likely, he is going through an emotional difficulty which does not come within the category of mental illness. He may be temporarily handicapped or out of action, but if some adjustment is made in the limited area of his disturbance, he will soon be able to function again.

Mental illness, on the other hand, distorts the *entire* personality — usually over a number of years. Very often, the person's thinking is so disturbed that it does not even occur to him to ask himself if he is mentally ill. (This is not always true, of course. A person whose men-

58

tal health is fast deteriorating into a full-blown mental illness may be aware of what is happening, but is unable to do anything about it.)

Symptoms of mental illness can develop gradually or can come on suddenly. A person may display progressively more "eccentric" behavior over a period of years, until it becomes apparent that he is mentally ill; or he may go along appearing to be altogether "normal," until suddenly he starts doing "abnormal" things.

One distressed young man described an acute episode of mental illness he went through:

> I thought I had died and was in Hell, where I had landed as pun-
> ishment for my greed. Everything looked Satanic; everything looked
> completely corrupt. Everyone was either a demon, a ghoul, a body
> without a soul, or the Devil in disguise. I thought my soul was gone,
> lost — that I couldn't possibly do anything of any worth. It was all a
> big cat-and-mouse game, with me as the mouse. Everything that any-
> one said I interpreted as an exquisitely elaborate torture. I thought I
> was on the other side of reality — on the other side of the mirror.

The mentally ill person may desperately want to get through to the world of reality (to "communicate"), but his entire personality is so affected that he cannot easily make himself understood. For instance, the young man quoted above wanted to say something about being in Hell, but during the most acute phase of his illness, he was unable to do so; he assumed that any conversation would inevitably be "corrupted" into a torture session.

Often, a mentally ill person feels that his body is like a machine that he can't control. He is eager for help, but at the same time he is convinced that he is beyond help. This explains in part why he may speak in disjointed, illogical phrases that convey no clear ideas. *He* understands what he is saying, but no one else does. For instance, the young man mentioned above, when asked where he was from, would make such replies as, "Across the River" (the River Styx), or "the Other Side" (life).

In fact, a mentally ill person may respond or behave in all manner of odd ways. He may be in the depths of despair, but his face bursts into uncontrolled laughter. He may fail to respond when spoken to, or he may suddenly break off a conversation and wander away. When people behave like this, we know they are in trouble and need our help. However, it is not always easy to tell if a person is mentally ill. He may make a deliberate effort to act "normally," and may succeed in giving this impression, even though he still feels hopelessly cut off from reality.

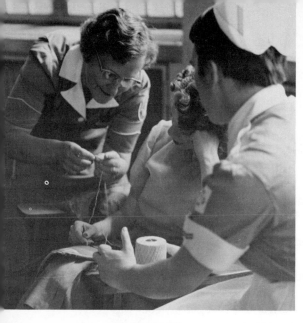

Mentally troubled persons sometimes derive considerable benefit from being taught to develop relatively simple but satisfying manual skills, such as sewing and weaving.

Some Basic Terms

The technical name for mental illness is *psychosis*. The term *insanity* is not commonly used by psychologists because it has an ugly association with "raving maniac" (although the word *sanity* is frequently used to describe mental health).

The psychoses are divided into two broad classifications — *organic* and *functional*.

The *organic* psychoses are those that have physical causes. In other words, they are the result of some type of brain damage. They include *paresis,* which is caused by infectious syphilis, and *senility,* which is caused by deterioration of the brain in old age.

The *functional* psychoses are those that were at one time thought to have mainly or exclusively psychological causes. In general, they are not the result of any easily detectable physical abnormality. However, there is some indication that a number of the so-called functional psychoses — particularly *schizophrenia* — may have organic as well as psychological causes. Specifically, a person may be born with a difference in his body chemistry that makes him more prone to mental illness when the psychological pressures are fairly strong.

Attitudes Toward the Mentally Ill

It is traditional in our society to jeer at and abuse the mentally ill. We have all heard, and perhaps told, our share of jokes about the "nut house," the "funny farm," and the "men in the white coats."

This attitude is no doubt based on thoughtlessness, rather than any intent to be cruel. Nonetheless, a great deal of harm may be done when we make fun of someone showing symptoms of mental illness.

Often it comes as a surprise to learn that the mentally ill, no matter how "removed" they may seem, in many cases know what is going on around them and are aware of how they are being treated. They resent it when people show a harsh and contemptuous attitude toward them, and all too often their illness is intensified as a result. Like everyone else (perhaps *more than* everyone else), they need and respond to understanding and sympathy — though you may not be able to tell immediately that they are reacting in a positive way.

But sympathy and kindness are not enough. If you know someone who is mentally ill, or who you think is mentally ill, the greatest service you can do him is to *help him get professional care.**

Does Mental Illness "Run in Families"?

There is a popular misconception that mental illness "runs in families."

Although there is some indication that mental illness is partly caused by inborn physical differences, there is little proof that any such difference is directly inherited from the parents, like eye color or blood type. Mental illness is such a widespread problem that if it does "run in families," there must be very few families which do not carry this hereditary factor. For example, according to one estimate, *one in every ten* Americans will be hospitalized for mental illness at some point in his life. In 1968, the number of patients receiving psychiatric care in the United States was almost 3.4 million — representing close to 2% of the population. Mental illness is so common that almost everyone knows or has heard of someone who is suffering, or has suffered, from mental illness.

In fact, many of us have relatives suffering from mental disorders. This sometimes leads to a secret fear that the same condition may show up in other members of the family. Most experts feel that this fear is unwarranted, and that, in this sense, mental illness does not "run in families."

Thus, if your Uncle Joe is mentally ill, this certainly does not mean that you will become mentally ill, even if you look like your uncle or have some of his mannerisms. Sometimes in this situation, family members or friends will make teasing remarks, such as, "Now you're behaving like Uncle Joe." Remarks of this sort are unfortunate and probably quite meaningless, and you should not allow them to cause you unnecessary worry.

---

* In the United States, every state and most large cities have a *Mental Health Association* which can help with information and referrals.

Emotional Problems vs. Mental Illness

Sometimes people worry needlessly and jump to false conclusions because they do not appreciate the difference between being *mentally ill* and having *emotional problems*. In the course of a lifetime, you can scarcely hope to escape some emotional problems, any more than you can go through life without some symptoms of physical illness or malfunctioning.

An emotional problem will make you feel disturbed and confused (anxious). You may react by eating too much, by withdrawing from social relationships, or by being generally overanxious. These are signs that something is bothering you. If these symptoms persist over a fairly long time, your emotional problem may even be severe enough to be called a *neurosis*. However, whether you are suffering from a short-term emotional difficulty or an obvious neurosis, your overall personality is not radically affected, and you are still able to communicate with other people to a fair degree. In fact, a key distinction between an emotional problem and a full-blown mental illness depends on the fact that one involves only a moderate impairment of the ability to communicate, while the other is characterized by ruinous breakdown of communication on almost every level.

Usually, if you have an emotional problem, you are aware that something is wrong and that it is necessary for you to make some kind of effort to help yourself. When you are able to face a problem squarely — for example, by admitting that a romance that meant a great deal to you is over and done with — the symptoms may ease off, and in time vanish entirely.

But a mental illness is a great deal more serious. It is a gross distortion or disabling of the personality that is reflected in every aspect of the person's life. As noted above, it has a long-term character, and it is almost always futile to hope for quick, easy, or dramatic cures.

There is also a widespread idea that anyone with an emotional problem who consults a psychiatrist or psychologist is in effect betraying the fact that he is mentally ill or "crazy." This too is a flagrant misconception. Psychiatrists and psychologists, to be sure, do treat the mentally ill, but they also help people with lesser emotional troubles. We certainly don't assume that anyone who sees a physician must be gravely ill with a disease that may require years of treatment.

Retardation and Mental Illness

Mental retardation means a low functioning of the intelligence capacity. This condition is sometimes hereditary.* Under favorable conditions, much can be done to help the retarded person to make good use of his limited capacities and to lead a relatively normal and satisfactory life.

Low intelligence is not in itself a cause of mental illness. However, retarded people, because they are likely to be treated without regard for their special needs, and because they are often cut off from normal social relations, may be more prone than most others to emotional disorders and mental illness.

It should also be noted that some victims of mental illness having normal, or even superior, intelligence may *appear* to be mentally retarded. This is a symptom of the illness, or a reaction to unsuitable or even cruel treatment, rather than a result of any inborn defect.

Changing Views on Mental Health

Mistreatment, rather than treatment, has traditionally been the fate of the mentally ill in virtually all the countries of the world.

In many primitive cultures (and in some not so primitive), it was believed that the bodies of the mentally ill were inhabited by "evil spirits," or that such spirits had "taken possession" of their souls. The spirits in question were thought to be responsible for the strange behavior. Chants, dances, magic charms, incantations, and special potions were commonly used to drive out the spirits, or to placate them,

---

*Mental retardation may be transmitted from parents to children as a *recessive hereditary trait*. Therefore, it is perfectly possible for two normal parents to have a mentally retarded child.

This engraving by William Hogarth shows conditions in London's main hospital for the insane in the 18th century. The official name of the hospital was St. Mary of Bethlehem, but it became popularly known as "Bedlam," and added that word to the English language.

so that they would allow their unfortunate victims to return to normalcy. Even such highly civilized peoples as the ancient Greeks and the Hebrews, except for a few enlightened individuals, shared the belief in "demonic possession."

In Europe during the Middle Ages, fear of mentally ill persons reached hysterical levels. These unfortunate people were often flogged or otherwise tortured to drive out the diabolical agents that "possessed" them. Then, as Europe emerged from the medieval period into modern times, treatment of the mentally ill became, if anything, even worse. Persons who showed symptoms of mental ailments were placed in the same category as "witches" — that is, allies of the devil. Many men and women who were guilty of nothing more than somewhat unusual or eccentric behavior were tried in court, forced to "confess," and then subjected to the most barbaric punishments, such as burning at the stake.

The belief that persons showing symptoms of mental abnormality were actually *ill* began to gain acceptance in the 18th and 19th centuries. A French physician named Philippe Pinel became aware that "lunatics" would often show encouraging responses if they were treated more like human beings. At the height of the French Revolution in 1793, Pinel took charge of the Bicêtre Hospital for the Insane in Paris. It had been customary here to chain the ragged or naked inmates to the walls and beds. They lived in squalor and filth, and were fed miserably. "Treatment" consisted mainly of physical restraint and beatings. On holidays, visitors paid an admission fee to walk through the hospital and gape at the "sights," as though the inmates were strange animals in a zoo.

To the amazement of his revolutionary contemporaries, Pinel unchained the inmates and began to clean up the hospital. Inmates were no longer brutally punished or exhibited publicly. Though he had few resources with which to treat his patients, Pinel found that sympathy and humanity could accomplish a great deal. People who had previously been considered dangerous now walked about freely with few or no difficulties.

The most significant change, however, was the development of the concept of *mental illness*. It became less and less common to describe a mentally ill person as "possessed by devils." In this enlightened view, such an individual was not an object for punishment or ridicule; he was simply a sick person who needed help. True, very little was known of why people became ill in this way, or of what could be done to help them, but the very idea that this was a proper subject for medical investigation must be considered a major advance. *Psychiatry* emerged as the branch of medical science that classifies and treats mental illnesses. Mentally ill persons were to be treated (not merely confined) in special institutions called *mental hospitals*.

Mental Hospitals

In the 19th century, mental hospitals were built in civilized countries in all parts of the world. In the United States they were usually located (by state governments) in isolated rural areas because of the popular belief that mental patients are dangerous. Yet the fact is that only a tiny percentage of mental patients are dangerous to others — certainly not enough to justify treating them all as prisoners.

Unfortunately, many of the state-run hospitals, particularly the larger ones, have too often been little more than a human dumping ground for society's misfits and "undesirables." They are so overcrowded that patients receive generally inadequate attention, to put it mildly. The emphasis, even today, is frequently on keeping the patients "quiet" and "safe." Overworked attendants sometimes fall back on force and punishment for this purpose.

There are, of course, wide disparities in the quality of care and treatment given to mental patients in this country's public institutions. Some of the newer hospitals are showing encouraging improvement. Many now have open wards, in which the doors are unlocked and the patients have considerable freedom of movement. The hospitals themselves are now being located mainly in or near urban areas, where they are more accessible to visitors — an important consideration because many patients benefit greatly from regular visits from their friends and relatives. The problems of overcrowding are acute, but some doctors and administrators are working hard and with considerable success to provide better care.

Outpatient Care for the Mentally Ill

In recent years, community mental health centers have been set up in many cities with the aid of the Federal government. These provide outpatient as well as inpatient care. In addition, there are now psychiatric outpatient clinics attached to some general hospitals.

By the early 1970's, about 45% of all mental patients in the United States were being treated through outpatient facilities. This means that the people in question continue to live at home, while they visit the medical institution at regular intervals for examination and treatment. There are several advantages in this: It saves a great deal of money. It reserves inpatient facilities for those who need it most. And, most important of all, it helps a great many patients who do not want or need the protection of a sheltered institutional environment, and who will be much better adjusted, and therefore more treatable, if they live at home.

An encouraging new development is the establishment of day-care, work, and recreational centers for disturbed persons. These "halfway houses" help people recently discharged from mental hospitals to return to society with some supervision.

Patients in mental hospitals may benefit from a planned program of exercise and physical rehabilitation.

Symptoms of a Mental Illness

The mental illnesses from which people suffer are frequently classified into the following major categories: *schizophrenia, involutional psychosis, manic-depression, psychotic depression, paranoid reactions.*

Each of these categories is usually broken down into sub-classifications. Such distinctions, however, tend to become very hazy and sometimes appear to depend on the subjective impressions of whoever is making the diagnosis, rather than on real, observable differences in the illnesses themselves.

People with any one of these illnesses invariably show one or more of the following symptoms: *disorientation, delusions, hallucinations, emotional disturbance, disruption of spoken communication, unusual or bizarre mannerisms.*

A *disoriented* patient acts as though he doesn't know who he is, where he is, or what time of the day, week, or year it is. Sometimes however, this impression of disorientation may not be an accurate reflection of the trouble. For example, recall the young man (described on page 59) who thought he was in Hell and who, when asked where he was from, answered, "From across the River" (meaning the River Styx in Hell). This patient was really suffering from a *delusion* — a grossly mistaken and distorted belief. If the questioner was not aware of the delusion, he would probably assume simply that the young man didn't know where he had come from. Often it is difficult to tell if an apparently disoriented person has actually lost his sense of time and place, or is for some reason unwilling to acknowledge the facts. Frequently, the individual's condition appears to be a mixture of both elements.

Hallucination refers to seeing, hearing, feeling, smelling, or even tasting something of which no one else is aware and which appears to have no actual physical basis. The most frequent type of hallucination is "hearing voices." Sometimes these voices are encouraging, but more often they are menacing and terrifying. The patient may believe that he is hearing the "voice of God," and may respond by some form of destructive behavior.

You may have experienced a mild hallucination during a long automobile or train ride, when the rhythmic sounds of the motor and wheels began to sound like the playing of an orchestra, or perhaps a repetitive chant of some familiar phrase. If you have had such an experience, you have some idea of how compelling an hallucination may be, even though on another level of awareness you realize perfectly well that your interpretation of the sounds is not based on reality.

The young man who thought he was in Hell experienced another type of hallucination. He reported later that during the period of this delusion, he didn't actually "see things that weren't there," but he did see them differently than under ordinary (normal) conditions. "Everything looked Satanic; everything looked corrupt." A patient in this condition may observe an ordinary dog or cat and hallucinate it into a wild beast that is about to tear him apart.

Persons suffering from mental illness sometimes show emotional reactions which are so far out of the ordinary that they must be considered *emotional disturbances*. Symptoms of this type include apparently unmotivated exuberance or elation, and erratic outbursts of extreme anger that may lead occasionally to uncontrollable violence. In contrast, the patient may appear to be completely passive, displaying no signs of any kind of feeling.

Disruption of communication occurs when the mentally ill person is unable or unwilling to respond to spoken questions or comments in a way that is ordinarily considered "logical" or "sensible." For example, if he is asked, "What did you have for breakfast?" he may answer, "Inside out." This is sometimes referred to as a "thought disorder."

Symbolic or ritualistic mannerisms are frequently an indication that a person is suffering from a mental illness. Such mannerisms are always compulsive and inappropriate, but they may cover a wide range of behavior. At one extreme are subtle shifts in facial expressions that would be noticed only by experienced observers. At the other extreme, the behavior may be so bizarre that it can scarcely be overlooked by anyone.

At this point, it should be noted that except in extreme cases, it is difficult for even highly trained professionals to make an accurate diagnosis of mental illness. What this means for you is that even if you observe what appear to be clear signs of "strange behavior" in someone whom you know, you will be ill-advised to assume that this person is mentally ill. You simply do not have an adequate basis for forming such a judgment. If the person in question seems to need help try to refer him, as a first step, to an experienced adult whose judgment you trust — for example, a clergyman, a teacher, a counselor, or a family physician. This individual can look into the situation and, if it seems justified, will probably refer the troubled person to a mental health specialist.

Schizophrenia

The Most Common Mental Illness

By far the most common of mental illnesses is *schizophrenia.* Fully half of all the beds in mental hospitals and wards in the United States are occupied by people regarded as schizophrenics.

The word *schizophrenia,* derived from Greek, means literally "splintered" or "fragmented" (*schizo-*) plus "mind" (*phrenia*). Some experts feel that this traditional name still describes the condition fairly well. In their opinion, the schizophrenic personality is fragmented into separate "control centers" or "identities," each of which may take charge of the person's behavior at different times.

Whether or not this is what actually happens, the personality of the schizophrenic individual does appear to be deteriorating or "breaking up." As far as the people around a schizophrenic can judge, he is cut off from reality, and specifically he is cut off from other people. The most compelling characteristic of this illness is an *inability to communicate* at a level understood by the average person.

Delusions are another symptom of schizophrenia. A *delusion,* as we have noted, is a false belief — not merely an inaccurate or questionable idea but a conviction which is obviously far beyond the bounds of reality. For example, a schizophrenic may announce in a hospital ward that he is Napoleon or Jesus Christ. There is no point in trying to use ordinary logic to convince him that this is impossible. Such an effort is doomed to failure because, as far as the schizophrenic is concerned, his belief is so obviously correct that denying it is a denial of reality and truth. The British psychiatrist R. D. Laing tells of a schizophrenic patient who, during a lie-detector test, was asked if he was Napoleon. When the patient replied "No," the machine registered a lie.

In a brilliant discussion of mental illness, Laing describes the schizophrenic's condition succinctly:*

> The schizophrenic is desperate, is simply without hope. I have never known a schizophrenic who could say he was loved, as a man, by God the Father or by the Mother of God, or by another man. He either *is* God, or the Devil, or in hell, estranged from God.
>
> Schizophrenia cannot be understood without understanding despair.

---

* R. D. Laing, *The Divided Self* (Tavistock Publications, 1959).

Ignoring Life — Catatonia

Life may become so unbearable for a schizophrenic that he simply withdraws from it. Since he sees himself as cut off from reality (or, one might say, he feels that he has lost his soul), he may well conclude that there is no point or purpose in making an effort to "go through the motions of living."

He may sit or lie in a curled-up position all day, ignoring the presence of anyone else. He may cause his body to go rigid for hours on end. If he is placed in a certain position by a nurse, he may remain that way without the slightest change for a long time. By such immobility and silence — called *catatonia* — he seems to be appealing to everyone, "Go away! Leave me alone."

Yet if these patients are "left alone" (ignored), or, worse, if they are mistreated, they are much more likely to become hostile than if they are treated with a reasonable amount of sympathy. Behind the appearance of catatonic withdrawal and unfeelingness, the schizophrenic *does* have some awareness of what is happening. If people continue to treat him like a human being, rather than an unfeeling lump of matter, he is more likely to give up this behavior when he is ready to do so. Unfortunately, in some hospitals, catatonics and other schizophrenics are taken at face value and are treated like objects — rather than people. This attitude is communicated to the patient and reinforces his behavior. In overcrowded institutions, where patients receive little individual attention, there are many schizophrenics in the "back wards" who for all practical purposes have been abandoned and will never get out.

Childish Behavior by Schizophrenics

Some schizophrenics express their condition in disordered speech, random giggling, and generally childish behavior. They seem ready to do whatever may occur to them, no matter how silly. It is very hard in the face of such behavior not to treat schizophrenics like small children.

Yet, if such patients are treated like children, with no attempt at understanding, they tend to get worse. The seemingly foolish, undirected, erratic behavior of a schizophrenic is really another manifestation of total despair. It is, in a sense, another means of appealing for attention and help, although at the same time it suggests a denial that any help is possible. There is some evidence that if a person showing such symptoms is treated sympathetically and like an adult, he may modify his childish behavior, at least for a time.

Schizophrenia and the Family

Some mental health specialists are convinced that the root of many schizophrenic disorders lies in the way that children and young people relate to other members of their families. This theory (which has strong but by no means universal support) holds that a person may be born with a tendency toward schizophrenia, but that this will be brought out and actualized only if the family relationships are significantly unhealthy.

The starting point, according to this theory, is a child living in a family with insecure or hostile parents, unsure of themselves and their roles. As such a child grows older, he typically discovers that what his parents want from him above all is to "be good," which means more than anything else not creating any disorder or asking for anything. The child is not allowed to behave spontaneously — to be himself. Often, these parents will say later, without realizing the implications, "He was always such a good boy! He never demanded anything."

Several points should be noted:

Parents in emotionally disturbed families rarely are aware of what they are doing wrong. They themselves may be the victims of similar childhoods.

Of course, not all children from such homes become mentally ill. In some cases the children become delinquents. And in others, somewhat surprisingly, the unfavorable conditions seem to produce exceptionally sturdy and independent characters.

On the other hand, a significant number of babies with schizophrenic symptoms are born into what appear to be well-adjusted families. On this basis, it seems possible that some types of schizophrenia are due more to genetic defects (such as abnormalities of body chemistry) than to psychological causes. However, the evidence to support this interpretation is far from conclusive.

When schizophrenic symptoms appear in childhood, the disorder is called *infantile autism*.

Treatment for Schizophrenia

There is no single highly successful treatment for schizophrenia. This is reflected in the fact that psychiatrists are continually seeking and experimenting to find a generally effective method of therapy for the disorder.

The treatments most often used in state institutions are typically more physical than psychological in approach. They include electrical shock to the brain and tranquilizing drugs.

Psychological approaches vary widely. One such type of therapy is described in Marguerite Sechahaye's fascinating account, *The Autobiography of a Schizophrenic Girl.* The treatment in question consists of psychological influences designed to guide the patient back to earlier stages in his life cycle until he reaches the point where he is behaving like a helpless infant. At this point, all of his desires are satisfied, even to the extent of allowing him to use baby bottles. This treatment, it is hoped, will recover for the patient a sense of security and well-being which normal people experienced as a result of being loved and cared for in infancy. This suggests that the only way a schizophrenic can be made to feel sufficiently secure to relate normally to reality is to teach him how to feel love in a genuine way.

Other Forms of Mental Illness

Other forms of mental illness occur with much less frequency than schizophrenia, but their frequency and the damage they do are still alarming. It is quite easy to apply verbal labels to these illnesses (as we shall do below), but in actual practice it is often difficult to distinguish one illness from another. A given individual may often show at the same time symptoms which appear to be associated with several different conditions.

For example, depression and paranoiac feelings appear in virtually all forms of mental illness, although in very different degrees. The depressive ailments, however, are traditionally classified into three main types: *manic-depression, psychotic depression,* and *involutional psychosis.*

Manic Depression

Virtually everyone has moods of depression from time to time. In some cases the depression may be quite pronounced and persistent, but the individual in question is still able to function reasonably well in the relations of everyday life. This is *ordinary simple depression* or *simple neurotic depression.* Since it is not disabling it is not regarded as a mental illness. The depression is sometimes followed by a mood of exuberance or elation, which in turn is not so extreme that it has a disabling effect.

The form of mental illness called *manic-depression* is also characterized by ups and downs in the individual's moods, but in this case the "swings" are relatively extreme. Deep depression may be succeeded by seemingly boundless enthusiasm or agitation (the *manic phase*). In either phase, the individual is so far separated from reality that he cannot relate normally to other people and carry out the ordinary responsibilities of life.

Not all cases follow the classic "up-and-down" model. The person may repeatedly become deeply depressed without ever going through a well-defined manic phase. Or he may repeatedly become elated or over-agitated without appearing to suffer from spells of deep depression.

Psychologists believe that a person in the manic phase of the cycle is basically still depressed. Struggling against his own unhappiness, he hopes unconsciously that a "show" of feverish activity and exaggerated optimism will help him overcome and forget his feelings of despair.

It rarely does any good to "argue" with a person in any phase of a manic-depressive cycle — to attempt to explain (however patiently or convincingly) that there is no rational basis for either the "low" of the depression or the "high" of the manic phase. The patient is disoriented from the reality of the outside world to such a degree that he is indifferent to demonstrations that there is no "real reason" for his extreme emotions.

The causes of manic-depression are far from being completely understood. There is growing evidence that genetic factors may be involved — in other words, that some persons may inherit special biochemical conditions that make them more vulnerable than others. On occasions, the illness seems to vanish spontaneously. Some scientists interpret this to mean that the body chemistry has somehow adjusted itself.

Involutional Psychosis

This is a form of mental illness that usually strikes in middle age, during the so-called "change of life." The causes may be *physical,* involving a change in the body chemistry. They may also be *psychological,* resulting from a panic realization that this milestone in the life cycle has been passed, and that "the future is here." Whatever the cause or combination of causes, the basic reaction is a profound depression.

Physical symptoms commonly include dizziness, sleeplessness, poor appetite, and general listlessness. Typical psychological symptoms are hypochondria (a morbid preoccupation with illness), self-pity, general anxiety, and a sense of uneasiness. People suffering from involutional psychosis often appear to be "unable to sit still"; they may break out into unmotivated crying spells; they experience hallucinations and delusions.

Chances of recovering from this condition are usually quite good, although the mood of depression may last as long as two or three years. Many people seem to recover spontaneously, and go on to lead more or less normal lives.

Psychotic Depression

This type of illness must be distinguished both from ordinary (neurotic) depression and from the "down" phase of the manic-depressive cycle. The basic difference lies in the fact that the psychotic depression is so profound and so incapacitating that the sufferer falls into a stupor and can do virtually nothing for himself. Often he must be spoon fed. Delusions and hallucinations are common.

This ailment often occurs in old age and is likely to be triggered by a traumatic event, such as the death of a husband or wife. Some psychologists believe that the depression may be in large part a reaction to growing awareness of the approach of death.

Paranoid Reactions

Paranoia is characterized by delusions of persecution. There are many neurotics who suffer from fantasies that other people are "against them" and are "talking about them." In psychotic paranoia, however, the patient's fantasies of persecution are so extreme and so pervasive that they create fears and hatreds which dominate his entire outlook on life. Serious difficulties frequently result.

Some of the most memorable characters in world literature are paranoid types. Don Quixote attacks the windmills, secure in his conviction that they are "wicked giants," bent on destroying him and bringing trouble to mankind.

For example, a person may be obsessed with the idea that some large organization (such as a major corporation or a government agency) is persecuting him. The only "basis" for this conviction may be perhaps some minor incident that occurred many years ago. Nonetheless, the paranoid individual somehow convinces himself that the company or agency in question is keenly aware of his existence and is using all its vast resources to "get him." Again, rational arguments to prove that this cannot possibly be so is highly unlikely to have any effect whatsoever. The paranoid personality often becomes surprisingly ingenious in finding "evidence" to back up his delusion.

An obsessive paranoid reaction of this type is believed to be a defense against feelings of unimportance and powerlessness. The individual in question is dominated by fears, and he tries to overcome these by unconsciously projecting them onto the outside world. At the same time, he builds up his feelings of self-importance. (*Obviously General Motors or the Internal Revenue Service wouldn't bother to persecute an insignificant individual!*) Also, he finds a ready-made excuse for failures. (*Who can succeed at anything when the whole world is against him?*)

Syphilis and Brain Disorders

In the 19th and early 20th centuries, doctors became aware of a disease called *paresis,* in which the victims show psychotic symptoms, such as delusions and hallucinations. Another typical symptom is unrestrained expression of emotions, varying wildly from depression to elation, with crying and laughing spells. Paretics may also show a shuffling gait, disturbed speech, and generally uncoordinated and inappropriate behavior.

Often the victims of paresis come to the attention of doctors because of the behavioral changes noted. However, there are also specific physical symptoms used in the diagnosis of the disease. (This is not true of schizophrenia or manic-depressive conditions.)

Paresis is now understood to be the last stage of neuro-syphilis. The syphilitic infection, transmitted by sexual intercourse (page 458), will remain in the person's body if it is untreated. After a period of time (perhaps 5 to 20 years), the nervous system, including the brain, becomes severely damaged by the organisms of the disease. It is this damage that results in the symptoms noted above.

The best way to avoid paresis is to avoid syphilitic infection. If the infection does occur, however, it is now treatable by penicillin and other antibiotics. Prompt and thorough treatment will usually kill the infection before it has done too much harm. (Incidentally, not all cases of syphilis, even prolonged cases, result in paresis. Many other organs of the body may be affected, in addition to the brain.)

There are other infectious diseases which affect the brain and thus result in abnormal behavior. They include *encephalitis* and *meningitis*. Victims of such disorders are not generally considered to be "mentally ill" and thus are not treated in mental hospitals.

Senile Brain Disease

This type of mental illness is essentially a process of degeneration or deterioration due to aging. With advancing years, many of the organs of the body are likely to become impaired — for example, eyes, heart, blood vessels, bladder. Worse than any of these, in a sense, is brain deterioration because it affects the *entire personality* of the individual.

Senile brain disease comes on gradually. The aged person's mental processes are seriously impaired — memory, awareness of other people, ability to think logically, etc. Eventually he may have great trouble taking care of himself. His emotional behavior may seem childish. These are the familiar symptoms of "second childhood." Paranoid reactions are common.

There may be a hereditary factor involved in this disease because it seems to occur at about the same stage of life for many members of some families. And there are many families in which the disease does not occur at all, even though some members may live to an advanced age. At the present stage of medical science, there seems to be little that can be done to arrest the degenerative process, or to correct it after it has occurred.

Like all mentally ill people, the senile require sympathy and understanding. Although the degeneration cannot be corrected, much can be done under proper conditions to keep the old people comfortable and to prevent them from being a burden to others and to themselves. When committed to hospitals, they may become very disoriented and appear far more helpless than they really are. Very often such people can get on much better when cared for in a familiar home setting.

One final point: As the life span lengthens, and more and more people survive into their seventies, eighties, and even beyond, we must expect more and more senile brain disease. Our society will be challenged to provide suitable treatment for these people.

Treatment of Mental Illness

Two Different Approaches

Victims of *organic* mental illness (paresis and senility) are treated according to more or less standard medical procedures.

For the *functional* disorders, however, methods of treatment vary widely. Particularly in cases of schizophrenia, many different approaches have been tried, usually with no more than partial success.

Mentally ill people without financial resources are likely to be committed to state institutions. Here the therapy is directed far more to *physical* than to psychological techniques. The most common forms of treatment are electric-shock therapy and use of tranquilizing and energizing drugs (described below).

For mentally ill persons who can afford the costs of private physicians and personal attention, the treatment is likely to be more on a *psychological* level. In general, an attempt is made to establish some form of personality interaction between patient and therapist, and also, in some cases, among the patients themselves.

Physical Treatments for Mental Illness

In the early 1950's, two *tranquilizing drugs,* one new and one very old, were introduced for the treatment of schizophrenics, who make up a large percentage of all mental patients.

The new drug is *chlorpromazine* (trade name: "Thorazine"), which was developed in France in 1952. Its general tranquilizing ef-

Various methods used in the past to "treat" mental illness appear grotesque and barbaric to us. This sketch shows a rotating chair used in the 18th century. The patient was strapped in the chair, and it was spun rapidly to "drive out the devil." It may be that some of the techniques now in common use will be judged harshly by later generations.

fect was quickly noted, and it was soon utilized in the treatment of schizophrenic patients.

The older drug was originally derived from the mandrake or snakeroot plant, whose medicinal properties have been known for centuries. In India, snakeroot is a popular folk medicine, and it has been used there for many generations to produce drowsiness in children and even to treat emotionally disturbed persons. In 1952, it was synthesized in American laboratories and was given the name of *reserpine* (trade name: "Serpasil").

These drugs, both referred to as "major tranquilizers," are not related chemically, but they are used for the same purpose — to calm mental patients. Although they have a calming or tranquilizing effect, they are *not* strong sedatives. Thus, the patients remain relatively alert and active, but their emotions are subdued. A fairly typical reaction is that they become less excitable, less fearful, less suspicious, less hostile.

The introduction of these two drugs had a tremendous impact on mental hospitals in this country and elsewhere in the 1950's. With patients so readily calmed (some would say "numbed"), hospital authorities felt much safer in discontinuing or at least modifying the traditional restraints. Patients now had more personal freedom. The general atmosphere of the institutions in many cases became less "custodial" and more pleasant and humane. And, probably most important, there was now more opportunity and more incentive to seek out methods of *treating* patients to bring them back to health, rather than simply "guarding" them to prevent them from doing harm to themselves and others. (It should be noted that the tranquilizing drugs in themselves are *not* cures for any mental illness, although they may help to make the patients more "accessible" to other types of treatment.)

Energizing drugs are stimulants. Some of the drugs in this category are classified as amphetamines. They may be given to severely depressed patients who do not seem to be able to function at all, in the hope that they will be stimulated or aroused enough to regain some interest in living. Experience has shown, however, that prolonged use of stimulants is very dangerous. With repeated dosage, the patient is overcome by fatigue and may become severely depressed. Since this occurs to a person who already has a condition of chronic depression, the results may be catastrophic.

In *electro-shock treatment,* a low-intensity electric charge is applied to certain areas of the brain. One theory about what happens as a result of this is that memories and associations with which the patient has been deeply preoccupied are temporarily "knocked out." They may gradually take shape again in the patient's mind, but perhaps with less obsessiveness and less harm to the personality than before. In any case, the period of respite may be beneficial. This, however, is only a theory. Actually, there is no satisfactory explanation of how or why electro-shock treatment seems to be beneficial to some victims of mental illness. There are psychiatrists who will not use this method of treatment at all because they fear it may do more harm than good. There are others who use it rather routinely, even in cases of relatively "mild" depression.

Psychological Treatment of Neuroses and Psychoses

Psychotherapy. In the past, the Freudian method of treating emotional disturbances (neuroses) has rarely been used for psychoses (mental illnesses). The reason for this is that a mentally ill person is rarely able to cooperate to any degree with the psychiatrist. Freud thought that people suffering from a psychosis had so little mature ego remaining in their personalities that they could not respond to psychoanalysis.

Today, however, psychotherapy is being used to some extent to treat psychoses. The method of therapy used is derived from psychoanalysis, but the techniques differ considerably. Often, psychiatric drugs (which were not available to Freud) are used to enable the therapist to "reach" the patient. One limitation of this method of treatment is that it is time-consuming and expensive.

Group Therapy. This is another form of treatment now widely used. Patients meet together as a group under the supervision of a therapist to discuss their feelings, ideas, and problems. An attempt is made to create an atmosphere that emphasizes informality but at the same time suggests that the group is a coherent body and will accept and support each of its members.

Group therapy has proved to have many positive benefits. Withdrawn patients have a chance to express themselves. Aggressive patients may learn to restrain themselves, in the interests of the group. Patients gain self-control and learn to assume some responsibility for themselves and others.

Fortunately, many hospitals today, unlike such institutions in earlier generations, recognize that mental patients respond much better in an atmosphere where they are given some opportunity to exercise their own judgment, make their own decisions, and control their own activities. This does not mean that the patients "run" the hospital but rather that they get a chance *to think of themselves as responsible adults* and to act accordingly.

Milieu Therapy. In some of the more progressive institutions to-day, a technique called *milieu therapy* is used to encourage a sense of patient responsibility and participation. Mental patients and staff members (including doctors, as well as nurses and attendants) meet together regularly to discuss their common problems. The patients are encouraged to state their ideas and complaints openly, and many specific improvements in procedures have resulted from this. Thus, patients feel more responsible for themselves and more hopeful of improvement. At the same time, staff members come to realize that the patients may have valid complaints and are able to present them reasonably. This increases the respect of staff members for patients — a sore point in most of the more traditional institutions. A significant improvement in day-to-day relations between staff and patients is likely to result.

Behavior Modification. This is a widely used method of therapy based on rewarding desirable forms of behavior and ignoring (if feasible) undesirable or inappropriate conduct. The theory is that this treatment is to be continued until the patient has learned to behave acceptably, even *without* receiving some immediate compensation. Usually, in hospitals, the "rewards" paid out are in the form of special privileges or of tokens which can be used to buy candy, cigarettes, and similar items.

Behavior modification appears to be particularly helpful to people who have been institutionalized for many years and have become thoroughly accustomed to having their lives closely regulated, with all their material needs provided by others. Patients of this type are likely to be passive, lacking the most elementary initiative and willingness to do things "on their own." Such people may respond positively to a system of treatment which recognizes that they *can* do something right, and which actually rewards them in small but tangible ways for good conduct. Small children also seem to benefit from behavior modification therapy.

Many psychiatrists and psychologists, however, are highly skeptical of the long-term value of this type of treatment. They maintain that any benefits which seem to result will be at the most temporary. If the *unconscious conflicts* causing the problem are not resolved, the symptoms will come back, perhaps in a somewhat different form. The behaviorists answer that the "essence" of the unconscious *is* the behavior itself, and that if behavior can be corrected, the illness will be cured.

Attitudes Toward Mental Illness

Traces of the Old Attitudes Remain

At the beginning of this chapter, we reviewed the historical development of attitudes toward mental illness. We noted that the mentally ill person was once regarded as a sort of outcast, possessed by demons, in some sense wicked and loathsome. He was likely to be subjected to physical "punishment" or at least to derision and contempt. We have come a long way since then. Most intelligent people today recognize that mentally ill persons are no more to be blamed for their maladies than the victims of pneumonia or cancer, and that it is the duty of society to care for them and to try to find ways of preventing and curing the disorders.

And yet some traces of the old attitude remain. Many of us still find it hard to regard those who are mentally ill in exactly the same way we do those who are physically ill. In a recent survey, about 60% of a group of people interviewed said that they would feel "uncomfortable" talking with someone whom they knew to be an ex-mental patient. Would they feel uncomfortable talking to someone who had recovered from pneumonia? Obviously not. In the popular mind, there is still a stigma — a suggestion of infamy or disgrace — attached to mental illness.

In part, this is probably because there is a confusion between the *mentally ill* and the *criminally insane*. A very small proportion of the persons committed to mental hospitals today are there for having committed violent crimes. Yet, most of us are keenly aware of these "raving maniacs" or "berserk killers" because they receive so much publicity in the mass media. Of course, such people exist, but a far greater number of mentally ill persons have never committed any crimes, are not violent, and represent little threat or danger to anyone. They are indeed far "more sinned against than sinning."

It is clear that mentally ill persons are hurt by our unjustified fears and revulsion. Being kept like prisoners in overcrowded state institutions is also harmful to them. The success of open wards, milieu therapy, and outpatient treatment shows that there are other approaches, more similar to the normal conditions of life, that offer far better hopes for helping these people, without creating any real danger to themselves or to others. The number of mentally ill people who are really "hopeless" or "incurable" is relatively small. In most cases, when they are treated in an enlightened, humane, friendly and positive way, they will respond favorably.

Why Do We Fear the Mentally Ill?

Why do so many of us fear the mentally ill so much? This is itself an interesting psychological question. Since the fear is certainly not a reasonable one, we must look for the answer in the realm of the irrational or unconscious. Perhaps it goes back to the fact that we have already mentioned — that virtually everyone at some time or another has asked himself, "Am I mentally ill? Am I losing control of myself?" The possibility of this is so frightening to most of us that perhaps we react by showing hostility and contempt to those who really *are* mentally ill.

Yet most people do not even recognize a mentally ill person when they see one. Their ideas of the symptoms of mental illness are likely to be all wrong. Also, they tend to confuse mental *problems* with mental *illness* and assume that anyone who seeks help by seeing a psychiatrist or psychologist is ill. As we know, however, mental health professionals help all kinds of people, a large majority of whom are not mentally ill.

The Road Back from Mental Illness to Normal Life

Suppose a person has been mentally ill, has undergone treatment, and has been discharged as "cured," or at least has been allowed to

The man shown here is being discharged from a mental hospital. His future history depends largely on the treatment he receives in the "outside world."

return home without outpatient status. What future awaits him? Obviously, this depends very largely on the reception he gets from other people. If he is shunned — if he finds it unduly hard to get employment — if he cannot establish a normal social life, his prospects are probably not too favorable. If his experience is extremely difficult, there may even be a relapse. In many cases, the crucial attitude will be the *attitude of the members of his own family.*

However, it has been found that ex-mental patients can also help each other. For this reason, self-help groups have been set up in many cities. The best known of these organizations is called "Recovery." The methods used are similar to those made famous by Alcoholics Anonymous. People who have been mental patients get together more or less regularly (preferably under the guidance of an experienced leader) and "talk things out." They tell their experiences; they offer practical advice; they warn of pitfalls; they offer hope and encouragement without suggesting that there are not real problems; they even have fun with each other. An ex-mental patient who may have been wondering if he can really "make it" in the competitive outside world will naturally take heart when he looks around a room filled with able, articulate, self-possessed people and realizes that everyone there was at one time a mental patient. This kind of experience may be a valuable adjunct for a person who is still receiving drug therapy or psychotherapy.

Our understanding of the causes of mental illness is still limited, and the methods of treatment at our disposal are still very imperfect. Yet, we do know a great deal, and there is little doubt that we can and should achieve better results than are being achieved at the present time. Whether or not there will be substantial improvement in the years ahead depends in part on the accumulation of knowledge and skills by the professional workers in the field, in part on the attitude of public officials, and in part on the understanding and awareness of the general public, which means all of us.

Is Mental Illness a Myth? — A Criticism of Traditional Views

Is the whole idea of mental illness a myth? Or is it at least *sometimes* a myth?

Such questions probably appear absurd to most traditional psychiatrists and psychologists. However, there are now some influential workers in this field who believe that prevailing attitudes toward the "aberrant" types of behavior we have been discussing are fundamentally wrong, and that the whole conception of "illness" in this connection is a distortion.

Laing. One of these critics is the British psychiatrist R. D. Laing, who has been particularly concerned with schizophrenia. In his view, it makes little sense to call schizophrenics "mentally ill" simply because they are alienated or cut off from the world around them. By using this label, says Laing, we are assuming that such people are separated from "normality," but the fact is that our whole society shows abnormal characteristics, in relation to what we now know it could and should be.

Laing feels that people undergoing an acute schizophrenic episode, if they receive the proper help and encouragement, have an opportunity to use it as a broadening and mind-expanding experience. Schizophrenics, in Laing's view, do have an important adjustment to make (so has virtually everyone else!), but they have a much better chance to do this successfully if they are not treated as inferiors or defectives. However, the "mentally ill" label practically insures that they will be treated in this way.

Laing emphasizes that the apparent "irrationality" of the schizophrenic is more often than not simply a reflection of the greater irrationality of the world in which he must live. Note the following typical interpretation*:

> A little girl of seventeen in a mental hospital told me that she was terrified because the Atom Bomb was inside her. That is a delusion. The statesmen of the world who boast and threaten that they have Doomsday Weapons are far more dangerous, and far more estranged from "reality," than many of the people on whom the label "psychotic" is fixed.

Szasz. Thomas S. Szasz, a noted American psychiatrist, thinks that most mental illness is in actuality a form of "malingering," which means in essence *pretending* to be ill. In other words, the "sick" person is trying to evade life's responsibilities, without discredit to himself, by assuming the status of a "patient." In our society, says Szasz, "being sick" is frequently rewarded, in the sense that the "sick" person is not required to *do* anything, and is usually provided with at least the essentials of life, as well as a good deal of sympathy. Being strong and independent, on the other hand, is not only not rewarded but may actually be punished.

It may be answered that the very need or desire to "malinger" is in itself a symptom of mental illness, but Szasz rejects this as an absurdly strained attempt to hold on to a familiar concept which has outlived its usefulness.

---

* R. D. Laing, *The Divided Self* (introduction to Pelican edition, 1967).

Szasz emphasizes that "physicians need sick people." Thus, anyone who "acts sick" will be labeled and treated accordingly, although what he is actually suffering from may be no more than a kind of "ethical confusion" — an unwillingness to assume life's responsibilities. Psychotherapy is an industry, and like all industries it is "looking for business." People spend money (their own, or someone else's) on psychotherapy, in the pursuit of happiness, just as they do on "religion . . . alcohol, tobacco, cosmetics, and various recreational activities."

Szasz is certainly not arguing against helping those who need help, but he says that "decency to our fellow man should not be conditional on his 'sickness.' " He feels that the principal job of the psychiatrist is to aid people in solving "moral dilemmas."*

Szasz has also emphasized the need to protect the *civil rights* of people who are labeled "mentally ill." They may now be committed to institutions for many years, or indeed for life, on the basis of diagnoses which he regards as arbitrary and unrealistic. Such a procedure, which would not be tolerated for any other class of citizens, is commonly justified by invoking the concept of "mental illness." Szasz condemns this as bad therapy and bad law, even though the patients may in a sense welcome the institutionalization as a "reward for malingering."

Quite possibly you will be puzzled to find such arguments and ideas being voiced by prominent psychiatrists. They seem to be rejecting, or at least questioning, much of what has been said in this chapter. They do not deny that the old idea of "demonic possession" to explain certain forms of behavior was a gross superstition, and that it led to terrible abuses, but they question whether we are now on much firmer ground by having substituted the idea of "mental illness."

In this book, of course, we cannot attempt to pass final judgment on ideas such as those of Laing and Szasz. We can say, however, that it is extremely significant that such criticisms are being made and are receiving respectful attention. There is a great deal about the human mind and human behavior (both in good health and in apparent disorder) that we do not understand. Our attempts to explain these phenomena and to set standards for dealing with them are certainly not final or complete. Therefore, it is to be expected, and is entirely proper, that our "accepted ideas" should be subjected to constant re-examination and vigorous criticism. It is as a result of such an approach that greater progress may be made in the years ahead.

---

* Thomas S. Szasz, *The Myth of Mental Illness* (Dell, 1961)

THINGS TO DISCUSS :: THINGS TO DO :: THINGS TO READ

1. "There is no great genius without some touch of madness" — SENECA. What is your reaction to this statement? Try to give some specific examples to support your judgment.

2. Would you say that any person whose behavior is strikingly "weird" or "abnormal" should be committed to a mental institution?

3. What criteria should psychiatrists and the courts use when they are considering whether to commit someone to a mental institution? Should a person's civil rights under the Constitution be suspended if the case appears to warrant it?

4. Schizophrenia is often described as a condition in which the victim is "cut off from reality." This means that he cannot distinguish fantasies from reality (which, as Freud pointed out, is a characteristic of the unconscious). There are times, however, when all of us feel to some degree alienated from reality, or unwilling to accept reality. Does this mean that we are all schizophrenics? Explain.

5. Are there any places in this chapter that gave you some uncomfortable moments? What are they?

6. Examine an art book containing a series of Vincent Van Gogh's paintings, and see if you can guess which were painted during periods of acute mental illness.

7. If you have the necessary fortitude and desire, you may volunteer to help out in a mental hospital. Report your findings to the class.

READINGS

One Flew Over the Cuckoo's Nest, by Ken Kesey (Viking, 1962). Though criticized as unduly grim and unfair to attendants and nurses, this is a brilliant and revealing novel of life in a mental hospital.

I Never Promised You A Rose Garden, by Hannah Green (Holt, 1964). A fascinating story of the inner world of a schizophrenic girl.

The Divided Self, by R. D. Laing (Tavistock Publications, London, 1959). Although now widely regarded as a classic, this is still a somewhat controversial study of schizophrenia.

The Politics of Experience, by R. D. Laing (Pelican Books, 1967). This relates schizophrenia to specific social conditions and problems.

Freud

and Freudianism

● ◉ ●

"It seems to be my fate to discover the obvious: that children have sexual feelings, which every nursemaid knows; and that night dreams are just as much a wish fulfillment as day dreams."

— *SIGMUND FREUD*

Freud's Early Career

Sigmund Freud (1856-1939) ranks with Charles Darwin as a thinker who has shaped our current awareness of the world. Freud, like Darwin, had to overcome strong opposition before his ideas gained widespread acceptance and became part of the intellectual and emotional background shared by 20th-century man in most parts of the world.

Darwin advanced the theory that *man's biological origins* could be explained according to natural laws. Freud some years later proposed the equally radical idea that *man's mind* could be examined and understood in the light of scientific principles. Freud fanned the fires of protest by claiming that children have sexual needs and desires — a shocking idea in the context of the Victorian tradition — but the very severity of the reaction was perhaps a good indication of the truth of the claim.

This man who has influenced the lives of all of us in so many ways was born of modest origins in the small town of Freiburg, Moravia (then under Austrian control, now in Czechoslovakia). At an early age, his family moved to the sophisticated intellectual and cultural atmosphere of Vienna, where he spent most of the remainder of his life.

Left: Sigmund Freud in 1922, at the age of 66.

Below: Freud's study in Vienna. At the left, note a few items of his collection of primitive art, in which he was keenly interested. The couch shown was the one used by patients undergoing analysis.

Photograph by Edmund Engelman

In Vienna, Freud studied medicine. As a young doctor he aspired to become a famous medical scientist, rather than a practicing physician. His burning ambition, combined with his youthful impetuousness and his inclination to independent thought and behavior, involved him in a major scandal.

Freud stumbled upon the then little-known drug, cocaine, and in his eagerness to make a name for himself, he became overly enthusiastic about its immediate beneficial effects. Without carefully researching the effects of this drug on humans, he vigorously propagandized for its use to treat many types of ailments, major and minor, and pressed it on friends and relatives. Before long, the harmful effects of using the drug in this way became evident, but by this time cocaine abuse had become an alarming social problem. Freud was severely criticized, and there is every indication that the reproaches of his own conscience were far more punishing. It is quite possible that he learned a lesson in this early episode that stood him in good stead during his long and epoch-making scientific career.

During the years in which he was involved in this episode, Freud also did some brilliant scientific work. It was at this time that he decided to specialize in *neurology* — the branch of medicine that deals with disorders of the nervous system. Again, showing his characteristic determination and independence of thought, he was attracted by the pioneering work of the famed French neurologist, Jean Charcot.

Charcot had transformed hypnotism from a charlatan's trick to a medical treatment for hysteria.* This condition had been observed since ancient times, but had never been scientifically investigated. The accepted idea was that it was caused by some *organic* (physical) abnormality. Charcot showed, however, that hysteria is *psychological* in origin. He did this by removing (or inducing) hysterical symptoms in various individuals purely by means of hypnotic suggestion.

Toward a Theory of Hysteria

Freud was much impressed by this evidence that *physical* symptoms, such as those of hysteria, could be corrected or induced primarily by means of *ideas* directed to the patient's mind. He went to Paris to study under Charcot and remained there for six months. Then in 1886 he returned to Vienna and set up medical practice in order to make enough money to marry. Freud was not much interested in general medical practice, and he began to specialize in neurology. As time went on, he saw many patients with neurotic symptoms, and he

---

* *Hysteria* is now known to be a severe neurosis (emotional disorder). It is usually accompanied by such symptoms as paralysis, muscle spasms, and insensitive skin areas.

used hypnosis on some of them. At this time, he began a long-term association with Josef Breuer, a highly respected physician and scientist who was also interested in the problems of the human mind.

In 1895, Freud and Breuer proposed the then novel, and indeed heretical, idea that hysteria could be traced to a distressing event in the patient's earlier life. In their joint book *Studies on Hysteria,* Freud made the radical suggestion that such distressing events always had a sexual basis. In treating hysterical patients, Breuer had found that if a patient could be persuaded to recall and retell the "forgotten" unpleasant experience, which presumably caused the symptom, there was frequently an emotional reaction contributing to a sense of relief and well-being.

The Power of the Unconscious

Freud gradually grew dissatisfied with hypnosis as a method of therapy because only some patients were able to respond. Moreover, of those who did respond, many reverted to their neurotic behavior after initial improvement. Instead, he developed *free association,* which became the basic tool in *psychoanalysis,* the Freudian method of treating disorders of the mind.

In free association, the patient is encouraged to relax (for example, while lying on a couch) and to say aloud whatever occurs to him, no matter how "trivial," "silly," or "immoral" it may seem. Although many of the associations may appear pointless or nonsensical, they may eventually expose a troubling idea in the background of the patient's mind and thus lead to the root of the difficulty.

The method of free association is simple, but it helped Freud arrive at some of his most brilliant insights. He came to realize that when the patient is relaxed, his thoughts and associations are not random or undirected but, rather, are governed by underlying motivations of which the individual is not even conscious. And since a person is most relaxed while asleep, Freud concluded that dreams are the key to these *unconscious motivations.* He thought that dreams are basically wish-fulfillments — the "wishes" in question being unconscious desires.*

In fact, any theory of the mind which does not include the *unconscious* is "incapable of solving the problems of dreams and hypnosis." Thus, the division of the mind "into what is conscious and what is unconscious is the fundamental premise of psychoanalysis." A mental process is unconscious if we must conclude that it is being

---

* See Chapter 8, "Dreams, A Language of the Unconscious."

"activated *at the moment,* though *at the moment* we know nothing about it."

The unconscious, as Freud analyzed it, is made up of a number of separate entities or components.

▶ "Memory traces" that come into consciousness through the *preconscious* (see below).

▶ A "reservoir" of instinctive drives.

▶ Material that was once conscious but has become so painful that it cannot be admitted into consciousness again.

The *preconscious* is the area in which thoughts and fragments of knowledge and awareness hover just below the level of consciousness, waiting to be "called up," if needed, and combined with conscious thought patterns. Freud, however, was more concerned with the deeper parts of the unconscious, which is where *hidden motivations* operate. By analyzing these unconscious motivations — through free association and dream interpretation — Freud found that patients revealed memories of sexual desires originating in *childhood*. On this basis he advanced the theory that many neuroses, including hysteria, have their roots in unresolved sexual conflicts dating from the early part of the life span. In fact, he thought that the most common single cause of neurotic anxiety is the blocking of infantile sexual urges.

These urges, and the memories which involve such urges, are kept unconscious by a "censorship" in the mind. The "censorship" operates because the urges and memories are too unpleasant to be admitted to consciousness. We do not want to be reminded of them. The process of keeping these mental components out of consciousness is called *repression*.

The Pleasure Principle

Freud proposed the theory that the mind is run by a certain amount of *psychic energy*. This energy is used by the human organism to avoid pain and concurrently to gain pleasure. In prehistoric man, this process (of avoiding pain and seeking pleasure) might be regarded as an aid to survival. This is less true today, but the human organism continues to try to get rid of and keep away from both physical pain and psychic pain ("unpleasure"), and to enhance and hold on to pleasure. Freud called this biological motivation the *pleasure principle*.

In the presence of unpleasure, psychic energy builds up (*tension*). Under such conditions, the aim of the organism becomes to reduce tension — the less tension, the more pleasure. But such pleasure is necessarily transitory because tension quickly builds up again in response to such basic needs as those for food and sexual satisfaction. The cycle is then repeated.

Thus, because of the conflict between primitive unconscious urges and the prohibitions set in the way of those urges — first by parents, later by society in general — the human organism comes to be motivated on the basis of reducing pain to the minimum, the principle of "lesser pain."

Freud's View of Childhood Sexuality

"The child is father to the man." This line by William Wordsworth was often quoted by Freud. He believed that some of the most powerful influences in the development of the adult personality come about in the first five years of life.

Freud pointed out that a newborn baby is *irrational* (he cannot think in accordance with reality); he is *amoral* (he has no concept at all of moral standards, of "right" and "wrong"); and he believes that he is the "center of the universe" (he can't distinguish the rest of the world from his own person). Only gradually are these limitations overcome.

A baby has little capacity to tolerate frustration. He demands and expects instant gratification of all his needs and wants. These needs are not limited to the intake of food and the expelling of wastes. He

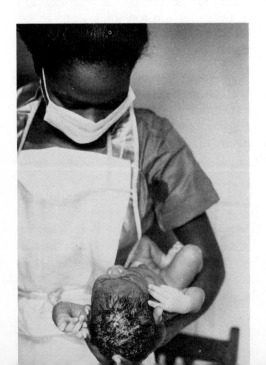

also wants love to be demonstrated to him by fondling, caressing, and cooing, all of which, Freud pointed out, is part of sexuality. Mainly, however, sexual feelings center around the mouth in this early stage, since the baby's pleasure is the greatest while he is feeding. Later, sexual feelings are associated with the pleasurable effects in the anus during defecation. Eventually, it centers around the genitals.

The suggestion that children could harbor sexual feelings and impulses shocked the sensibilities of most "respectable" people during the Victorian era. The accepted or idealized picture of children at this time was that they were altogether "pure" and "innocent." Freud was angrily attacked for "soiling the innocence" of little children, and seeking to "undermine" the supreme values of the family, of morality, and indeed of civilization.

Many people were even more unresponsive to the idea that they themselves might harbor repressed feelings of hate, jealousy, and greed related to childhood sexual conflicts. After analyzing his own dreams and the dreams of other people considered to be more or less mentally healthy adults, Freud found that normal people could and did hold these unconscious feelings. In the 1890's and early 1900's, it was generally taken for granted that there was a sharp dividing line between health and sickness. A person was simply healthy or sick, normal or abnormal. Thus, it was inconceivable to most people that a normal adult could have "crazy" wishes and impulses like those which Freud insisted were revealed in dreams. Freud answered that these irrational strivings do exist and that they represent "the child in the man."

The Oral Stage

The newborn babe lives through and loves with his mouth (oral-ly). The mouth works in five main ways: by taking in, holding on, biting, spitting out, and closing. Each of these modes of behavior is a model for later developments in the individual's behavior (personality traits).

Freud believed that taking in through the mouth is the behavioral model for *acquisitiveness;* holding on, for *tenacity* and *determination;* biting, for *destructiveness;* and closing, for *refusal* and *pessimism.*

The particular trait that is dominant in the adult personality depends largely on the degree of frustration experienced in connection with the childhood models. For example, a baby who is weaned (shifted from breast or bottle feeding to other forms of nourishment) too soon or too abruptly may develop a strong tendency to hold on to things. Adult greediness or acquisitiveness may result from not getting enough food or love during infancy. Such an individual can never be satisfied so long as his personality is dominated by this infantile drive because whatever he may be acquiring — whether money, fame, or power — is only a substitute for what he really wants: food from a loving mother.

In Freud's view, there is ample evidence that traces of this oral stage are carried over into adulthood. This can be seen, for example, in the ways people gratify themselves orally, even when such gratification is not really necessary for the physical well-being of the organism. A bottle of beer, a cigarette, a stick of gum, or even the singing of a song are, according to Freudian interpretation, substitutes for the maternal nipple. This does not mean that it is "bad" to chew gum or to sing songs. For all practical purposes, most people have overcome the personal problems involved in the oral stage, even though they may still indulge in such forms of oral gratification. Also, it is conceded by Freudians that the need for oral gratification is not the *sole* factor leading to such activities as singing.

The Anal Stage

The anal stage comes in the second and third years of life, when the child has enough muscular coordination to control his bowels. Sexual energy and pleasure now center around defecation. Freud believed that the manner in which the child is toilet-trained becomes the model for generosity (or the lack of it) later in life.

To clarify this, Freud explained that at the outset of toilet training, the child's "own feces produce no disgust in him; he values them as part of his own body and is unwilling to part with them; he uses them as the first 'present' by which he can mark out those people whom he values especially." At this stage the child shows no self-consciousness in relation to his bowel functions. It is only later that he is taught "that everything connected with these functions is 'improper' and must be kept concealed."

Prior to toilet training, the child has no notion of the meaning of "giving." But now he learns that he must give (his feces) when expected, in order to get something else: the approval of his parents. Thus, people who become exceptionally or even compulsively generous in later life may be motivated by a strong need for approval (love), associated unconsciously with the idea of "giving" freely. Conversely, when toilet training is too early or too strict, the child may grow into an adult who shows a compulsive need for "orderliness" — who is stingy, finicky, and "tight" in matters of affection, time, and money, as well as in managing his bowels. Or, as a reaction to this, the person in question may become disorderly, messy, irresponsible, wasteful, and extravagant.

The Phallic Stage

"There is no possible doubt that one of the most important sources of the sense of guilt which so often torments neurotic people is to be found in the Oedipus complex."

Oedipus is a figure in Greek mythology who unwittingly slew his father and married his mother. (See Chapter 9.) This analogy was used by Freud to describe the wishes, and their results, characteristic of children in the phallic stage (ages four and five).

In the male Oedipus complex, the boy wishes physically to possess and dominate his mother and get rid of his father, whom he unknowingly considers a rival. It should be remembered that the child has no realistic conception of death, which he simply equates with being not present or "gone."

This is also the time that the male child usually discovers that his penis is something "special." He becomes aware of the fact that some people do not have this organ — for example, his sister or a female playmate. Since he can't conceive of a person being born different from himself, he assumes that in such cases the penis has been cut off. If this unfortunate event has happened to other people, it may also happen to him. This assumption may sometimes be reinforced by playful (and not so playful) parental remarks about the possible removal of the penis. In boys, this pattern of experience leads to a fear called the *castration complex*.

The boy thus fears his father will castrate him as punishment for wishing to take over the father's rights to his mother. This hostility toward the father is counterbalanced by a love for him. In healthy people, the fear and the love combine to force the boy to renounce the goal of actually possessing his mother, thus resolving the conflict. Many adult neurotics, however, have not resolved this conflict, which continues to rage on and to dominate their personalities, although repression prevents awareness of it.

In girls, the Oedipus complex (sometimes called the *Electra complex*) takes a somewhat different form and has considerably different results. Before the arrival of the phallic stage, "the girl's father is only a troublesome rival" and, like the boy, she regards her mother as a "love-object." However, once the girl becomes aware that she does not have a penis, she turns against her mother, who has always provided nearly everything else. The girl holds her mother responsible for this "loss," which she bitterly resents. Noting that her mother also lacks a penis, she turns to her father as a love-object, hoping that he will give her the desired organ. Penis envy in Freud's view is the basis of the "feminine castration complex."

However, since the girl has no reason to fear castration, "girls remain (in the Oedipus complex) for an indeterminate length of time; they demolish it late and, even so, incompletely." This combined with the "instinctual (female) passivity," which manifests itself later, leaves even adult women expecting and demanding that they receive love, a basically infantile attitude. Thus, in Freud's view, women's natural heritage is the passive, dependent role, which he thought was the basis of "normal" femininity.

It is hardly surprising that this view of the feminine role advanced by Freud has been strongly contested by those people (both men and women) who refuse to accept the idea that women are "naturally" subordinate to men in all the essential relations of life. In our own day, Freud has been bitterly criticized by the proponents of the "Women's Liberation" movement. (See Chapter 16.)

In fairness to Freud, however, it should be pointed out that he believed that males normally have some feminine traits, and that females have some masculine traits. This situation points to the existence of *bisexual impulses* in all human beings. Since there is such a mixture of traits in individuals, it cannot be assumed (in Freud's view), that all women are completely subordinate, and that all men show a natural impulse to dominance.

The Period of Latency

After the phallic stage, the child enters a period of *latency*. This begins between the ages of six and eight and usually lasts until about age twelve, or the time that puberty begins. During these latency years, sexual feelings are repressed, and the child's energies are directed primarily into school and play. Little interest is displayed in the opposite sex: boys prefer the company of boys, and girls prefer the company of girls.

With the onset of puberty, sexual impulses begin to reassert themselves, and the adolescent directs his interests to members of the opposite sex. As he matures to adulthood, he learns what society considers the proper balance between control and expression of his impulses. How well he is able to do this depends in large part on how well conflicts were resolved during the oral, anal, and particularly, phallic stages.

"Beyond the Pleasure Principle"

The bulk of Freud's theory on childhood sexuality appeared in his book, *Three Essays on Sexuality,* published in 1905. The years between 1900 and 1910 were highly productive years for Freud, witnessing the publication of some of his most important works, including *The Psychopathology of Everyday Life.* In this he analyzed the influence of the unconscious on such everyday occurrences as slips of the tongue, errors, and "accidents." Today, the widespread use of such catchphrases as "Freudian slip" reflects the pervasive influence of these ideas on our entire mental background and mode of thinking.

At the time of his greatest productivity, however, Freud was virtually ignored by the scientific community, or dismissed as a "crank" by all but a few. One of the few was Stanley Hall, President of Clark University in Worcester, Massachusetts. In 1908, Hall invited Freud and one of his followers, the Swiss psychiatrist Carl Jung, to visit Clark University to lecture on psychoanalysis. Elated, Freud made his first (and last) trip to America, where he was presented with his first honorary doctorate. Much moved, Freud said, "This is the first official recognition of our endeavors."

However, Freud's theories did not receive wide popular attention until the mass bloodletting of World War I had shattered the comfortable illusions of millions of people regarding "normality," "morality," and the forces that control human behavior. Many people were now far more receptive to revolutionary theories regarding the role of the unconscious in human life. Freud also felt the impact of the war on his thinking, and in 1920 he wrote an important book called *Beyond the Pleasure Principle.* In this book he proposed for the first time the concept of a death instinct* in man. Such a death instinct, as Freud saw it, lay behind the aggressive and destructive behavior which had manifested itself in the war. This was also a significant development in Freud's thinking because (as the title of the book suggests) he had moved beyond the idea of the "pleasure principle" which loomed so large in his earlier writings.

He recognized this urge to self-destruction in many "normal" people, as well as in obvious neurotics, who repeatedly, though unconsciously, entangle themselves in unpleasant and dangerous situations. Thus we have, "the man whose friendships all end in betrayal by his friend; or the man who time after time in the course of his life raises someone else to a position of great authority and then, after a certain interval, himself upsets that authority and replaces him by a

---

* See Chapter 19, "Why Does Man Kill?"

new one; or, again, the lover each of whose affairs with a woman passes through the same phases and reaches the same conclusion." To such a pattern of behavior, Freud applied the term *repetition compulsion*. He noted specifically that we cannot assume that a person involved in such a pattern is seeking, however mistakenly, to experience a particular pleasure, since the *first* such experience was undoubtedly disappointing or positively unpleasant.

Does this contradict the idea that the basic drive motivating the organism is to avoid "unpleasure" and to obtain pleasure? In short, does it mean that Freud was wrong in his earlier interpretations?

To answer this, Freud first had to make clear distinctions among *fear, fright,* and *anxiety*. While *fear* is a reaction to an obvious or identified external danger, *fright* is more specifically "the state a person gets into when he runs into a danger without being prepared for it." There is an element of surprise or unpreparedness involved. *Anxiety* "describes a particular state of expecting the danger or preparing for it, even though it may be an unknown one." Thus we might say that a soldier feels *fear* when he has to go out on a patrol in enemy territory that he knows will be highly dangerous. His *anxiety* at this time is emotional preparation or adjustment to face the dangerous situation. But when a man runs into a burglar entirely unexpectedly in his own home, his reaction is one of *fright*. There has been no previous buildup of anxiety to help him face this situation.

Fright then comes typically with overwhelming shock or *trauma,* which Freud suggested is a time when the brain is overloaded with more stimulation than it can handle. Having clarified this distinction between anxiety and fright, Freud could now explain that when a person repeats "compulsively" the behavior that has already led to the trauma of fright, the brain is trying to develop the appropriate anxiety and to "master the situation retrospectively." In other words, the person is trying to work out the situation by building up the anxiety that will take the element of surprise out of the experience and thus get rid of the fright. This "repetition compulsion" takes immediate priority over the pleasure principle, but it does not negate the fact that the pleasure principle is still at work in other areas of the individual's behavior.

The explanation is ingenious but there is no doubt that Freud had modified, or at least expanded, an earlier pronouncement regarding the basis of human behavior. He was also obliged to concede that, contrary to his earlier theory, some dreams are not wish fulfillments. Specifically, some repeating dreams, with their origin in a traumatic experience, are not dominated by the pleasure principle.

Freud at Clark University in 1909. Freud is seated at the left. The man seated at the right is Freud's disciple, Carl Jung. President Stanley Hall of Clark University is seated between them. Standing (from left to right) are Abraham Brill, Ernest Jones, and Sandor Ferenczi, all of whom became important figures in the history of psychiatry.

For Freud, the clarification of this exception to the pleasure principle meant that the mind, as he now saw it, was to be divided into a conflict between *life forces* and *death forces*, whereas previously he had interpreted it as divided between the repressive "censorship" and sexual drives. In addition, Freud's revised view included a reinterpretation of "sexual instincts." These instincts now suggested more than a relatively simple drive toward sexual relations and satisfaction. Indeed, the "sexual instincts" in this later view were very nearly equivalent to the life force "which holds all living things together." In this context, Freud developed the concept of the *libido,* meaning life-sustaining energy in general.

The Id, the Ego, the Superego

It was not long after publication of *Beyond the Pleasure Principle* that Freud revised his presentation of the dynamics of personality. He explained in *The Ego and the Id* (1923) that whereas previously he had thought of personality primarily in terms of unconscious versus conscious, this view could no longer be considered adequate.

Prior to this it had been unclear whether there was any difference between the *ego* and the *conscious mind*. Now, however, Freud explained that although it is to the ego "that consciousness is attached," much of the ego must be unconscious. In fact, Freud added, it is impractical to describe behavior in terms of consciousness. Consciousness does not determine personality. To describe the forces that shape and regulate personality, Freud divided the mind into three principal "agencies": the *ego* (in its revised concept), the *id,* and the *superego.* The id is never conscious, and the ego and superego may or may not show themselves in conscious thought.

The Id. For a newborn there is only one "agency" of the mind — the *id.* (This is the Latin word for "it.") Since the infant is all id, as far as he "knows," he is the "center of the universe," and he cannot distinguish between the rest of the world and himself. Since the rest of the world does not exist, only he can have needs and wants. The id has no awareness of the existence of other people, much less of their feelings.

The id does not think. It is the wellspring of urgent needs and desires, which it transforms into wishes ("the mental equivalents of instincts"). It is without fear and consequently demands immediate gratification of its wishes. The id has no morality or values and cannot distinguish between good and evil. It becomes the burying ground of "impressions" which have been "sunk" into it by repression. And many years after these impressions are first experienced, the id may act as though they had just happened, since it has no sense of time.

The Ego. As the child matures, the *ego* grows gradually out of the id until it has enough strength to act as a more or less independent agency.

The ego is formed by the experience of pain, and thus the ego knows fear. If an impulse from the id causes behavior which brings punishment from the external world, this behavior is remembered. Thus, the ego becomes the mind's "defense department" against pain. The complicated processes of judgment and rational thought which take place in the ego are originally developed as a means for keeping the id out of difficulties.

However, the id cannot be neutralized or "squelched." The ego can only act as a referee between the forces of the id and the outside world — which the ego learns to know as distinct from itself. Therefore, the ego can only delay, limit, or modify pleasure, which it does by causing behavior to conform with reality. This detouring of energy into patterns of behavior acceptable to parents, and later to "society," is known as the *reality principle.*

As a phase of the defense network, the ego houses the "censorship," which prevents painful memories from reaching consciousness, repressing them back into the id. This censorship usually comes under the influence of the superego, which develops in strength as the child gets older. Thus, the ego must contend with the demands of the id, the superego, and the outside world, so that it feels "hemmed in on three sides."

The Superego. As the ego grows out of the id, so the *superego* grows out of and is a part of the ego. The superego is the agency that comprises the individual's moral code. The strength of the superego varies widely from one person to another. In some it is so active that it causes an unreasonable amount of self-criticism and even self-hatred. In others, it scarcely seems to function at all.

Freud believed that the manner in which the superego develops in an individual depends in large part on how successful he was in resolving the Oedipus complex (page 95). The ego of a small boy becomes aware (because of the fear of castration) that the id's goal of possessing the mother must be given up. However, since the ego is still weak at such an early stage, it must provide a substitute "object" for the id's goal. This it does through a process of *identification* with the parents; the child "builds them into" himself. Thus the superego takes shape. As the individual grows older, the superego is also shaped and developed by the ideals and values of other "parent figures," such as teachers, religious leaders, and admired public figures. But where the Oedipus complex is not transcended successfully in this way, the development of the superego tends to be stunted.

There may be a conflict or a disparity between the exacting demands of the superego and the ego's ability to handle the id. This situation results in a sense of guilt. "A great part of the guilt must normally remain unconscious, because the origin of the conscience is intimately connected with the Oedipus complex, which belongs to the unconscious."

Anxiety and Ego Defenses

The biological value of *anxiety* is the same as that of *fear*: to increase immediate alertness to danger in preparation for flight or fight.

But fear, as Freud defined it (page 98), is a response to a danger in the external world that actually exists or appears to exist on the basis of evidence at hand. It is essentially rational. Anxiety, in contrast, may not be rational at all. Thus, when a situation arises which is unconsciously associated with a painful event in the past, the ego may experience anxiety; this serves as a danger signal and alerts the body to prepare for attack or retreat, although objectively there may be no need for such behavior. The ego, however, often finds that it must deal with a situation by some means other than physical resistance or retreat. Under such conditions it cannot tolerate long continuation of the anxiety, which is "demanding" immediate action. When this happens, the ego will set up defenses (defense mechanisms) which are designed to protect it from the *anxiety,* rather than from a danger in the external world.

Typical ego defenses include: *repression, projection, rationalization, reaction-formation, regression, displacement,* and *sublimation.* We all employ such defenses at times, but when they become exaggerated or obsessive, the person is considered neurotic.

Repression. Repression, as we have noted, means the process whereby mental material by which the ego feels threatened is "sunk" into the id. Such material includes largely traumatic memories; although these memories are unconscious, they are not forgotten.

A repressed memory is either painful in itself, or is associated with something painful. For example, you may forget the name of someone with whom you had a humiliating or otherwise painful encounter. Memories associated with traumatic experiences, such as automobile accidents, are often repressed. A child (or adult) may repress deepseated hostility toward his parents, thus sparing himself the pain his ego feels this hostility would bring — from either the superego or the external world — if the hostility were acknowledged in conscious thought.

Repression should not be confused with a conscious decision to *suppress* a desire from being carried into action. For example, you may have an impulse to steal something from a store shelf, but you consciously "turn aside" this impulse because you know the brief feeling of satisfaction that might result would not be worth the pain and trouble that would also be involved. You may even have an "argument" with yourself before overcoming or *suppressing* the impulse, but throughout you know pretty much what you're doing. In contrast, a person is not aware that he has *repressed* a memory or wish. The repressed material remains active "underground," in the unconscious, and may be expressed in disguised forms — for example in dreams, slips of the tongue, jokes, "forgetting," or "accidents."

Repression is part of everyone's personality development. Often, it is the only way the ego knows by which to keep the id from getting the person in trouble. The growth of such repressive "censorship" goes hand in hand with the growth of the ego and the superego. And since civilization, by its structure, places so much emphasis on controlling sexual behavior, the impulses and memories which are most intensely repressed usually have a sexual content.

Reaction-Formation. Sometimes a person's reaction to a threatening and repressed feeling or wish is to act in a way that appears to be the complete *opposite* of what the unconscious desires to do. Such counter-behavior is known as a *reaction-formation.* Since reaction-formations are always compulsive forms of behavior, the appearance of this type of ego defense is a sure sign of neurosis. A person tormented by an urge to soil, for example, may "overcompensate" by being clean and neat to an exaggerated degree. Or a person who fears his own homosexual impulses may react by continually maligning homosexuals.

A reaction-formation betrays its origins by its tendency to go too far — to take excessively great pains — to explain or justify too much. As Shakespeare put it in *Hamlet*: "The lady doth protest too much, methinks."

Projection. A person may set up a defense against motives, desires, and character traits which he is not willing to recognize in himself by attributing them to others. This is called *projection.* The aim is to convert the source of anxiety from an inner shortcoming to an outer "danger." Instead of saying, "I hate *him*" — which might make you feel guilty — you say: "He hates *me.*" A student who has failed a test because of his own inadequate preparation may say that the teacher did a poor job in preparing the class. A woman who has repressed her sexual desires believes that men are constantly making advances to her.

Rationalizing. This term refers to the familiar device of interpreting motives and behavior in a way that makes a person "look good" to himself and (he hopes) to others. The person makes an unconscious effort to defend or enhance his self-concept in a potentially threatening situation. Thus, a mother may be overprotective of a child because she fears that if the child becomes more independent, she (the mother) will no longer be needed. The mother then justifies or rationalizes her behavior by explaining in great detail that the child is exposed to many dangers, and that everything she is doing is in the child's best interests.

Regression. A retreat from a higher level of personality development to an earlier stage is called *regression.* For example a three-year-old child who has already been toilet-trained may "forget" his training when he discovers he has a "rival" — a new brother or sister. The three-year-old is unhappy at not being the center of family attention any longer, and he hopes, on an unconscious level, to regain this lost status by becoming a helpless infant again.

Even generally healthy and mature people may regress occasionally to relieve anxiety — to "let off steam." Such regressive behavior may take the form of temper tantrums, getting drunk, "silly" antics at a party, and daydreaming.

Displacement. This refers to the process of shifting an emotion from one person or object, for whom it was originally intended, to another person or object. For example, a man angered by his wife may displace or vent his aggression by reckless driving. A child who has been punished may strike another child, since he can't strike his parents.

Sublimation. Sublimation, like repression, is found in all growing human beings and cannot be considered a neurotic response to "reality." Freud saw all civilization and social behavior as a process by which the ego redirects id urges to forms of activity which are more useful, or pleasing, or socially acceptable. The id urges are then said to have undergone *sublimation.* For instance, an artistic activity, such as sculpting with clay, may serve an unconscious need to "mess" or "soil."

However, there is also always more than one other instinct or need involved in a "higher-level" activity, and these various impulses, drives, and instincts are fused into a single behavior pattern. The sculptor creates in his medium because of a number of motivations that combine to direct him to this type of artistic expression (sublimation).

What motivations or drives may be involved in the creation of an artistic masterpiece such as Michelangelo's "Moses"?

Psychoanalytic Therapy

The method of therapy most associated with the work of Sigmund Freud is *psychoanalysis*. Basically, psychoanalysis is a method of helping the ego mature so that it can deal with reality realistically, instead of in a neurotic — that is to say, infantile — manner. It is a technique designed to reveal to the patient his own inappropriate ego-defenses, so that he can proceed to correct them.

In order to do this, however, part of the ego must retain some elements of maturity. This is why psychoanalysis has had most of its success in treating neurotic adults. Children's egos are too immature to be reached effectively by psychoanalysis, and the egos of psychotics are usually too far out of touch with reality. (For such individuals, other forms of therapy are needed.)

The process of helping the patient understand the significance of his dreams and of helping him uncover the things that are bothering him through free association may take as long as five years. Obviously, this is likely to be very costly in terms of money as well as time and energy. Freudian psychoanalysts* say that this much time is needed because the patient must do more than understand his problem intellectually. Mere intellectual understanding is too superficial or limited to have significant effects on the patient's behavior. Rather, his *entire ego* must comprehend the problem so that his behavior can become more mature — more in accordance with reality.

The beneficial change comes about through a process of *transference,* in which the patient unconsciously transfers powerful emotions associated with a figure from childhood (usually a parent) onto the doctor. The analyst sees his role in respect to these emotions as neutral. He doesn't reward or punish neurotic behavior; he slowly encourages the patient's ego to realize that the neurotic reactions are infantile and not in harmony with reality.

Thus, a major part of treatment consists of aiding the patient to "work out" his difficulties by learning to see the analyst as an independent, mature person, rather than as a substitute parent. The theory is that if the patient can do this with the analyst, he can also do it with other people, and thus develops a more mature, realistic, effective personality for meeting the problems and the opportunities of life.

The Psychology of Groups

Although Freud is usually associated with the one-to-one relationship of psychoanalysis (one therapist treating one patient), the

---

* There are today several major schools of psychoanalysis, all of which have somewhat different ideas about the therapeutic process.

fact is that he explained how psychoanalytic theory might be applied to groups. In *Group Psychology and the Analysis of the Ego,* he wrote: "The contrast between individual psychology and social or group psychology, which at first glance may appear to be full of significance, loses a great deal of its sharpness when it is examined more closely."

Freud then asks how a group of people is able to "acquire the capacity for exercising such a decisive influence over the mental life of the individual." In order for this to happen, the group must advance beyond being a mere assembly of individuals. It must have some essential unity of its own. "If the individuals of a group are combined into a unity, there must surely be something to unite them, and this bond might be precisely the thing that is characteristic of a group."

Before elaborating on the nature of this bond, Freud made a few pertinent comments about groups: "In groups the most contradictory ideas can exist side by side and tolerate each other, without any conflict arising from the logical contradictions between them." Thus, "groups have never thirsted for truth," and "they demand illusions, and cannot do without them."

Freud continued: "Since a group is in no doubt as to what constitutes truth or error, and is conscious, moreover, of its own great strength, it is intolerant as it is obedient to authority. It respects force and can only slightly be influenced by kindness, which it regards merely as a form of weakness. What it demands of its heroes is strength, or even violence. It wants to be ruled and oppressed by its masters." Nonetheless, "under the influence of suggestion, groups are capable of high achievements in the shape of self-denial, unselfishness, and devotion to an ideal."

How is it that a person can lower himself, or raise himself, when he is acting as a member of a group? Is there some kind of "herd instinct" that accounts for a form of instinctive attraction between people, as some scientists had supposed? Actually, Freud said, it is love that gets people together.

Love, he said, is an excellent word to describe the activity and effects of libidinal energy. Libido is "the energy . . . of those instincts which have to do with all that may be comprised under the word 'love.' " He adds: "The nucleus of what we mean by love naturally consists . . . in sexual love with sexual union as its aim."

However, although libidinal energy, which springs from the id, powers the urge toward sexual intercourse, the ego, as we have noted, forces this energy into other channels (sublimation) in the interests of self-preservation. In the early years this turns into self-love or *narcissism.** In most cases, however, as the person matures, narcissism recedes, and libido is "transformed" into "desexualized" forms of love and friendship, including, "love for parents and children, friendship and love for humanity in general, and also devotion to concrete objects and to abstract ideas." It is these "love relationships, or, to use a more neutral term, emotional ties, (which) also constitute the essence of the group mind."

A well-known characteristic of stable, long-lasting groups, such as a religious body or an army, is that a threat of punishment is "employed to prevent them from disintegrating and to check alterations in their structure." However, what is not generally understood is that libidinal force is also at work, acting to push people into each other's company, even though this may threaten personal survival.

One problem is that the greater the strength of libidinal ties within the group, the more intense the cruelty to and intolerance of outsiders is likely to be. Since group members identify themselves with each other (that is, see themselves in other group members), much of their love for each other is really narcissistic — a disguised form of self-love. Strangers, however, may present a threat to a group member's ability to indulge in self-love, since he unconsciously interprets any difference from "his own particular line of development" as a criticism of himself. This would account for the intense hostility which members of well-established groups so often show to outsiders.

Love in Freud's Life

It is evident from all that has been said that Freud was concerned above all with a scientific analysis and understanding of love. Because of this, young students of Freud's work sometimes get the impression that his attitude toward love was cold and impersonal — that he tended to dehumanize it and rob it of its unique value.

But the fact is that Freud, for all of his intellectual powers and his ceaseless quest for understanding, was a very human person, and love played a vital part in his own life. This was amply shown in his relations with his parents, his wife, and his children. His relations with his students and colleagues, while not without personal clashes, were marked for the most part by loyalty, affection, and sincere regard.

---

* *Narcissus,* a character in Greek mythology, was a handsome youth who refused all offers of love. As punishment for this rejection, he was made to fall in love with his own image, which he saw reflected in a mountain pool. The word *narcissism,* accordingly, has come to mean erotic feeling aroused by one's own body and personality. In Freud's view, this is a normal stage of sexual development.

In 1938, Freud, now 82 years old and in failing health, had to flee from Vienna to escape Nazi persecution. He sought refuge in England, and he was greatly touched by the warm reception given to him and his family. He spoke with evident emotion and appreciation of the many letters received "from strangers who only wish to say how happy they are that we are in peace and safety." These are not the words of a "cold intellectual," detached from ordinary human emotions.

Three weeks after the outbreak of World War II, Sigmund Freud died in his sleep of cancer of the jaw.

The Spread of Freudian Ideas

The basic Freudian ideas of repression, of the significance of childhood sexuality, of the scientific recognition of sex, and of unconscious motivation, have taken a strong hold in the everyday knowledge and general mental background of people living in Western countries and indeed in all parts of the world. Freudian concepts and Freudian language are utilized freely today even by people who have had no training in psychology and have no specific awareness of the life and work of the founder of psychoanalysis.

Following World War I, when it became fashionable to talk about sex more openly, psychoanalysis gained a certain notoriety, particularly among upper-class people in metropolitan centers of Europe and the United States. For many "sophisticates" the concepts of psychoanalysis were bandied about like new toys and soon thoughtlessly tossed away. However, psychoanalysis gained more solid acceptance among informed, serious-minded people in all walks of life. Undoubtedly some of this prestige was due to the fact that many well-known individuals underwent psychoanalysis. Benefiting from their experiences on the psychiatric couch, such individuals often carried Freudian ideas and concepts into their own specialized activities, such as the arts, literature, historical interpretation, and journalism.

For instance, much of the serious literature written in the past fifty years has unconscious motivation as a basic theme, and the portrayal of the unconscious is often along recognizably Freudian lines. This is true, to mention just one instance, of the dramas of the great American playwright Eugene O'Neill, such as *The Iceman Cometh* and *Long Day's Journey into Night*.

Psychologists, of course, can be found today everywhere in American life — in hospitals, in schools, in universities, in business, in government, in penal institutions, in the armed forces. And even though many of these psychologists are in disagreement with Freud, they are still indebted to him for basic insights that are now considered to be part of the common knowledge and intellectual orientation of modern man. This is an achievement which can be matched by few individuals in the entire history of Western civilization.

THINGS TO DISCUSS :: THINGS TO DO :: THINGS TO READ

Answer the following questions in relation to the Freudian concepts and standards presented in this chapter.

1. Under what circumstances may behavior be described as "infantile"?

2. What is the difference between a *mature decision* and an *unconscious urge* which is rationalized on the conscious level? Give hypothetical examples.

3. When may guilt feelings be regarded as a form of self-punishment?

4. *Projection* is a fundamental concept in psychology. Why?

5. *Repression* is another fundamental concept. Under what conditions may it be useful to the individual? When may it be harmful?

6. How can you tell the difference between *narcissism* (self-indulgent love) and *self-respect?*

7. Are there any places in this chapter that gave you some uncomfortable moments? What are they?

8. One of Freud's chief therapeutic tools was *free association*. Try this on yourself. Can you get some feeling of what the unconscious is like?

9. Note that conversations between people often start off on one topic and then move on to areas that have nothing to do with the original theme. Try to identify the irrational impulses that cause conversation to take such strange "twists and turns."

10. Hold a class debate or round-table discussion on Freud. Try to elicit contrasting or opposing ideas on such matters as repression, ego, the Oedipus complex, feminism, and transference.

READINGS

A General Introduction to Psychoanalysis, by Sigmund Freud (available in many editions). Written in everyday language, it gives a good survey of Freudian theory. (Some parts are a little steep, but these may be skipped.)

The Brothers Karamazov, by Fyodor Dostoyevsky (available in many editions). Freud considered this one of the world's greatest novels. Can you see why?

The Greening of America, by Charles A. Reich (Random House, 1970). What might be the relationship between Reich's "Consciousness III" and Freudian depth psychology?

THEORIES OF PERSONALITY AFTER FREUD

6

FOLLOWERS, SUCCESSORS, RIVALS

● ●

"... the child expresses what the parent represses."

— *ERIK H. ERIKSON*

Challenges to Freud

As the founder and guiding spirit of the psychoanalytic movement, Freud has continued to exert a powerful influence on psychologists and psychiatrists until the present day. Indeed, as we noted, Freud's ideas on personality and on mental health have become an important part of the intellectual background of great numbers of educated people in all parts of the world.

However, Freud's ideas have certainly not gone unchallenged. Some of his early followers later developed doctrines which in some respects amplified and in other respects broke away from "orthodox" Freudian theory. Prominent among these innovators were Alfred Adler and Carl Jung.

They were followed by a group of so-called "neo-Freudians" who stayed within the Freudian framework but objected to what they considered the exaggerated emphasis on sexual motivation. In place of this biological factor, they tend to emphasize *cultural* and *interpersonal* influences. Erich Fromm is one of the leading "neo-Freudians."

Erik H. Erikson, who is often called a "humanistic psychologist," has stayed pretty much within the Freudian fold. Following the lead of Freud's psychoanalyst daughter, Anna Freud, he has concentrated more on the ego and its relations to society.

Karen Horney, also trained as a Freudian, later refuted Freud in many respects and has emphasized particularly the "need for security."

Altogether opposed to the Freudians, to the neo-Freudians, and to any other "introspectionist" psychologists are the *behaviorists,* who take their cue from the pioneering work of the Russian physiologist Ivan Pavlov.

Alfred Adler (1870-1937)

Alfred Adler was an early Viennese disciple of Freud and the first to openly break with him. Following the split in 1911, he founded his school of "individual psychology" — so named to distinguish it from Freud's "psychoanalysis."

Basic Ideas — The Feeling of Inferiority

The *"feeling of inferiority"* is the central idea in Adlerian thinking. In his psychological scheme, the goal of everyone, in some degree or other, is to overcome this feeling by manifesting superiority. This striving toward superiority may be expressed as an attempt to dominate others, which is negative, childish, and neurotic; or at the other extreme, it may take the form of a striving to master life's difficulties "courageously."

In fact, Adler thought that "neurosis is the weapon of the coward, and the weapon most used by the weak."* He added, "We cannot ignore the heavily-veiled aggressive or vindictive element in most neuroses."

Adler pictured personality development as a continuous process of "compensating" for inferiority. Inferiority feelings are thus essential to psychological growth, for they stimulate healthy strivings and desires for competence and for the surmounting of difficulties.

Adler's Theory of Neurosis

A child who has been "spoiled" or "pampered," so that he becomes overly dependent on others, tends to develop a mistaken "style of life"† — that is, a *neurosis*. Adler taught that neurosis represents a negative handling or avoidance of one of the three critical areas of adult life: *society, love* and *work*. Psychotics, he said, are unable to function in any of these areas.

Adler thought that neurotics are basically behaving in a selfish manner, whereas mature people have a strong "social feeling" or sense of responsibility for other people. Neurotics "expect to be appreciated *before* they have done anything of social value, instead of *after*

---

* All quotations in this section are taken from Adler's *Problems of Neurosis* (Routledge & Logan Paul, Ltd., 1929).

† The phrase "style of life" (usually rendered as *life style* in English) was originated by Adler.

having done it, thus expecting the natural course of things to be reversed in their own favor." They also want to "take without giving," they want "everything for nothing," and they want "all or nothing."

One of the essential characteristics of the neurotic personality, in Adler's view, is that he needs to suffer in order to justify his failure. He is in effect saying to the world, "If only I didn't have something wrong with me, such as a neurosis, then I could succeed."

Adler's theory of neurosis grew out of his idea of "organ inferiority," an idea Freud found objectionable because it placed sexual motivations in a secondary position. Adler believed that many people are born with some naturally weak body part or function which is more subject to disorder than other parts. For example, some people have delicate stomachs; others have weak lungs; others get headaches easily. A person who is prone to neurosis, instead of overcoming the weakness as he matures, or learning to "live with it," uses it as an excuse for his failings, and so makes it worse. He vomits chronically; he shows the symptoms of asthma; or he conveniently comes down with migraine headaches whenever his anxiety is too great.

Such a person characteristically will be reluctant to undergo treatment for his disability. In a sense, he *needs* the disability because he lacks the courage "to return to the useful side of life." It is this which causes the patient to "put up a defense against treatment, for fear that his relation to the psychologist should force him into some useful activity in which he may be defeated."

People with positive styles of life are actively engaged in contributing to other people, without any specific expectation of gaining favor. The way out of neurosis lies in the acceptance of social responsibility. "It is also impossible to exaggerate the value of an increase in social feeling. The mind improves, for intelligence is a communal function."

Importance of the Early Years

Adler, like Freud, thought that the first four or five years of life are of critical importance in shaping the person's character, or style of life. During this time, Adler thought, "the most vital factor is the mother . . . for it is in its mother that every child makes its first contact with a trustworthy fellow man." If, for some reason, the mother has inadequately discharged her responsibilities and "spoiled" the child, it becomes the therapist's job to take over the mother's role and provide the patient with the standard or idea of a human being whom he can fully trust and respect. In this way, it is hoped, normal social feeling will be developed.

Compensating for Feelings of Inferiority

Even mature people must strive to overcome some feelings of inferiority. However, they do not become "stuck" in their feelings of inferiority; they do not allow these emotions to dominate their personalities. In short, unlike neurotic personalities, they do not develop an *inferiority complex* (another Adlerian phrase).

A characteristic of mature, healthy people is that they *compensate,* or sometimes *"overcompensate,"* for their feelings of deficiency in a *positive* manner. Adler cites, for example, the case of a man who, as a baby, suffered from a paralyzing disease. Although he recovered, he became preoccupied with the idea of motion. As a small boy, he had the fantasy of being changed into a horse. As an adult, however, he became a successful automotive engineer. Thus, he used the motivation provided by a deficiency or weakness to direct him into a useful and successful career.

The same basic pattern is illustrated in the well-known life story of Demosthenes. As a boy in ancient Greece, he was a wretched stutterer. He worked long and hard to overcome his speech defect, even going so far (tradition tells us) as to practice speaking with pebbles

Napoleon Bonaparte was only about 5 feet, 3 inches tall. His consciousness of his small stature and his need to compensate for it may have been a factor in the tremendous drive that made him the dominant military and political figure of his generation. Napoleon liked to be represented standing on an elevation of some kind or on horseback. This painting by Meissonier is typical, although it was done many years after Napoleon's death.

in his mouth. Eventually, he became the greatest and most famous orator of the Greek world.

Life offers us many other familiar examples of people who attain a satisfactory adjustment to life (and sometimes outstanding success) by compensating or overcompensating for deficiencies. We all know, for example, of physically small people who are motivated to make extreme efforts to show that they are as formidable and as "tough" as much larger men. Napoleon is the classic example of this. A girl who feels she is not physically attractive may seek to develop social charm, wit, and conversational ability. A childless woman may find an occupation that brings her into close contact with children, and may show notable ability at this work. Adler believed that one indispensable element in genius is the expression of an urge to compensate for a shortcoming, real or imagined.

The long-range goal of people with a positive life style is "perfection," Adler thought. And although this goal, in the very nature of things, is never fully achieved, mature people constantly move toward it by devoting themselves in a positive way to other people — that is, to life.

Carl Jung (1875-1961)

Carl Jung, a Swiss psychiatrist, was early in his career a follower and colleague of Freud's. For a time, in fact, Freud regarded Jung as his "true heir" to the leadership of the psychoanalytic movement. Jung, however, was much too individualistic to follow docilely in the footsteps of another man, however great. In 1912, the master and his disciple parted company, and Jung set to work on the development of his own "analytic psychology."

The Collective Unconscious — Archetypes

According to Jung, there are two areas of the unconscious — the *personal unconscious* and the *collective unconscious*. The personal unconscious corresponds closely to the unconscious as described by Freud. It consists of the person's repressed memories and feelings.

The collective unconscious is Jung's distinctive idea. Jung believed that there has been "a deposit of ancestral memories from untold millions of years," and that this has produced a "racial inheritance" which is shared by all groups of mankind. Buried in the minds of all men are certain archaic memories or *archetypes* which profoundly influence human personality and behavior.

The "mother archetype," a familiar theme in Western art, as represented in Michelangelo's *Pietà*.

These archetypes appear in dreams and in the works of art produced by cultures in all parts of the world. They are mysterious, essential concepts around which images are built. For example, there is the *"mother archetype"* — symbolizing the experience with mothers which all human beings have had. She represents the miracle of life, and in the depths of the mind she is associated with the nourishing earth, the warming sun, the hearth, the milk-giving cow, and the security of the home. The *"father archetype"* symbolizes the fact of fatherhood in human experience. He represents power and authority and is linked in the imagination with winds, storms, violence, battles, war, and the fury of wild animals. Other similar images are the *"hero archetype"* (the deliverer, savior, messiah, strong man), and the *"wise man archetype"* (the teacher, sage, prophet).

Jung asserted that his idea of a collective unconscious is supported by the fact that there are essential similarities in the legends and myths of peoples widely separated in space and time. (See Chapter 9.) For example, the concepts of sacrifice and rebirth are common to nearly all religions. So is the idea of identification with the Deity. This is represented among many primitive peoples by eating the flesh of the totem animal of the tribe, which has the symbolic value of "eating" the tribal god. In the Christian tradition, there is the sacrament of the mass, in which wine and wafer represent (or are believed actually to be) the blood and body of Christ.

Archetypes emerge in fairy tales, folk legends, and religious traditions. For example, the theme of men fighting against giants appears in the stories of Jack and the Beanstalk, St. George and the Dragon, and David and Goliath. The story of Cinderella, which originated in China and has traveled all over the world, and the story of the Ugly Duckling portray the ignored and neglected individual coming into his own. In many religions there is a story of a fall from a lost paradise, and of a crucial battle of angels or gods.

The "Persona" and the "Shadow"

These terms represent two other basic concepts in Jung's analytic psychology.

The *"persona"* is the social front, the façade, or the mask that each person presents to society. Each of us has a persona that constitutes the public self. We identify a person, for example, as a judge, a church worker, a housewife, a teacher, a student, a social worker, an athlete. Jung's point is not that the persona is fraudulent but rather that it constitutes only *part* of reality — the part which the individual chooses to expose, and which society chooses to accept and emphasize.

The *"shadow"* is the undeveloped part of the human personality, the "other self," distinguished from the persona. In Jung's words, it is the inferior or less commendable part of a person. Our recognition that the "shadow" exists is reflected in such phrases as "He forgot himself," or "He acted out of character." The "shadow" personifies the *personal unconscious.*

Four Basic Psychological Functions

According to Jung, there are four basic psychological functions: *thinking, feeling, sensation,* and *intuition.* All four are used in varying degrees, but each of us tends to emphasize one particular function (or several functions) in relation to the others.

▶ *Thinking* refers to active, logical, directed thought. A person dominated by thinking tends to be detached and to view experience as a series of problems to be analyzed and solved in a rational way.

▶ The opposite of thinking is *feeling,* a predominantly subjective approach to life that emphasizes personal values and emotions.

▶ *Sensation* is direct awareness through the senses.

▶ *Intuition,* the opposite of sensation, refers to such mental processes as "hunches," non-rational insights, awareness of the implications and possibilities in a situation. An intuitive type of person is usually at home with abstract ideas and inferences, but weak in practical matters.

In Jung's view, the conscious functions of *males* are usually thinking and sensation, while feeling and intuition are unconscious. In the *female* personality, feeling and intuition usually dominate; thinking and sensation tend to remain on the unconscious level. However, no individual is purely "male" or "female" in Jung's psychology. Every male has a submerged feminine side, which is called his *anima;* every woman has a masculine aspect, called her *animus.* The anima and animus are archetypes that appear in dreams.

Introverts and Extroverts

Jung further classified people as being *introverted* or *extroverted* according to their basic outlook toward the world. Again, every individual shows both tendencies to some degree, but one is more or less dominant.

The *extrovert* lives mainly according to external demands. He is oriented toward the objective world of things and events, and he tends to be "realistic" and socially active.

The *introvert* is primarily interested in the inner world of imagination, ideas, and emotions. He stresses his own values and feelings, and tends to be sensitive, idealistic, or defensive against the outer world.

Whichever attitude prevails in a given person almost always conflicts with the opposite attitude that the individual also holds to a lesser degree.

Karen Horney (1885-1952)

Karen Horney, a German-American woman psychiatrist, rejected the biological emphasis of traditional Freudianism and focused on *interpersonal influence.*

Basic Anxiety

In Horney's psychological scheme, *basic anxiety* is the driving force of personality. This anxiety arises from the child's experiences of being isolated and helpless in a potentially hostile world, rather than from, as Freud taught, the ego's need to control the id. She stressed that anxiety is expressed essentially in interpersonal relations. Thus, the child can move *toward* people, *against* them, or *away from* them. When moving toward people, he accepts his own helplessness and, despite his fears, tries to win the affection of others. When moving against people, he takes for granted the hostility around him and decides to fight. When moving away, he wants neither to belong nor to fight, but simply to withdraw. Each of these reactions represents a general personality orientation.

In her influential book *The Neurotic Personality of Our Time,* Horney describes the typical neurotic personality in direct, uncomplicated terms. The neurotic, she said, often creates an idealized image of himself which he substitutes for realistic self-confidence and pride. He may choose, for example, to think of himself as a brilliant intellectual, or as a model of the social graces, or as a person who is extremely attractive to the opposite sex, even though in cold fact there is little basis for any of these self-representations.

To a degree, the image is reassuring to the person involved, but it is also rigid and generally inadequate. Thus, it is likely to generate a new rift or trauma in the personality. Having placed himself on a pedestal and made himself an object of admiration, the neurotic can tolerate his real self even less than before, and may start to rage against it. Thus, he wavers between self-adoration and self-hatred.

Symptoms of Neurotic Conflict

One symptom of neurotic conflict, according to Horney, is a general indecisiveness in life situations. This may extend from trivial matters, such as choosing what to eat for breakfast, to deciding whether or not to marry. Another symptom is sluggishness — an aversion to getting started promptly, to making a real effort, to carrying something through to completion. Most important is the fear of changing anything in oneself — a feeling probably grounded in the fear of losing the idealized image and thus becoming a rejected and depressed version of one's own personality.

However, "neurotic trends," such as these, are actually "safety devices" and if they don't work, then anxiety makes itself felt. It is not the so-called ego that is threatened, "but the individual's security, inasmuch as his security rests on the functioning of his neurotic trends."*

Repressed Hostility

The neurotic's "basic feeling of helplessness in a potentially hostile world" comes about because of repressed hostility (toward parents). "Repression of hostility helps to render a person defenseless be-

---

* All quotations in this section are from Karen Horney's *New Ways in Psychoanalysis.* Copyright, 1939 by W. W. Norton & Co., New York, N. Y. Copyright renewed 1966 by Marianne von Eckardt, Renate Muntz, and Brigitte Swarzenski.

cause it makes him lose sight of the danger which he should fight. If he represses his hostility it means that he is no longer aware that some individual represents a menace to him; hence he is likely to be submissive, compliant, friendly in situations where he should be on his guard."

Perfectionism and Neurosis

Horney taught that a neurotic sense of guilt does not go back to the formation of the superego, as Freud maintained. Rather, "self-recriminations are an unavoidable consequence of the (neurotic) need to appear perfect."

> For the neurotic individual any failure to maintain a semblance of perfection means defeat and danger. Therefore he must be angry at himself for any move, whether in thought, feelings, or actions, which to him means failing to be perfect.

> Perfectionist persons . . . are deeply afraid of anyone recognizing that their façade is only a façade; hence their . . . fear of criticism and reproaches. In this regard their self-recriminations are an attempt to anticipate reproaches and, by raising them themselves, to prevent others from making them — even more, to appease others by demonstrating their apparent severity toward themselves and to elicit reassurances.

Horney emphasizes the inability of neurotics to understand that life is inherently "incalculable and uncontrollable," and their characteristic unwillingness to face up to this fact.

> The practice of shifting reproaches from others to oneself is often based on the philosophy that *someone* has to be blamed whenever anything adverse happens. Usually, if not always, persons who build up a colossal apparatus to maintain a semblance of perfection are highly apprehensive of impending disaster. They feel as if they were living under a suspended sword which may fall down at any moment, although they may not be aware of these fears. They have a fundamental incapacity to face life's ups and downs in a matter-of-fact way. They cannot reconcile themselves to the fact that life is not calculable like a mathematical task, that it is to some extent like an adventure or gamble, subject to good and ill luck, full of unpredictable difficulties, risks, unforeseen and unforeseeable perplexities. As a means of reassurance they cling to the belief that life is calculable and controllable. Hence they believe it is the fault of someone if something goes wrong, for this makes it possible to avoid the un-

pleasant realization that life is incalculable and uncontrollable. If such persons are for any reason stopped from reproaching others they will take on themselves the blame for adverse happenings.

Horney said that "in the last analysis neurotic dependency of whatever kind is based on the fact that the individual has lost his center of gravity in himself and shifted it to the outside world."

Erich Fromm (1900-   )

Erich Fromm, born and educated in Germany, has lived in North America since 1934 and has gained wide renown for his application of the findings of contemporary sociology and anthropology to psychoanalysis.

"Escape from Freedom"

Fromm believes that culture is the major shaper of personality. As the child grows, he gradually gains freedom from parents and other persons dominant in his life. This newly-won independence is stimulating, but it also separates him emotionally from others, causing loneliness and fear. Therefore, the child wants to *"escape from freedom,"* in Fromm's phrase. He tries to regain security either by forming new and productive relationships with other people, or by submitting to authority and conforming blindly to binding rules laid down by social authorities.

A person's method of seeking to regain security depends on how his society meets man's basic needs. These needs include: a sense of *relatedness* to other people in order to overcome basic loneliness and isolation; a sense of *rootedness,* of belonging to some social group or groups; a sense of *identity* — of one's uniqueness as an individual; a sense of *transcendence* — the capacity to create and to feel that you are in control of your life, rather than being the passive victim of events; and a frame of *orientation and devotion* — a philosophy of life or religion that provides direction, meaning, and purpose for existence. Personality depends on how these needs are met, and on the specific restrictions and opportunities for gratification found in the particular society.

Fromm shows how each society — communist, fascist, feudal, socialist, or capitalist — tends to mold a particular type of personality. The sane society, in Fromm's view, would be one that meets the basic human needs in the best way, effectively counteracting feel-

"Escape from freedom." The charismatic and all-powerful leader in a totalitarian society relieves his followers of the burden of individual judgment and responsibility.

ings of loneliness, isolation, and despair. In contrast, the frustration of basic needs and capacities creates deep guilt within the individual.

Character Types

Fromm distinguishes between two types of conscience. *Authoritarian* conscience is roughly equivalent to the Freudian superego. It is the voice of authority, represented for example by parents, that a person has internalized. *Humanistic* conscience is the voice of the person himself, the expression of his enlightened self-interest, intelligence, and honesty.

Fromm describes several character types fostered by a capitalistic society, such as our own. The *receptive* character depends on others for support and needs above all to be liked and accepted. The *exploitative* type takes things from others by force, cunning, or domination. The *marketing* type regards people as commodities to be bought and sold. The person with a *hoarding* orientation bases security on saving and keeping what he has. The *productive* outlook implies full use of one's capacities, especially creative tendencies and the ability to love.

Forms of Relatedness

Fromm states that man needs to be *related* to his fellow man, in order to overcome a sense of loneliness and isolation. There are, however, many forms of relatedness.

A common form is *symbiotic union*. A man can make himself part of another person, who guides him, provides for him, protects him. In thus relating himself to a strong personality, the individual gains a feeling of strength and importance. Or he can relate himself by *dominating* — by incorporating a lesser person into himself. In either case, the two partners become interdependent. The powerful one needs to dominate, and the dependent partner needs to submit, so that each meets the other's needs. These needs, of course, are very often not conscious.

A healthier form of relatedness is *love,* which Fromm defines as "union under the condition of preserving one's integrity." Love always implies care, responsibility, respect, and knowledge. We often think of responsibility as a "duty," something imposed from the outside. In the context of this relatedness, however, responsibility implies that one person responds sensitively and willingly to the needs of the other. Respect implies the ability to see another person as he actually is, without illusion or wishful thinking. If you respect a person, says Fromm, you don't want to "mold" him according to your own character and needs; you want to see him develop according to *his own* character and needs. Thus, respect implies the absence of domination and exploitation.

Fromm disputes Freud's contention that every person has only a fixed amount of libidinal energy. He rejects the idea that the more *libido* (page 106) a person directs at himself, the less he will have available for loving relationships with others. Fromm asserts that a person who loves himself is *more* capable of loving others. Even the Biblical injunction "Love thy neighbor as thyself" recognizes this.

Alienation in Modern Man

Fromm contends that modern man is characteristically alienated from himself, from his fellow man, and from nature. In Western societies, human relations have become those of automatons, trying to gain security by staying close to the crowd and by not being "different" in thought or deed. As a result, people remain utterly alone and experience insecurity and anxiety. A strict routine of bureaucratized, organized work is reassuring because it helps to make Western man less conscious of his separateness. So does passive consumption of movies and TV, as well as the satisfaction of continually buying new things. In explaining how everything, emotional and spiritual as well as material, has in our society become an object of exchange and consumption, Fromm states: "The world is one great object for our appetite, a big apple, a big bottle, a big breast; we are the sucklers, the eternally expectant ones, the hopeful ones — and the eternally disappointed ones."

Fromm suggests that most of us go astray by seeing love primarily as a matter of *being loved,* rather than *loving.* A second common fallacy is that we think that loving is simple and guided by instinct, although in fact finding the "right" object to love — or to be loved by — may be exceedingly difficult. Our culture is based on the appetite for buying, on the idea of a mutually favorable exchange. Thus, "attractive" usually means a "nice package" of qualities that are popular and sought after on the current personality market. Fromm suggests that we should recognize that love is an art, which we have to learn just as we have to learn any other art form — music, painting, medicine, sports, or dancing.

Erik H. Erikson (1902-   )

"If everything goes back into childhood, then everything is somebody else's fault, and trust in one's power of taking responsibility for oneself may be undermined." This statement is typical of the views and the style of the influential European-American psychologist, Erik H. Erikson.

Erikson, originally an artist, came into contact with Freud in Vienna and studied psychoanalysis under Freud's daughter, Anna. Moving to the United States in 1933, he established himself as a child psychoanalyst and became interested in the growth of the ego.

Psychosocial Development

While Freud described the development of personality in psychosexual terms, and concentrated particularly on early childhood as the key to personality development, Erikson became more interested in *psychosocial* development — in how the personality is affected by *culture* and *society.*

Erikson uses the concept of *identity* to describe the interaction of forces on the developing individual. Identity is some sense of inner continuity and wholeness, a feeling of knowing who you are, where you came from, and where you are going. At each stage of development, a person's identity is the product of three forces: his body, his mind, and his environment.

Each stage in the life history represents a crossroads, a point at which, because of physical change and widening social interaction, the developing personality may move toward growth or fail to achieve it. Each successive step, then, is potentially a crisis — a time of danger but also a time of opportunity.

Eight Stages of Life

In his book *Childhood and Society,** Erikson identifies eight stages of the life cycle, each characterized by certain basic attitudes, and each involving certain dangers for personality development.

1. *Basic Trust vs. Basic Mistrust.* In the first year of life the baby acquires his basic orientation toward the world, which will usually extend throughout his life. "The first demonstration of social trust in the baby is the ease of his feeding, the depth of his sleep, the relaxation of his bowels."

> In his gradually increasing waking hours, he finds that more and more adventures of the senses arouse a feeling of familiarity, of having coincided with a feeling of inner goodness. Forms of comfort, and people associated with them, become as familiar as the gnawing discomfort of the bowels. The infant's first social achievement, then, is his willingness to let the mother out of sight without undue anxiety or rage, because she has become an inner certainty as well as an outer predictability.

People suffering from schizophrenia and chronic depression appear to have been deprived of the basic trust deriving from this first stage. Thus, the treatment of such mentally ill people is aimed at reestablishing a state of trust. (See Chapter 4.)

2. *Autonomy vs. Shame and Doubt.* In this period, the child learns the "ratio of love and hate, cooperation and willfulness, freedom of self expression and its suppression." Erikson adds, "From a sense of self-control without loss of self-esteem comes a lasting sense of good-will and pride; from a sense of loss of self-control and of (outside) overcontrol comes a lasting propensity for doubt and shame."

"Autonomy" or independence of mind, comes about when the positive aspects of this stage are fulfilled.

3. *Initiative vs. Guilt.* This period comes when the child is able to move around by himself and when he is "on the make." This ability to move gives the child an exhilarating sense of his power to manipulate aggressively his environment, including possibly his parents. Erikson believes that the "danger of this stage is a sense of guilt over

---

* All quotations in this section are taken from Erik H. Erikson's *Childhood and Society* (W. W. Norton, 1950, 1963).

the goals contemplated and the acts initiated in one's exuberant enjoyment" of the new-found power.

4. *Industriousness vs. Conformity.* In all cultures, at this stage, children receive some *systematic instruction,* "whether the school is field, jungle or classroom." Unfortunately, "many a child's development is disrupted when family life has failed to prepare him for school life, or when school life fails to sustain the promise of earlier stages." A fundamental danger is that the attitudes instilled at this time may have the effect of limiting the individual's horizons to such a degree that everything centers on his daily work. "If he accepts work as his only obligation, and what works as his only criterion for worthwhileness, he may become the conformist and thoughtless slave of his technology and those who are in a position to exploit it."

5. *Identity vs. Role Confusion.* Erikson sees adolescence as the key stage in the development of identity, and he emphasizes the importance of the "adolescent identity crisis." Psychologically, the individual ego requires a sense of continuity amid change. But in adolescence, all sense of continuity is called into question, because the body is growing and changing so rapidly, and because of the impact of newly acquired sexual maturity. As a result, young people become concerned "with what they appear to be in the eyes of others, as compared with what they feel they are," and they worry about how to connect all the skills and roles learned previously with some occupation or career in future life.

Many typical adolescent behavior patterns can be seen as a result of the identity crisis. For instance, adolescents band together in *cliques* as a way of temporarily seeking identity as part of a group. The group provides standards for behavior. It helps to define what is "in" and what is "out" and thus provides some protection against the unsettling influence of rapid change.

Temporarily, the adolescent may adopt roles that are displeasing to the community around him, such as drop-out, hippie, cynic, or delinquent. We say "temporarily," but the fact is that individuals sometimes become "frozen" in these roles because the community overreacts and condemns the adolescent too sharply. Such dangers are real, but Erikson stresses that the *adolescent identity crisis* is necessary to the development of the personality, and that youth needs this interlude to experiment with new ideas and new roles.

The concept of identity crisis is particularly important in our time of rapid social change. Indeed the adolescent identity crisis seems to be taking place in the midst of a similar national and international "crisis."

The question "Who am I and what is my place in society?" is a crucial one to young people everywhere, and they need help and guidance in arriving at viable answers. However, in Erikson's view, the individual in the last analysis must still trust in his own capacity to take responsibility for himself, if his answer is going to be a good one for him.

6. *Intimacy vs. Isolation.* Young adulthood is the time when a person, "emerging from the search for and insistence on identity, is eager and willing to fuse his identity with that of others." According to Erikson, "He is ready for intimacy, that is, the capacity to commit himself to concrete affiliations and partnerships and to develop the ethical strength to abide by such commitments, even though they may call for significant sacrifices and compromises."

Avoidance of such experiences "because of fear of ego loss may lead to a deep sense of isolation and consequent self-absorption."

7. *Generativity vs. Stagnation.* By "generativity" Erikson means "productivity" and "creativity," as well as the "concern of establishing and guiding the next generation." The denial or frustration of this capacity means that the individual is stagnating, failing to take advantage of his potentiality.

8. *Ego Integrity vs. Despair.* Ego integrity, which comes in the last phase of life, is "a post-narcissistic love of the human ego — not

of the self — as an experience which conveys some world order and spiritual sense, no matter how dearly paid for."

On the other hand, "The lack or loss of this accrued ego integration is signified by fear of death" or despair.

Erikson neatly brings the life cycle together by saying that "healthy children will not fear life if their elders have integrity enough not to fear death." And elsewhere he comments that "the values of any new generation do not spring full-blown from their heads; they are already there, inherent if not articulated in the older generation." He adds that "the younger generation makes overt what is covert in the older generation; *the child expresses what the parent represses.*"

Behaviorism

Psychoanalysis and psychodynamics are not universally accepted. At about the same time that Freud was formulating his theories, Ivan Pavlov (1849-1936), a Russian physiologist, was discovering the principles of conditioning which are the basis for the school of psychology called *behaviorism*.

Pavlov's Experiments

Pavlov conducted a famous series of laboratory experiments with dogs. When food is given to hungry dogs, they will salivate in anticipation. This is a normal or *unconditioned* response. Over a period of time, Pavlov gave food to his laboratory dogs at regular intervals, and rang a bell whenever the food was made available. The dogs salivated on each occasion. After this had gone on for some time, Pavlov waited for the dogs to become hungry and then rang the bell *without serving the food*. The dogs salivated even though no food was present. They had learned to associate food with the ringing of the bell. The response (salivation) had been *conditioned* so that it was triggered not only by the original stimulus (food) but by a secondary stimulus (the ringing bell).

Behaviorists are a school of psychologists who see all behavior as responses to stimuli. Some responses are "built in" by nature — for example, the salivation of a dog in response to food, or the crying of a baby who is uncomfortable. Others are learned by conditioning. Man excels all other animals in the number and complexity of the conditioned responses he can form, but according to these theorists the process in man is not essentially different from the behavior of the dogs who learned to salivate in response to a ringing bell.

vibrating
tuning fork (ss)

SS

food
(os)

food
(os)

secretion
of saliva

1.   **2.**   **3.**

This diagram summarizes Pavlov's classic experiment on conditioned reflexes. In *1*, the dog responds to the food (the original stimulus, *os)* by
salivating. In *2*, this response is *conditioned* by supplying a secondary stimulus (*ss*), such as a ringing bell or a vibrating tuning fork, each time the food
is served. In *3*, the dog responds by salivating when only the secondary
stimulus (not the food) is present.

Denial of the Unconscious

Behaviorists deny the existence of the unconscious. In their view,
neurotic symptoms are simply bad habits — unsuitable or poorly
adapted responses to stimuli. They claim that mental or emotional
disorders which have resulted from a process of "bad conditioning"
can be corrected by a process of "good conditioning."

The behaviorists attack vigorously the record of psychoanalysis
and allied techniques in curing mental illness. They point out that
such treatment is protracted, costly, and difficult, and assert that there
is no proof, in the scientific sense, that it is effective. They say that
they have had far greater success than psychoanalysts in helping people by using conditioning to relieve the symptoms of mental illness,
without worrying too much about the life history or psychic conditions that led to the trouble, perhaps decades previously.

Perhaps the crux of the disagreement between psychoanalysts
and behaviorists regarding the effectiveness of their respective methods lies in different interpretations of the word "cure." Behaviorists
feel that if symptoms have been eliminated, the patient has been re-
deemed from his illness; the malady no longer exists. Psychoanalysts
say that if only the symptoms are treated, without achieving an understanding of the conditions that caused the symptoms in the first
place, then the alleged "cure" may do more harm than good. Either
the original symptoms will return, or the patient will develop new
symptoms which are simply another expression of his continued, un-
cured illness.

Forms of Treatment Used by Behaviorists

In treating people with psychological problems or behavioral disorders, behaviorist therapists employ basically two forms of treatment.

In the first place, patients are rewarded for making good, healthy responses, while maladaptive responses are either ignored or sometimes punished ("aversive therapy"). The "reward" may take the form of the commendation and approval of the therapist or of other persons important to the patient. In some institutions, the patient may actually be "paid" for appropriate behavior by being given candy, cigarettes, movie admissions, etc., or tokens that will buy these things. In this way, the behaviorists say, the patient's behavior is gradually conditioned toward standards of health and normality. And when he learns to *behave* normally, he *is* normal.

Hypnosis, long discarded by the Freudians, is used freely by the behaviorists for therapeutic purposes. Andrew Salter, a leading behaviorist, believes that hypnosis is essentially nothing more than a form of conditioning, and that it is exceptionally well adapted to impose other forms of conditioning that will help people to solve problems and overcome bad habits. For example, heavy smokers who wish to stop smoking are hypnotized, and while they are in this hyper-suggestible state (page 255), they are conditioned to associate tobacco with a nauseated, miserable feeling. After several treatments, some people who are "excellent hypnotic subjects" have not only lost their desire to smoke but can't stand the smell of a cigarette or cigar. The difficulty is, as Salter admits, that most people are not "excellent hypnotic subjects."

Behavior therapy at its present stage appears to be a useful technique for certain purposes, but it does not seem to be adequate to come to grips with all aspects of human psychology, both applied and theoretical.

*   *   *

There can be no doubt as to the tremendous importance of Freud's pioneering contributions to the understanding of human motivation and behavior. There can be no doubt, too, that his successors (both followers and challengers) have added to his original perceptions, and that in the years ahead much more will be learned of the psychic aspects of man's life. Since human society — the setting within which men function — is always changing, there can never be any final or complete answers to the questions of why we think, feel, and behave as we do.

THINGS TO DISCUSS :: THINGS TO DO :: THINGS TO READ

1. Erik H. Erikson once observed that "You will not see in another what you have not learned to recognize in yourself." What connection do you see between this judgment and the concept of *identity?*

2. In Erich Fromm's view, "Happiness is an achievement brought about by man's inner productiveness and not a gift of the gods." What does Fromm mean by "inner productiveness"? How can you apply this judgment to your own life and problems?

3. Behaviorists place great emphasis on accumulating and using objective data. What does *objective* mean in this sense? If other schools of psychologists are more "subjective" than the behaviorists, does this necessarily mean that they are less "scientific," or that their conclusions are less valid?

4. What psychologist or school of psychology presented in this chapter and the preceding chapter seem to you to make the most sense and to have the most value in explaining human conduct and dealing with life problems? Prepare a brief statement in which you summarize the psychological ideas in question and explain why you consider these points of view more valuable for you than the others, in the sense indicated.

READINGS

Man for Himself — An Inquiry Into the Psychology of Ethics, by Erich Fromm (Holt, Rinehart and Winston, 1947). This is an interesting, well-written book which discusses in depth the relationship between psychology and morality.

Gandhi's Truth, by Erik H. Erikson (W. W. Norton, 1969). Erikson won the Pulitzer Prize for this book, which is a psychological study of the great exponent of non-violent political activism, Mohandas K. Gandhi.

Problems of Neurosis — A Book of Case Histories, by Alfred Adler (Cosmopolitan Books, 1930). This is a short book written in a clear, straightforward style. It gives an interesting perspective on the causes and symptoms of neurosis.

New Ways in Psychoanalysis, by Karen Horney (W. W. Norton, 1939). Much of this book is designed as a refutation of Freud. It contains many interesting passages — especially in regard to "perfectionism."

Four Archetypes — Mother, Rebirth, Spirit, Trickster, by Carl Jung (Princeton University Press, 1969). This book presents the essence of Jung's ideas. The presentation, however, is so complicated and specialized that you will probably find it more rewarding for "browsing" than for sustained reading.

Growth
and
Self–Actualization

● ●

". . . we're not Beatles to each other, you know. It's a joke to us. Everybody lookin' at us sees the Beatles. But we're not the Beatles at all. We're just us."

— *JOHN LENNON (before the breakup of the Beatles)*

Superstars and Ordinary People

"Am I as good as he is?" *Translation*: Am I as strong, clever, witty, good-looking, sophisticated, sexually attractive as that other person appears to be?

Just by asking the question, of course, a person, reveals that he has doubts that the answer is favorable. The next step in such a train of thought is often:

▶ "I *could be* as good as he is if I didn't have . . . ." You can fill in the blank with asthma, a bad back, insomnia, unsympathetic parents, weak eyes, an oversized nose, or any other malady or shortcoming that seems appropriate.

or

▶ "I *am* as good as he is, no matter what anybody says." The *anybody* refers to the speaker himself, identified by *I*. The person he must really convince is himself.

or

▶ "I *will be* as good as he is, no matter what." This person is determined to measure up to his standard of excellence, to become the center of admiration, by hook or by crook.

131

It is clear that envy acts as a basis for much social competition, in an active, positive sense. It may also be a basis for neurotic forms of behavior to *avoid* such competition. As people mature, they usually begin to accept the idea that in any particular area, there will always be *someone* whom they cannot hope to match. Thus, the need to compete, or to find excuses for avoiding competition, in the sense indicated, is seen to be absurd. There are only a few heroes, geniuses, and "superstars." The rest of the world, beyond these few, is made up of ordinary people, and most of us, like it or not, fall into that category.

It is striking, however, that the relatively few who have emerged in the competitive process as "superstars" are not necessarily outstanding for being happy or well-adjusted. The luminaries whom so many millions know and admire may turn out, on closer inspection, to be very imperfect indeed. For example, movie stars receive mass adulation; they have fabulous incomes; they are the "beautiful people." Yet we all know of the high rates of divorce, alcoholism, drug abuse, and suicide among these people, and of the relatively widespread delinquency and alienation among their children. Even the captain of your school's football team and the prettiest girl in the senior class may have their hang-ups!

This does not mean that it is worthwhile to go searching for defects or shortcomings in people who seem to receive more attention than we do. This is just another way for envy to reveal itself. The point is, rather, that being widely admired is not necessarily the criterion for maturity and happiness. In fact, constant desire to be the center of attraction and the shaping of one's behavior toward that end shows an infantile frame of mind.

A Changed Attitude Toward "Popularity" and "Adjustment"

Our attitudes toward such stereotypes as "popularity," "adjustment," and "delinquency" are changing. Instead of assuming uncritically that popularity is a "good thing," we are now more likely to ask, "Popular with *whom?*" Maybe it's better for a young person to be *unpopular* with snobs, bigots, and crass materialists.

Similarly, we may ask, "Well-adjusted to *what?*" To intolerable social conditions? To dominating and possessive parents? To a job that provides no opportunities for growth or personal fulfillment? Would you approve of a slave being well-adjusted to his status as a thing, rather than a human being?

The other side of the coin is that we are now likely to show more tolerance for people who are quite obviously *not* well-adjusted. Even social delinquents, such as alcoholics and drug addicts, customarily receive a certain amount of understanding — certainly more than in the past.

Some of these matters have been discussed in Chapter 3, "Problems of the Self." Here we want to continue exploring the concept of "adjustment" by examining some ideas about mental and emotional growth. The key question is, "Where am I headed? And why?"

A New View of Mental Health: Humanistic Psychology

By what standards can we judge that a person is in excellent mental health? According to the humanistic psychologists, the answer is directly tied in with the question, "What does it mean to be a good human being?"

The humanists, including such figures as Abraham Maslow, Carl Rogers, Erich Fromm, Erik Erikson, and Sidney Jourard, believe that if people can satisfy or neutralize their *primary needs* (see below), they have a tendency to grow to be healthy and "good." Some psychologists of this school contrast themselves in this respect to Freud, who felt that people can never altogether satisfy their basic needs.

Although the humanists differ to a degree among themselves, there are some main views that are common to all of their opinions. These are the views we shall emphasize in this chapter.

Good mental health is not always dependent on good physical health or even normality. An outstanding example of this is Helen Keller, who lived a long, successful, and happy life, marked by distinguished public service and many fine human relations, in spite of having been deaf, dumb, and blind since early childhood. Miss Keller is shown here shortly after World War II on a special mission to aid European children who had been blinded during that conflict.

As you proceed, however, bear in mind that we are presenting here only a *model,* or imaginary person, who includes all the traits of mental health. The healthiest people seem to be moving in the direction suggested — but no one has gone all the way. This is another way of saying that there is no such thing as a perfect human being.

Primary Needs and Growth Needs

One of the most striking facts about human beings is that, while each person is unique, all of them have basically the same inner nature. The humanistic psychologists believe that this inner nature is not "evil." We do observe destructiveness, hate, and cruelty in people, but they are not building blocks of human nature. Rather, say the humanists, these undesirable qualities develop from the thwarting or frustration of primary inner needs, which *are* part of our basic nature.

These primary needs must, in some way, be satisfied or neutralized before a person is able to continue his growth healthfully — in both a physical and mental sense. Some of these needs include love, security, safety, belongingness, self-esteem, and "survival" in general.

Since our essential nature is not evil, and possibly good, the humanists assert that we should allow it to *express* itself, rather than to keep it *repressed.* In order for it to express itself, however, we must arrive at a satisfactory way of dealing with our primary needs. If we deny our essential nature, or thwart our primary needs, we develop neurotic symptoms. Sometimes these symptoms are obvious, such as compulsive behavior, chronic anxiety, and facial tics. Sometimes the symptoms are more subtle — for example, passivity, projecting problems onto others, and fear of intimacy.

The primary needs for love, belongingness, safety, security, self-esteem, and respect come before all others. The basic characteristic of these needs is that they can be fulfilled only from an *outside source.* For instance, a person who wants love gets it from *another person.*

A person who finds it necessary to put most of his energy into getting these needs fulfilled is said to be *deficiency-motivated.* In other words, his needs are being insufficiently satisfied, and he is under constant strain to obtain the basic satisfaction and reassurance he feels he must have.

If this situation grows acute, and the person becomes entangled in trying to get what his unconscious demands, psychic conflicts result. The first step in remedying such a disturbance and regaining mental health is to resolve the problem by making sure that the needs will be adequately satisfied. The person can then cease to be deficiency-motivated.

Only when there is not an urgent need to supply the primary needs can a person activate his own unique potentials and live in a manner that is not predominantly mechanical and "ritualistic." In other words, only then can he assume a *creative outlook on life.* Capacities and potentials that spring from our inner nature "press forward" begging to be put to use and exercised, in much the same way that an athlete doesn't "feel right" unless he uses his muscles. In fact, he *has* to use his muscles to feel healthy. Capacities such as intelligence, artistic talent, the ability to work usefully and efficiently, and the capacity to love all clamor for active use.

Thus, capacities and tendencies toward a creative approach to living can also be seen as *needs.* They are, in fact, called *growth needs,* as opposed to primary needs.

Just as an undeveloped arm muscle limits the amount of lifting a person can do, so an unused mental or spiritual capacity limits the whole person. For example, a man who keeps silent when he knows the truth, and when he realizes that the truth should be openly expressed, punishes himself with guilt. He also limits himself in his ability to enjoy living, and therefore in his ability to do anything worthwhile. Another person may have a great love for music and perhaps some musical talent. What he must do is to integrate some satisfying musical activities into his life — not necessarily as a professional musician but in some role as a participant, creator, or appreciative audience. Otherwise, he is likely to become intolerably frustrated, and as a result is likely to limit his accomplishments in other areas of his life.

People who have resolved or somehow adequately worked out their primary needs are not deficiency-motivated. Rather they are motivated mainly by their *growth needs.* The noted psychologist Abraham Maslow referred to the activating of these capacities and talents as a process of *self-actualization.* Ideally, if all such capacities were to be developed to their full, then a person would be completely self-actualized and perfectly happy. But, as we have noted, the perfect (that is, completely self-actualized) person exists only as a sort of theoretical goal or abstraction.

Means and Ends

We can enjoy an activity *for its own sake* — that is, because it is helping us fulfill a growth need. In contrast, if an activity is simply a means toward an end, we often don't enjoy it at all — we are gratified only by the goal attained. This is why so many people live only for isolated moments of triumph, achievement, climax, or satisfaction of

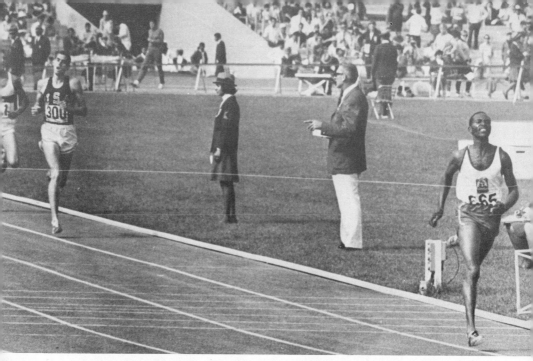

A "peak experience" — an athlete climaxes years of training and preparation by winning an event at the Olympic Games. Was the training and preparation merely a means to an end, or did it have value of its own?

appetites. They are intensely "alive" only in certain fragments of time or "peak experiences" (to use Maslow's phrase).

An athlete, for example, must go through an exhausting routine of training, conditioning, and practice. He may find this an almost unbearable drudgery, but he keeps at it . . . and perhaps he gets his "reward" when he wins an Olympic medal or scores a touchdown before 70,000 people.

In contrast, self-actualizing people (and of course athletes may be self-actualizing) enjoy more of life more of the time. Certainly they have dreams, goals, and ambitions, but these concepts of the future do not dominate the present to such a degree that the person is scarcely aware of the here-and-now. There is much less distinction between means and ends than is true for deficiency-motivated people.

The enthusiastic and skilled gardener, for example, gets pleasure out of everything he must do — preparing the soil, planting the seeds, tending the growing plants, etc. When the flowers finally bloom, he is of course gratified, but this is merely one phase of a *continuously* rewarding experience.

Tolerating Frustration

Even unsatisfied needs can be accepted and enjoyed if they have been dependably satisfied in the past, and if one can count — at least with reasonable confidence — on their being satisfied in the future. If you eat well day after day, and if there is good food on the table awaiting you, a keen appetite is something to be welcomed, rather than dreaded.

This is not to say, however, that in order to be self-actualizing, a person must have all his needs and wants immediately gratified. A self-actualizing person must have learned to *tolerate frustration of his needs and desires* to a considerable degree. His long-range goal of self-actualization need not be hindered because he arrives at the table famished, only to learn that there won't be a good meal until the next day. Even though he is hungry, he is still able to enjoy whatever he is doing, and even more importantly, he is still able to do it. (Of course, if the hunger turns out to be severe and prolonged, he will find it hard to move toward self-actualization. Under such conditions, he would probably have to put most of his energy into obtaining food, and he would then be deficiency-motivated.)

Furthermore, healthy people usually have worthwhile long-term goals, and they enjoy the movement toward the goal, as well as its ultimate attainment. In fact, they are continually attaining the goal at one level, and enjoying it, only to discover that there is more yet ahead of them. *Life becomes a succession of opportunities to be used — not of burdens to be endured.*

Dependence and Independence

Until a person's *primary needs* have been filled, and as long as a person is deficiency-motivated, he remains heavily dependent on the rules and wishes of others. For example, an adolescent whose primary need for belongingness has not been resolved in the family or in friendships may join a clique and seek to gain status by dressing in a certain way, or learning to smoke with the rest of the group. He may not like smoking, but he will conform, rather than risk the group's rejection. Thus, in a sense, the young person has forfeited his right to decide his own conduct.

The self-actualizer is likely to be recognized as much more independent in his decisions. He is self-directed or "autonomous." He is more governed by inner laws than by outside social pressures. (The reverse is true of the deficiency-motivated person.) The laws that guide him are more in line with the filling of his growth needs. Such a person is less worried about rejection by others and is not likely to be an eager conformist. In general, his behavior is expressive of himself, rather than fashioned to cope with others (that is, to get something out of them, such as love, security, or approval).

Such independence means that a healthy person is less likely to be shattered by adverse external circumstances. He can "bounce back" from disappointments, reverses, and even tragedy.

The deficiency-motivated person, whether he is aware of it or not, tends to see other people in terms of their usefulness as need-gratifiers. Whatever he doesn't believe is needed for his immediate purposes is likely to bore, annoy, or threaten him.

One way of expressing this is that the deficiency-motivated person typically envisions other people as fulfilling specific roles, such as waiters, policemen, or cab drivers. When you are in a city and want to get somewhere quickly, one cab driver is as good as another. You look for a cab (*any* cab), and when you get into it, you don't think of the driver as an individual but only as the provider of a specific service *for you*. The same situation applies when you need the services of a policeman, or of a waiter in a busy restaurant. Similarly, for the deficiency-motivated person, one supplier of security, for example, is about as good as another. All that counts is his pressing need. He is not really interested in people as people. True, his need for love, security, and admiration (status in the eyes of his friends) may lead him into various relationships, such as romantic "crushes," but these are likely to be transitory and basically unsatisfactory substitutes for more selective and meaningful ties.

The self-actualizer, in contrast, is less driven, less needful. His relationships with other people are intermixed far less with wavering and hostility. *Since he does not feel threatened easily by other people, he is less inclined to judge and label them according to stereotypes.* He accepts them for what they are, individual human beings, and he tries to bring out and enjoy the best in their personalities.

How Many "Selves"?

You may think you have just one self. Think again.

Think of the sleepy self in the morning; or the miserable self overcome by nausea and vomiting; or the buoyant self at the peak of physical vigor; or the self aroused by sexual excitement. Think of your body naked in the dark, or exposed in the light. How does your actual physical structure compare with the body you would like to have? All these things, and many more, combine into what is called the *body self*.

Now consider your *competent self,* doing something at which you excel, such as swimming or playing the piano. Contrast this with your *powerless self* — in a dentist's chair, for example, or in a crisis beyond your control, or in a situation where you feel incompetent. Perhaps your car has broken down on a lonely road and you don't know the first thing about making the necessary repairs.

Think of all your *public selves*: yourself among friends; yourself as you interact with your parents; the "you" your teachers know; the "you" your younger brother or sister knows.

Remember yourself as you were in grade school some years in the *past*, and picture the self you will be some years in the *future*. All these different roles, stages, and aspects of your personality combine to make up your *self-identity*.

Next, consider your typical reactions to various life situations. If you were asked to describe yourself, what terms would you use? Honest? Lazy? Short-tempered? Sensitive? Good sense of humor? Sincere? Self-indulgent? Generous? Your own beliefs about your qualities and characteristics — about the kind of person you are — form your *self-concept* (or *self-image*).

Finally, think of yourself as you would *like to be*. How do the expectations of your parents, the standards of your friends, and the current ideals of your cultural background influence this picture of yourself? The version of yourself you develop on the basis of these and other models represents the *ideal-self*.

Your level of mental health is reflected to a large extent by how well you fit together all these selves into one reasonable "whole." And the more "together" you are, the less these various selves contradict

each other, and the harder it is to tell them apart. After all, the idea of "wholeness" or "unity" refers to a collection of parts, even very "different" parts, that work together purposefully, smoothly, effectively. As Erikson noted, we recognize this in everyday speech when we talk about *whole*heartedness, *whole*mindedness, and *whole*someness. Of course, achieving such unity of personality is easier said than done.

A self-actualizing person feels at ease with his body, with his ideal-self, and with his self-identity. Moreover, he has a sense of inner continuity — a sort of natural flow, through his past, present, and future selves. Such a person's various roles in life — son or daughter, brother or sister, student, friend, and eventually husband or wife — seem to "fit together" harmoniously and satisfyingly.

The fully functioning person becomes "all of one piece." The word used by Maslow and Rogers to describe this unity of personality is *integration*; Erikson calls it the *sense of identity*. An older term is *inner harmony*.

Mental Totalitarianism

Are you familiar with Charles Schulz's comic strip *Peanuts*? If so, you probably know about the little boy named Linus who panics when there is even the threat of his being separated from his "security blanket." Many small children, of course, cling to a doll, a teddy bear, or a blanket as a symbol of security.

Later in life, the physical symbol of security is given up, but the person may find a substitute in passionate *loves* and *hates,* in sudden *conversions* (to a cause or an ideology), or in strong *aversions* (to a culture, a set of ideas, a race, etc.). The adolescent or adult may become extremely attached or bitterly hostile to a person, a group, an idea (or almost anything), and this emotional conviction becomes essential to his sense of security. Literally everything appears to depend on this object of his devotion (or hatred). There are suggestions of total gain, or forebodings of total loss, from this source. We call this type of mental structure a *totality*.

You know what a *totalitarian* country is. The government has complete control over the people, and governmental power is concentrated in a dictator and in a tight party structure. The dictator and his program are absolutes, not to be questioned by anyone on pain of drastic punishment. A psychological totality has the same quality of *absoluteness*. In this frame of reference, there are no "ifs, ands, or buts." Everything is either for or against, "black or white, with no shades of gray." Perhaps, the best word to describe this attitude is *rigidity*.

All of us show this totality tendency to some degree or other. At times we yearn for total dependence or total independence; we become wildly hopeful or profoundly despairing; we think and act in terms of absolute goodness and unqualified badness. But eventually mature and healthy people will modify this pattern of mental totalitarianism. They realize that life almost always lies somewhere between absolute black and white. They learn that the way to adjust to reality is not to take a fixed position and to defend it undeviatingly, but rather to select what is usable and valid from various positions and to combine them appropriately.

Less mature and healthy people, in contrast, show limited elasticity. The trend toward totality is stronger and influences more of their decision-making. In their personal affairs, in their work relationships, in their political judgments, they tend to act on the "all or nothing" basis. This attitude is believed to originate in infancy, when the child expects to have all his desires immediately and fully satisfied. Children characteristically cannot tolerate any frustration. Fanatics who see everything in terms of good or bad, black or white, salvation or ruin, are often emotionally infantile and show the typical infantile inability to tolerate frustration. This helps us to understand the all but incredible cruelty and bitterness which fanatics sometimes show when they are in a position to "punish" their opponents.

Openness to Experience

A fully functioning, self-actualizing person is open to experience. This openness means, first of all, that he is aware of his own feelings and the forces that motivate him. The more self-aware he is, the more he is aware of what is motivating him *at the moment,* without, however, being unduly preoccupied with this introspection.

The more "open" a person is, the more freely he will experience what is happening around and to him — without distorting what he sees and hears to fit preconceived patterns. When a new situation occurs, instead of *anticipating* that he will be pleased or displeased, attracted or repelled, he lives the situation as it develops. He realizes that every situation embodies an element of the old and an element of the new, so that he must continually adapt his behavior to the here-and-now. He seeks to be creative rather than fixed and reactionary in his approach to life.

He doesn't erect barriers to prevent the full experiencing of whatever happens. In Ernest Hemingway's words, "He lives all the way up."

To put it another way, this kind of openness means that the integrated self and the personality emerge naturally from experience.

Experiences are not molded or twisted to fit expectations, prejudices, and the self-image. Thus, the open person is not static; he is not rigid. Growth to him means a continuous *becoming,* which goes hand in hand with his *be-ing.* To open yourself to what is happening *now,* and to let yourself change fluidly, attuned to what is best, is a sign of maturity.

Making Your Own Decisions

Accordingly, in order to be "natural," rather than stilted and artificial in your life style, you must avoid being fooled or intimidated into accepting values that are not necessarily valid for you. For example, consider a college student taking a pre-med course. He has undertaken this not because he is attracted to it but because his parents urgently desire him to become a doctor. Now he finds himself getting failing grades, although he has always been a better-than-average student. Is he a failure in life because he has not lived up to his parents' fond dreams? Or should he draw the conclusion that he has allowed himself to be forced into a mold that is not right *for him,* and that his poor work may well be a symptom of unconscious rebellion against this? Instead of feeling crushed, should he not react by looking for another type of activity or training that will correspond more nearly to what *he* wants and what *he* can do effectively?

The point is that this young man in the last analysis must make his own decision as to what is good or bad, right or wrong, productive or counter-productive. He has reached a stage in life at which he must move toward self-actualization or continued control by others. He is not a "failure" because he has done poorly in a few examinations but only because he is not accepting what must be his own responsibilities.

The self-actualizing person is undoubtedly influenced by religious and moral principles, by society's laws and customs, and by the advice and expectations of relatives and friends. He understands that, in the last analysis, he cannot fall back on any of these as a substitute for his own decision-making.

The humanistic psychologists feel that it may come as a shock to many people to realize that their values must, ultimately, unfold from within themselves, rather than be laid down by outside forces. It is only when values develop as an expression of the person himself that they foster self-actualization. Nonetheless, the humanists assert that the so-called higher values (the "eternal values" of civilization) are more or less the same as the values chosen spontaneously by the most healthy adults.

The reason that the values of one self-actualizer tend to be fairly close to those of another self-actualizer is that all healthy people incline to prize and to choose experiences that enable them to grow stronger and more complete as human beings. The "eternal values" are inherent in man because they spring from that most profound self-actualizing experience: the *giving of love freely*.

Trusting Yourself

We still have not discussed one of the most important aspects of mental health: a positive *self-concept*. Remember that your self-concept consists of all the beliefs and ideas you have formed about yourself.

Your self-concept is dependent on how "together" or "integrated" your personality is. If your ideal self, which consists of the demands and expectations of those important to you and the standards you have set for yourself, is unrealistic or inappropriate, you probably doubt your own worth. Similarly, if your *public self* is sharply at odds with your *real self*, you probably live with anxiety, guilt, and a fear of being "found out."

You will recall that we included· *self-esteem* among the primary needs that must be supplied to a person by other people. The reason is that the self-concept is not automatically generated from "inside" but is *learned*. The way you conceive of yourself is usually a reflection of the way "significant others" treat you and respond to you as you are growing.

If "significant others" (parents, friends, teachers, and other persons whose opinions are important to you) have loved, accepted, and prized you for what you are, you probably accept yourself and feel that you have something worthwhile to give to other people. But if "significant others" have consistently criticized and rejected you, it is easy for you to become hostile and/or to withdraw.

A person with a positive view of himself accepts risks as they come, instead of being constantly assailed with indecision and ineffectiveness. Just as a well-constructed ship can venture boldly into dangerous waters, a healthy person can launch himself confidently into new and undetermined situations. He can afford to be generous and to give freely of himself. He can become more involved in a variety of relationships without worrying about losing his own integrity. *He can even risk being rejected*.

A healthy person is a loving person. This doesn't necessarily mean that he is popular, or that he needs to be constantly surrounded by people, or that he is always "in love." In fact, a self-actualizer is *less concerned with being loved than with giving love.* For the healthy person, to give love is at the same time to express strength.

Many psychologists, humanists or not, regard *the ability to love as a sure sign of the overall state of a person's mental health.*

Spontaneous or "Up-Tight"?

Spontaneity — free, uninhibited, trusting, and unpremeditated expression of the self — is possible in dreams, imagination, friendship, love, and creativity. There are a number of necessary "brakes" on spontaneity that we identify by such terms as "self-control," "practical judgment," and "politeness."

But too many of us have other brakes. We may disapprove of our deeper selves, and expect that others will too. We grow too inhibited and defensive. We are afraid to feel. Our behavior becomes planned, cautious, "tight," "super-cool." We are afraid of making mistakes and we are timid about being wrong. As a result, we almost lose the ability to react spontaneously and to "be ourselves."

In contrast, a person who trusts himself can relax. He can even afford to let himself be flooded by emotion on occasion. He does not get overly fearful of his own thoughts, even when some may consider them "stupid" or "weird," and he is not worried about being an object of disapproval or ridicule. Thus, healthy behavior is more spontaneous, more natural, less self-conscious. In one sense, it is at times more innocent and childlike.

A person who accepts his real inner self has less need to "put up a front." He is honest and outspoken. This type of honesty does not mean that he blurts out anything that comes into his head, especially if it may be harmful or unnecessarily unpleasant to someone else. It is possible to be "unphony" without reporting in detail everything of which you happen to be aware. On the other hand, such a person is not afraid to say something if he feels that it is right and helpful to say it, even if it may not be welcomed.

Healthy Problems

You may get the impression that the self-actualizer we have been describing is always happy, or that he has no problems. Not so! First of all, growth is always accompanied by difficulties and pains, trials and tribulations, as well as by rewards.

Each step forward is a step into the unknown, and is therefore potentially dangerous. Growth means, in part, giving up what is familiar, satisfying, and "comfortable." Often it involves a separation or

Young people look forward eagerly to "going away to college," but there may be a challenging problem of adjusting to a new way of life. Freshmen are shown here registering at a large university.

parting — from familiar scenes, routines, or people. This may lead to nostalgia, loneliness, and a sense of deprivation.

For example, a young person takes such a step when he or she goes away to college, or enters the Armed Forces, leaving behind the security of childhood. In fact, we may think of a period of growth as a sort of death and rebirth.

Growth takes place despite inevitable reverses or disappointments. The question is whether the growth will be distorted and limited, or whether it will proceed in a natural, robust way. This depends on the strength of the individual, as well as the protection, authorization, and encouragement of others.

It should not be thought that a self-actualizing person always maintains an outward display of unbroken calm and self-possession. After all, sometimes it may be necessary to get disturbed. However, people on the road to self-actualization squarely confront and deal with the real shocks and dilemmas that are always found in life.

An Example from Real Life

We have discussed self-actualization mainly in general terms. A letter written by a 19-year-old girl may help to illustrate how it takes place in real life.

At the time of writing, Dee had just broken up with her boy friend after three years together. This, combined with the normal trials of adjusting to life as a freshman at a large university, made her think deeply about many things she had previously accepted without question. She expressed some of her reactions in these words:

> Here on campus there is a service called Center for Human Growth. Anyone can go . . . or call at any hour, any day. One night when I was feeling very non-existent I, a little timidly, went there. I've gone there several times and I've been learning about my inner self more and more. . . .
>
> I have realized that my actions too many times are decided by the opinions of those around me, not by my real desires and wants. Because of this, I needlessly create inner frustration and conflict, and I am the only one to blame for this. Now because I am consciously aware of my deficiency I am gradually making myself more serene inwardly. I'm learning to listen to my physical thoughts — for example, a headache when I have to face an uncomfortable situation. Also I'm becoming less rigid in my daily life — more flexible, and I'm liking myself better for it.
>
> My parents constantly tell me I'm my own worst critic and enemy. So I'm perhaps having negotiations and working out a friendly settlement. . . . I'm gradually learning the reality of integration of the many facets of my personality into one whole being. For a while the conflicting facets were unsettled in my physical structure but now they are mingling reasonably easily and smoothly.
>
> Am I making sense? I feel now an inner peace. I'm ready to extend myself to others but in a slow and gradual process, lest I may leave myself too open for rejection and denial. . . .

Clearly, this is the statement of a young woman who is groping for and growing toward self-actualization.

Self-Actualization Reviewed

Each individual has primary needs for love, safety, security, respect, belongingness, and self-esteem. Only when these needs have been gratified by other people can we activate our own unique potentials and respond to our creative impulses.

A self-actualizer is a person who has gratified his basic needs. He is motivated mainly by growth needs.

A self-actualizer is independent (self-determining); mere conformism plays a minor part in his life. His behavior is self-expressive, rather than determined by a need to "get by."

A healthy person sees life basically as a series of opportunities — not of burdens.

Since a self-actualizer is less driven by unsatisfied needs, he can see others more clearly and accept them for what they are. His human relationships are less wavering and less hostile than those formed by immature and not fully functioning people.

A healthy personality is a unified whole. Impelling wishes and compelling demands tend to balance out satisfactorily — between the public self and the private self — between self-ideal, self-concept, and self-identity. The varied roles and stages of life fit together.

A healthy personality avoids the psychological pattern of totality. He does not look for absolute values of "good" and "bad" in the real world. He does not expect people, or ideas, or institutions to be all one thing or all the other.

A fully functioning person is open to life. He is aware of his own feelings and of the forces that activate him. The self emerges naturally from experience, rather than the reverse — experience being molded to fit the self-concept or values. The person is *becoming,* as well as *being.*

Valuing is a process, not a rigid system. Values are uncovered in the individual and selected because they foster growth and self-actualization. The values of different healthy people turn out in practice to be quite similar.

The self-concept is learned from "significant others." A healthy person trusts himself because others have trusted him. He accepts himself because other people who are important to him have loved, accepted, and prized him for what he is. He is, therefore, a more loving person. Giving love helps to actualize the giver as well as the receiver. The ability to love is regarded as a dependable sign of overall mental health.

A healthy person shows a high degree of spontaneity. He is able to "be himself" and to allow free, uninhibited expression of his own feelings. He is playful, with a lively sense of the paradoxical and ridiculous in human life.

The most favorable mental health is experienced as a sense of mental and social well-being, a feeling of being at home in one's body, an awareness of knowing where one is going, and an inner assuredness of recognition from those who count.

A self-actualizer is not free from problems. Growth involves pains and burdens as well as pleasures. But healthy people confront confidently the unavoidable dilemmas inherent in man and his environment.

THINGS TO DISCUSS :: THINGS TO DO :: THINGS TO READ

1. Divide the class into groups of three or four. Each person asks the others in his group, "Who are you?" Then he asks "Who would you *like* to be?" What insights or points of view do the answers suggest?

2. Think of a person who you feel could validly be described as "on the road to self-actualization." This person may be a character from history, an important current national or world figure, or just someone you know. List the qualities that you think make him (or her) a "self-actualizer." Then give a short presentation before the class. Invite questions from the audience, and defend your selection of this person and your interpretation of his personality.

3. Hold a class debate on self-actualization and "mind drugs." Is there any validity to the claim that use of such drugs may help one to achieve self-actualization? (See Chapter 12, pages 242-253.)

4. Life can be seen as an opportunity — a process of striving. But for what? See if you can find a satisfactory answer for this question from your own knowledge and experience. Bear in mind the ideas expressed in this chapter.

5. Consider a society or country where food is in short supply. If a person has become accustomed to using a good part of his total time and energy to obtain enough food to survive, will it still be possible for him to be self-actualizing? Explain.

6. What do you understand by an "all or nothing" attitude toward life? Give some examples of this from your own experience.

7. The humanist credo or program might be summarized as cultivating the ability to give love unselfishly through "good works." Is this rational? Wouldn't it be more logical and "efficient" to concentrate on promoting *one's own interests?*

8. But the humanists also say that a person must resolve his own primary needs. Which comes first — yourself or other people? Can these priorities change, depending on the situation? Give examples.

READINGS

The Transparent Self, by Sidney M. Jourard (Litton, 1971). This is a fascinating and easy to read and understand book about a "revolutionary" psychologist's approach to life. (Be sure to get the revised 1971 edition.)

On Becoming a Person, by Carl R. Rogers (Houghton-Mifflin, 1961). Rogers presents a brilliant analysis of the growth of personality.

The Master Game, by Robert S. deRopp (Delacorte, 1968). Written by a biologist, this book is a perceptive discussion of striving for self-mastery.

Toward a Psychology of Being, by Abraham Maslow (Van Nostrand, 1962). This is considered one of the "breakthrough" books of humanistic psychology.

Dreams
A LANGUAGE OF THE UNCONSCIOUS

● ●

*"Who alive can say
'Thou art no Poet — may'st not tell thy dream'?
Since every man whose soul is not a clod
Hath visions and would speak."*

— *JOHN KEATS*

The Need to Dream *Introduction*

Every night we enter a different world — the world of dreams. There, the laws of logic are temporarily suspended, and time and space, which in waking life limit our activities, have no power. We dream of events and people we have not thought of in a long time — perhaps of people who have been dead for many years. We seem to tap a vast store of experience and memory of which we are unaware in our waking hours.

Dreams are in the present tense. Usually they tell a story. They embody events that occurred as recently as yesterday, and as long ago as infancy.

Dreaming serves a double function. In one sense, we dream in order *to sleep;* and in another sense, we dream *to become more fully awake.* We shall explore both of these functions in the pages that follow. *If we are awaken several times a night during our dream we become very cranky and could become*

Lost Dreaming Time *mentally disturbed. Thats why we need our dream sleep.*

Everyone knows that lack of sleep can have serious conse- quences, ranging from fatigue and crankiness to a marked increase in nervous tension and even hallucinations. Deprived of sleep for several

149

nights, a person seems to need to "catch up" on sleep. He also needs to make up for lost dreaming time. If deprived of dreaming time, a person will tend to break all his familiar patterns of sleep and dreaming until he has compensated sufficiently. This reflects the fact that dreaming is of great importance for the maintenance of normal waking behavior.

Content of Dreams

What do people dream about? In one study, 10,000 dreams were analyzed with respect to setting, cast of characters, plot, and emotions.

The most frequent setting was part of a house. The most popular room, it was found, was the living room, followed by the bedroom, kitchen, stairway, and basement. Some other settings were vehicles (most often automobiles), an entire building, a place of recreation, and a street or road.

Thus, the typical dream occurs in commonplace surroundings — a living room, car, or field. In relation to the amount of time that most of us spend in places of work (offices, schools, stores, factories, etc.), these places appear infrequently in dreams. On the other hand, vehicles or recreational places occupy a larger sector of dreams than of waking life. Thus, in our dreams, it appears that we tend to avoid work, study, and business transactions, and prefer play and "going places." An alternative explanation is that we tend to *remember* mainly dreams connected with recreation and "having fun."

Of the characters that appear in dreams, about two of five seem to be strangers (really people we know, but in dream disguise). An almost equal proportion are friends or acquaintances, and most of the rest are close relatives. Among family members, mothers appear most often. People in the news, whose names and faces we know but whom we do not associate with personally, rarely show up.

Action in Dreams

What do people do in their dreams? Contrary to popular belief, falling or floating is rare. Because of their rarity, perhaps, such dreams tend to be remembered vividly. About a third of dreams involve movement — walking, running, riding. A tenth emphasize talking. After that, in descending order, come sitting, watching, playing, thinking, struggling, arguing, and acquiring.

Many dreams deal with passive or quiet episodes. Dreamers go places more often than they do things when they get there. Actions, when they do occur, are more likely to be vigorous play activities, such as dancing or swimming, than any form of work.

In dreams, hostile acts (by or against the dreamer) outnumber friendly acts by more than two to one. The most common dream emotion is fear — in the form of anxiety and confusion. Next come anger, happiness, and excitement. Least common of all is sadness. Thus, most dreams deal with unpleasant emotions — apprehension, anger, and confusion.

Conflicts in Dreams

A few conflicts regularly stand out in dreams. Often the individual is torn between growth and independence on the one hand and infantile security and dependence on the other. This tug-of-war appears most often in the dreams of adolescents and old people.

Then there is the moral dilemma — the conflict between good and bad, between immediate impulses and conscience. The dreamer kills a character and is punished for it. He expresses some sexual urge and then suffers a misfortune. He steals and is exposed.

Another conflict arises out of opposition between the life-maintaining and loving tendencies of man, which promote harmony of personality, and the opposing tendencies of hate, fear and greed, which promote neurosis.

No Dreams Are Meaningless

What is the psychological significance of dreams? Freud was the first modern authority to suggest that no dream, even the "silliest," is psychologically meaningless. Erich Fromm gives us an example*:

> A young woman, interested in the problems of dream interpretation, tells her husband at the breakfast table: "Last night I had a dream which shows that there are dreams which have no meaning. The dream was simply that I saw myself serving you strawberries for breakfast." The husband laughs and says: "You only seem to forget that strawberries are the one fruit which I do not eat."

Fromm offers this comment on the dream:

> It is obvious that the dream is far from being meaningless. She offers her husband something she knows he cannot accept and is of no use or pleasure to him. Does this dream indicate that she is a frustrating personality who likes to give the very thing that is not acceptable? Does it show a deepseated conflict in the marriage of these

---

* Erich Fromm, *The Forgotten Language: An Introduction to the Understanding of Dreams, Fairy Tales, and Myths* (Rinehart, 1951).

two people, caused by her character but quite unconscious in her? Or is her dream only the reaction to a disappointment caused by her husband the day before, and an expression of the fleeting anger she got rid of in the revenge contained in the dream? We cannot answer these questions without knowing more about the dreamer and her marriage, but we do know that the dream is not meaningless.

Language of the Unconscious

Dreams are the language of the unconscious. According to Jung, the dream is "the small hidden door in the deepest and most intimate sanctum of the soul." . . . When we discover its real meaning, we find ourselves deep in the dreamer's secrets and discover with astonishment that an apparently senseless dream is, in the highest degree, significant and that it speaks only of extraordinarily important and serious things." Furthermore, says Jung, "One must never forget that one dreams primarily, and so to speak, exclusively, *about oneself and out of oneself.*" This is obvious from the content of dreams, which involve the dreamer and people close to him, and deal with basic life conflicts.

Dreams are impartial, spontaneous products of the *unconscious*. The dream has little respect for the dreamer's conscious attitudes and beliefs, or for his view as to how things *should* be. It simply reflects the way things *are* in the depths of his unconscious. Dreams, in short, "tell it like it is" — if you know how to read them.

Our dreams are real to us while we are dreaming, and the deeper the sleep, the more real they seem. In fact, dreams may be so vivid that throughout history men have wondered: How do we know that what we dream is unreal, and that what we experience in our waking life is real?

A Chinese poet expressed this nicely: "I dreamt last night that I was a butterfly, and now I don't know whether I am a man who dreamt he was a butterfly, or perhaps a butterfly who dreams now that he is a man."

History of Dream Interpretation

Throughout the ages, people have interpreted the symbolic language of dreams in many different ways. In ancient times, it was accepted in many religions or mythologies that dreams represented the voices of demons, or the dreamer's disembodied soul, or messages from the dead. In some societies, events in dreams were often taken as seriously as events in waking life. For example, if a tribal leader dreamed about a neighboring village launching an attack, this might be considered adequate reason to get ready for battle, or even to strike before the "enemy" could carry out the plans revealed in the dream. In the tradition of the Ashanti people of West Africa, if a man dreams of committing adultery with another man's wife, his soul and hers have had intercourse, and they are subject to penalties for this "misconduct."

In the early cultures of the Middle East, which have so profoundly influenced our own culture, there was a tendency to interpret dreams according to a detailed religious and moral symbolism. Each action, object, or situation, had a definite meaning, in terms of human life. The Old Testament, for example, tells us of the Pharaoh's dream of seven fat sheaves of corn and the seven lean sheaves. Joseph interpreted this as referring to seven years of plenty throughout Egypt, followed by seven years of famine. Accordingly, the Pharaoh ordered granaries to be set up to store reserves of food. When the crop failure came, as predicted, famine was avoided. For saving Egypt from such a catastrophe, Joseph was raised to great power. In Biblical times,

dreams were considered communications from God or from the gods. They were also regarded as prophetic visions — which amounts to much the same thing because the prophets were believed to be divinely inspired.

For many years, there was a widespread tendency in Western cultures to regard dreams as senseless and unworthy of serious attention. Adults concerned themselves properly with organizing aspects of "reality," such as business, political affairs, or physical science and technology. Dreams in contrast were considered mere will o' the wisps, which were unrelated to "real life."

One explanation of this attitude is that dreams are so often contradictory and puzzling. We dream of hating people whom we "know" we love, and of being attracted to people in whom we "really" have no interest. Ordinarily submissive people dream of being very bold and domineering, and "big, strong" men may reveal childish fears. Faced with these and innumerable other contradictions, Western thinkers found it convenient and reassuring to assume that dreams simply make no sense and have nothing to tell us.

Psychology Rediscovers Dreams

A profound change in our attitudes toward dreams has taken place in the 20th century — a change initiated primarily by the work of Sigmund Freud. Beginning with the aim of helping people suffering from emotional illnesses, Freud went on to study dreams as a universal human phenomenon. He recognized that dreams are similar in many ways to myths and fairy tales. He advanced the theory that to understand the language of one of these is to gain a major insight into the other, and that both reveal to us important but hidden aspects of human experience and the human personality.

Today, there are various schools of dream interpretation. Freud believed that all dreams are essentially wish-fulfillments, and that they express the irrational and asocial nature of man. Carl Jung maintained that dreams reveal knowledge of unknown potentials. Erich Fromm teaches that either of these views may be true, depending on the individual, and that in either case dreams provide insights into the human personality and suggest possible solutions to some of our deepest conflicts.

Kinds of Symbols

In dream interpretation, we deal necessarily with *symbols* — things that stand for other things. In general, there are three types of symbols.

Conventional symbols include primarily words. These, of course, are different for each language, but within a given linguistic group they are used and recognized by everyone. For example, in English, the letters *c-h-a-i-r* stand for a certain type of physical object. Also, the sound pattern represented by these five letters is a symbol for the same object. There are conventional symbols which represent the nation (a flag), a religion (the cross), a direction (an arrow or index finger), and many, many others which we all recognize.

Accidental symbols are those which are based on the individual's own experience. For example, you may associate a certain song with a particular event in your life, such as graduation from school. You may think of a certain city in terms of a theater which you attended there. These are personal or accidental symbols which may come out in your dreams.

Then there are *universal symbols,* which have been used over the ages and are still valid for people in all parts of the world. Here we are dealing with natural phenomena which suggest certain inherent qualities. Fire, for example, symbolizes power, energy, light, grace, and constant movement. It may convey such emotions as aliveness, warmth, and pleasure, as well as terror and powerlessness. Water is slow, heavy, deep, and "eternal." It may carry the idea of destruction; it may also be associated with security feelings, as in unconscious memories of being in the womb.

As we shall see, only accidental and universal symbols express inner experiences as though they were sensory experiences. These are, therefore, the only types of symbols that appear in our dreams.

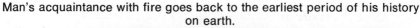

Man's acquaintance with fire goes back to the earliest period of his history on earth.

The Dream as Wish-Fulfillment

Freud interpreted the great majority of dreams as expressions of unconscious wishes or "impulses." (Remember that Freud did not use the word *wish* in its ordinary sense, but rather to denote the mental counterpart of an instinct.) Most wishes in the Freudian view never become conscious and are not clearly defined. They have a primitive and driving quality. Often they have sexual or aggressive roots. In fact, many wishes are quite unacceptable to the conscious part of the personality. They are irrational and often amoral.

Freud believed that the wishes expressed in our dreams are rooted in childhood. This view is based on his general picture of the child as irrational and amoral, and on his theory of psychosexual development. Many of the sexual strivings which in an adult are considered perversions or abnormalities are aspects of *normal* sexual development during the first five years of life. The child's sexual strivings, his narcissism (self-love), his intense jealousy, and his exhibitionism are later repressed because of the demands of parents and society. But when the individual falls asleep, the repression weakens and "childish" impulses come to life again.

When we are asleep, the moral "censorship" in our personality relaxes its control. But often it is still alert enough to bar our forbidden thoughts from appearing in clearly recognizable form. Otherwise, we might wake up and defeat the purpose of the dream. That is why dreams are "written" in symbolic language. According to Freud, the symbols represent a compromise between the driving forces of the *id* and the checking forces of the *ego* and *superego*. (See pages 100-101.)

Most of the dream symbols Freud identified are sexual in nature. The male genital is frequently represented by sticks, trees, umbrellas, knives, swords, pencils, rockets, and many other objects similar in shape or function. The female genital is often symbolized by caves, boxes, doors, gardens, or flowers. The sex act is often represented by flying, going up or downstairs, and dancing. Loss of hair or teeth can symbolize castration. Other symbols are related to the experiences of a child. For example, king and queen symbolize mother and father; journeys may stand for death or going back in time; and small animals represent children.

Dream Disguises

In Freudian terms, the material that makes up the dream picture as we remember it is the *manifest content* (symbolic content). The true dream — that is, the hidden desires, and therefore the real significance of the dream — is called the *latent content* (hidden meaning). And the process of distortion or disguise is the *dream-work*.

Freud believed that the manifest dream is much shorter than the content of the latent dream would seem to indicate. A person, object, or event occurring in a dream rarely has a single meaning. These symbols often represent a variety of thoughts, feelings, and memories. Thus, the dream image brings together, in highly abbreviated form, a wide range of meanings. The living room of one's childhood, a familiar landmark on the way to school, the bathing of a brother or sister — to cite a few fairly typical examples — all call up a host of associations.

The manifest dream leaves out some elements of the latent content, combines fragments of other elements, and condenses them into a single new entity. For example, suppose you dream of a male authority figure for whom you feel fear. You might see in the manifest dream an individual whose hair looks like your father's, whose face resembles that of a feared teacher, and whose manner of dress is like that of your present boss or supervisor at your place of work. That the father, teacher, and boss are objectively different is unimportant. What matters, on an unconscious level, is that they express the same inner experience. And they do so with extraordinary condensation and brevity.

Freud explained that an element of great importance in the latent dream may be expressed by a seemingly trivial detail in the manifest dream. The dream often treats the most crucial images as though they were of no particular significance. Thus, the true meaning is further disguised from the watchful censor (the suppressor of "forbidden" thoughts).

In the process of dream-work, gaps in the manifest dream are filled in, and inconsistencies are corrected, giving the manifest dream some apparent unity, which again helps to disguise the drama underneath.

Freud also pointed out that dream symbols often stand for their *opposites*. To be fully dressed may symbolize nakedness; to be rich may stand for being poor; a feeling of affection may mask hostility or rage. This is still another way to evade the censorship.

Dreams as a Primitive Form of Thinking

Dreams are a primitive form of thinking. Freud said they represent a *regression* — a return to an earlier stage of development. In this case, the earlier stage is that of pre-verbal, pre-logical thought.

The dream cannot logically express ideas and relationships which we convey by terms such as "but," "although," "as if," "therefore," and "because." Logical connections between ideas are expressed, rather, as events that happen at the same time. Cause and effect may be represented by something changing before the dreamer's eyes. Similarity or agreement is expressed in the dream by unity, by simply being together. For example, a person may dream of someone who stands up and raises his arm, and then is changed into a chicken. In waking life we would say, "He gave the appearance of being strong, but he is really weak and cowardly, like a chicken." In the dream this whole idea is expressed by a sequence of two images.

In the dream, figurative terms and slang expressions are often restored to their original meanings. For example, we speak of being "in a tight place," meaning to face uncomfortable choices. In the dream, the individual may actually appear in a tight corner or at the bottom of a hole. The expression "You make me sick," might be suggested by an actual feeling of nausea in the dream.

Examples of Freudian Dream Analysis

The following example of a common class of dreams is adapted from Freud's book *The Interpretation of Dreams*.

A dream of nakedness commands our attention most when we feel ashamed and embarrassed, when we wish to escape or hide but feel rooted to the spot. Almost everyone has had this dream at some time.

The nature of the exposure is usually vague. The dreamer may say later, "I was in my underwear," or "I forgot to wear my tie, or blouse, or shoes." Generally, the lack of clothing isn't serious enough to justify the intense shame actually felt.

The spectators are almost always strangers whose faces remain vague. In the typical dream, we are never reproved or even noticed because of our lack of clothing. On the contrary, the people in the dream typically appear to be indifferent.

This is an apparent contradiction here. At first consideration, the dreamer's feeling of shame would seem to be more justified and more intense if the strangers looked at him in astonishment or anger, or if they laughed at him. However, this offensive behavior (on the part of the spectators) has been changed to indifference by wish fulfillment, while the embarrassment remains.

Such a dream, according to Freud, is rooted in a childhood memory. In our society, childhood is the only time when we may be seen by members of our family, as well as by visitors and strangers, in a state of undress, without being ashamed of the nakedness. In fact, for many children being undressed is exciting, rather than embarrassing. They may laugh, leap about, and slap their own bodies.

Thus, according to Freud, childhood, when the sense of shame was unknown, seems like a lost paradise. It is to this paradise that dreams return us at night.

In this exhibitionist dream, the dreamer appears not as a child but as he is at present. He wears some clothing, because he is so used to being at least partly clothed, and because he has learned that it is wrong to go about naked. The people who were actually the objects of the dreamer's sexual interest in childhood do not appear in the dream. They are replaced by strangers. The strangers represent a counter-wish — a camouflage of someone intimately known, for whom the exposure of the body is really intended.

Finally, the reason for the embarrassment is that the censorship, following orders from the conscience, condemns the individual's desire to be exposed and naked.

Following is a passage from *The Interpretation of Dreams** in which a "typical" dream is analyzed.

> A child of under four years old reported having dreamt that *he had seen a big dish with a big joint of roast meat and vegetables on it. All at once the joint had been eaten up — whole and without being cut up. He had not seen the person who ate it.*

> Who can this unknown person have been whose sumptuous banquet of meat was the subject of the little boy's dream? His experiences during the . . . day must enlighten us on the subject. By doctor's orders he had been put on a milk diet for the past few days. On the evening of the dream . . . he had been naughty, and as a punishment he had been sent to bed without his supper. He had been through this hunger-cure once before and had been very brave about it. He knew he would get nothing, but would not allow himself to show by so much as a single word that he was hungry. Education [learning] had already begun to have an effect on him: it found expression in this dream, which exhibits the beginning of dream-distortion. There can be no doubt that the person whose wishes were aimed at this lavish meal — a meat meal, too — was himself. But since he knew he was not allowed it, he did not venture to sit down to the meal himself, as hungry children do in dreams. . . . The person who ate the meal remained anonymous.

---

* Taken from James Strachey's translation (Basic Books, 1965).

Unconscious Wisdom in Dreams

According to Jung, the purpose of the symbolic language of dreams is not (as Freud said) to distort or disguise, but rather to *communicate more clearly*. Thus, for Jung, there is no "latent content" in dreams. What Freud called the "manifest content" is for Jung the true significance of the dream, and not a mask for a message hidden underneath. The dream is saying what it actually means.

In interpreting dreams, Jung increasingly dispensed with free association. Freud looked at dreams from the standpoint of *cause* — where the dream images come from, what infantile wishes they relate to, what problems they reveal. Jung interpreted dreams in terms of *purpose* — the personal needs they indicate, and where the unconscious is leading the individual.

Thus, in Jung's view, if you dream constantly that you are doing silly things, your unconscious may be saying that you are too formal, too conventional, and too concerned about not making a fool of yourself. Maybe you need to be more spontaneous and not take yourself so seriously. That, at least, is what the unconscious is "advising" through the dream. Or if you consider yourself objective, practical, or detached, but in your dreams appear to be highly emotional, or even sentimental, your unconscious may be protesting a tendency to repress a vital part of your personality — the ability to feel deeply.

In Jung's view, then, dreams represent a kind of unconscious wisdom, regarding personality, behavior, and life style.

Dreams That Solve Problems — The Biological Theory

According to the so-called biological theory, the purpose of dreams, by reproducing the conflicts of waking life in altered form, is to help us *solve these conflicts*.

For example, suppose you dream that someone you love has died. Dreams of this type are common when the dreamer is extremely dependent on the person who dies in the dream, or when this person is seriously ill. Such a dream acts as an emotional safety valve. It prepares the dreamer for the blow that may actually come by giving him a chance to experience it in advance, on a dream level. When death or the breakup of the relationship occurs in real life, the dreamer has already gotten rid of some of his grief. He is in part "inoculated" against the painful new situation.

This suggests one important function of dreams: *they stand in the place of experience*. Consider another example. A student argues with a teacher but is forced to yield; he must do as the teacher says. The next night he dreams about the argument, but this time he "stands up" to the teacher — and finds to his surprise that the teacher respects him more for his courage. If another similar situation occurs in real life, this time the student may actually have the courage of his convictions and defend what he thinks is right. Thus, the dream has taken the place of experience and has suggested what may be a viable solution for the student's problem.

The tendency of the mind to reproduce worrying situations and unsolved problems is sometimes called *perseveration*. A familiar example is being in a situation where someone has insulted you or "put you down," and you can't think of an effective comeback. Perhaps you are annoyed at yourself for not having shown up too well in this encounter. You try to forget the incident but find yourself involuntarily reliving it in your imagination. Eventually you will probably complete the episode in a more satisfying way in your mind — perhaps by silencing the other person with a crushing and witty rejoinder.

This is essentially what happens in dreams. They reproduce again and again difficulties we have avoided facing, obligations we have not fulfilled, problems we have been unable to solve, opportunities we have not utilized. According to this theory, a dream is likely to be repeated in one form or another until a satisfactory solution of some kind has been worked out.

Recent Research on Dreaming

Since Freud's time, developments in technology have influenced scientific research on dreaming. The electro-encephalogram (EEG)

EEG tracing of currents generated by the brain during *orthodox sleep*, usually described as "thinking."

rapid eye movement periods

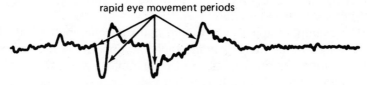

EEG tracing of currents generated during *rapid eye movement sleep*, usually described as "dreaming."

now makes it possible to monitor changes in brain activity during sleep. The brain produces tiny amounts of electrical energy which are measured by electrodes attached to the sleeper's scalp and connected to a recording device.

The main discovery made in this way is that dreaming occurs during a specific stage of sleep which repeats itself in cycles throughout the night. This stage is marked by a characteristic pattern of electrical activity in the brain, and also by "rapid eye movements" (abbreviated REM). In one experiment, when volunteer subjects were awakened during the REM stage of sleep, they reported about 80% of the time that they had been dreaming. During the non-REM stages of sleep, in contrast, the same subjects did not report vivid dreams at all. Instead they indicated that they had been occupied with the more usual types of thinking, such as memories of events from the day before. Mental activity during sleep is continuous, and much of it resembles ordinary waking thought, as Adler suggested. But during the special REM stages, activity very much like Freud's dream-work appears to be going on.

According to the experiments, subjects dream about 20% of their total sleeping time each night. Dreams seem to occur on a regular cyclic basis, so that they are part of the normal pattern of everyone's sleep. In other words, even if someone had no problems at all (if we can imagine such a thing), he would still dream. Such a view appears to contradict the idea that dreams are prompted only by unresolved problems, as Freud and others believed.

Dreams as Warning Signals

Ideation is the ability to form images and ideas in the mind in the absence of the actual experience. If these images are concerned with the past, we call them *memories;* if they refer to things which haven't happened yet (or may never happen), *imagination*. Ideation helps us work out problems, at least in part, without the immediate necessity of living through the actual experiences. If you are planning a journey, for example, you can go through it in imagination — decide what you will need, work out a schedule, visualize possible hazards or delays, and recall past experiences of the same type so that you can avoid the mistakes that may have been made on a previous occasion.

Dreams are another, more primitive form of ideation. For example, suppose that while you are driving a car, you grope for something in your pocket. In doing this, you change your grip on the steering wheel, causing the car to swerve and perhaps barely avoiding an accident. After a moment's fright you make light of the whole situation, and possibly forget all about it. The next night you dream that the car is swerving, but this time you *do* have an accident. The dream has re-presented the problem to you in vivid form and has forced you to face up to the situation. It has in effect warned you of the possible consequences of repeating this unwise behavior.

Dreams Reveal Emotions

The emotion accompanying a dream may be more intense and more overt than that which was consciously felt in the actual experience leading to the dream. Thus, the dream produces a deeper impression than the original experience and may lead us to a better understanding.

For example, a girl has a date with a boy, who fails to appear. She is hurt at being "stood up," but she pretends indifference and perhaps even convinces herself that she "doesn't care." But that night in a dream she lives through the painful feelings she has repressed, and she wakes up crying. This dream experience has given her an insight into the way she really feels. She may now know how to cope with situations more realistically in the future.

Nightmares

Many dreams relate to startling and painful experiences of the past — to events of infancy, and even to birth itself. These events have left behind psychic problems which the helpless child could not solve at the time. In fact, any painful situation may leave a residue of grief, guilt, and anxiety. In this view, guilt represents the energy used for continually repeating unpleasant thoughts, both in waking life and

"Out damned spot! Out I say!"

in dreams. We continue to dream about "unfinished" situations until we work through the guilt or anxiety. (Freud called this a "repetition compulsion.")

This pattern is illustrated vividly in Shakespeare's *Macbeth*. Lady Macbeth has encouraged her husband to murder Duncan and to take his place as King of Scotland. Lady Macbeth, at first, seems untroubled about her part in the murder. However, her sense of guilt shows itself in a nightmare. She walks in her sleep, crying out, "Out, damned spot! Out, I say!" as she goes through the motions of washing her hands. She is attempting to wash away the stain of guilt she refused to acknowledge in her conscious mind.

Prophetic Dreams

Is there any truth to the ideas that dreams can predict (or *foreshadow*) the future?

Since Biblical times, many people have regarded dreams as signs of what is actually going to happen. We have all heard many stories which illustrate this. A mother dreams that her child is ill, and the next day he has a fever. A businessman dreams that a plane on which he is due to fly crashes, and postpones his out-of-town appointment.

The plane does crash. A secretary dreams that she will be fired, and lo and behold . . .! The details vary but the pattern is a familiar one.

One famous prophetic dream is attributed to Abraham Lincoln. A few days before his assassination in 1865, he dreamed he heard weeping and saw, in the East Room of the White House, soldiers standing guard over a casket. "Who is dead?" he asked. "The President," replied a soldier. "He was killed by an assassin."

Premonitions of disaster in dreams are very common. And in some situations, they may be based on hard facts. In the case of Lincoln, the nation had gone through four years of bloody and bitter civil war. Washington was known to be swarming with Confederate sympathizers, and there had been repeated threats against the President's life. Several earlier plots had miscarried. Lincoln was well aware of all this, and, as the war approached its end, it is quite possible that he began to brood about the possibility of being killed. It is not surprising that these unwelcome thoughts should come out in his dreams. That the dream in question occurred just a few days before the actual assassination is what makes it seem remarkable. But this could be no more than a coincidence.

We can provide a somewhat similar "naturalistic" explanation for the mother's dream about her child's illness. She knows the child's appearance and behavior so well that she senses any small changes which may be the first signs of an oncoming illness. Almost unconsciously, she starts to worry about these signs. The worries are expressed in her dreams — and the illness actually occurs. As for the secretary, she may be aware, without actually admitting it to herself, that she is not doing her job efficiently. Or she may be apprehensive that business is not good, and that there is not enough work in the office to keep her busy. So she dreams of being fired — and the dream comes true.

Besides, think of how many times mothers have dreamed of children becoming ill, and employees have dreamed of losing their jobs, *without* the event occurring in actuality. But these "non-prophetic" dreams tend to be quickly forgotten. The ones that "come off" are naturally remembered.

Other apparently prophetic dreams can be explained in terms of the fulfillment of rational wishes. Our dreams may indicate healthy strivings and insights into our problems and neuroses. That we sometimes get what we want, or that we change and grow, is not extraordinary. The potential is already there, and the dream simply acts as a catalyst. Thus, a high school student may dream of winning a college scholarship. He then decides to compete for such a scholarship, and applies all his abilities and energies until he actually does win it.

The dream in this case didn't "predict" the future. It simply indicated the direction in which the young man was already motivated to move.

Fromm's View of Dreams

In his book *The Forgotten Language**, Erich Fromm defines dreaming as "any kind of mental activity under the condition of sleep." Fromm believes that dreams express both the worst and the best in us, the primitive and the wise. His stand is somewhere between those of Freud and Jung. The problem, as he sees it, is to discover when a particular dream expresses an irrational wish and its fulfillment, *or* a simple fear or anxiety, *or* an insight into inner and outer forces and events. "Dreams are like the microscope through which we look at the hidden occurrences of the soul."

Fromm relies heavily on free association in analyzing dreams. The dream must be understood in the light of significant recent events, and the dreamer's life history. The following dream, reported in *The Forgotten Language,* illustrates the use of free association in interpreting dreams:

> A 28-year-old lawyer reports this dream: "I saw myself riding on a white charger, reviewing a large number of soldiers. They all cheered me wildly."

What do *you* think this dream means? A summary of Fromm's interpretation follows:

> The first question the analyst asks his patient is rather general: "What comes to your mind?" "Nothing," the man answers. "The dream is silly. You know that I dislike war and armies, that I certainly would not want to be a general." And in addition, "I also would not like to be the center of attention and to be stared at, cheering or no cheering, by thousands of soldiers. You know from what I told you about my professional problems how difficult it is for me to plead a case in court with everybody looking at me."
>
> The analyst answers: "Yes, that is all quite true; but it does not do away with the fact that this is *your* dream, the plot *you* have written and in which you assigned yourself a role."
>
> When the analyst urges the lawyer to focus on the charger, the patient remembers a picture he used to like as a teen-ager showing Napoleon on a white horse riding before his troops. It is similar to the picture in the dream.

---

* This discussion is based on material from *The Forgotten Language* by Erich Fromm. Copyright 1951 by Erich Fromm. Reprinted by permission of Holt, Rinehart and Winston, Inc.

The patient, embarrassed, says that at age fourteen or fifteen he was quite shy, poor at athletics, and somewhat afraid of "tough kids." Once, however, he liked one of the "tough kids" very much and wanted to become his friend. He invited the boy to his house to look at his microscope. The boy humiliated him, calling him a "sissy." It was then that he began to read books about Napoleon and to day-dream about becoming a famous general. Like Napoleon, he was small in build and was something of an "outsider." In his fantasies during this period, the patient *was* Napoleon and was widely admired and envied. When he went to college, he got over his hero-worship and had not since thought or spoken about it.

The analyst asks what else could have happened the day before to trigger the dream. The lawyer replies that the day had been much like any other. He went to the office, worked to gather material for a brief, went home, ate dinner, went to a movie, and went to bed. The analyst says, "That does not seem to explain why you rode on a white charger in the night. Tell me more about what went on at the office."

". . . . I remember . . . but this can't have anything to do with the dream." His boss, the senior partner of the firm, had discovered a mistake in the brief and criticized the young lawyer. For a moment the lawyer was upset, thinking perhaps that this failure would prevent him from being taken into the firm as a partner, as he had hoped. But he then realized that he was making a mountain out of a molehill, and he forgot the whole affair. He was not nervous or depressed after-wards, but simply tired. That night he was deeply moved by a film about a poor, despised boy who grew up to become a great national hero.

The analyst says, "We understand a little better why you had this dream, don't we? As a boy you felt shy, awkward, rejected. We know from our previous work that this had a great deal to do with your father, who was so proud of his success but was so incapable of being close to you and of feeling — to say nothing of showing — af-fection and of giving encouragement." Building on this foundation, the analyst brings in the other elements revealed in the free associa-tion. The rejection so many years ago by the "tough kid" reinforced the boy's belief that he could never amount to anything or be ac-cepted by the people he admired. So he escaped into a fantasy world where he achieved the admiration and self-respect he lacked in reality. At college, where he was less dependent on his father, he decided to make a new start and put away his "childish" daydreams. But this new-found confidence was deceptive. He was still frightened before exams, nervous with girls, and later, after graduation, afraid of his boss's criticism.

The boss's critical comments on the day before the dream revived the old feeling of inadequacy. But the patient pushed it aside, reacting by feeling tired instead of consciously anxious. Then he saw the movie and identified himself with the hero. The film, therefore, influenced the imagery of his dream. The dream indicates that the lawyer still tended to withdraw into his private realm of fantasy whenever reality was disappointing and troubling.

Could we understand this dream even without the associations supplied by the dreamer? Only to a degree. You have probably guessed that the man on the white charger, being cheered by troops, is a symbol of power and success. If we knew only this much, we could say that the dreamer had a fantasy of triumph. But with the added background of his adolescent idolization of Napoleon, we understand that the dream revives an old fantasy which compensated for a feeling of defeat and powerlessness.

Notice also the significance of (in Freud's term) the "day residue" — the events of the day before the dream. *Consciously,* the dreamer overcame his disappointment and apprehension at the boss's comments. The dream shows, however, that the criticism had hit him again at his sensitive spot — the fear of inadequacy and failure — and had reproduced the old avenue of escape, the dream of fame and power. The important point is that past and present, personality, and actual events, are woven together in a design which tells us a great deal about the dreamer's motivation, the dangers he must be aware of, and the goals he must work toward for greater health.

A Dream Culture — The Senoi People of Malaya

Although the technique is not practiced in Western cultures, there is evidence from the experience of other peoples that dreaming can be guided and utilized to produce social benefits.

For example, the Senoi people, a primitive* tribe living on the Malay Peninsula in Southeast Asia, use dream analysis techniques to help raise their children and to maintain harmony in the community. It is reported that they have not had an instance of violent crime or an intercommunal conflict in many years. Their level of mental and physical health is so high that (according to the testimony of one observer) they have no need of police, jails, hospitals, or insane asy-

---

* The word *primitive,* as used by psychologists and anthropologists, does not imply that the people in question are "simple" or "childlike," or that their culture is necessarily "inferior" to our own. It suggests only that the people in question live on a simple level in a technological sense — in the tools and machines that they use to meet their needs. Other phases of their culture, such as religion, family institutions, and language, may be exceedingly complex.

lums. Their affairs are controlled in accordance with a democratic consensus, yet individuals retain a wide area of personal freedom and responsibility.

The Senoi have an official, known as the *Tohat,* who is the equivalent of a "tribe psychologist." He is the highest authority in the social group. Their psychology has two parts, dream *expression* and dream *interpretation.* Senoi children relate their dreams each morning to the father and older brothers of the family, who then interpret them. Then the adults discuss these dreams, as well as their own, at a common council meeting in the village.

Children are taught not to be afraid of dreams which might ordinarily be considered "fearful." For example, in the case of a "falling" dream, they are encouraged to fall with trust and confidence, and to learn whatever they can about the place where they "land." The children then share such knowledge with others. By the time they have become adults, falling dreams have customarily changed to flying dreams.

The importance of the community is taught early, and dreams are used to reinforce this idea. For example, aggressive feelings, which are potentially antisocial, may be handled through dream interpretation. Thus, if a child dreams of conflict between himself and another person, he may be advised to give that person a gift to help resolve the conflict. Children are also encouraged to bring back from dreams some useful or creative knowledge to share with the rest of the tribe. For a sexual dream, the child is taught that he must demand from the dream-lover a poem, a song, or a dance which will express the beauty of the relationship.

In adult life, dreams are more often used to deal with a waking problem, such as an accident or a social conflict. Many changes in the social customs of the Senoi people have come about through dream interpretation. For example, it is said that women were granted equal status as the result of a dream by the Tohat.

This experience of the Senoi people tends to confirm the view that dreams represent a door to the unconscious, and that they may reflect, influence, and possibly direct much of our behavior. On the basis of evidence such as this, researchers in recent years have taken a new interest in dream consciousness. Since Freud, the interpretation of dreams has been used in therapy for individuals, but we are still far from employing dreams as a collective, social resource in the manner of the Senoi psychologists.

THINGS TO DISCUSS :: THINGS TO DO :: THINGS TO READ

1. Focus on one of your recent dreams which you remember reasonably well. Who are the people in the dream? Do you have any reason to believe that some of them represent other people?

2. What fears, problems, wishes, hopes, or opportunities does this dream reveal to you? Explain carefully.

3. In Freud's view, most dreams are unconscious wish-fulfillments. Why would the unconscious, particularly the id, be satisfied, at least temporarily, with a fantasy, rather than the reality?

4. According to Freud's later writings, some dreams are products of a "repetition compulsion" and are not strictly wish-fulfillments. According to this interpretation, what unconscious purpose do such dreams serve?

5. Have you ever had a dream that seemed to suggest a helpful solution to a problem? If so, explain how you benefited from the suggestions offered by the dream.

6. In what ways is dreaming similar to other activities of the unconscious?

7. Choose a record of a "psychedelic" song with lyrics that don't seem to make much sense. Play it in class. For the sake of discussion, assume that the verses (and the music) convey dream imagery. Identify the wishes and fears expressed in the record, and try to analyze them "in depth." How do these conclusions compare with your interpretations of your own (or anyone else's) dreams?

8. Select a short story from a science fiction or fantasy magazine, and analyze it in the same way you did the record.

READINGS

The Interpretation of Dreams, by Sigmund Freud (available in many editions). This is a massive work but not unduly difficult to read. Freud writes in an interesting, conversational style. Anyone who manages to get through it will probably find that he has achieved the beginning of a deep insight, not only into dreams, but into the unconscious — and into life. This is one of those rare books that has the capacity, almost by itself, to "expand awareness" (although, of course, it won't magically solve problems). If you give it adequate time and attention, it is quite likely that even though you may not understand much of it all at once, it will have a profound impact on your thinking throughout your life.

The Forgotten Language, by Erich Fromm (Harper, Row and World, 1951). Also a major pioneering work in the field. Fromm adds a "humanistic" perspective to dream interpretation.

Book of Dreams, by Jack Kerouac (City Lights Books, 1961). A collection of dreams by the late writer and early "beatnik" who wrote *On the Road* and *The Dharma Bums.*

Mythology

and Psychology

●●●●●●●●●●●●●●●●●●●●●●●●●●

*"Given a universe full of uncertainties and mysteries, the
myth intervenes to introduce the human element."*

— PIERRE GRIMAL

What Are Myths?

All cultures have myths. Anthropologists have not yet discovered
any society in any part of the world which does not have its own
group of traditional stories about gods, angels, the creation of the
world, and ancient heroes and sages. It is true that some cultures have
a much more complex system of mythology than others, and it is also
true that in some cultures, such as our own, many of the stories our
ancestors knew intimately have been forgotten, or are remembered
only fragmentarily. On the whole, however, myths are an example of
what the anthropologists call "universal phenomena" — social features which are common to all social groups.

Are Myths True?

When a psychologist calls a story a *myth,* he does not necessarily
mean that it is not true. He means rather that it is a story which people have created and which they keep alive in order to explain their
beliefs about the universe, about divine powers, about society, and
about man himself. Older members of a culture tell myths to their
children in order to explain to them what life, according to their own
beliefs, is all about.

For example, a culture may have a myth about a great hero who
was the ancestor of the group and gave it his name. The hero may
have brought the group sacred knowledge of the gods and of the
creation of the world. He may have made possible the group's survival

171

by teaching it a skill such as farming or hunting, or by slaying a destructive monster. For the people involved, this story has profound significance because it answers basic questions about their place in the overall scheme of things. It is this belief together with its influence on the thinking, feeling, and behavior of the people that interests the psychologist. The factual or historical authenticity of the story is not his concern.

The psychologist is concerned about truth on a different level: What does the myth reveal to us about the nature of man and about human society? Myths are not just interesting anecdotes which people tell to pass the time. They have immediate and far-reaching significance for the people who tell and hear them, even if the events narrated are supposed to have occurred thousands of years ago in remote parts of the world, or possibly "out of this world." The visions of Mohammed, for example, by which he received the inspiration to compose the Koran, occurred almost 1500 years ago in a cave, located outside what was then an obscure city of Arabia. But for untold millions of people this continues to be a supreme event of world history.

Resemblances Among Myths

If the mythology of each culture were totally different from all the others, myths would be of little interest to the psychologist. What makes myths particularly significant is the extraordinary degree of *similarity* between those belonging to widely different cultures.

There are various religions or cultural traditions which have a myth about a great hero who brought the gift of fire to mankind. One of these is the Greek mythological figure, Prometheus, who stole fire from heaven, and then was punished for his presumption. There are essentially similar stories in the myths of the Aztecs, certain African groups, and other peoples.

The ancient Norse tradition tells of a cosmic tragedy involving the downfall of the established gods. (This "Twilight of the Gods," or *Götterdämmerung,* is the theme of Richard Wagner's great opera.) The Greeks had a similar story of ancient gods, such as Cronus and Oceanus, overthrown by the Olympian gods.

Many other examples of this kind might be given. The important point is that these similarities are not just coincidences. The same ideas and images are used by different cultures because these ideas and images seem to possess a common meaning.

Jung's Archetypes

We have already noted in Chapter 5 that the Swiss psychiatrist Carl Jung explained these similarities among myths by the concept of the *archetype*. An archetype in this sense is a mysterious essential element on which patterns of thought and images are based. In terms of mythology, it refers to an elemental theme or idea to which varying details are added to make a story. Jung believed that these archetypes ("archaic remnants") are hereditary and common to all human beings, having been passed down from man's primitive beginnings to the present day.

For example, there are a great many myths from all over the world telling of a battle between a hero and a monster. The Norse hero Siegfried killed the dragon Fafnir; the Greek hero Perseus slew Medusa, a snake-haired woman whose gaze turned men to stone; and the Chinese hero Yu, controller of floods, destroyed Hsiang-yao, a serpent-bodied creature with nine heads who fouled springs and marshes. According to Jung this archetype is based on man's constant fight against the hostile forces of the world which seek to destroy him.

Man against monster — Perseus slays Medusa.

Stories such as these make a deep impression on the emotions of the members of the culture, and are therefore passed down from generation to generation as myths. Moreover (according to Jung), because the psychological tendency is inherited, the archetype continues to influence even people who have never heard about the myths, or who have apparently forgotten them. These unconscious influences may then emerge spontaneously in the form of dreams. To continue with our example, a man living in the United States today, and who does not consciously know any myths about monsters, may nonetheless dream about one. This image of the monster would have just as much psychological meaning to his unconscious as it had for the ancient Greeks or Chinese.

Another Explanation of Myths

Jung's concept of hereditary archetypes has been challenged by other psychologists, who reject the idea that such tendencies are biologically inherited. They would say that these unconscious tendencies are a result of *man's reaction to his environment.* This reaction begins at the moment of birth, continues with the development of the child, and remains an on-going process throughout the entire life of the individual. The child's first encounter with a hostile world creates a fear in him which makes him both dependent on his mother and ready to lash out against those forces which seem to threaten him. The critical confrontations and adaptations that the child must make toward his environment are common to all men, whether they are members of a complex industrial society or of a primitive tribe.

The basic episodes or experiences which all human beings must pass through include birth (the moment the child emerges from the protection of his mother's womb), competition with other family members (particularly the father) for the attention of the mother, adolescent initiation into the role of an adult, and the certainty of death. These experiences affect the psychological development of an individual in a way shared by all other members of his species. As a result all human beings develop the same psychological needs, and these are reflected in the myths of the various cultures, however different they may seem to be.

The Myth of Oedipus

To give concrete content to these ideas, let us examine one of the best known mythological models — the ancient Greek story of Oedipus. Sigmund Freud analyzed this in great detail and based on it his theory of the *Oedipus complex.*

According to the Greek myth, Laius, King of Thebes, was told by an oracle that his son would eventually kill him. Thus, when his wife Iocaste gave birth to a son (Oedipus), the King had the infant taken away and left on a mountainside to die. A shepherd found the baby boy, and took him to Polybus, King of Corinth. Oedipus grew up in the King's palace, thinking that Polybus was his father. When he had grown to young manhood, he was accused by a Corinthian of being a foundling, whose real parents had abandoned him. Oedipus questioned the King about this, and Polybus reluctantly admitted the truth. Oedipus then left Corinth in search of his real father, and consulted the oracle at Delphi. This oracle was well-known for giving vague and ambiguous ("delphic") answers which left a great burden of interpretation on the questioner. The Delphic oracle told Oedipus that he would kill his father and marry his own mother.

The young man was naturally disturbed by this strange revelation and left Delphi wondering what it could mean. He concluded that since it was impossible to know who his real parents were, the oracle must have been referring to his adopted father and mother, Polybus and Periboea, and he resolved never to return to Corinth for fear of what he might do there. As he was proceeding on his journey, he happened to encounter Laius, who was riding in a chariot along a narrow road. Laius' herald ordered Oedipus to step aside, but the young man was in no mood to inconvenience himself for the sake of a stranger. When he refused to move, the herald killed his horse, and Oedipus in anger killed both the herald and Laius.

Oedipus continued along the road until he arrived at the gates of Thebes, where he encountered the Sphinx, a monster that was half lion and half woman. The Sphinx had been terrorizing the Thebans by stopping passersby and asking them a riddle; if they failed to answer correctly (as all did), the Sphinx then devoured them. Oedipus solved the riddle, and the Sphinx jumped into a ravine and dashed herself to pieces among the rocks. The Thebans, happy to be rid of the monster, wanted to make Oedipus their King, since Laius had failed to return from his journey. Oedipus accepted and married the Queen, Iocaste, who unknown to him was actually his mother. All went well for several years. Then a plague fell upon Thebes. Creon, the brother of Laius, went to Delphi to find out why the gods were punishing Thebes, and the oracle told him that the plague would continue until the murder of Laius was avenged. Oedipus swore a horrible oath against the murderer, whoever he might be, and began an investigation to find him. Eventually the dreadful facts were revealed, and Iocaste hanged herself. Oedipus, horrified by the sins which he had committed, put out his own eyes with Iocaste's brooch, and left Thebes in voluntary exile.

The blinded Oedipus in exile, led by his faithful daughter, Antigone.

Freud's Theory of the Oedipus Complex

Freud used this myth as a model for a psychological pattern which he believed to be common to many people in all parts of the world. According to the theory of the Oedipus complex, when the developing child finds that he is in competition with his father for the affections of his mother he develops a desire to get rid of the father. The child may indulge in fantasies wherein the father goes away and the child must remain to comfort the mother. Freud thought that the widespread stories of a hero rescuing a maiden by killing the dragon which holds her captive are based on this Oedipal desire. The maiden, pure and loving, represents the mother; while the evil dragon, who certainly does not treat the maiden as she deserves, represents the father. Most people as they grow older adjust to the fact that they cannot maintain a monopoly on their mother's affections, but for some the complex develops into an unhealthy obsession which is often played out in the unconscious, in the form of neurotic behavior and dreams. In the play *Oedipus the King,* by the Greek playwright Sophocles, Iocaste tells Oedipus at the beginning of his investigation into Laius' murder:

> Many a man hath seen himself in dreams
> His mother's mate, but he who gives no heed
> To such like matters bears the easier fate.

Some men, however, continue to be unconsciously affected by this fantasy, with the result that they may develop a resentment against the father of which they are not themselves aware. The marriage of such a man may be unsuccessful because he remains overattached to his mother and expects his wife to give him the same selfless devotion he received as a child from his mother.

This is just one example of how an ancient myth can continue to have meaning for modern man, even for an individual who has never heard the story. The Greek who first told the story thousands of years ago, and the man who dreams of killing his father today, have both passed through the same types of emotional experience. In Jungian terms, the Oedipus story is an *archetype*.

Symbols in Mythology

Symbols are an important element of mythology. A symbol may be in the form of an incident or a situation, such as a man being swallowed by a huge beast. It may also be a concrete recognizable object, such as the solid red disk by which the Japanese represent the sun-goddess and the divine origin of their country. In either case, the symbol stands for some concept or doctrine which is not immediately evident. A symbol, in sort, is a "visible sign of something invisible."

On the surface, the idea of a man being swallowed by a beast is no more than an interesting and rather fanciful story. At a deeper level, it is a portrayal of a highly significant psychological process. It symbolizes a spiritual death, followed by an emergence from the tomb (the animal's stomach), after which the hero is at peace with God and with himself, having discovered a truth of which he was not aware before.

The Squared Circle

Symbols, like myths, are universal; they can be found in all parts of the world. Let us take as an example the symbol of the squared circle, that is, a circle divided into four parts. (See the illustrations on page 178.) Religious pictures based on the squared circle were employed by, among others, the Chinese, the Tibetans, and the Aztecs. Now, of course, it does not take much imagination to think of dividing a circle into four parts, so it is not at all strange that these different peoples all created the same symbol. But what is striking indeed is that these three cultures in different parts of the world all used this symbol *to represent the same basic idea.*

A bronze mirror from 8th-century China shows a square earth at the center of the circle, surrounded on four sides by the ocean in which it floats. Surrounding the ocean are the four animals representing the cardinal points: a dragon in the east, a phoenix in the south, a tiger in the west, and a tortoise in the north. These animals are also connected with the four seasons. Each direction is also marked by a mountain which was formed from part of the body of the first creature, Phan-ku. Phan-ku was born when the cosmic egg broke apart. He grew at the rate of 10 feet a day for 18,000 years, separating those parts of the egg which became the sky from the parts that formed the earth. When he died, his head became the eastern mountain, his left arm the southern mountain, his right arm the northern mountain, and his feet the western mountain. His stomach became the mountain of the center. The human race began, humbly enough, from the fleas which covered his body.

A Tibetan *mandala,* a design used by the Buddhists for meditation, usually has two circles one inside the other. In the "Amitayus Mandala," the central circle is occupied by Amitayus, who is the Buddha of boundless life and light. At four points around the circle are the *lokapalas,* the "guardians" of the cardinal points or directions. Between the inner circle and the outer circle is the "pure land" over which Amitayus rules.

An Aztec calendar stone has grimmer implications. In the Aztec system of recording time, the years were named according to four signs, which also represented the four directions. The reed was the east, flint was the north, the horse was the west, and the rabbit was the south. These four year-signs surround the inner circle of the stone. (See page 180.) Around these is a complex representation of the days, each of which belonged to a god. Some of these gods represented various aspects of the sun, but in the center circle is the Sun-God himself, Tonatiuh. He is shown with his mouth open and his tongue hanging out, eager for human blood. The Aztecs believed that it was necessary to offer blood to the sun in order to keep it moving in the sky. This was the basis for their practice of human sacrifice.

The Concept of Wholeness

We can see that these squared circles all represent the earth with its four directions (north, south, east, west). However, they symbolize much more than that. They are expressions of the idea of *wholeness,* of the essential *unity* of all things in the universe and the *totality* of human experience. For example, in Chinese mythology a primeval being named Phan-ku contained in his body the whole world. He was the first man, from whom everything that exists today was derived.

Within the basic form of the "squared circle," there are many variations of the mandala to express individual feelings and ideas. Two such forms are shown here. The one on the left was designed by a young artist "to reach a good balance between the dynamic and the passive, the symmetrical and the asymmetrical."

The four animals surrounding the earth represent not only the four directions and the four seasons, but also the four "elements" of which the Chinese thought everything was made. The dragon was wood, the phoenix was fire, the tiger was metal, and the tortoise was water.

All men were originally joined in the body of Phan-ku. Accordingly, the Chinese design described on page 177 is not only a pictorial representation of the world but a symbol of the basic unity of all existence.

The idea of four basic "elements" of which everything (including man) is made was also developed by the ancient Greeks and transmitted by them to Western Europe. The "elements" in question were air, water, earth, and fire. It was not until the rise of modern science, beginning in the 16th century, that this idea was finally dropped. Symbolically, the four "elements" suggest again the unity of the universe and the essential oneness of mankind.

The Tibetan mandala is another symbolic representation of wholeness. Its basic idea is the unity of the realm of consciousness (thought) with the realm of form (the physical world). When the Buddhists use this figure as an object of meditation, they let their thoughts travel from the outer circle, which represents the world, to the innermost circle, where Amitayus is sitting. Amitayus represents the highest spiritual nature which man can attain and, simultaneously, the very basis of being — the force that lies within and beneath all things that exist. By meditating upon the Amitayus Mandala, the Buddhists aspire to attain *Nirvhana* — a vision of wholeness and a state of divine union with the universe.

There is a clear similarity between the mandala and the practice in medieval Europe of building cities in the form of a circle. The circle was divided into four parts by two main roads, which intersected at the center of the city. The cathedral, or main church, was located at this intersection. This plan is interpreted as an attempt to symbolize the idea that man's spiritual life is the very center of his existence on earth. The position of the church at the center of the city unites this world with the world above.

The Aztecs and the Order of the Universe

The Aztecs would seem, at first glance, to have had a very different idea of the world than that held by the Chinese and the Tibetan Buddhists. The religion of the Aztecs was in one sense extremely pessimistic. They believed that everything was in conflict, male powers against female powers, night against day, the sun against the moon and stars, good against evil. Someday these battles would become so fierce that the world would be destroyed. Indeed, the Aztecs believed it had already been destroyed no fewer than four times.

As a result of their fear that the world was subject to such disruption, the Aztecs were very concerned with order. Each god had his own time, color, space, and collection of beliefs. Everything that existed and every event that occurred was a manifestation of a god. The order of the world was based on the dependence of the gods on each other, and also on their dependence on men.

The source of the Aztecs' idea of their responsibility and involvement in the survival of the universe was their belief that they were a chosen race. They thought it was their special duty to help the sun in its task, which was to make it possible for the world to continue. They helped the sun by giving it the food it needed — human blood. The Aztec calendar was not just a means of recording time; it was also a religious statement, showing the relationships between the days, the gods, the seasons, the directions of the compass, the elements of the earth, and mankind. Human destiny depended less on the will of the gods than it did on this strict ordering of the universe.

The Aztec calendar stone is thus a symbol of wholeness and unity, and the bloodthirsty god at its center represents that point where man can participate in the life of everything which exists.

The Aztec calendar stone.

Wholeness and Self

The idea of wholeness is very important in modern psychology. Jung has pointed out that the "self" is often characterized as having a fourfold nature. He theorized that there are four functions of consciousness. There are *sensation, intuition, feeling,* and *thought,* as explained in Chapter 6. In a healthy, mature, well-adjusted person, each of these forms of consciousness is developed to more or less the same degree, and each is dependent on the others. There are, however, some people who have overdeveloped one function at the expense of the others. For example, a man may be keenly aware of everything going on around him, but may be deficient in intellectual understanding of these events. He has sacrificed thought to sensation. Another man may be so "lost in thought" that he is scarcely aware of events in the outside world. He has overemphasized thought at the cost of sensation and intuition.

Ignoring one of the areas of consciousness in this way, Jung taught, may result in a neurosis. The natural union (the wholeness) between thought and emotion is disrupted, and as a result the individual loses touch with the world and with part of himself. This, he said, is the reason so many people today feel an acute sense of loneliness — they are separated from other people by their inability to relate to them emotionally. This can also lead to a sense of personal artificiality. A person may feel somehow "unreal" because he is cut off from part of his basic nature. The individual cannot be at peace with himself and with the outside world unless he has achieved a firm sense of wholeness.

The Circle and the Square

In many mythological traditions, the square, as a symbol of the earth, is a representation of the physical part of man. The circle, on the other hand, represents the psyche, the spiritual side of man's nature. The squared circle is therefore a union of these two aspects. This union between darkness and light, emotion and thought, physical life and mental life, is essential for psychological health.

The Navajos, a tribal group of American Indians, employed the squared-circle design in their curing rituals. They believed that it enabled the sick person to return to harmony with himself and the cosmos, and thus to cure his illness.

It should be noted also that there are five points in the squared circle — the four directions and the center, where the lines meet. These five points suggest the five senses. This is yet another way in which the squared-circle symbolizes the totality of human experience.

This design appears on a goblet found at Susa, Persia. It dates from the 2nd millenium B.C. What ideas discussed in this chapter does it illustrate?

The squared circle has been discussed here because it is a symbolic representation of an idea which is basic to all mythology. It is an ideal picture of the cosmos, and at the same time indicates to a person what his role is within that picture.

There are many other universal archetype symbols. One is the tree, which will be discussed later in this chapter. Others are the snake, the hermaphrodite (a creature who is half male and half female), the earth mother, the sorceress, the monster (half-human and half-animal), and the sun and the moon. Whenever one of these symbols appears in a myth in any part of the world, many scholars feel that it almost always has the same essential psychological meaning.

Modern man is the heir to these symbolic traditions. Moreover, the same symbols may appear in his dreams, where they have essentially the same meaning.

Symbols and the Unconscious

The symbols which appear in so many mythologies, and which still have significance for modern man, were probably not consciously or deliberately devised by anyone. It is unlikely that an Aztec priest sat down and said to himself, "Now, what would be a good way to illustrate the idea of the unity of all things?" Mythic symbols originated not in conscious thought but rather deep in the *unconscious*.

If such symbols were the product of conscious ideas, they would cease to have any meaning or acceptance after the ideas connected with them had been forgotten. But historically, as we have noted, this has not happened. The symbols continue to have meaning because *in themselves* they suggest some psychological relationship or need to the unconscious mind. The conscious mind in many cases has no idea at all what the symbol means.

For example, if a man had a dream about being married to a she-bear, he would probably dismiss it as total nonsense. However, in both Greek and Celtic mythology, the she-bear was the symbol of the totally feminine mother-goddess. If the man in question had been trying to avoid becoming involved with a woman, this dream might have been a way in which his unconscious was symbolizing his need to allow the feminine aspect into his life. The rational, conscious mind rejects the idea of being married to an animal, but the unconscious uses it to express something which is important to the individual.

The symbol of the monster (part animal, part human) appears in the traditions of many religions. Shown here is a painting from prehistoric times, found on the walls of a cave in Southern France. It represents a shaman or priest whose costume is composed of the antlers of a reindeer, the ears of a stag, the eyes of an owl, the paws of a bear, and the tail of a horse. The beard and the feet are clearly human.

Indeed, a symbol may have more important psychological meaning to a person who is entirely unfamiliar with it than to someone who has consciously accepted it as part of his religion. This is because symbols which are in constant use tend to gather subsidiary ideas and "overtones," added to them by the conscious mind, which they did not have when they first sprang from the unconscious. For example, the mandala has become a highly intellectualized symbol in Buddhism. Volumes have been written interpreting its meaning. As a result, the central emotional impact of the mandala may become diluted in this sophisticated religious intellectualizing. But when the mandala appears in the dreams of a modern Western man, according to Jung's interpretation, it carries with it the essential meaning of unity and wholeness being expressed by the unconscious.

It is precisely this power of symbols to tap some rich emotional vein deep within the psyche that makes them such an essential part of mythology. Man uses symbols to communicate ideas which cannot be easily expressed in words, yet which play an important role in his psychological life. The most common object may be invested by this process with a wealth of hidden associations. This is one way in which myths and symbols tend to involve man more deeply and intimately in the world around him. The entities that make up our environment do not exist as mere "things" which have nothing to say to man. The unconscious transforms them into outside pictures of inner truths. We shall now consider how this principle is applied to one of the most common objects in nature, the tree.

The Tree as a Symbol

Growth is one of the most important aspects of human life. The development of a child into an adult involves both physical and mental growth. The mysterious process by which this occurs has always been of great concern of mankind, and it is for this reason that there have been countless attempts to explain the meaning and the secrets of growth.

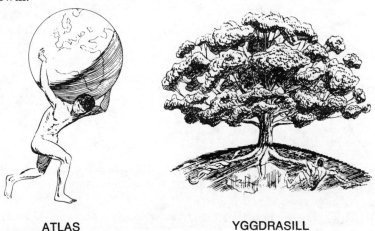

ATLAS   YGGDRASILL

The tree is a natural symbol for the process of growth because it originates as a tiny seed and develops into an organism of size, majesty, and exceptionally long life. The study of mythological trees can therefore be very rewarding in terms of what they tell us about the human mind.

The Greeks pictured the universe as being supported by a giant (Atlas), but the Nordic people of pre-Christian Germany and Scandinavia thought it was held together by a huge, fantastic tree named *Yggdrasill*. This ash tree connected all the parts of the universe, for its roots went deep into the earth and its topmost branches reached into the heavens, where they were eternally bathed in a cloud of light. The entire world was in the shadow of its branches. Its leaves were always green, despite the fact that they were always being eaten by animals.

Serpents, particularly the evil dragon Nidhoggr, tried to destroy the divine tree by eating away at its roots, but the tree survived because new strength constantly flowed into it through one of its roots, which reached to Urd's Well, the Fountain of Youth. This well was guarded by one of the *Norns*, the goddesses who ruled over the course of time and the destinies of men. Perpetual life was also insured by a miraculous dew which fell from the sky.

A second root of Yggdrasill passed through Niflheim, the land of ice, and reached the fountain of Hvergelmir, which overflowed to provide the waters for all the great rivers of the earth.

A third root of Yggdrassil passed through the land of the giants, eternally covered with frost, to reach a magical fountain. This was the Fountain of Wisdom, guarded by a giant named Nimir (literally, "He who thinks"). The miraculous powers of this fountain, providing knowledge of all things in the universe, were so highly prized that even Odin, the chief god of Norse mythology, traded one of his eyes for a sip of its waters.

Through its triple roots, the tree was connected with the three worlds of gods, giants, and men. It also connected the past, known to Nimir, to the future, known to the Norns. A golden rooster sat at the top of the tree, scanning the horizon to warn the gods whenever their enemies, the giants, were preparing to attack them. Heydrun a goat fed on its leaves, and her milk provided the food for Odin's warriors.

Trees of Good and Evil

Other mythologies feature the tree as a pillar of the universe. The natives of the Caroline Islands in the South Seas tell the story of how the first god, Solal, planted a giant tree on the rock of the universe — the primeval rock which existed before anything else. Solal then climbed the tree, stopping halfway up to create the earth. At the top of the tree he made the sky.

The Yakut people of Siberia picture the cosmic tree as growing on a hill in the middle of a flat plain. Its resin was transparent and sweet-scented, its bark never cracked or dried, its sap was silver, and its leaves never wilted. The souls of unborn children inhabited its branches like small birds. The tree rose up through the North Star, the center or navel of the sky, and extended above the seven floors of heaven. The god Yryn-ai-tojon tethered his horses at its top. The tree was the dwelling place of the ancient Earth Mother, the source of all life.

The *druids* were the priests of the ancient Celtic people who inhabited the British Isles when the Romans under Julius Caesar invaded the area in 55 B.C. We know from Caesar's reports and from other evidence that this religion involved the worship of a pantheon of ancient nature deities, symbolized mainly by trees. The druid religious ceremonies seem to have been performed largely in tree groves. In particular, the oak and the mistletoe that grows on the oak were held sacred. In the druid tradition, in short, the tree was regarded as the most overt manifestation of divine forces, and tree worship was man's means of making contact with those forces.

The Tree as a Symbol of Immortality

The Norse god Odin also sacrificed himself upon the Tree of the World. One of the *Eddas* (the epic poems of Norse mythology) tells how Odin hanged himself from the branches of Yggdrasill.

> I know that I hung
> On the wind-rocked tree
> Nine whole nights,
> Wounded by my own spear,
> And to Odin offered
> Myself to myself;
> On that tree,
> Whose roots go down
> Men know not where.

Odin waited for nine days and nights for something to come to relieve his agony. At last he saw some *runes* lying on the ground beneath his feet. These were magical stones inscribed with secret formulas. Groaning with the effort, he finally managed to raise the stones to a level where he could read them. Their miraculous powers put an end to his suffering; he immediately fell to the ground completely rejuvenated, with all his youthful strength and vigor restored. Nimir then gave him permission to drink once more from the Fountain of Wisdom, so that he regained all the knowledge that he had lost. This regeneration was the purpose and the meaning of Odin's voluntary death upon the tree. It also represented a form of immortality, for it gave the god back his youth.

This story is similar to many others in which the tree serves as an archetypical symbol of immortality and restored youth. A significant parallel can be found in the ancient legend of Gilgamesh from Sumer, in the Middle East. In the story, the hero Gilgamesh, after a long and arduous journey, was able to obtain the plant of rejuvenation from the bottom of the ocean. It was his intention to take the plant back to his city for the old men to eat, "and at last I shall eat it myself and have back all my lost youth." The story does not end happily, however. On the return journey, the plant was stolen from him by a serpent. The trickery of the serpent is a recurrent theme in many mythic traditions.

The Sun as a Symbol of Immortality

Immortality is also often associated with the sun, which dies every night to be reborn in the morning. A Shinto myth from Japan concerns the beautiful sun-goddess, Amaterasu. Her brother, the storm-god Susanowo, had been misbehaving disgracefully. She tried to appease him, but he continued to destroy her rice fields and to annoy her in every way he could think of. Finally he dropped a skinned horse through the roof of her weaving-hall. Amaterasu was so terrified by the sight that she hid in a heavenly cave and closed the door behind her. With the disappearance of the sun, the whole universe went dark, and evil spirits ran freely through the world.

The gods gathered together to figure out a way to get Amaterasu out of her cave, for if she stayed there much longer, the universe would surely come to an end. Finally they devised a plan. A great tree was set up in front of the cave and decorated with jewels. They filled the tree with crowing roosters, so that it seemed that dawn was about to break at any moment. Then they hung a mirror, eight feet long, from the middle branches of the tree, and began to engage in loud festivities. Amaterasu heard all the noise and could not understand what was going on. Finally, her curiosity got the better of her, and she opened the door of her cave to inquire what all the laughter was about, since she had expected that everyone would be grieving over the loss of the sun. The gods told her that they were rejoicing because there was now a new goddess, even more illustrious than she was. Amaterasu looked out and saw herself in the mirror. Astonished, she hesitantly moved closer to get a better look at this goddess who was taking her place. As soon as she had left the cave, a god stretched a rope across it so that she could not return. Thus, the light of the sun was restored to the world because Amaterasu saw herself in a mirror suspended from the cosmic tree.

What Are Myths Good For?

Human experience indicates that an idea is often most easily remembered when it is in the form of a story or a picture; that is, in the form of a myth or a symbol. But what are these ideas which are so important that man develops myths and symbols to explain them? In other words, *what are myths good for?*

The famous mythologist Joseph Campbell has proposed that myths have four basic functions. He identified these as the *mystical,* the *cosmological,* the *sociological,* and the *psychological.* Here, we are most concerned with the psychological function of myths, but we shall discuss the other three functions as well.

Mystical Function of Myths

The object of mysticism is to unite the individual with the world in which he lives. It is quite natural for people to think that the world is "against them." Any number of unfortunate events, either natural or caused by man, can destroy a person's livelihood or take his life. Such misfortunes may make a person wonder whether there is any sense at all to life because the world so often seems, for no recognizable reason, to be working against his own interests.

The mystical function of mythology is to demonstrate to the individual that the world does, somehow, "make sense." Myths attempt to do this in a number of ways. They may teach, as in Hinduism, that the material world is an evil illusion, and that man must rise above this in order to join with the God-head. They may suggest, as many myths of primitive people do, that man must make a better adaptation to the natural order of things in the world. The object of many primitive initiation rites is to guide a person into accepting the way things are — to say, in effect, "Yes, life is hard, but you have to get used to it, because you can't change it." By accepting this, the individual will come to understand that he is part of nature, and this understanding provides him with the personal strength he needs to survive.

On the other hand, myths may give a picture of the world as having fallen from a perfect state. The evil of the world, according to these traditions, resulted from man's failure to obey the will of God, and it is only by following the will of God that the world can be restored to its proper state. Many myths, such as those of the Greeks tell of a "Golden Age" that man enjoyed in the past and to which he may be able to return, given the proper attitudes and behavior.

In all cases, the mystical function of mythology is to show the individual what the world means to him, and how he can learn to live within the context of that meaning.

Cosmological Function of Myths

A *cosmology* is a theory about the way in which the universe (the *cosmos*) is shaped. Man has always felt a need to have a working picture of the world, and to understand just how he fits into the overall scheme of things. Examples of such "pictures" are the squared circle of Chinese tradition, showing the world and the animals at its four corners, and the Cosmic Tree from Norse mythology, which connects all the parts of the universe. These are both cosmological symbols. They give a picture of the world in which all things — rocks, animals, plants, the sun, the seasons, time, and man himself — are parts of a great wholeness.

Because everything that exists is part of the whole, we may be able to uncover the mystery of the universe by examining a single aspect, such as the way a flower grows, or the movements of the stars in the sky. Men use a cosmology in an attempt to understand how the world fits together, and how they fit into the structure.

Sociological Function of Myths

A human society, composed of many individuals and groups, is a complex and delicately balanced organism. If the society is to function reasonably well and survive, there must be general agreement among the members on values, standards of conduct, and the "rules of the game." It is not to be expected that *everyone* will conform to the rules, but if there is too much basic dissent or anti-social conduct, the social organization will be in trouble.

The sociological function of mythology is to help insure that the rules and standards recognized by the society will be generally observed. Usually, myths serve this purpose by giving a *sacred* or *supernatural* character to the laws and taboos which the society considers vital to its survival. Anyone who violates these basic rules is not merely breaking a man-made commandment; he is doing something that will bring down heavenly wrath on himself, and perhaps on his group.

The Greeks symbolized this in the story of *Pandora,* a beautiful young woman whom the gods had endowed with every charm – but also with curiosity and deceit. Among many other gifts, the gods gave Pandora a box which they warned her she was not to open. But she had an irresistible—and all too human—urge to see what was in it, and one day she threw back the lid and peered in. There then emerged from the box all kinds of misery to afflict mankind. Envy, discontent, pain, anger, hunger, plague, crime – these and many other ills flew out over the earth before Pandora could slam down the lid. She wept for the evil she had done to mankind – and to herself – by her transgression, but to no avail. She could not call back the ills.

In Norse tradition, only warriors who showed great courage while dying in battle would be privileged to go to *Valhalla,* the legendary banquet hall of the gods. This belief presumably encouraged Norse fighting men to behave with the "fearlessness" that their militaristic culture expected of them.

The Aztecs believed that the sun would die unless it was fed human blood. This idea made the practice of human sacrifice beyond question for members of the Aztec culture. The Aztecs' faith that they were a special people, chosen to help the universe survive, was a strong unifying force.

Such examples show how myths often serve the important sociological function of inducing people not merely to obey but to support actively the basic rules of their society.

Psychological Function of Mythology

It is not enough for people merely to accept and conform to the rules of their society. The members of the society must also be shaped in their minds and personalities so that they will adjust favorably to the difficulties which they are bound to encounter in their lives.

This is the psychological function which is at the very root of mythology and forms the basis of all its other functions. Cosmologies and social rules differ markedly from one culture to another, but the essential problems and key events of life remain the same throughout the entire world. Both an Australian aborigine and a banker in New York City pass through the crises of birth, change from childhood to adulthood, marriage, birth of children, and death.

In mythology, we find symbolic representations of these life crises, and also a great deal of practical wisdom about the meaning of such events for man. Perhaps the most critical of these experiences is the juncture at which a person leaves the world of childhood and takes on the role and the responsibilities of an adult. In all species other than man, the new-born organism is equipped with almost all the instincts which it needs to survive. Its parents must look after it long enough for it to develop the strength to live on its own, but they do not have to teach it very much about the techniques of survival. The young animal already knows them instinctually.

This is not the case with man. The child has to be taught slowly and systematically the facts and the skills which it must have at its disposal in order to deal with the problems of life. For many years, the young human remains under the protection of his parents, guided and sustained by them until the time comes when he is ready to go out in the world on his own. This is a very critical and psychologically disturbing point in the life cycle, because even though the individual may have learned all that he has to know, he is still emotionally dependent on his parents and is accustomed to looking to them for support. He must overcome this dependence if he is to take on the role of an adult. He must learn to think for himself, to rely on himself, to do whatever is necessary, without having his parents around to help him. In the Oedipus myth, we see a representation of the psychological distress a man will experience if he has been unable to overcome his dependence on his mother. Instead of looking for a wife to share his life with him, the man suffering from an Oedipus complex is always seeking a woman who will take his mother's place and provide him with the security of childhood. Such a man has been unable to become a complete adult. He has not conformed to the normal life pattern symbolized in the mythology of his culture.

A great many myths deal with the idea of rebirth. Brahma, Dionysus, Odin, and many other traditional figures are represented as having died, after which they were reborn, or arose from the dead. In the initiation rites of primitive tribes, the idea of rebirth plays the central role. The object of this ceremony is to introduce the young male into the role of adulthood. The initiation rites follow a typical pattern. When the boy comes of age, he is "torn away" from his mother by the men of his tribe. He is taken to a special place and told the myths which reveal the secret truths of the universe. After that he is left by himself to think about the mysteries that have been revealed to him,

At this special ceremony, young boys are initiated into the Fly River tribe of New Guinea. The men wearing the masks assume the role of oracles, answering questions and revealing tribal secrets to the boys. No women are present.

or to receive a vision which will have an important meaning to him in his adult life. During this time he is symbolically dead. Finally, he is reintroduced to the tribe in a special ceremony. In this ceremony he is wrapped in an animal skin, or simply surrounded by the men of his tribe in a close circle. In either case he has to fight his way to the outside world. This symbolizes his rebirth. The entire initiation rite represents his death as a child and his birth as a man.

And now the whole tribe has become the parents of the young man. In other words, he has left his first mother and has been given a new mother, his society. Now he must take on the responsibility and self-discipline demanded by his new mother, and abandon the dependence on his natural parent. In this way, both he and the entire tribe acknowledge that he has entered a new stage of life. The mythology symbolizes, parallels, and reinforces a basic psychological change in the normal life cycle.

Myths and Modern Man

In this discussion, we have seen how and why mythology was important to our ancestors. But what about us today, living in the United States in the last third of the 20th century? Do myths still have meaning for us? Is it true, as some people have said, that we have somehow "advanced beyond the stage" where man needs myths, or can even take them seriously?

It is clear that there is no longer any general body of myths which are accepted by everyone within our culture. This has happened for a number of reasons. First, the "Age of Reason," which began in the 18th century, has placed great emphasis on establishing rational or intellectual truths on the basis of scientific evidence — meaning observation, experimentation, and rigorously logical thinking. In this climate of rationalism, there has been a strong tendency to dismiss mythology as "nonsense" and "fairy tales." Secondly, the very size and complexity of modern society make it difficult for all people to agree on a single set of beliefs. Even among those people who accept a religious frame of reference for their thinking, there is much diversity. Every one of the major world religions today is divided into a number of branches or sects, representing somewhat different interpretations and applications of the same basic tradition.

However, the fact that we no longer have a common mythology does not mean that we do not *need* a mythology at all. To the extent that we have given up our mythic tradition, we have had to pay a heavy price. If we consider the functions which myths serve, as summarized above, we can see that we are still very much in need of something which will take their place. Many people today have the feeling that the universe "makes no sense," that it is no more than a "jumble" of impersonal, meaningless forces in which man has no special place. Our accepted scientific cosmology gives us a picture of an infinite universe in which human life seems to be only an accident. Many of the rules of our society seem outdated and no longer serve a useful purpose. Flagrant and deliberate violations of these rules are commonplace, as is revealed in crime statistics. Our whole society seems to many to have "lost its way." Because of a prevailing sense of uncertainty, many people feel detached from the world and from themselves — an attitude which we have already referred to as *alienation*. All of these characteristics and symptoms are typical of a society which no longer has a dominant mythology to tell people how they fit into the world and what the world is all about.

Will We Develop a New Mythology?

Of course, the fact that we see the need for a mythology to help bring order and meaning into our lives doesn't mean that we can simply invent one, or borrow one from another source. Many young people today seem to be trying to do something very much like this by "exploring" Zen Buddhism and other philosophy-religions of Asia. But a mythology cannot really be "borrowed" or transplanted in this way. It must grow naturally out of the culture itself. It must fit into the prevailing way of life because it is in itself a product of that specific social and physical environment.

Are we developing, or will we develop, a new mythology in our society? Thus far, this has not happened. To be sure, we do have some traditional stories about national figures and movements which have very nearly taken on a mythic quality. Prominent among these is the story of Abraham Lincoln — the backwoods boy who became one of the greatest Presidents of the United States.* In many respects, this story embodies basic values of American society: the rise of a boy from extreme poverty on the basis of his own efforts and abilities; the success in going "to the top" — attaining the position of highest power; the selfless devotion to the preservation of the nation; the qualities of honesty, humanity, and compassion; the unassuming "common man"

---

* We are not suggesting here that the familiar story of Abraham Lincoln is not historically true. In the main it is. But it has taken on an idealized and generalized quality which, in a sense, is beyond history. Such terms as "Father Abraham" and the "Great Emancipator" show a tendency to convert a remarkable but very imperfect human being (like all human beings) into an archetypical national symbol. The symbol is virtually beyond criticism and is to be regarded with reverence and love. Obviously this has more of the quality of a myth than of an actual historical figure.

The making of a legend — "Young Abe, the Rail Splitter." This picture was widely distributed during the Presidential campaign of 1860 and helped to bring about the election of Lincoln, until then a relative unknown on the national political scene.

personality, in spite of great talents and achievements; and finally the martyrdom in the service of his country.

But perhaps the Lincoln story (or myth) does not have as much meaning for young people today as it once had. For the most part, they admire him, but they see grave shortcomings in the society which has emerged in the century since the Civil War. They note particularly that even the cause of black emancipation, in which Lincoln played such a notable part, has not fulfilled its promise. We are still struggling with the heritage of racism — still trying to make equality a reality rather than a slogan. This in itself does not impair Lincoln's stature, but it does impair his value as a mythic or semi-mythic figure who can embody and symbolize the values of the group.

Significant changes are occurring rapidly in the United States today. Among other things, many of our old ideas are disintegrating, and many new ideas are being introduced. In any period of major change, cultures learn to direct themselves toward new goals. Perhaps out of this redirection, there will emerge a new mythology, based on what we know of life today. Then man may be better equipped to find a state of peace with himself and the universe.

THINGS TO DISCUSS :: THINGS TO DO :: THINGS TO READ

1. How do you explain the fact that the same, or strikingly similar, symbols and stories are found in widely separated places and historical eras in the form of myths, folk-tales and dreams? (Try to prepare a theory other than the "universal unconscious" proposed by Jung.)

2. What elements or characteristics make a story a *myth?*

3. Do we really need a system of myths to provide meaning and reassurance for the individual and his values? Are there other ways for a person to be reassured of the meaningfulness of his actions and basic beliefs?

4. The Theory of Organic Evolution is only vaguely understood by many people, who nonetheless accept its authenticity and regard Charles Darwin as a "wise man," in much the same way that people of other times and places have regarded priests and prophets. In the light of this, might it be meaningful to say that for such people Darwin's theories have a "mythical" character and function? Can you think of any other myths (in this sense of the term) accepted in areas that are supposed to be "scientific" and "objective"?

5. Some people pin their future, their hopes and their aspirations (their "meaning of life") on a single legend. Give an example of this. In what sense may such an approach be dangerous? What might be a more reasonable alternative?

6. Select a team of five students, each of whom will briefly relate to the class a myth, legend or folk-tale. The team should make sure that each story represents a different culture or period of history. For greater interest, an effort should be made to select materials which will be unfamiliar to most members of the class. Then hold a class discussion. Can you recognize any similarities among these various tales? What are they? How do you explain them?

7. Select another team of five students, each of whom will narrate a dream which he or she has had recently. Can you recognize any similarities between the dreams and the myths previously narrated? Explain.

   Do you think that any similar patterns recognized in the dreams and the myths may be *archetypes?* In other words, do any of these represent basic themes which have been employed by men in many different times and places? Explain.

READINGS

The Larousse World Mythology (Prometheus Press, Paul Hamlyn Ltd., 1965), edited by Pierre Grimal. This is a treasure house of "far-out" pictures and stories.

Man and His Symbols, conceived by Carl Jung (Doubleday, 1964, 69). The pictures are particularly fascinating.

Man, Myth and Magic — An Illustrated Encyclopedia of the Supernatural, edited by Richard Cavendish (Marshall Cavendish Corp., 1971). The best illustrated and written materials on the subject are found in this encyclopedia.

Totem and Tabu, by Sigmund Freud (available in many editions). If you want to get into some deep reading, Freud presents a "radical" view of mythological themes.

The Psychology of
Magical Beliefs

●●●●●●●●●●●●●●●●●●●●●●●●●●●●●

*"It's a fact the whole world knows,
That Pobbles are happier without their toes"*

— *EDWARD LEAR*

*"Human kind
Cannot bear very much reality"*

— *T. S. ELIOT*

Magic in Human History

Magic has been with us for a very long time. Primitive man used it in his daily activities, turning to magical practices to help track game, or to make sure that crops would grow, or to keep away diseases or other disasters that he thought were brought on by evil spirits. As civilization advanced, magic came to play a smaller role in the life of most people. Some scholars suggested that magic would soon disappear altogether in modern, scientific societies. So far, however, this has not turned out to be true. Magic certainly is no longer accepted by everyone, as it was in primitive societies, but it hasn't died out either. Moreover, in recent years, there has been what might be called a "boom" in magic — a great increase in the number of people who are interested in the supernatural.

Many scholars have tried to explain why magic has played such a prominent and persistent part in human affairs. A great deal has been written on the subject by anthropologists, sociologists, theologians, and psychologists. These studies have arrived at many different conclusions and explanations, but, with few exceptions, they all started with the same basic assumption: *Magical beliefs are invalid.* It is generally taken for granted by scientifically-minded people that magic does not work. These studies have sought to discover why so many people believe in something that appears to the investigators to be useless.

Magic and Psychic Phenomena

But are we justified in assuming that magical practices are totally ineffective? Magic as it is practiced today is often associated with so-called "psychic powers" — telepathy, clairvoyance, prophecy, and other "super-normal" abilities of the mind. All of these are included under the general label of *extrasensory perception* (ESP). As we shall see in the next chapter, some scientists today are giving serious consideration to the possibility that ESP powers and phenomena may be real. Because magical practices and psychic phenomena appear to "overlap" in this way, there is a widespread tendency to confuse the two and even to assume that they are the same thing.

But there is a significant difference between these two areas of human experience. Magic usually attempts to make use of powers or influences which are "beyond" man and even beyond the operation of natural laws. Thus, the lives of people are said to be controlled in some inexplicable way by the "vibrations" of the planets; the future may be revealed by the fall of the cards in a deck, or by the lines in a person's hand. In contrast, psychic powers, if they are real, exist *within* the human mind and are human in orgin. They may be part of the general operation of natural laws and, some scientists feel, have nothing to do with any "supernatural" forces.

With this distinction in mind, we shall make two basic assumptions in the present treatment:

▶ It is possible, although not yet fully proven, that human minds are capable of exercising so-called "psychic powers" (ESP). This subject will be treated in some detail in the next chapter.

▶ There are no "magical" forces operating in the universe which control human destinies. Therefore, any system of ideas or set of practices which depends on influencing such forces cannot possibly be true. This is not to say that all natural laws are fully understood. There is much that remains to be learned. But there is no accepted evidence to support the existence of forces beyond or outside of natural laws, and a great deal of opposing scientific thinking that such forces do *not* exist.

In this chapter, we shall seek to understand the psychological significance of magic, particularly as it is accepted and practiced by some young people in the United States today. We shall try particularly to answer this question: If magical practices fail so often and so conspicuously (as they do) to achieve the results claimed, why do many people continue to believe in them so strongly?

Magic in Our Society

The chances are very good that you own a zodiac poster or pendant. You may also have in your possession a paperback edition of the *I Ching* or a deck of tarot cards. For the last few years, our culture has been producing and distributing such articles in large quantities. This acceptance reflects our growing interest in magical beliefs thousands of years old.

To be sure, only a small proportion of the contemporary students or practitioners of magic are aware of its origins or of the significant role it has played in the lives of people of other cultures. Indeed, it is often studied in a most hasty and superficial way. But the important thing, from the standpoint of the psychologist, is the nature of magical beliefs and the emotional needs and tendencies which they reflect.

Two Basic Forms of Magic

There are two basic forms of magic. *Manipulative magic* refers to the use of supernatural forces to produce observable effects in the physical world. This includes such activities as casting spells, levitation (causing heavy objects to float in the air), and alchemy (the conversion of common metals into gold). *Divinatory magic,* or *divination,* is the attempt to gain knowledge about the future through the use of supernatural means.

Manipulative magic and divination are often closely related. For example, both medieval alchemy (manipulative) and astrology (divinatory) relied heavily on the signs of the zodiac, the twelve divisions of the "heavenly year." It is useful, however, to separate these two forms of magic, because at various times greater emphasis has been laid on one than on the other. Among primitive peoples, most magical practices are manipulative; among practitioners in our society, divination clearly has the upper hand.

Magic and Science

Magic is sometimes called a "pseudo-science," or false science. This is not strictly accurate. It is true that in the past some forms of magic have been closely related to branches of science then being developed. For example, the study of the movements of the planets, the

One of the purposes of magical practices is to help people cope with the recurrent problems and emergencies of life. Among these is childbirth. An expectant mother always hopes for an easy delivery and a normal child. She may put her reliance on an expert obstetrician. Or in some societies, she may carry a "fertility doll," such as the one shown here (from the Ashanti tribe of Ghana, West Africa).

stars, and other heavenly bodies was developed by early astrologers, who relied on these movements to predict the future. To a large extent, modern astronomy grew out of astrology, and in some societies the same individual might be both an astrologer and an astronomer. He attempted to predict the future, but he also observed and charted the movements of the heavenly bodies.

In general, however, magic operates in a very different realm from that of science. Science is concerned with the *material world,* and with establishing the laws which describe what processes take place in that world. Magic deals with the *spiritual world,* which is outside the realm of matter and not subject to the laws which control matter. A scientist gathers his facts primarily from observation. The magician relies on "secret knowledge" which he simply assumes to be correct and on certain special skills and techniques which in some inexplicable way can control physical processes in the universe. The magician sees the universe in terms of invisible spirits and immaterial forces which can be manipulated or predicted to some degree (by magical practices) but cannot really be understood and analyzed in a rational way.

When a person claims to be "working magic," he is operating in the realm of the *supernatural,* as opposed to the *natural.* If a man raises a table by lifting it with his hand, the effect is considered natural — fully understandable by the laws of physics. The effect can be described in terms of the weight of the table and the size of the force exerted by the man's hands. But if he raises the table without any direct physical contact, or if he makes it float in midair with no means of support (*levitation*), we say that he is a magician practicing magic. Presumably, there is no "natural" explanation for the effects produced; they are beyond nature or "supernatural." Similarly, it is a basic law of physical science that matter can neither be created nor destroyed (except in the special case of nuclear reactions). Thus, making something "disappear," or making it appear "out of thin air," is also a magical feat.

Magic cannot be described simply as a group of ideas that are wrong, in the way that a scientific theory may be proved wrong. Magic and science are fundamentally different ways of looking at reality. Much of the attraction of magic is due to the fact that it does not have to operate within the confining limits of rationality and science. It offers people a look into a new world, freed from the restrictions of everyday life.

The Black Mass

In the year 1679, shocking news was circulated throughout France which caused a sensation among the aristocracy and indeed among all classes of society. A special court which had been set up by King Louis XIV to investigate cases of poisonings among the nobility began to turn up evidence not only of poisonings, but also of black magic and sorcery. The investigations soon began to center around one woman, a fortune-teller known as La Voisin, who had become wealthy by supplying high-ranking ladies with poisons, charms, and black magical ceremonies, and by arranging for the murder of unwanted children. La Voisin confessed that she had burned in her furnace and buried in her garden over 2500 infants. Some of these children had been sacrificed in ceremonies held in a strange chapel in her house. The chapel was draped in black, with a black altar upon which stood black candles.

La Voisin was burned alive in February, 1680. The evidence also implicated Madame de Montespan, who was none other than the mistress of the King and who had borne him several children. It was revealed that Madame de Montespan had been employing the services of La Voisin for years. Madame de Montespan apparently believed that the magical powers controlled by the "Black Mass" would enable her to keep her position as the King's favorite. During these blood rituals, babies were sacrificed to a pair of demons in order to obtain their cooperation.

The story of Madame de Montespan is the best-documented record of a true Black Mass (or "Witches' Sabbath") which has come down to us in the foggy history of magic. It shows vividly the criminal extremes to which some people will go to achieve their purposes, and it reflects the extraordinary faith in the efficacy of magic. The people engaged in these practices knew that they were exposing themselves to savage punishment if caught, but they were so sure of the great benefits to be obtained from the rites that they apparently did not hesitate to risk their lives.

It is difficult to say what degree the Black Mass celebrated by La Voisin and her collaborators resembles all the similar *"Black Magic"* rituals that have been performed throughout the centuries, and to some extent are still being performed today, even in the United States. However, the reports of what went on at the La Voisin ceremonies do seem to share certain elements with the few other Black Masses of which we have information. These elements include the black candles, the summoning of demons, and the use of the naked body of a woman as an altar. In the Black Mass celebrated by Madame de Montespan, it appears that the prayers were offered to the Christian God, but the reports of most other rituals of this type suggest that Satan (not the Deity) is being worshipped. In short, an effort is made to use magical rites (a travesty of the Christian Mass) in order to enlist the powers of the supreme *evil* force in the universe. This is called *Satanism*.

Witches and Witchcraft

Since ancient times, there have been reports of Satanism or Black Magic carried on by evil women known as *witches*. The great "witch hunts" of the Middle Ages resulted in the deaths of untold thousands of people, most of whom were innocent of anything, except being in most cases old, ugly, friendless, and perhaps somewhat "strange" in their behavior. As late as the end of the 17th century, hundreds of people in Salem, Massachusetts Bay Colony were accused of witch-craft, and 20 were executed. It appears that the accusations which led to these trials and executions were the result of widespread public hysteria, as well as specific personal grudges. In many cases, accused witches confessed fully to their satanic crimes, but such "confessions" usually came only after unspeakable tortures.

On the other hand, it is likely that "witch cults" *have* existed in some times and places. It has been suggested that these cults were actually the remnants of the pagan religions which prevailed in Europe before the coming of Christianity. Christians of the time might have identified these old religions as witchcraft simply because they be-lieved that any non-Christian religious practices were the works of the devil.

The most likely explanation, however, is that devil-worship in the Middle Ages was a combination of old pagan beliefs and the dominant Christian ideas. Since Christian religious leaders were' con-stantly issuing strong warnings about the vast powers of Satan, it is

The Salem witchcraft trials of the 1690's show the extraordinary obsessions which belief in this form of magic can produce. In the scene illustrated in this painting, the "afflicted" or bewitched young girls in the foreground are going into tantrums, while the accused parties are brought before the court.

not too surprising that some people might try to appeal to him for aid in achieving their desires. There is no proof, however, that witchcraft actually existed as an organized religion, with its principles being passed down from one generation to another. A person in the Middle Ages who wanted to practice witchcraft or Satanism probably had to improvise or "make up" most of the rituals to be used, just as a similar person would have to do today.

As suggested above, there is some evidence that witchcraft, as well as forms of Black Magic or Satanism, is being practiced today in the United States and other countries. This, however, represents a rather rare exception. The most common forms of present-day magic center on various types of divination, or foretelling the future. We shall describe below the techniques used for this purpose, including astrology, palmistry, tarot cards, and the *I Ching*. A large body of literature, some of it handed down from ancient times, has grown up in connection with these occult practices.

Mysticism and Magic

All forms of magic, and particularly divination, appear to be closely connected to the doctrine or the frame of mind called *mysticism*. There are many variations of mysticism, but the basic idea on which they all rest is that *the universe is an organic whole or unity*. All the innumerable and diverse entities that make up the universe exist only as parts of this unity. However different and unrelated they may *appear* to be, they are all closely connected, forming part of an all-encompassing plan or "great design." The mystic believes that if he gains an understanding or appreciation of this basic pattern of existence, he can reach total spiritual awareness. This is to be achieved not by intellectual understanding alone but rather by an act of faith and by spiritual purity, or saintliness.

Mysticism has a long history in the Western world and is certainly a recognizable part of the Judaeo-Christian religious tradition. The Western religions, however, are not as exclusively or predominantly mystical in their teachings as are the religions of the East. Within recent years, mystical emphases or points of view borrowed from these Eastern religions have gained considerable acceptance in the United States and Western Europe, particularly among young people.

Divination (Foretelling the Future)

As indicated, the form of magic called *divination* is based essentially on mystical ideas. Since everything is organically related to everything else, we can learn about.one part of the whole by observing something which, on the face of it, has no connection with the former element. Thus, the future events in your life may be revealed by studying the heavenly bodies, or by observing the order in which tarot cards show up after being shuffled.

In magical belief, and also in the basic theory of divination, there is no such thing as an accident or chance. Everything happens for a purpose because it is part of the universal plan. If an event has a purpose, it also has *meaning* for everything else in the universe. Thus we can use the occurrence of these events to make predictions about the future because the future too is part of the "great design."

The major forms of divination are much the same in all parts of the world, regardless of how different the various regions may be in religion and in other aspects of civilization. The reason basically is that in all cases there is the same underlying mystical idea of a "great design" that controls all aspects of reality.

Astrology

Many thousands of years ago, man became interested in the passage of the stars through the heavens and learned how this movement might be correlated with the divisions of the year into various time divisions and into seasons. At first this knowledge was used as a guide to determine when crops should be planted, or when one might expect the return of migrating animals which provided man with food and other necessities. As time went on, however, man began to attach additional significance to the movement of the stars in the heavens. Gradually the conviction developed that the rhythmic passage of the heavenly bodies was closely related to man's destinies on the surface of the earth. There grew up a body of ideas, doctrines, and specific interpretative techniques that is now called *astrology.*

Astrology is one of the oldest forms of divination still in use today. It is impossible to say exactly when and where it began, but there is evidence that it was employed as far back as 4000 B.C. in both China and the ancient Middle Eastern kingdom of Chaldea. In these early times, astrology was not used to make predictions about individuals, unless the individual happened to be a key figure such as a high priest or king. It was reserved, rather, for specially trained functionaries (usually priests) who used it to determine the destinies of nations and to make major decisions, such as those involving war and peace. Today, astrology is most commonly used to cast personal horoscopes. (A *horoscope* is a prediction made on the basis of the rules of astrology.)

According to the principles of astrology, a person's character and fate are decided by the positions of the heavenly bodies at the moment of his birth. The basic unit used in making astrological predictions is the *sun sign,* which refers to the sign of the zodiac the sun occupied at the time that the person was born. Note the accompanying diagram which shows how the path which the sun appears to trace through the heavens (the *ecliptic*) is divided into twelve areas, each designated by a special sign.

As an example of the interpretation of a sun sign, let us take the zodiac symbol *Taurus* (the bull). According to astrology, people born under the sign of Taurus (April 20 to May 20) have the qualities of selflessness and generosity. They enjoy providing entertainment and are often looked up to as leaders and organizers. They possess great energy and rapidly overcome obstacles to obtain their goals and rise to the top. Their magnetic personal qualities quickly draw supporters to their sides.

One book on astrology lists John James Audubon (birthday, April 26, 1785) as a classic example of a Taurus personality. He was born on the island of Haiti, the son of a French naval officer and a Creole woman. He had to cope with many problems, but he succeeded in being trained as an artist. He developed a great interest in birds, and eventually became world-famous for his beautiful and remarkably accurate paintings of birds in their native habitats. Audubon's whole career, the astrologer would say, reflects the drive, the determination to excel, and the refusal to accept conventional standards that mark people born under the sign of Taurus.

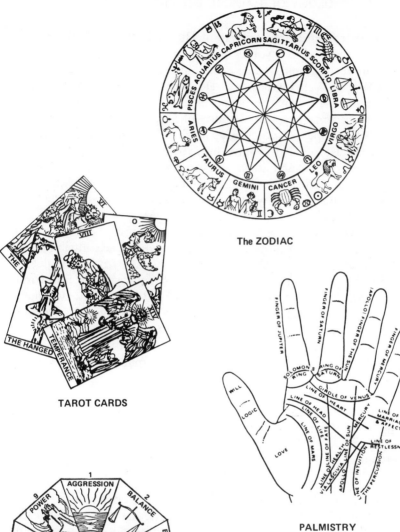

The ZODIAC

TAROT CARDS

PALMISTRY

NUMEROLOGY

I CHING HEXAGRAMS
The eight basic figures
(trigrams) shown here are
combined in pairs to form
64 hexagrams.

Another Taurus figure is Adolf Hitler, born on April 29, 1889. Hitler, too, planned as a young man to become an artist, but he failed to gain any recognition, and he turned his formidable talents to politics in post-World War I Germany. He founded the National Socialist (Nazi) Party. Although he began in utter poverty and obscurity, he eventually became absolute dictator of Germany and the conqueror of much of Europe. His career was marked by fanaticism, cruelty, and ruthlessness. He seemed to have an extraordinary ability to sway the emotions of people and to inspire unquestioning loyalty among his followers. It is hard, however, to imagine anyone more lacking in the "selflessness and generosity" that are supposed to be characteristic of Taurus individuals.

Can we recognize any common element in the lives of two famous men such as Audubon and Hitler which are attributable to "zodiacal" influences? It would appear that apart from their determination to excel and their refusal to be discouraged by unfavorable circumstances, these two men are about as dissimilar as two human beings could be. And such determination in the face of adversity is certainly not limited to people born under the sign of Taurus.

In general, there seems to be very little objective evidence to support the claim of astrologers that the personalities and the life histories of people are determined by their zodiacal signs. "Successful predictions" by astrologers usually rest on careful selection of the particular facts that will support their claims, and on just as careful ignoring of the facts that do not "fit in."

Tarot Cards

A tarot deck consists of 78 cards, each marked by a picture or symbol. The cards are shuffled and are then laid out in a certain pattern. When this is done in relation to a particular person, the reading of the cards is supposed to reveal information about his personality and about the future course of his life.

The tarot deck is the ancestor of modern playing cards. According to occult tradition, the tarot was invented in ancient Egypt and was later brought to Europe by the Gypsies. Actually, the origin of the tarot is unknown. The earliest reliable reference to the deck dates back only as far as the 14th century in France.

Numerology

Numerology is a technique of reading personality and telling fortunes based on the spiritual significance of numbers. All numbers are said to carry "vibrations," which influence our lives.

For example, *1* is a good number because it represents the unity of all living things in God. In contrast, the number *2,* while possessing the "feminine" qualities of gentleness and diplomacy, also carries implications of deceit and evil because it is the number of Satan, who broke away from God and destroyed the unity of the universe.

The particular numbers that apply to and influence a given individual are usually determined by attaching numerical values to the letters of the alphabet (from 1 to 26). Then the numerical value of all the letters in the person's full name is computed. The number arrived at in this way represents the "character" belonging to the name.

Numerology is said to date back to Pythagoras, the pioneering Greek philosopher and mathematician of the 6th century B.C.

Palmistry

This is a technique of fortune-telling based on a study of the shape of a person's hand and of the lines on the palm of the hand. Egyptian records concerned with palmistry go back thousands of years before the Christian era. Acceptance of palmistry as a method of divination appears to be extremely widespread, even rivaling astrology. It has been practiced in India, China, and Japan, as well as Egypt, and is now popular in the Western world.

There are many conflicting interpretations of the significance of the shape and lines of the hand. Some of the most common interpretations accepted by palmists in the United States today are as follows:

▶ The fleshy part of the palm below the thumb is called the "Mount of Venus." A large "mount," is supposed to reveal a passionate, animal nature. A small or thin Mount of Venus indicates little interest in sex.

▶ The "life-line" is the long line curving around the Mount of Venus. A long, unbroken life-line is supposed to mean a long and happy life. Breaks in this line indicate disasters.

▶ The "head-lines" start on the palm between the thumb and first finger, just above the life-line. If a person's head-line is horizontal, it means that he tends to be practical; if it slopes, he tends to have a more creative and imaginative mind.

▶ The third line across the palm is the "heart-line." There are two kinds of heart-lines — "masculine" and "feminine." The "feminine" type is straight and horizontal, and indicates little interest in sex; the "masculine" type curves upward and supposedly signifies a strong sex drive.

The *I Ching*

One of the most fascinating types of divination in use today comes from ancient China. It is known as the *I Ching* or "Book of Changes." Its earliest origins are obscure, but it was probably written by many different people over a long period of time, prior to the third century B.C. The great Chinese philosopher Confucius is supposed to have contributed to the final text.

The *I Ching* is based largely on the Eastern philosophical concept that everything is in a constant state of change within a basic pattern that remains the same. Within this pattern, there is tension between opposites. This tension sometimes increases to such a degree that opposites change into each other. The *I Ching* reveals what tensions and forces are in play at any given moment.

As with the tarot, all the secrets of life are supposed to be contained within the *I Ching* — to those who know how to read it. The usual method of divination nowadays involves the use of three coins. A numerical value is attached to each possible result of a coin toss, and these numbers are used in a special way to produce a six-line figure called a hexagram. Each line of the hexagram may be broken or solid, and each hexagram has a different meaning — pertaining to the subject's future. The interpretation of each hexagram is derived in part from the fact that according to ancient Chinese lore, the unbroken lines represent the aggressive, masculine, rational forces of the universe; the broken lines, the feminine, passive, and unconscious forces. The first is called the *yang* principle; the second is called the *yin* principle. *Yang* is also associated with light; *yin* with darkness.

Can Magic (Divination) Work?

Anyone who has ever had his fortune read, whether it was by astrology, the tarot, palmistry, or any other form of divination, has probably noticed that much of what was said seemed to be a fairly accurate picture of his personality and of the events in his life. The magic actually appeared to reveal something about him! Many people would say that this is all the "common sense" proof that is needed for one to accept the reality of divination. But is it? There are other explanations for these apparent accuracies, without assuming the existence of any "supernatural" faculties or events.

The key point is that most fortune-telling is carefully cast in vague, generalized terms. Thus the reading can be applied to any number of persons and situations. For example, following are some of the qualities which are supposed to be related to a particular sign of the zodiac. Do you think that most of these characteristics might apply to you? Is there anyone you know to whom they do *not* apply — at least in his own estimation?

▶ You are a person of both thought and action.

▶ Your thoughts and beliefs are revealed by your conduct.

▶ You are always searching for new knowledge.

▶ You are tolerant of others.

▶ You like to travel.

▶ You are a good talker.

Almost anyone might agree that he possesses some (or all) of these qualities. In fact, most of us would probably be somewhat flattered to be told that we are "tolerant," that we are "always searching for new knowledge," and that we combine "thought and action." But these qualities are specifically assigned to people born under the sign of *Gemini* (the twins), between May 21 and June 20. The fortune-teller in this case is not likely to be told by the "subject" that he has gone wrong.

In short the vagueness of divinations enables them to be applied to the personality and life of almost anyone. The individual himself fills in the details to round out the picture. Sometimes people will actually change their view or interpretation of things that have happened to them so that they will fit in more accurately with the reading. This is done quite unconsciously. For example, if a girl is told that a sensitive, imaginative man will influence her life, she may start attributing poetic qualities to the football hero she has been dating, even though she never before thought of him as being particularly sensitive or imaginative.

Another factor that works in favor of acceptance of magic is the tendency of people to pay special attention to the parts of the reading that seem accurate and to disregard the parts that seem wide of the mark. For example, a person born under the sign of *Gemini* might think of himself as possessing all the qualities listed above, except for the one about being a good talker. He might well be inclined, however, simply to ignore that particular point and to conclude that the astrological description of a typical Gemini fits him remarkably well.

On the other hand, divinatory methods may under certain conditions actually bring out certain elements of truth that the subject was not fully aware of before. For example, if a person conducting a reading of tarot cards has a perceptive, sensitive mind, the symbols on the cards may serve as a means of organizing his thoughts about the subject. In other words, the symbols may "cue" a train of ideas and responses which, taken together with what he already knows about the subject, enable him to arrive at some accurate and revealing conclusions. It may be the unconscious mind, rather than the consciousness, which responds to these symbols. Just as a psychoanalyst uses word associations and responses to Rorschach tests ("ink blot" tests) to bring out material buried in his patient's unconscious, the tarot cards may bring to light ideas and information of which the reader was not consciously aware. These ideas may have some value in widening the individual's awareness of the conditions of his life.

The late Carl Jung (pages 114-117) argued that such divinatory practices as the *I Ching* offer valuable methods for furthering self-awareness. In interpreting the answer which the *I Ching* yields in a particular case, the subject must try to fit it into his own experiences and to make it apply to his own situation. This process is highly subjective, and from the purely rational point of view, invalidates the claim that the *I Ching* is an accurate way of revealing the future. But Jung suggested that the *I Ching* may be valid precisely *because* the process of interpretation is so subjective — it allows the user to become aware of things in his unconscious which he had previously never thought about. In this sense, the *I Ching* is doing exactly what it is supposed to do — reveal hidden knowledge.

There is another possibility which could account for the surprisingly accurate findings that sometimes result from divination — the diviner may conceivably possess *psychic powers*. Instead of learning about the future from the tarot cards, for example, he may be "picking up" information directly through the use of his psychic ability to perceive things about which he has no direct knowledge, and even things which have not yet happened. (We shall explore this type of possibility in the next chapter.)

Why Is Magic Popular Today?

In times of profound social stress and change, many of the traditional values and ideas of a society tend to lose their significance. The United States is going through just such a period of change at the present time. Many of the "eternal verities" which have sustained Americans throughout the nation's history are being called into question. For example, one traditional American belief is that anyone who is willing to work hard and to observe the "rules of the game" will be able to get ahead — to "make it to the top." Today, many young people are not at all sure that this is so, and (even more significantly) they are questioning whether it is worthwhile trying to get to the "top" in the first place.

The advanced technology developed in this country has made possible the highest standard of living in the world. But it has also been the source of a great many problems — to mention just a few: jobs which involve a deadening, dehumanizing routine; environmental pollution; concentration of population in huge urban centers, with all the attendant difficulties of transportation, housing, crime, etc. Besides, tens of millions of Americans do not share the benefits of our great national productivity, for they live under conditions which the government itself has characterized as "poverty." Accordingly, many Americans are skeptical of the value of an advanced technology, and of a society which is organized largely to further such a technology.

Again, our society is highly mobile — families and individuals are constantly moving from place to place. They never stay in any one place long enough to "put down roots." This, it is said, has contributed to a widespread sense of loneliness and alienation among many Americans. They have left behind their pasts and feel "lonely and afraid in a world they never made."

Our society is so complex that it often seems difficult to "make any sense of it." People understand only the fragments of experience with which they are directly concerned. For example, if a man has a job in a huge factory, he knows what is being done in his own department, but he may have only a vague idea of how this function contributes to the operation of the factory as a whole — to say nothing of how the factory fits into the needs of the community and of the entire nation. People in such a situation are likely to feel small and insignificant. They do not have a strong conviction that their lives and their work mean very much in terms of society as an overall entity.

The problems which have taken shape in our society in recent years are sometimes so overwhelming that they seem to defy solution. In particular, they may make the efforts and the contributions of the individual appear to be utterly futile. What can one person do, for example, about war, racism, pollution, crime, urban blight, and overpopulation? In the face of such massive problems, and without a strong set of traditional values to provide firm guidelines, many people feel lost and helpless.

The people in our society who usually feel these problems most deeply are the young. A boy or girl growing up in the United States sooner or later is faced with a crucial decision. What is he going to do with his life in a society which is so confusing and complex that he doesn't understand it and cannot relate to it? A satisfactory answer is not easily arrived at. Young people often have a sense that they are just "drifting," with no goals to strive for and no firm principles to guide them. This, in highly general terms, is the reason for the sense of

alienation from the larger society that characterizes the youth culture today. (We shall consider this further in Chapters 13 and 14.)

The charge is made that in pursuit of material progress, mastery of nature, and accumulation of wealth, Western society has largely ignored *spiritual values*. These are the values that relate to man's "inner life," to his relationship to the world as a whole, to his conviction that both he and the world he lives in have some ultimate meaning. Many young people today are devoting themselves to a search for spiritual values. And there is reason to think that it is this search which leads them, in some cases at least, to turn to a cultivation of the ancient forms of magic.

It is sometimes said that the resort to magic by the younger generation represents a form of "rebellion" against established society. This theory, however, does not tell us very much about why young people turn to *magic* in particular, as opposed to other forms of rebellion. Besides, there is the undeniable fact that some forms of magic, such as astrology, are very popular among older people, including highly "respectable" members of the middle class. The "rebellion" explanation, therefore, would appear to have little value.

At a time when there is so much uncertainty about the future, what could be more appealing than something which offers to reveal the future to us, to lay it open so that we can understand where we are headed? This is exactly what divination claims to offer. By giving people a way of anticipating what tomorrow will bring, magic provides a kind of emotional security. This can be extremely comforting in a world that is plagued with crucial uncertainties — even the uncertainty of whether man can survive in the face of environmental pollution and nuclear war.

Magic is a ritual and, like all rituals, it serves as a means of declaring and reaffirming one's beliefs. This is why people continue to use magical practices, no matter how many "proofs" are given that such practices do not really "work." Perhaps they do not "work" on an objective, rational level, but they may be effective on another level. For some, magic is above all a means of expressing *hope in the future.*

A person practicing "light" magic, such as fortune-telling, is in effect testifying that he needs to regard the world as having a meaningful pattern, and that he himself is meaningful as a part of that pattern. He is not just a speck of matter in an infinite universe subject only to random physical laws. If that were the case, then any attempt to foretell the future of an individual human being, or of a group of human beings, would be the height of futility.

There is evidence, therefore, that some types of magic *do* help people to cope with the stresses created by modern life. Can we judge, on this basis, whether it is "good" or "bad" to use magical practices? From the purely psychological point of view, we might say that magic is "good" when employed as a source of hope, reassurance, and meaning; it is "bad" when it serves as an escape from the real world and an excuse for not assuming personal responsibility to try to solve life problems. The judgment must be made by each individual for himself.

It should be added, however, that people who delve deeply into what we have called "Black Magic" are exposing themselves to serious dangers. This form of magic involves attempts to manipulate the unconscious elements of the mind. Any exploration of the unconscious may cause severe psychological harm unless it is undertaken in a serious, conscientious way, probably under the direction of a trained psychotherapist. A dabbler in the "black arts" may come under the influence of a self-styled "witch" or "sorcerer," who will take sadistic satisfaction in implanting suggestions in the unconscious, and in creating a relationship of dependence based on fear.

Hallucinogenic drugs (such as belladonna — also known as "deadly nightshade" — and jimson weed) have been used for centuries in ceremonies connected with witchcraft and devil worship. These are dangerous drugs; in fact, overdoses have been known in some cases to be fatal. They are similar in some ways to the hallucinogenic drug LSD (page 247). Indeed, belladonna is sometimes mixed with illicit, low-grade LSD to "spice it up." A person under the influence of an hallucinogenic drug, such as belladonna, is extremely open to suggestion. Taking part in Black Magic practices while in such

"You see, Reggie, I've evolved. You're still in yang-yin macrobiotic, and I'm in psychokinesis."

a condition of hypersuggestibility may have destructive psychological effects that cannot even be anticipated. Whatever may be said for the "harmlessness" of some forms of magic, combining these practices with the use of drugs is dangerous and should be strictly avoided.

THINGS TO DISCUSS :: THINGS TO DO :: THINGS TO READ

1. A house is struck by lightning, and considerable damage is done. How might this be explained according to (*a*) the doctrines of magic, (*b*) the ideas of science? What basis is there for believing that one explanation is more valid than the other? What action might be recommended by the magician and by the scientist to prevent a recurrence of the event?

2. It has been said that the more comprehensive and accurate a tradition of magic becomes, the more it tends to evolve into a science. Give an historical example of this process. Is the reverse also possible — that is, may a science take on some of the aspects of magic? Explain.

3. Psychologists have speculated that for some people the practice of magic is a substitute for the ability to give and feel love. In substantiation of this idea, it is pointed out that in typical systems of magic, love plays no part as a motivational force, or the ideas about love are badly distorted. What is your feeling about this? Can you see any reason why it is difficult to reconcile faith in magic with healthy love relationships? What psychological condition does this bring to mind?

4. Tie a ring to a piece of thread at least 1 foot long. With one hand, hold the thread so that the ring is hanging motionless above the floor. While trying to hold the thread as still as possible, begin to concentrate on causing the ring to move back and forth. Speaking aloud, "command" the ring to move. It is quite likely that the ring will now begin swinging, even though you have no sensation that you are causing this by moving your hand holding the thread.

In this case you are consciously suggesting that the ring is to move in a certain way. Do you think it is possible for *unconscious* commands to operate in the same way, so that you cause a physical body to move, even though you are not consciously willing yourself to do so? Could this relate to the way a ouija board works? Devise an experiment with a ouija board.

5. Obtain a paperback copy of the *I Ching*. Read the directions carefully. Then submit a question, and obtain the answer in accordance with these directions. What is your impression of the answer? Does it have any value for you? Do you think there may be more to the *I Ching* than can be explained by chance or from a "psychological" viewpoint?

6. Here's a test you can try — whether you are pro-astrology, against it, or neutral. Select, at random, an astrology book that provides fairly detailed passages interpreting various zodiacal signs. Find someone who knows little about astrology but is curious about it — and ask him for his sign (as indicated by his date of birth). Then tell him you are reading him the interpretation for his sign — but actually read him the interpretation for a different sign, substituting words here and there as may be necessary to avoid giving away the game. (Tell him of your subterfuge afterwards.) During the reading, note his reactions. Do many suggestions strike a sympathetic or responsive chord? Does he seem at least partly convinced? Ask him immediately afterward, "Would you say that this was pretty close to the mark?" What conclusions do you draw from the experiment?

READINGS

Diary of a Witch by Sybil Leek (Prentice-Hall, 1968). This is a highly readable, entertaining autobiography of a self-professed witch, a practicer of the "Old Religion" of the Celts and an adept at "white magic." Her account is so straightforward, interesting and intelligent, that it is not so easy to dismiss her fantastic claims as "crazy."

The Autobiography of a Yogi, by Paramahansa Yogananda (Published by Self-Realization Fellowship, 1946). This is a splendidly readable book which tells some fantastic tales of its own in the context of mystical development and revelation. There are striking parallels with Sybil Leek's book.

The Teachings of Don Juan: A Yaqui Way of Knowledge, by Carlos Castaneda (University of California Press, 1968). This is a two-part book. The first part is a first-person account of a young South American anthropologist who apprenticed himself to an Indian *brujo* (magician) and "man of knowledge." It tells remarkable tales of experiences induced with and without the help of "Mescalito" (a spiritual "ally" who manifests himself when raw mescaline in the form of peyote is correctly consumed). The second part of the book is a scholarly interpretation of the effects of the hallucinogenic properties of mescaline and other drugs used in Mexico.

Parapsychology 11

The Frontiers of the Mind

●●●●●●●●●●●●●●●●●●●●●●●●●●●●

". . . if you see someone giving a performance of ESP on stage or on television, you can be pretty sure it's not on the level."

— J. B. RHINE

What Is Parapsychology?

Magic involves the use of individual will-power and other special powers to foresee the future or to bring about changes which are normally beyond human control. In the traditional practice of magic, this was often done by seeking aid from "spirits" and "demons" whose powers were thought to be greater than those of human beings. However, many people who believe in magic today largely ignore the idea of "invisible spirits" in favor of the claim that the human mind itself possesses powers which enable it to see into the future, or to read the thoughts of another person, or to cause something to happen without using the normal means of cause and effect. Magic has become involved with a belief in the "paranormal" or "supernormal" powers of the mind. The study of these powers is known as *parapsychology.*

There is, however, another aspect to this picture. While believers in magic have been attempting to give parapsychology a central position in magical theory, a small number of psychologists have been trying to remove parapsychology from the realm of magic, so that it can be studied *scientifically,* in the laboratory and in the processes of everyday life.

Researchers in parapsychology, in short, have been looking for objective evidence that the human mind *does possess paranormal*

216

powers. The phenomena in which they are interested fall into two major classes.

The first is *extrasensory perception,* commonly known as ESP. ESP is the ability to receive information from the outside world without the use of any of the known senses. In other words, sight, hearing, touch, smell, and taste are not involved. Three main types of ESP are recognized:

▶ *Telepathy* — "Mind reading"; awareness of what is going on in the mind of another person without use of any of the usual means of communication.

▶ *Clairvoyance* — Awareness of objects or events which can neither be apprehended by any of the individual's senses, nor "picked up" from the mind of another person by means of telepathy.

▶ *Precognition* — Awareness of events which have not yet happened; divination or prophecy.

The second main division of parapsychology is *telekinesis,* or *psychokinesis,* which is defined as the ability to move objects by the power of thought alone. Levitation and controlling the roll of dice are examples of telekinesis.

Communication with the Dead

Parapsychology has also been concerned with the question of whether or not it is possible to communicate with the dead. In the early period of the scientific study of parapsychology, at the end of the 19th century and at the beginning of the 20th century, a major part of the research in this area was concerned with *survival.* In terms of parapsychology, this means the continued existence of an individual's personality after the death of his body. Such research was carried on with the use of *mediums,* people who were supposedly able (by means of certain inborn faculties and special training) to receive "messages" from the dead.

However, scientific investigation into such survival after death has ceased almost completely within the last 50 years. For one thing, there are relatively few people today who even claim to have the special "sensitivity" needed to serve as mediums. Moreover, experience has shown that it is all but impossible to subject the claims of mediums and their believers to scientific testing. For example, suppose a medium claims to have acquired some information by receiving it from a "departed soul." This cannot be given any credence, from a scientific point of view, unless *it can be shown beyond any possible doubt that*

"Communication with the dead" has a long history of fraud and self-deception. At this *séance,* held in 1874, a medium supposedly brought about the materialization of the "spirit body" of a girl dead for two centuries.

the information in question could not have been obtained by means of normal communication. Without such proof the credibility of the medium is open to question, and there is no basis for a serious scientific investigation.

The same principle applies to the other types of parapsychological phenomena mentioned above. As we shall see later, scientific research in this area depends on establishing the fact that there is no possible way in which the results of the experiments could have been obtained by normal means.

Magic and Science in Relation to ESP

Scientists do continue to devote attention to the other phenomena mentioned (telepathy, clairvoyance, precognition, and telekinesis). Such phenomena have been and are being investigated in parapsychology laboratories in many parts of the world.

It should be noted that all these phenomena (as well as survival after death) are integral parts of magic as it is practiced today in the United States and elsewhere. The practitioners of magic simply take it for granted that the human mind possesses these faculties, and that almost anyone with the right training or indoctrination can use them. Scientists, in contrast, regard the existence of ESP as open to question. They insist that a body of objective, detailed, authentic evidence must be built up before the existence of such phenomena can be conceded, and before their character and limitations can be accurately described.

Suppose that science is able to establish eventually that the human mind is sometimes capable of exercising extrasensory perception. It must be borne in mind that this would *not* prove the validity of various forms of magic. Thus, if experiments were to show that some individuals possess the faculty of precognition, this would not by any means suggest that particular magical practices which seek to predict the future (such as astrology and the tarot) actually work. Even if some form of precognition does exist as a faculty of the human mind, what reason is there to suppose that it depends on the positions of the planets in their orbits, or on the order of the cards in a certain deck?

Is This a Genuine Case of ESP?

On occasion, you have probably heard someone tell of an experience which he thought showed the existence of some parapsychological phenomenon. You may even have had such an experience yourself.

Such experiences can be very convincing to the people who undergo them. And they may be perfectly honest and sincere in claiming that it is impossible to offer any "natural" explanation for what has happened. Nonetheless, in the great majority of cases, outsiders are justified in being skeptical because it can be shown that the "evidence" offered does not meet the requirements of scientific proof. There are other ways of explaining what has happened than the theory that a parapsychological phenomenon has taken place. Scientists in general believe that the validity of these phenomena must be established, if at all, in the laboratory, under carefully controlled conditions.

On the other hand, it cannot be denied that some reports of paranormal events which occur "spontaneously" in everyday life have been attested to by reputable persons and cannot be easily dismissed. A typical case of this type was reported in 1954 by a psychiatrist named Jan Ehrenwald.

One day, during an analytic session in his office, a woman patient told Dr. Ehrenwald of a dream she had had recently. In the dream the woman was at her dressmaker, who told her that she had a second-floor apartment which she wished to rent. The woman looked at the apartment, which she described as follows:*

---

* This incident, including the description quoted, is taken from *New Dimensions of Deep Analysis,* by Jan Ehrenwald (Allen and Unwin Ltd., London and Grune and Stratton, New York, 1958).

It consisted of a beautiful long, well-shaped living room, spacious, with a high ceiling. It opened out to a nice open terrace where the sun shone. The terrace stretched along the whole building across the front . . . some 50 feet or so. It had a brick wall, and the floor was made of planks with cracks in between. There was not much furniture in the room. . . . There was no carpet, only Oriental rugs, a big one in the middle with figures like the one you have here in your office. There were smaller rugs at either end. . . . There were also a few mahogany chairs and an open fireplace. A French door and two French windows opened to the terrace. A dingy little hall led into the bedroom and into the bathroom. I thought this would be the apartment I would like to live in, except that it did not have a maid's room and no extra bathroom.

This dream on the face of it does not seem too significant, but Dr. Ehrenwald found it very curious indeed. A week before the interview in question, he had moved into a new apartment, located on the second floor of a large building in a New York suburb. The apartment had a spacious living room from which a French door and two French windows opened onto a terrace. The terrace stretched along the whole front of the building, but only about 50 feet of it belonged to his apartment. It was surrounded by a brick wall. The living room was sparsely furnished, with no carpeting, but the floor was partly covered by one large and two smaller Oriental rugs. A small hall led to the bedroom and bathroom. Unlike the patient's description, however, there were no mahogany chairs in the living room, and no fireplace. (It turned out that those items reminded the patient of the house she had lived in as a child.) When Dr. Ehrenwald asked his patient to draw a plan of the apartment in her dream, she produced a picture almost identical to the plan for his own apartment.

The woman, according to Dr. Ehrenwald, did not know where he lived, was unaware that he had recently moved into a new apartment, and had no way of knowing what his apartment looked like.

How are we to interpret this strange case? If it is to be explained on a purely "natural" basis, we must accept one of the following:

▶ The psychiatrist was either lying about the whole incident, or was suffering from a delusion, or for some other reason confused and misrepresented the facts.

or

▶ The woman patient somehow became familiar with the appearance of the doctor's apartment, and she was lying when she said that she had never seen it and knew nothing about it.

or

▶ The similarity between the actual apartment and the apartment which the woman reported she had seen in her dream was a coincidence.

The one remaining possibility is that the patient had unconsciously employed ESP — either telepathy, or clairvoyance, or both — to become familiar with the appearance of her analyst's apartment, and that this knowledge had "come out" in her dream.

The explanation which a given person accepts as being most probable will depend largely on his own background of beliefs and experience. Someone who is hostile to the whole idea of the existence of ESP will either have to assume a "coincidence" (which seems an extremely remote possibility), or will have to question the reliability of the psychiatrist or his patient. In this connection, it should be pointed out that a man who holds a license to practice psychiatry is not necessarily honest or free from delusions. Also it is a familiar fact that a person undergoing psychoanalysis is sometimes extremely anxious to relate personally to the analyst, and may go to a great deal of trouble to "make an impression." In this case, Dr. Ehrenwald indicated that the woman patient had transferred onto him much of her strong attachment to her father. It is possible that she deliberately sought information about the analyst's new home so that she could, in a sense, "share" it with him — just as during her childhood she had shared with her father the house with the fireplace and the mahogany chairs.

But this is no more than a theory, and it does not rule out the possibility that there *is* no "natural" explanation, and that we must accept the existence of ESP. The most basic assumption of science is that there is a rational explanation for everything that occurs in the world around us. So far, the main body of qualified scientific authorities are not willing to accept ESP as a "rational explanation" for observed events. But the case described above does raise an important question: Is there a point at which "normal" explanations for possible paranormal events have to be made so complex and elaborate that they become more improbable than the existence of ESP? Many people might feel that this characterization would apply to the theory that the woman patient in some way spied on the analyst's home so that she might have the satisfaction of describing it to him later.

Deception and Self-Deception

Many observers are hostile to the claims made for ESP because there has been a great deal of deliberate deception connected with this type of experience. Much of this is relatively harmless — perhaps in the form of professional entertainment — but in some cases there have been calculated efforts to exploit or defraud.

More important is the fact that people in general have a great capacity for *deceiving themselves* as to what has actually happened. This is particularly true in an emotionally charged situation, such as the death of a loved one.

For example, a man may have an aged mother living in another city, to whom he is very much devoted. He thinks of her quite often. He cannot be unaware that, with the advance of the years, her life expectancy is not very great. One day he learns that she has just died. "I was thinking of her only a few minutes ago," the man says to himself, "and I was worried that she might not be well!" Under such circumstances, it is probably easy for him to convince himself that he had a full-fledged premonition ("precognition") of her death. But how many times has he thought of her in the past *without* the simultaneous occurrence of her death?

Also, it must be understood that a great many instances of what may appear to be intuitive or extrasensory knowledge is actually based on experience and on physical observation. For example, a high school student may ask his father for permission to use the family car. When the father refuses, the boy says, "I knew he was going to say no. I could read his mind!" But there is really no "mind-reading" (telepathy) involved. In the first place, the boy might well be able to guess in advance, on the basis of past experience, that his father would not want him to use the car. Second, even before the father said anything, the boy could very probably observe certain mannerisms (perhaps a tightening of the mouth, a frown, a clearing of the throat) which he had learned to associate with disapproval. The father was probably unconscious of these actions, but they "spoke" to the son quite as loudly as words.

In evaluating claims of telepathy, clairvoyance, and other forms of ESP, we should make careful allowance for the possibility of such instances of self-deception. To be of any value in supporting the idea of paranormal phenomena, an ESP experience must be fairly precise and possess *many* points in common with the event to which it is supposed to be related. It must also be clearly demonstrated that knowledge of the event could not have been gained by "natural" means. Most experiences which are claimed to be paranormal do not meet these standards. In the laboratory, however, scientific researchers have based the study of parapsychology on the principle that these standards must be rigorously maintained.

Parapsychology in the Laboratory

One of the founders of the scientific approach to parapsychology is Dr. J. B. Rhine, who began research in ESP at Duke University in 1927. Many of his experiments were concerned with investigating clairvoyance. The tests involved the use of two-person teams. The "sender" shuffled and dealt a specially prepared deck of cards. The "receiver," who was positioned so that he was not able to see the cards, tried to guess which card was being dealt at any given time.

Matching test of clairvoyant ESP. The girl (by pointing) guesses which of the five key cards will match the top card in the deck held face-down by the tester behind the screen.

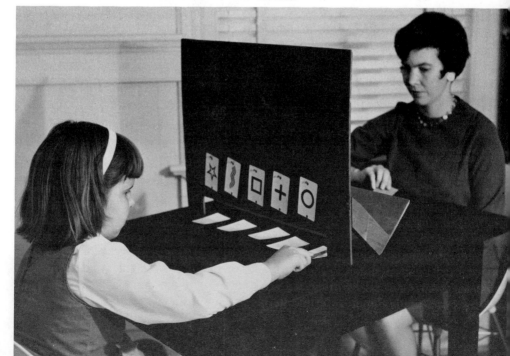

The best known of these tests, carried out in 1933-34, used as the receiver a student named Hubert Pearce. In this experiment, Pearce and the sender sat in different buildings while the test was being conducted. The sender did not even look at the cards that he was dealing; he simply laid them face-down on a table in front of him. Pearce tried to guess the cards. Over a large number of trials, he had a much higher percentage of correct guesses than could possibly be expected or accounted for by mere "chance" — that is, by the operation of the statistical laws of probability.

Gertrude Schmiedler, a psychologist at Harvard University, conducted somewhat similar experiments. One hypothesis which she tested is that persons who believe in the possibility of ESP will do better on a mental telepathy test than those who flatly reject it. She divided her subjects into two groups — those who accepted ESP, and those who did not. Members of both groups were asked to guess the order of cards in a deck being dealt out in another room 40 feet away. Those who believed that ESP is possible scored considerably higher than would have been predicted by the laws of probability; those who rejected ESP did not score higher than would be expected.

Margaret Anderson and Rhea White, psychologists at Duke University, divided a group of school children into two sub-groups, on the basis of whether they expressed positive or negative feelings toward a certain teacher. In a telepathy experiment, this teacher acted as a "sender," and each child acted as a "receiver." The results indicated that those students who had favorable feelings toward the teacher were able to score a significantly higher number of correct guesses than those students who had negative feelings. The highest scores were achieved in the cases where the student and teacher had positive feelings toward each other.

Experiments run during World War II by the British researchers S. G. Soal and F. Bateman sought to test the precognition ability of a man named Shackleton. Instead of being asked to guess which card the sender was looking at, Shackleton was asked to guess which card the sender would *look at next*. Again, the results were considerably higher than would be expected on the basis of probability.

Criticism of Parapsychology Experiments

The experiments described above are among the best known which have been conducted in the field of parapsychology in recent years. The results indicated have had the effect of creating a more open-minded attitude toward parapsychology among some scientists. Many other scientists, however, remain unconvinced and critical.

One line of criticism is that the parapsychology experiments, by and large, have used methods which are so lax and "sloppy" that they do not rule out the possibility that the information in question was transmitted in ways other than by ESP. And in fact there is some evidence for the conclusion that, as the researchers have tightened the controls on their experiments, the ESP test scores (that is, the deviations from what would be expected on the basis of probability) have tended to decline.

The statistical methods used to interpret the results of the experiments have also been questioned. The Rhine experiments at Duke have been criticized on this level, although the American Institute of Mathematical Statistics has testified that his conclusions cannot be invalidated on purely mathematical grounds. But some other researchers have been accused of using statistical methods that are highly questionable to make their findings look impressive.

The major reason that many psychologists are reluctant to accept the existence of ESP and telekinesis is that the *results of the experiments are not "repeatable."* In traditional scientific research, the validity of a finding is dependent on whether other scientists can repeat the experiment and get essentially the same results. In parapsychological research, however, attempts to repeat an apparently successful experiment have often yielded disappointing results. Related to this is the problem that paranormal phenomena seem to be inconsistent. Some experiment volunteers appear to be skilled in both clairvoyance and telepathy; others are skilled only in one of these areas; and still others possess no skills in direct telepathy or clairvoyance but seem to be adept at precognition. Others show different skills (or varying levels of skills) at different times. Critics assert that such fluctuations and inconsistencies make it impossible to assemble data which have the precision and the definiteness needed for conclusions of scientific validity.

Supporters of parapsychology answer that we must simply recognize the fact that ESP skills vary widely from one individual to another, and that even the performance of a given individual may be affected by circumstances (such as the relationship between "sender" and "receiver" in card-guessing experiments). This is why it is so difficult to repeat experiments with different subjects, and at different times and places, and obtain substantially similar results. All that this proves, it is argued, is that we still have a great deal to learn about ESP — *not* that the phenomena do not exist.

Until more work is done in this field, it is advisable to withhold final judgments. In short the most sensible attitude would appear to be to concede that ESP may be a possibility while recognizing that it has not yet been proved beyond any reasonable doubt.

The Nature of the Paranormal

It should be emphasized that even those scientists who are most confident of the existence of ESP phenomena do not regard them as supernatural. These phenomena may be "mysterious," in the sense that we do not now fully understand them, but the premise is that they are not beyond rational understanding and that they do not violate the laws of nature. This attitude obviously is very different from the premises of magic.

In the past, scientists have observed many natural phenomena which they could not understand or account for *at the time*. Later, when more information had been gathered, and a more satisfactory theoretical framework had been developed, the phenomena were explained in purely scientific terms. This may eventually prove to be true of some types of so-called "psychic phenomena."

One possible element of apparently "paranormal" powers is *subliminal perception*. Subliminal perception is the *perception of sense data at a level below that of conscious awareness*. There is nothing mysterious or paranormal about subliminal perception; psychologists have studied it intensively in the laboratory. Subliminal sense data seem to be transmitted to lower levels of the mind without passing through the consciousness. For example, a person can be conditioned to expect an electric shock every time he sees a certain word. The word can then be flashed on a screen so faintly that the individual is not consciously aware that it is there. At the same time, however, his skin may respond as if it were preparing for an electric shock. *He has actually perceived the word and reacted to it without being consciously aware of it.*

The important point is that a person's body and mind can respond to external stimuli which are below the threshold of conscious recognition. There is good reason to believe that unconscious mechanisms pick up such stimuli and reorganize them for their own use. Dreams often reflect events or images of the past day or days which the individual was not even conscious of experiencing. As we noted earlier, in the chapter on magic, the unconscious can organize data in ways unknown to the conscious.

An Example of Subliminal Perception — Does it Explain ESP?

It is possible that an individual may have an experience which he is sure involves ESP, but which is actually due to the fact that

information acquired through subliminal perception has emerged into consciousness. For example, imagine a man who is driving home from work one night with his mind completely absorbed with some business problems. Later that night, his son borrows the car. The father goes to bed and wakes up from a nightmare in which his son was in a car accident. In the dream the son had tried to stop the car and the brakes had failed. Suddenly the telephone rings. It is the police, informing him that his son has been involved in an accident. Later it is revealed that the accident was a result of brake failure.

The father in this story might very well imagine that he has had an ESP experience. After all, he had no reason for believing that his son would be in an accident. But it is possible that the car brakes have been faulty for some time, and that they were not performing properly when the father drove home from work that night. However, he was not aware of this because he was so wrapped up in his business troubles. But the fact that the brakes were faulty did register *unconsciously,* and the data relating to this fact were then organized and presented in the form of a dream. The dream simply reflected the result which might logically be expected if someone were to drive a car with bad brakes. There is no need to use ESP to account for this experience.

There may also be subliminal stimuli which the consciousness would not recognize even if it were aware of them. Some people may be more open to receive such stimuli than others. There are fairly reliable reports of people who are able to recognize the colors of objects by touching them with their fingertips. Visual images are usually received through the eyes, but there are also light-sensitive cells scattered throughout the body. Some people are apparently able to make use of the stimuli which reaches these cells. It is possible that some ESP "flashes" represent those moments at which unknown types of subliminal stimuli are suddenly put to intelligent use.

Of course this is only speculation, and it is not meant to imply that all ESP experiences can be explained in terms of subliminal perception. There is a possibility, however, that it may eventually be shown that subliminal perception can account for a large number of "ESP-type" experiences.

Brain Electricity — An Attempt to Explain ESP

There have been some attempts to provide a scientific basis for "true" ESP — that is, perception which does not involve even subliminal use of the known sense organs. One possible approach is based on the well-known fact that the brain produces electricity. When electrodes are attached to the head in a certain way, various frequencies of brain waves are recorded. One such frequency is the "alpha rhythm," which is from 8 to 12 cycles per second. Some experimental psychologists have been able to train subjects to control their alpha rhythms so that they can produce them voluntarily. Although these people do not actually know how they control the rhythms, they are aware of the difference in feeling between an alpha and non-alpha state. People describe themselves as being tranquil, calm, and alert when they are in the alpha state.

This voluntary control of brain electricity bears a striking resemblance to certain phenomena connected with meditation (pages 234-239). Thus, researchers have asked masters of the Yoga and Zen disciplines to submit to electrode experiments. It was found that Zen meditators could learn control of their alpha rhythms much more quickly than ordinary subjects, and that mystics with 20 or more years of experience could produce slow alpha waves, and even slower theta waves. (A theta wave has a rhythm of 5 to 7 cycles per second.)

Some people can also produce alpha waves simply by closing their eyes. T. D. Duane and T. Behrendt, opthalmologists at the Jefferson Medical College in St. Louis, Mo., used this fact to study a possible form of telepathy between identical twins. The investigators recorded the brain waves of both members of a pair of identical twins when only one twin actually closed his eyes. In two out of the fifteen pairs studied, they found that whenever one twin closed his eyes, both of them would generate alpha rhythms, even though they were in separate rooms and neither had any idea of what the other was doing. This happened every time one of the twins closed his eyes. This raises the possibility that telepathy may be the result of some type of "connection" between the brain waves of two individuals.

It is much too early, of course, to draw up any elaborate conclusions from these limited data, but such experiments do illustrate the kind of approach which may provide scientific explanations for various "supernatural," "mystical," and "occult" phenomena. The field of parapsychology raises some very challenging questions about the nature of the human mind. It may be a long time before these questions can be adequately answered. Until then, it is good to remember that *all* psychology is an exploration of the unknown territories within our minds, and that in parapsychology, as in other areas of study, these territories continue to be fertile ground for disciplined research, logical thinking, and fascinating speculation.

THINGS TO DISCUSS :: THINGS TO DO :: THINGS TO READ

1. It has been pointed out that psychic phenomena are most often reported in connection with an urgent emotion or feeling — usually distress of some kind. It has also been noted that psychic perception is rarely strictly verbal, but is more likely to be in the form of images. Considering that the unconscious is urgency-oriented and is able to express itself in vivid images, why might telepathy possibly operate better in an unconscious, or at least non-verbal, manner? This is strictly a "fun question," so feel free to speculate.

2. One form of ESP which scientists generally reject is *telekinesis* — that is, using the force of the mind alone to cause a material object to move. If this were possible, it is said, it would violate the law of conservation of energy. However, it is also argued that this law is violated when a person says to himself, "I *will* stand up," and actually does so. He is causing a material object — his body — to move by exerting the will, or force of an intangible phenomenon called "the mind." Do you feel that the effects of the "will" on the body are an example of telekinesis? Is there any way that this can be reconciled with the law of conservation of energy?

3. In the case of telepathy, clairvoyance, or precognition (page 217), some scientific investigators think we may be dealing with phenomena explainable by natural physical processes of which we are now only dimly aware. Is it conceivable that the human brain may be capable of sending and receiving "signals" through a medium we have not yet identified? In what ways would such "signals" be similar to radio and television waves? In what ways would they be different?

4. It is common knowledge that apparent ESP phenomena are often the result of deliberate deception — either for entertainment purposes, or with fraudulent intent. Also, there is often an element of unconscious *self-deception*. Even if we concede that this is so in a great many cases, does this necessarily prove that ESP does not exist as a genuine phenomenon — a fact of life? Explain.

5. Test your telepathic power. Take the four aces from a deck of cards and place them on a table face up. Shuffle the other cards in the deck and then, without looking at them, try to identify what suit they belong to by placing them beneath the corresponding ace. Run through the deck in this way ten times. If you make as many as 150 correct guesses in this process, you are probably exceeding the laws of chance. Does this prove that you are clairvoyant?

6. Stare quietly at a person who is within ten yards of you and who has his back to you. Try to select someone who is not engaged in any particular activity at the moment. Do this if possible from behind a window or glass door (to reduce the possibility that the person may subliminally sense faint sounds and odors). Will that person turn around uneasily and look at you? What conclusions — if any — can you draw?

READINGS

The Occult — A History, by Colin Wilson (Random House, 1971). The theme of Wilson's book is that parapsychological phenomena are central to a "new awareness."

ESP in Life and Lab — Tracing Hidden Channels, by Louisa E. Rhine (Macmillan, 1967). Discusses the scientific and sociological aspects of ESP.

Mental Radio, by Upton Sinclair (Macmillan, 1936). Albert Einstein suggests in the preface that this book by a noted American novelist and social reformer deserves serious consideration by scientists.

ESP Curriculum Guide, by R. A. McConnell (Simon and Schuster, 1971). A scientist seeks to probe the reality of extrasensory perception.

Mind Bending

ALTERED STATES OF CONSCIOUSNESS

●●●●●●●●●●●●●●●●●●●●●●●●●●●●●

Changing the State of Consciousness

▶ During an initiation ceremony, a tribesman goes into a trance. His body is "possessed" by tribal spirits.

▶ A Zen Buddhist monk meditates each day for many years and finally attains the state of "complete enlightenment" (*satori*).

▶ A young American soldier taken prisoner by the North Koreans becomes "detached from reality" after several weeks of intensive political indoctrination.

▶ A 16th-century Christian monk, through fasting and self-denial, achieves an ecstatic religious vision.

▶ At a demonstration of hypnosis, a volunteer from the audience runs about on all fours when the hypnotist suggests to him that he has taken the form of a dog.

▶ A man awakens in the middle of the night, confused by a dream which seems exceptionally real.

▶ A group of young people "tripping" on LSD report that they are seeing the world "as if for the first time."

What do all these experiences — widely separated in space, in time, in the type of person involved — have in common? They all represent a change in *a person's state of consciousness.*

What Is an "Altered State of Consciousness"?

This concept is not easily defined. Yet anyone reading these words knows whether or not he is awake and in a "normal" state of consciousness. Similarly, a person whose consciousness has been altered in some way generally has little difficulty in knowing that such a change has taken place. He becomes aware of a *qualitative* shift in his mental functioning, one in which his perception and thinking have been modified noticeably.

We all experience slight changes in consciousness under ordinary circumstances. For instance, boredom and excitement can be regarded as distinctive or modified patterns of consciousness. However, an altered state of consciousness involves a *major shift in perception,* so that reality appears different in every way.

The distinction is not always easy to make. When does ordinary boredom become a trance? When does random, aimless thinking develop into a daydream?

Nevertheless, certain kinds of consciousness can clearly be recognized as "altered states." A familiar experience of this type is *dreaming.* Other solitary activities that produce altered states of consciousness include *meditation, self-hypnosis,* and *daydreaming.* In all of these cases, there is a reduction of sensory stimulation, and the physical functioning of the body becomes markedly relaxed.

We can also recognize without much doubt altered states of consciousness resulting from the interaction of two or more persons. One example is *hypnosis,* in which the subject responds to suggestions from the hypnotist. Subjection to high-powered propaganda may have somewhat similar results. This may occur either on an individual basis, or in small groups, as in so-called *"brainwashing."* Similar results can be produced in larger crowds — for example, when an effective speaker addresses a political rally or some other audience. Even an ordinary crowd activity, such as a rock concert or a football game, may change an individual's state of consciousness noticeably.

Finally, there is the class of altered states produced by changes in body chemistry. It is a familiar fact that various drugs, including alcohol, can produce such changes. These states may also result from fasting, dehydration, hyperventilation, or lack of sleep.

Regardless of the cause, the person with altered awareness knows that there has been a change in his thought processes, in the way his sense organs function, and in his emotional reactions. He may experience joy, fear, ecstasy, hate, or depression to a degree that causes him to lose his "self-control." His sense of time may be distorted as compared with his "normal" state of mind.

Other effects are harder to describe, although they are very real and very important to the person going through them. He may feel that there is a split between his mind and his body, so that he is living simultaneously in two entirely different dimensions — mental and physical. He may sense that the boundaries between himself and the outside world have melted away, so that his individuality no longer exists. He may undergo a profound change in his standards for judging significance. What ordinarily seems trivial may take on dimensions of great importance, and perhaps vice versa.

In some types of awareness changes, people report feeling "rejuvenated." There is a sense of newness in their lives; everything has begun afresh.

Still another change is hyper-suggestibility. This means that the subject suspends his critical faculty. He accepts the truth or value of whatever he may be told by a particular person or perhaps by the representative of a given authority. In such a state he may be easily deceived — "truth" may become just another illusion.

Obviously only a person who has actually undergone such experiences knows what they are like. Attempts to describe them in words are at best unsatisfactory.

A New Attitude Toward Altered States of Consciousness

There is every reason to believe that men have experienced altered states of consciousness since before the beginnings of civilization. The fact is, however, that there has been relatively little study of such phenomena in Western cultures. For the most part in our society, the prevailing attitude has been that normal consciousness is "good," and that any other type of awareness is "sick" or "crazy." If these mental states were to be studied at all, the purpose was usually to find some way of bringing them back to normal.

In recent years, however, there have been signs of a change in these negative attitudes. For one thing, we are now aware that there are altered states of consciousness, such as dreaming, which are a perfectly normal — indeed an inevitable — part of human experience. Also, it is now widely recognized that activities such as meditation, which may bring on a change of consciousness, are not at all "sick." On the contrary, they may be highly beneficial — even to Western man.

Dream Consciousness

There is one altered state of consciousness which all human beings have experienced. Psychologically, it is so important that sanity would be impaired without it. This is the state of *dreaming*.

Dreams have played a part in religion and literature throughout man's history. Many cultures have used dreams as a basis for prophecy. It is known, for example, that Alexander the Great would hesitate to make any important decision, such as engaging in a battle, without consulting his dream interpreter. The peoples of the Middle East have a similar tradition, as we know from the Old Testament story in which Joseph interpreted the Pharaoh's dream and thus won his way out of prison and gained the ruler's favor.

Because the interpretation of dreams was generally associated with such "unscientific" areas of knowledge as religion, poetry, and folklore, scientists scoffed for a long time at the idea of making productive use of an understanding of dreams. However, by the middle of the 19th century, many researchers had begun to study dreams seriously.

Recent experiments have shown that dreaming is as necessary to man's mental health as sleep is to his physical health. Volunteers who are continually interrupted during their dreaming stage of sleep soon begin to show signs of mental stress. Many become unduly anxious, hallucinate, and are unable to cope with the strains of daily life. It appears that dreaming is one altered state of consciousness that we cannot do without.

NOTE: For a more detailed discussion of dreaming, see Chapter 8.

Meditation

What Is Meditation?

In the part of the world that we call "The East," meditation is a widely practiced spiritual discipline. There are various meditative techniques practiced in Buddhism and in Hindu Yoga to achieve higher spiritual development within the traditions of those religions.

Some of these techniques, or bits and pieces of them, have been adopted in the West. Many Americans have found the exercises of Hatha Yoga physically beneficial, without being aware of the higher (spiritual) aims of this discipline and other forms of Yoga as practiced in India. Recently, techniques of Yoga have been popularized in the United States and other Western countries by *swami* ("wise

This painting shows a Hindu sage or *swami* who has retired from the world and is sharing his wisdom with a younger disciple. Meditation plays an essential part in Hinduism and in many other religious traditions.

men"), some of whom appear to have put their instruction on a profitable business basis. Many of the paying followers of these mentors have no idea what they may be getting into.

Meditation may be defined as an attempt to stabilize the mind around a single thought or object, producing a state of deep passivity, combined with a heightened awareness of the self. The meditator aims at muting all the usual functions of the mind; his goal, ideally, is to "empty the mind and make it a blank page." If he achieves this, it is claimed, the meditator will come to a knowledge of his true self, free of the ordinary distractions of his conscious thinking.

Preparing for Meditation

If you would like to experiment with meditation, the first thing you should know is that body position is important. You should be relaxed but aware. The cross-legged "lotus position" is commonly used, although often difficult for beginners. This is a sitting position, with the right foot resting on the left thigh, while the left foot rests on the right thigh. If you find this unduly difficult, try a "half lotus," with only one foot resting on the opposite thigh, and the other foot tucked close to the buttock. Or, as a substitute, you may sit in a chair with both feet flat on the floor, slightly apart. In all positions your back should be straight, but settled comfortably, and your head erect, eyes open, and focused a few feet ahead, with the hands resting in the lap. Before beginning, sway back and forth gently a few times, and breathe deeply.

There are many techniques and objects of meditation, but they have a number of essential characteristics in common. All are aimed, as we have noted, at increasing awareness of one's inner thoughts, in a detached frame of mind. It is important, however, not to try to conform to any rigidly preconceived idea of meditation because the detached self-awareness at which the meditator is aiming comes only from a relaxed and, so to speak, "natural" observation of the flow of thought. If someone tries to *force* himself into the desired frame of mind, he will probably fail.

Distractions are the enemy of concentration. However, you cannot avoid distractions entirely, and how you handle them will go far toward determining success or lack of it. If distractions take the form of your own thoughts, examine them and let them pass without trying to control them, interpret them, or become involved with them. If the distraction is something external, such as a noise, don't try to "fight" it. Just patiently bring back your attention to the object of meditation. You may concentrate on a part of your body, such as the tip of your nose, or on a picture or some other simple object. Another technique involves repetition of a "holy word" a *japa* or *mantra,* as a method of stabilizing the mind.

One word of caution: If you plan to meditate for more than an hour, have someone check on you at a predetermined time. People have been known to become "lost" in the "altered consciousness" of meditation.

Exercises Used in Meditation

Experienced meditators have recommended several exercises or techniques that help the subject reach the desired level of consciousness.

One of them has to do with focusing attention on the individual's own body:

> Breathe through your nose "allowing" the air to come in, rather than drawing it in. Exhale completely to the count of one, inhale again, and exhale to the count of two. Continue to ten and repeat. Your mind will probably wander but keep at it, and bring your mind back to the process of counting.

Another technique focuses on the mind. One form of this involves thought activity:

Relax. Resolve to do nothing, to think nothing, to "let go" of your body and mind. Step out of the stream of your ideas, and watch the flow. Do not get carried away with the current.

Frequently objects outside yourself can be used for meditation:

Concentrate on a simple object, such as a blue vase. Do not analyze it but try to see the vase as it is. Exclude other thoughts and bodily sensations. Fill your mind with the vase.

Zen monks in Japan meditating in the hall of their temple. The monk with the wooden stave will use it to arouse anyone who appears to be "dozing off."

Types of Responses to Meditation

Researchers have recognized five levels of responses to meditation.

The first response is likely to be a feeling of dizziness.

At the second level, the meditator feels calmer and more relaxed, although concentration may not be very sustained.

Pleasant body sensations occur at the third level, and concentration is generally increased.

The fourth level brings vivid experiences of breathing; the person's body seems to be filled with air, and concentration is effortless.

On the fifth level, there is a lucid state of consciousness, and the subject reaches a "nonstriving" attitude. He observes thoughts and feelings in a calm, detached manner. Concentration is easy and complete, usually accompanied by loss of bodily sensations.

These, of course, do not represent all of the responses to meditation, but they do suggest the most common pattern among beginners.

In one experiment where a number of volunteers meditated on a vase, there were some responses common to all of them, and others which varied with the individuals. All the meditators reported an altered perception of the object of meditation, usually with an increase of vividness, or with a change of shape. They usually lost an accurate sense of time. They often reported conflicting feelings of agitation and pleasure. Some said, however, that they found their feelings too confused even to attempt to describe them. The meditators also became aware of eventually building up "barriers" to keep out distractions. Some people experienced feelings of being "merged" with the object of meditation. Others said that the vase radiated light and warmth and brought about a "sexual" sensation.

How Meditation Is Used

Meditation is used regularly by practitioners of some Eastern religions to achieve a state of heightened religious awareness. Also, in Japan and the United States, efforts have been made to use meditation for *psychotherapy* (the treatment of emotional disorders). In such cases the therapist in effect meditates with the patient. He directs the meditation toward a carefully chosen subject and then discusses the results with the patient. The patient, in meditating on a "neutral" subject, often reveals his troubled thoughts and may be urged by the therapist to surmount his difficulties. This method has the advantage of aiming toward health or wholeness, instead of dwelling on past troubles. It is, however, an extremely subjective process, and meaningful results cannot be expected unless the therapist is highly dedicated both to the practice of meditation and to his subject.

The Western way of life and the practice of meditation may seem basically opposed to each other. In our society, most people are concerned primarily with purposive action and control, while meditation emphasizes passivity and the free flow of thoughts. We tend to be preoccupied with the conscious self, almost excluding the possibility of any direct knowledge of the unconscious or inner self. The spontaneous mental processes and the deep explorations of the self that meditation entails may appear to have little to offer to the practical, "busy," goal-directed mind of modern man.

But events may prove that meditation is not entirely irrelevant to or incompatible with our way of life. More and more people in today's world complain that they feel they are caught up in a "rat race," of ceaseless, exhausting, and ultimately pointless activity. Perhaps the practice of meditation in some form can provide a wholesome corrective influence — as long as it is not undertaken lightly or faddishly. It is never a good idea to "play around" with your inner being.

Brainwashing

Use by the Chinese Communists

Brainwashing or "thought reform" is a technique developed by the Chinese communists as a means of making people receptive to the Marxist ideas and programs formulated by (among others) Mao Tsetung. The basic method is prolonged and intensive indoctrination carried out through small groups, each of which is headed by a discussion leader well versed in group dynamics, applied psychology, and communist ideology.

The group discussion emphasizes the official teachings regarding such matters as economic affairs, the government system, family structure and relationships, and foreign policy. The "line" is laid down in the sharpest possible terms, with no suggestion that any deviation from it is even thinkable. In addition, the discussion leader requires each member of the group to examine his own attitudes and behavior, and also to criticize those of his neighbors. The purpose is to enable each individual member of the group to see how, where, and why "wrong thinking" began, and how to guide the erring brothers back to the right road.

Throughout, the discussion leader draws attention to the selfishness, injustice, and inefficiency of the "old" ways of thinking and behaving. He makes it evident that it is only within the communist framework (as exemplified in China, North Korea, or North Vietnam) that brotherhood, equality, democracy, prosperity, and a good life for all can be achieved.

These discussions are continued and repeated until the leaders are satisfied that everyone is fully convinced, not only intellectually but emotionally, that the official policies represent truth and goodness, and that any deviation from them is nothing short of criminal folly. Contrary to some rumors, there is no evidence that drugs, hypnotism, or any other special types of manipulation are used in these campaigns. However, there is reason to believe that in most cases the constant battering of propaganda, the repetition of simple formulas, the emotional pressures of the group, and the eloquence of the leader are simply overwhelming.

Brainwashing of American Prisoners of War

Americans have become familiar with brainwashing primarily as a result of the experience of our servicemen who became prisoners of the North Koreans and of the Chinese communists during the Korean War (1950-53). Later, prisoners of the North Vietnamese seem to have suffered somewhat similar treatment.

The methods used by the Chinese were probably the most typical and effective. First the prisoners usually experienced a long period of undernourishment and poor medical care. This was justified by saying that the Americans had bombed food depots, hospitals, and non-military convoys. In other words, the prisoners were suffering because of their own countrymen.

At the same time the prisoners were exposed to lectures, group discussions, radio programs, moving pictures, and literature that hammered away at one theme — the decadence of "capitalist imperialism" in the United States and the virtues of communism. If any men attempted to question these "arguments," they were answered with torrents of "facts" and "documentary evidence." (In many cases, the arguments were made more convincing by the undeniable fact that all through the 19th century China had been ruthlessly exploited by Western countries.)

Those prisoners who showed signs of being hard to convince were exposed to "special treatment." They were deprived of sleep for long periods of time; they were given especially inadequate food; they might be placed in solitary confinement. Above all, they were given

Two captured United States airmen are manacled together and paraded through the streets of Hanoi (North Vietnam). This picture gives some conception of the physical and psychological pressures to which prisoners of war may be subjected.

reason to fear that their health, their sanity, and their very survival were endangered, even more than those of the other prisoners, unless they went along with the ideas being presented. Those men who failed to break down even under these conditions were usually separated from the other prisoners, so that the more pliant majority would not be "infected" with anti-communist ideas.

Fear and mistrust were fostered among the prisoners by publicizing "confessions," by planting rumors designed to create dissension, and by encouraging informers. Threats of mass punishment, and actual use of it, acted as a psychological prod to stimulate informing. The prisoners who showed themselves somewhat receptive to the communist ideology might be rewarded with extra food rations, more personal liberty and other favors. Such men were often given especially intensive instruction and were then returned to the general prisoner population to propagandize the other prisoners.

"Criticism meetings" were held in which the men were urged to criticize themselves and each other. This might then be extended to include criticism of Americans as a whole and of American policies on the world scene and especially in Asia. The communists welcomed particularly "confessions" that United States forces had been making use of terror bombing of civilians and of indiscriminate germ and gas warfare. It appears, however, that the real aim of the brainwashing was not to obtain false confessions, offered cynically in the hope of pleasing the all-powerful captors. Rather, the "brainwashers" actually hoped to *convince* the prisoners that they came from a corrupt and decadent society, and that the communist system and way of life were vastly superior.

Reactions of the Brainwashed Prisoners

How did these prisoners of war react to brainwashing? Few, if any, were entirely unaffected, but the symptoms differed widely according to the personalities, the physical and moral stamina, the age, and the past histories of the men. Some "put on an act" in the hope of warding off punishment. Some became apathetic and dulled — "walking zombies" as the press put it. A startling number had what we might call "nervous breakdowns," showing uncontrolled and hysterical behavior. When they emerged from this condition, they might be highly receptive to the communist teachings. Some developed "guilt" symptoms and seemed actually anxious to be punished, so that they might atone for their misdeeds, real or imagined.

In the Korean War, there were 21 American servicemen who officially defected. They stated openly that they were convinced that the United States had been guilty of criminal aggression, and that the communist society was superior in every way. They confessed in writing and on the radio to every crime of which the communists accused them. They stated that they did not wish to return home, even after a peace treaty and exchange of prisoners had been arranged, and they made plans to spend the rest of their lives in mainland China.

Most of these men ultimately did ask to be returned to the United States, even though by their conduct they had exposed themselves to severe punishment. Some went to other countries. Few, if any, retained their first enthusiasm for Chinese communism.

There has been much discussion of the "weakness" of our servicemen under the influence of brainwashing. But it is necessary to bear in mind the extraordinary circumstances to which they were exposed — thousands of miles from home, completely in the power of the enemy, and subject to unremitting psychological pressures by dedicated and highly ingenious propagandists. It would have been remarkable if this regimen, continued for many months, had *not* brought about marked changes in their state of consciousness and behavior.

It is true, however, that the American prisoners were so confused that, even though they were often lightly guarded, there was not *one* successful escape attempt during the entire episode.

As for the 21 defectors, they showed a remarkable similarity in their personal backgrounds. They were all young — the oldest in their early 20's. They came from small towns or rural areas. They had very little education, and in particular had only the most rudimentary knowledge of history and political theory. Their personal lives prior to their military service had been generally unhappy, with a record of broken homes, school failures, unemployment, and menial, low-paid jobs. These were the "converts" made by the brainwashing of the Chinese communists.

Drugs

For thousands of years, men have altered their consciousness by means of drinking, eating, or smoking various substances that occur in nature, or that can be prepared from cultivated or wild plants. Every society has its favorite drugs whose use is permitted by law or custom. In our society, these include caffeine, nicotine, and alcohol.

The use of these substances is so familiar and (in most cases) apparently harmless that it may seem strange to call them "drugs" — much less drugs that alter consciousness. Yet this is what they actually are and what they actually do. Caffeine and nicotine are both mild stimulants; alcohol is an anesthetic and depressant.

Hallucinogens

Another group of drugs used to alter consciousness are known as *hallucinogens.* In contrast to the "accepted" drugs of our society, these have provoked a tremendous amount of concern and controversy. One reason for this is that they are relatively new and unfamiliar in our culture. As we shall see, however, there are more solid grounds for questioning the use of these and other drugs.

Users have claimed all but magical properties for the hallucinogens — for example that marijuana can somehow stimulate creativity, and that LSD can provide profound religious and philosophical insights. Such claims seem to have great appeal, especially for people who hope to achieve clarity of mind and release of anxiety by some easy shortcut. By the same token, some of the propaganda *against* these drugs has been irresponsibly overstated, thus obscuring the very real problems and dangers people face when they use hallucinogenic substances.

Marijuana and Hashish

The hallucinogenic drugs may be thought of as a sort of spectrum, ranging from the relatively mild *marijuana,* through the stronger *hashish,* to the much more potent *LSD, mescaline* and *psilocybin.* Some of these drugs, like marijuana, have been part of human experience for thousands of years; others, like LSD, are recent laboratory developments. All of them alter consciousness to a lesser or greater extent.

Marijuana is the second most popular intoxicant in the world — alcohol being the first. It was described by the Chinese over 5000 years ago, and was used medically in ancient India as a mild relaxant.

Marijuana is produced from the resinous leaves of the hemp plant, known to botanists as *Cannabis sativa.* Hashish is a concentrated form produced from the resin alone; it is much stronger than marijuana.

The leaves of the marijuana plant are cleaned, dried, and chopped up. When this substance is smoked, the user experiences a change in consciousness. The drug reduces the normal level of anxiety and sometimes results in a condition of intoxication or "high." In this state, music is more beautiful, jokes are funnier, companionship is more pleasant, and the simplest objects are more interesting. Strong doses of the drug may cause minor hallucinations — which explains why marijuana is classified as a "mild hallucinogen."

Some users have reported occasional unpleasant effects as a result of using "grass." Among these are extreme anxiety and paranoia:

Cannabis sativa, the plant from which marijuana is derived. The active hallucinogenic agent in marijuana is believed to be tetra-hydrocannabinol (THC).

the person has unfounded fears that he is being criticized or that someone is out to "get him." Most psychologists agree that a single use of marijuana is not likely to produce a psychotic reaction in previously normal people.

There is no reliable evidence that smoking marijuana incites people to violence.

The purely physical effects of marijuana on a long-range basis are not definitely established. Some veteran smokers apparently suffer no harm. There is, however, some evidence of eye damage among life-time smokers in the Middle East.

It is generally agreed that marijuana is not physically addictive. It does not create a physical need or craving, so that the body "demands" more and more of the drug. A heavy smoker can stop using "pot" without suffering the painful type of reaction (withdrawal symptoms) associated with heroin and other "hard" drugs.

On the other hand it is quite easy for someone to become psychologically dependent on marijuana. This happens when the drug becomes a central part of the person's daily life, a means of avoiding or disguising problems. The heavy user of marijuana often tends to "turn in on himself" — to become passive and non-productive. Rather than face problems, he likes to pretend they don't exist. Thus, he weakens his capacity to tolerate frustration, and he may neglect the skills that enable normal people to face and overcome reverses. Rather than try to overcome difficulties, he prefers to retreat to a pleasant drug-induced state. He becomes dependent on marijuana to give him the satisfactions others achieve through seeking to develop themselves in the real world.

Apart from the dangers of psychological dependency, marijuana is illegal in the United States. Punishment for possession ranges from a misdemeanor in some states to a felony in many others. Despite pressure to change marijuana laws, it is still true that an arrest can have a serious effect on a young person's future. Persons who have once been convicted of a felony are usually not allowed to enter such professions as law, medicine and teaching and may be barred from civil service jobs. They may forfeit voting and property rights.

Does Marijuana Lead to the Use of "Hard" Drugs?

The charge has often been made that smoking marijuana may not be so bad in itself, but that it leads a young person to experiment with the "hard" drugs, such as LSD, heroin, cocaine, and the barbiturates. This charge is emphatically denied by defenders of marijuana, including those who are pressing for its legalization. What are the facts?

In a *physiological* sense, use of marijuana does not lead to use of heroin and other "hard" drugs. It is perfectly possible for a person to smoke marijuana for years without feeling any need to "graduate" to something stronger. Indeed, there is reason to believe that this is actually true of most marijuana users.

Sociologically, however, the picture is different. Since the drug is illegal, there is a good chance that the user will be offered other illegal drugs being handled by the same sellers ("pushers"). He may hear boastful stories of how great it is to get "stoned" on these drugs. He may feel challenged to play "follow the leader" — to do what older, more "sophisticated" drug users are doing. Many of these users (who may also be dealers) have a "missionary" attitude. Some tortured individuals want to see other people get "hooked" in the same way that they are. Some misguided youths actually believe that drugs such as LSD will cure the world's ills. Such propagandists are always ready to extol the joys of using drugs and to ridicule the dangers. Aside from these factors, drug users often need money to support their habit, and selling LSD, heroin, and the others is an "easy" way of raising cash.

The drug threat

State Unit to Propose Tighter Laws on Drugs

Proposals for tightening state controls over "dangerous" drugs, increasing penalties for their sale and possession but reducing penalties in the case of marijuana, will be presented to the Legislature before the end of the year.

Scores 'Coddling' of Heroin Users

Cocaine Is Re-emerging as a Major Problem,

Drug Abuse in Schools No Surprise

CONSULAR SUSPECT CLAIMS IMMUNITY

French Aide Here Declines to Appear Before Grand Jury in Heroin Case

Doctor Alarmed At Rise Of Heroin Use In County

"There is no such thing as the controlled addict," Dr. Robert Adams told the Community Service Council this week.

methadone maintenance an ex-heroin addict, just a program, but this is certainly not a cure, it is merely a substitute, he warned. Adams pointed out that his

Drug Abuse

'Hard' and 'Soft' Drugs All Dangerous

School Situation Not New—

Legal Drugs and Alcohol Is More a Peril Than Heroin

Sleeping pills become habit

Parents often implant narcotics idea in teens

"Our current official policy on addiction is doomed to failure"

LSD and Related Drugs

LSD (lysergic acid diethylamide) is a compound prepared in the laboratory that, like marijuana, has hallucinogenic properties. However LSD is vastly more potent — a true hallucinogen capable of producing major personality changes in some people who use it. It is a drug "without a history." There is no record of any earlier culture making long-continued use of a drug as powerful as LSD. We might say that it is a drug that has largely created its own culture — and its own problems for the people who use it.

To be sure, related (although weaker) substances have been used in the past. Examples are the "magic mushrooms" (*psilocybin*) used originally by Mexican Indians of Oaxaca province; and *mescaline,* derived from peyote cactus. Both these drugs were used within the Aztec and Navajo Indian cultures to help provide a religious experience, in connection with specific rites. They were not taken indiscriminately to help people "feel better" or as part of the routine of everyday life.

How do the hallucinogens alter consciousness? LSD in particular seems to affect both the senses and basic thought processes. The effect on the senses has been described as an "opening of the flood gates." Colors may appear more vivid and satisfying; the shapes of objects seem to stand out with greater sharpness; patterns emerge more strikingly. The overall effect, it is reported, is that the sense of sight is intensified. The same holds true for hearing. Thus, music may become more pleasurable; individual sounds, more distinct. Sometimes a blending of the senses seems to occur, so that sounds are not only heard but also "seen" as colors, and colors take on the quality of smells.

There is an equally turbulent effect on the thought processes. Although time may seem to slow down, thoughts come rushing into the brain in rapid succession. The LSD user often has the sense that he is making one marvelous intellectual discovery after another, although all too often these "great ideas" seem pretty ludicrous the next morning. Or, even worse, they may not be recognized as unworthy until much later.

Emotionally, a person on an "acid trip" becomes extremely open to suggestion and may be easily influenced, often in an adverse way, by those around him. In some cases, the drug releases such an enormous amount of energy that the subject feels like a "superman," all but invulnerable to ordinary dangers and limitations. Thus, there have been cases reported in which "acid heads" jumped out of windows, believing that they could fly, or walked into a stream of traffic, apparently convinced that the oncoming cars could not harm them.

LSD is so powerful that it may be dangerous not only in the long run but even after a single dose. In some cases, the effect of the drug may not be a euphoric hallucination, such as we have described above, but rather a terrifying fantasy — a veritable nightmare, only far more vivid and much longer lasting than anything experienced in a dream. This is called a "bad trip" or a "bummer." An episode of this type has been known to result in commitment of the user to a mental hospital. It may also end in suicide, and on rare occasions in murder.

The long-term effects of LSD use, even if the other dangers are avoided, are on the *personality*. The user tends to withdraw from life, to become much involved in his own ideas and feelings. He finds it increasingly difficult to work with others, to plan realistically, to carry through any project to conclusion. Above all, in his preoccupation with himself (and with acid) he is impaired in his ability to enter into close relationships of friendship and love.

Amphetamines and Barbiturates

These two types of drugs are usually taken in the form of pills. Unlike marijuana, LSD, or heroin, these preparations are not illegal as such. They have their uses in medicine and may be prescribed by doctors for various purposes. However, vast numbers of the pills enter into illegal channels, and they are taken not for a medical purpose but simply to make the user "feel good."

Amphetamines. The amphetamines are strong stimulants. Thus, they are sometimes called "uppers" or "pep pills." The commercial names for these compounds include *Dexedrine, Benzedrine,* and *Methedrine.* (The name "speed" is often applied today to all the amphetamines, but particularly to Methedrine.)

The effect of an amphetamine is to stimulate the nervous system and increase the heart beat. Thus a person taking a large dose feels a tremendous infusion of energy. He becomes extremely active mentally and physically, but this activity usually has an obsessive-compulsive character. The user may spend hours in a non-stop talking jag, or in arranging and rearranging every article in a room. He becomes overly involved with details in a way that shows a seriously distorted sense of judgment.

There are also well-established physical dangers in taking amphetamines. The drug places severe strains on the heart. The user may drive himself into exhaustion by pushing his body too hard. Sleep becomes difficult, if not impossible. If the abuse continues for some time, there is likely to be severe overall physical deterioration, even in young people.

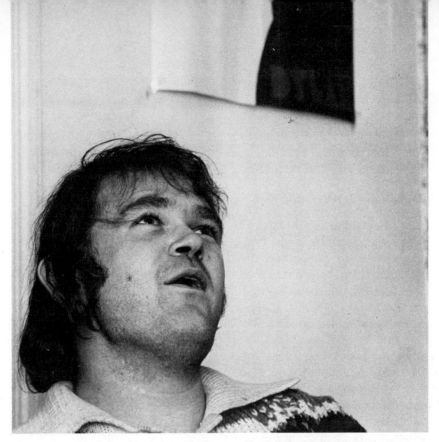

Life seems pretty wonderful during the amphetamine high. It will seem much less wonderful when the user has to "come down" to reality.

There is no purely physical addiction to amphetamines, but there is strong psychological dependence. When use is discontinued, the user has to come down from his "high," and this return to reality (called "crashing") can be extremely difficult. Abrupt withdrawal from the drug by a heavy user ("speed freak") may result in deep and sometimes suicidal depression.

Barbiturates. The barbiturates are sedatives or "downers." They have just the opposite effect of amphetamines — that is, they depress or slow down the body. Among the common trade names for the preparations are *Amytal, Seconal,* and *Nembutal.* Some of these are used in "sleeping pills." The users ("pill heads"), however, are not concerned with going to sleep but rather with the enjoyable effects of becoming intoxicated or "out of this world." They may sometimes take doses many times larger than a doctor would ever prescribe for a patient. An overdose interferes with respiration. The user becomes drowsy, passes out, and in some cases may die.

The barbiturates are physically addictive. Withdrawal from the drug is usually painful and dangerous, and may require a long period of hospitalization. During the withdrawal period, the patient may die from convulsions, or from sheer exhaustion.

It is particularly dangerous to mix barbiturates with alcohol. Many fatalities and near-fatalities have resulted from the practice of drinking heavily and then taking a large dose of "sleeping pills."

Heroin and Other Opiates

The *opiates* are a class of drugs which act as depressants — that is, lower the activity of the body. They are all derived from the opium poppy. The unripened seed pods of this flower yield a milky juice, which is treated to prepare a substance called *opium*. Opium itself has been used as a narcotic* drug for thousands of years but its main importance today is that it is the source of such synthetic drugs as *morphine, heroin,* and *codeine. Morphine* is widely used in medicine as a pain killer, but it also plays a part in the illegal drug trade. Moreover, morphine may be converted into *heroin,* the most powerful and dangerous of the opiate drugs. Heroin has no medical uses; it is illegal in this country for any purpose. (*Codeine* is relatively weak and of minor importance.)

Heroin† is considered "the end of the line" in drug use. A user stands a very good chance of becoming *addicted* or "hooked." Once he is a confirmed "junkie," he simply must have "fixes" of the drug regularly, or suffer severe withdrawal symptoms as well as psychological deprivation that he cannot tolerate. Chances of curing a heroin addict are very poor — even under favorable conditions probably no more than 10 to 15%.

Heroin is a white powder. It is either sniffed ("snorted"), or heated and dissolved in water ("cooked") and then injected into the body with a hypodermic needle. (In Vietnam, some of our servicemen were known to smoke it mixed with tobacco.) The injection may be under the skin or into a muscle ("skin popping"), or directly into a vein. This last, the most extreme form of heroin use, is called "mainlining" or "banging."

The "mainliner" feels a sudden overwhelming thrill (a "rush") as the drug races through his body. This is followed by a powerful

---

* The term *narcotic* usually is taken to mean any drug which depresses the activity of the body. In moderate doses, such a drug may relieve pain and produce deep sleep. In excessive (poisonous) doses, it results in stupor, coma, or convulsions. All of the opiates are true narcotics, as are belladonna and alcohol. However, *any* drug used illegally to produce pleasurable reactions may sometimes be called a "narcotic." Federal laws and many state legal codes classify cocaine, marijuana, and hashish (in addition to opiates) as "narcotics."

† Some nicknames for heroin include: *H, horse, stuff, smack, junk,* and *skag.*

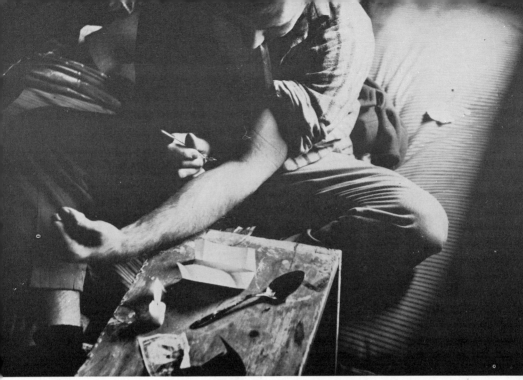

The heroin "fix."

"high" or period of *euphoria,* which means simply that the user feels very "nice." Tension and worries float away; pain is subdued; muscles are relaxed. After the "high" the user gets very drowsy and will doze ("nod") wherever he may be. Side effects include constipation, runny nose and eyes, sensitive stomach, yawning, and itchiness.

As an addict continues to take the drug, he will need larger and larger doses to produce the same effect. But an overdose (the dreaded "O.D.") can stop the workings of the lung and heart and result in death. No one knows for sure how many hundreds or thousands of addicts (including young children) have died from heroin O.D.'s in recent years. The danger of this is increased by the fact that when heroin is peddled on the streets its strength varies greatly, so that the user is never really sure how much of the drug he is taking.

But even if the heroin addict doesn't die quickly from an overdose, he is killing himself by degrees. The drug takes the place, to a large degree, of sex, aggressiveness, and hunger for food. A regular user of heroin (or some other opiate) has for all practical purposes given up the struggle to live. He is "flying low and dying slow." Frequently, he doesn't bother to eat properly or even to keep himself clean. He is an easy target for all kinds of diseases, including some transmitted by dirty needles.

The "junkie" needs considerable sums of money to meet his needs — an average in New York City, according to one estimate, of $10,000 a year. His chances of making such money legitimately are very poor. So the addicts commonly resort to crime, including thefts, muggings, pimping, and prostitution. Even worse, they may become pushers, supplying other addicts and trying to find new customers for the deadly drug. Police officials in cities in all parts of the United States testify that their massive crime problems are the result in large part of the desperate efforts of heroin addicts and other drug users to get the money they need to "feed their habits."

Cocaine

Cocaine, prepared from the leaves of the cocoa plant, is like the amphetamines, a powerful stimulant. The leaves are treated to make a white powder which may be either sniffed or dissolved in a liquid and injected. Among the nicknames for this drug are *coke* and *snow*.

The user of cocaine feels an exhilarating high, which usually lasts between 10 and 30 minutes. Persons "up" on cocaine sometimes feel so invigorated and powerful that their inhibitions against violence are greatly lowered. They may take risks which they would not even consider under normal conditions.

An overdose of cocaine can be fatal. The functioning of the lungs and heart is disrupted, and convulsions may occur.

Cocaine is not physically addictive, but like all forms of drug abuse it may lead to a condition of psychological dependence. The heavy user finds it hard to live without the illusion of strength and virility that the drug gives him. Moreover, "coke" is often used with drugs that are addictive — heroin and the barbiturates. With this deadly combination of a stimulant and a depressant, the user gets pulled two ways at once, for a "smoother high."

Some Advice about Drug Use

It is very easy (in a sense, *too* easy) to preach about the dangers of drug abuse. Young people in recent years have been all but inundated with advice and warnings about drugs, and the results of this, quite clearly, have not been too good.

Why do so many young people tend to tune out the well-intentioned advice of their elders? They often feel, for one thing, that the warnings are hysterical and exaggerated. There may be something in this. Certainly the dangers of using marijuana have sometimes been overstated, and the legal penalties prescribed have been excessive. (In many states the penalties have recently been reduced, or probably will be reduced in the near future.) It is said, too, that the advice is often hypocritical — that the same middle-aged "establishment type" who storms most strongly against drugs will stupefy himself every night with three Martinis before dinner. It is hard to deny that this charge has a lot of validity.

But perhaps the main reason for rejecting the anti-drug arguments and warnings is the belief that drugs are somehow an integral part of the life style of the younger generation — a style that older people can't or won't understand. Some young people apparently feel that drugs are "fun" — that they make life easier, more interesting, generally more rewarding. They resent efforts to deprive them of such a "life-expanding" experience.

It is difficult to argue against "fun." We all go through life looking for rewards, trying to enjoy as many interesting and satisfying experiences as possible. *But it is precisely here that drug use is self-defeating.* For example, what is more satisfying than meeting a problem head on and overcoming it by positive, intelligent action? But drugs tend to fog over problems, to convince the user that they don't really exist, and that in any case he needn't do anything much about them. When reality is tough (as it inevitably will be at times), it's so much easier to turn one's back on it and to belt down another drink, pop another pill, smoke another joint, or drop some acid.

There are plenty of horror stories to tell about drugs — early deaths, suicides, insanity, crime convictions, ruined lives. And most of them unfortunately are true. But even if we discount these dangers, the big charge against drugs remains: *they are life-defeating.* Their overall effect, for all of the momentary "euphoria" they induce, is to weaken the capacity for enjoying the satisfactions and joys, as well as the disappointments and the complications, that are the essential stuff of real living.

No one can become a wholer, better, saner person by introducing chemicals into his nervous system. As for altering your consciousness, try something that requires discipline, thought, and control, such as Yoga, meditation, or best of all perhaps, falling in love.

Hypnosis

What Is Hypnosis?

Hypnosis may be defined as a trancelike state, resembling normal sleep, except that the subject is under the influence of another person (the hypnotist) and is extremely suggestible. A person, however, cannot be hypnotized against his will. Even when hypnotized, the subject can usually "snap out of it" if pressured into an act which violates his normal values and standards of behavior.

The practice of hypnotism has long been associated with "magic" shows and other forms of entertainment. Accordingly, many people tend to regard it as something bizarre and mysterious, if not utterly fraudulent. It is true that hypnotism is not fully understood, and it is also true that it has sometimes been exploited by charlatans. Nonetheless, it has been intensively investigated by psychologists, who have attempted to develop scientific theories to explain how it works. Also, it has been found useful in certain types of psychotherapy (treatment of mental and emotional illnesses). These various aspects of hypnosis will be considered in the following pages.

How Hypnosis Is Induced

The first thing the hypnotist does is reduce the amount of stimulation impinging on his subject. He generally dims the room, excludes outside noise, and talks only in a dull monotone. Usually, he attempts to limit the subject's body movement, perhaps by saying things such as "You will relax as much as possible . . . sit quietly without moving . . . let go of all your muscles. . . ." Then the hypnotist proceeds to direct the person's attention to some specific localized area. Usually he tries to alter the subject's awareness of his own body. ("Your little finger will move by itself" . . . "Your arm is rising without your help. . . .")

As an alternative, the hypnotist may try to confuse the subject about his orientation in time and space. He may do this by shifting from one topic to another, by rapidly changing figures of speech, and by speaking quickly and uninterruptedly so that the subject finds it difficult to follow him.

Lastly, the hypnotist tries to establish an intimate relationship between himself and his subject, on a level which may be described as "special" or "magic." He may actually promise some "magical" results, or he may indicate that the person will be able to probe the depths of his own mind, or perhaps enter some new realm of experience.

After this "induction period," the hypnotist may give the subject specific commands, or he may leave him free to do whatever he wants. The person is now in a trance-like state, which will end normally whenever the hypnotist commands it.

Characteristics of the Hypnotic Trance

The main characteristic of the state of hypnotic trance is *hypersuggestibility* — a higher degree of suggestibility than normal. Many other effects can follow from this, for under the influence of the hypnotist, the subject is more capable of controlling certain semi-voluntary reactions, such as response to pain, perception, or memory. It is possible, for example, to suggest to a hypnotized person that he will not feel a pin prick. Someone who is faking would not be able to do this, but a hypnotized subject is capable of "allowing" himself to feel no pain. A similar effect that can be produced readily is *anesthesia,* or loss of all feeling in a part of the body. The hypnotist may suggest that an arm or a leg has become lighter, or even that it does not exist at all. The subject will react accordingly.

In general, perception can be altered dramatically. In one experiment, a hypnotist suggested to a young woman (under hypnosis) that a man who had been in the room with them had left. This man actually had not left, yet when he asked the subject questions, she acted as if he were not there. He even came up to her and moved one of her arms up and down. Still the young woman was convinced that he was not there. Later she said that she had no recollection of having moved her arm in this way. However, she "supposed" that she had done this because the hypnotist had told her that the arm would move by itself! The hypnotist's suggestion had controlled her perception to such a degree that she could not see a person directly in front of her, and even found "explanations" for things which that person had done to her.

Subjects under hypnosis are often less self-conscious in their behavior than under ordinary circumstances. Hidden impulses may be expressed and acted out. For example, hypnotized persons have been known to suck their thumbs, or to react with intense outbursts of crying, anger, or excitement, without any suggestion from the hypnotist. These emotional reactions are believed to have something to do with conflicts from early childhood that remain unresolved.

Therapeutic Hypnosis

When hypnosis is used as a means of treatment for persons troubled in some way, it is said to be *therapeutic*. During therapeutic hypnosis, the relationship between the subject and the hypnotist is likely to be altered in some significant way. Generally, the hypnotist takes on the role of some person important in the individual's early development — a father, mother, lover, teacher, or some other figure who has had a strong influence. The hypnotized person may then "transfer" repressed impulses and patterns of behavior to the hypnotist — for example, he may use the hypnotist as a target for aggressive tendencies or sexual drives.

> Arthur L. was a rather quiet young man in his early twenties who was being treated by a psychotherapist. Although he did well in school, he was very shy and withdrawn and never participated in sports or other aggressive activities. Under hypnosis, he was free to express any deeply felt wish that he might have. Surprisingly enough, Arthur answered that he would like to strike his therapist in the mouth. It turned out that he had deepseated aggressive tendencies against his father, and that under hypnosis he transferred his feelings about his father to his therapist.

If the therapist so directs, the subject may regress or "go back" to some earlier period in his life history. He may re-enact conflicts or painful experiences which took place many years ago. He may become consciously aware for the first time of why certain things trouble him.

> William J., a long-time stutterer, was referred to a psychologist by his speech therapist when it appeared that the usual speech therapy was doing him little good. Under hypnosis, the psychologist directed William J. to speak without stuttering, and found that he was able to do so, without any problem. The psychologist then asked him why he stuttered, and William responded, "So that people will feel sorry for me." Under hypnosis, William revealed that he *needed* his stuttering as a "crutch" to help him get along in the world.

When hypnosis is used with people with emotional problems, it is generally accompanied by psychotherapy.

Theory of Hypnosis

When hypnosis was first observed, its effects seemed so extraordinary that attempts were made to explain it on some magical or semi-magical basis. For example, it was suggested that the power of the hypnotist was due to a kind of "magnetic fluid" flowing between him and the subject. The term "animal magnetism" was used to refer to this effect. However, since the existence of such a "fluid" could not be demonstrated, psychologists have had to rely on explanations based not on imaginary substances and forces but on what we actually know of human behavior.

Hypnosis is now seen as an *altered state of consciousness,* different from sleep, and certainly different from the state of wakefulness. Ordinary waking alertness is characterized by a constant shifting of attention, by a capacity to focus in rapid succession on various aspects of any situation at hand. The person is free to do this because he has a structured *frame of reference* in the background of his mind. For example, a student in a classroom knows *where* he is — in which room, in which school, in which city. He can shift his attention repeatedly — from his teacher, to the clock on the wall, to something written on the blackboard, to a book on his desk, to his fellow students, etc. — without losing this background framework. He is oriented to reality — to the overall pattern of facts that answer the questions *Who? When? Where? Why?* A student who falls asleep, in contrast, has momentarily given up such a structured framework. He has allowed it to fade away, thus losing his orientation to reality. For the time being, he doesn't know where he is, what time it is, what he is supposed to be doing, and other relevant facts.

The hypnotic state of consciousness is somewhere in between being awake and being asleep. The orientation to objective reality is not completely lost, as in real sleep, but it is limited by the hypnotist's suggestions to a very small area. Awareness of reality can be made to fade away markedly, and the mental energy that is normally used to maintain it can be redirected by the hypnotist to different ends.

Hypnosis, then, is a state of consciousness very similar to drowsiness. In ordinary drowsiness, a person may forget for the moment where he is and what the specific occasion is. In other words, the normal frame of reference may fade away. In hypnosis, this process is combined with another element — the hypnotist's suggestions regarding a new frame of reference as a substitute for objective reality.

It is the responsibility of the hypnotist, once the subject's ordinary frame of reference has faded out, to avoid leading him into unsafe areas. This is why it is extremely unwise to engage in hypnotism as a sort of "joke," or as a form of "entertainment." Hypnotizing anyone should be undertaken only for a worthwhile purpose by a person who has been adequately trained in the field.

*   *   *

Should We Seek Out Altered States of Consciousness?

At the beginning of this chapter, we quoted the great American philosopher and psychologist, William James. Take another look at that statement (page 231).

James expressed the conviction that there *are* states of consciousness other than the one which dominates us in "normal" everyday life. Many other distinguished thinkers and investigators of the human mind confirm this opinion. In this chapter, we have reviewed briefly some of the altered states of consciousness which have been part of the experience of large numbers of people.

The question you may have in mind now is whether the individual should deliberately and actively seek out these other levels of consciousness. It is impossible to give a hard-and-fast answer to this. It cannot be denied that there may be a certain amount of risk in altering consciousness in this way. On the other hand, there is a certain amount of risk in all the experiences of life. The risk must be assessed in relation to the benefits that may result from desirable changes in perception and from an increase in general awareness of who and what you are.

It is safe to say, however, that if you are going to err at all, it should be on the side of *caution*. We have already expressed emphatic warnings regarding the indiscriminate use of drugs. Also, no one should "fool around" with hypnosis. It is not a parlor game and should be attempted only by a qualified psychiatrist or psychologist.

In short, you may want to do a lot of living and learning before you project yourself beyond the "world of our present consciousness" into different levels of awareness. But to know that these other levels of awareness do exist, and to appreciate their main characteristics, is essential for anyone seeking a broader understanding of the human mind.

THINGS TO DISCUSS :: THINGS TO DO :: THINGS TO READ

1. On page 242, we noted the personal backgrounds of the 21 Korean War prisoners who actually defected to the Chinese Communists. Does it surprise you that men of this background, rather than "university intellectuals," were most susceptible to Communist propaganda and brainwashing? Explain your assessment of this situation.

2. Select one method of "altering the state of consciousness," and try to explain what may be happening to (a) the unconscious, (b) the ego, during this process.

3. Recently a young serviceman who had become addicted to heroin in Vietnam was interviewed on television. In answer to a question, he said that while he knew the drug was extremely dangerous, he might not be able to resist using it again at the first opportunity. When asked why, he answered, "I dig the high." How do you explain this response? What might be said to this young man that would be appropriate and constructive?

4. One altered state of consciousness you can investigate on your own without danger is meditation. Try it for a period of 5 to 30 minutes, following the procedures outlined in this chapter. It is a good idea to have a friend or several friends perform the experiment with you. Then you can exchange notes on your impressions. In any case, do not attempt the meditation for longer than you feel comfortable. In other words, if you get a headache, feel extremely restless, or have some other "annoying" reaction, discontinue.

READINGS

Man, the Manipulator, by Everett L. Shostrom (Abingdon Press, 1967). "The inner journey from manipulation to actualization."

Sense Relaxation — Below Your Mind, by Bernard Gunther (Collier Macmillan, 1968). "A book of experiments in being alive."

The Highest State of Consciousness, edited by John White (Doubleday Anchor Original, 1972). A fascinating selection of writings, including "This Is It" by Alan Watts.

Drugs From A to Z: A Dictionary, by Richard R. Lingeman (McGraw Hill, 1969). An excellent reference providing authentic, up-to-date information.

Where to Get Help If You Have a Drug Problem, edited by Nancy McCarthy (Award Books, 1971). A state-by-state guide.

Drug Youse — A Survivor's Handbook, by Roger Conant (Ed-U Press, 1972). A compact, colorful comic book containing straightforward information about widely-used drugs, including sections on what to do about overdoses and bad hallucinogen trips. Single copies may be obtained by sending 25 cents to Ed-U Press, 760 Ostrom Ave., Syracuse, N. Y. 13210. Bulk rates available on request.

THE ADOLESCENT IN THE 1970'S

CULTURE AND COUNTER-CULTURE

PART I

13

> *"Something new is happening here.*
> *What it is ain't exactly clear."*
>
> — *BUFFALO SPRINGFIELD*

Toward Adulthood

Long hair, "weird" clothing, drugs, sexual permissiveness, rock music, militant "protests" — these are images typically associated with teen-agers in the 1970's. Is this picture rather extreme? Or is there a good deal of truth in it? Is it due to the "kids" themselves? Or is it a reaction to self-indulgent parents who live in and defend a life style and economy which seem to emphasize excessive consumption and consequently excessive seeking of immediate gratification?

We often hear that the youth of today is reacting against society's evils, but is it possible that many youngsters are failing to come to grips with *their own* problems of self-indulgence?

Why is it that young people today appear to be even more frustrated and confused, yet more aware and idealistic, than were their parents when they were teen-agers?

To begin to cope with such questions, we must first recognize that adolescence is a particularly stormy time of life for people in any culture. It is the time when some degree of social awareness and the sense of responsibility that goes along with it start to emerge. It is also the time when unconscious impulses, particularly sexual drives, begin to

make themselves felt, usually setting up inner conflicts of which the teen-ager often has only a limited understanding.

In our society, adolescence is considered to begin at roughly the same time as puberty, at about the age of 12, and to continue on to age 18, 19, or possibly older. Some time between age 10 and 15 is when the adolescent is biologically ready to have children. In some simple, "primitive" cultures, an adolescent takes on the role of an adult shortly after reaching sexual maturity, but in most cultures all the duties, responsibilities and privileges of an adult do not come until the late teens or early twenties.

This is simply because adolescence is the time when a person is supposed to master some of the essential skills for taking care of himself and others as an adult, and in all but a few economically simple cultures a number of years of preparation is needed. Thus, in a tribe of hunters each father teaches his adolescent sons how to track animals, how to handle weapons, how to prepare the carcass, and so forth. Among the ancient Romans, the sons of aristocratic families were sent to special schools, where they trained to serve as statesmen and soldiers. In the medieval era, many boys were apprenticed to established craftsmen for a fixed number of years, so that they might eventually master a trade. In all these societies, girls too were prepared (usually in the home) to assume the roles of adult women — that is, to become wives and mothers.

In our modern culture, with its advanced technology, its complex economic structure, and its far-flung (if imbalanced) freedom of choice, the route to adulthood is not so simple or clearly defined. For one thing, the future of an adolescent is not so completely "mapped" for him by social custom and law. He must choose from among hundreds, perhaps thousands, of possible careers; a person today is often well into his twenties before he is ready to work and make a living. Moreover, social changes are occurring so rapidly and on such a vast scale that the career training received by an adolescent often proves inadequate to meet his current needs. The result of this combination of circumstances is that the individual is often ill-prepared to take his place in modern society.

Adolescence has *always* been a difficult period of life, but adolescent boys and girls in the 1970's find themselves in a particularly confusing situation. They are trying to prepare themselves for adulthood at a time when our society is in deep conflict and is perhaps changing more drastically than at any other time in its history. The adults of this culture are not agreed on what is needed for survival, and this sense of uncertainty adds immeasurably to the challenges that adolescents must face and the obstacles they must overcome.

Development of Identity

Often when we think of adolescence, we have in mind particularly the radical physical changes the boy or girl undergoes, including increases in height, maturation of the sex organs, appearance of secondary sex characteristics, and muscular development.

In addition to the physical changes, however, the mind is also going through a far-reaching development. In modern societies, at least, adolescence is primarily a period of *self-definition*. The young person begins to develop a *sense of identity*, a *concept of himself*. He is starting seriously to ask and to attempt to answer the crucial question: *Who am I?*

This process is extremely complex because it involves not only the individual, but also his family, his friends, his teachers, his heroes, and indeed everyone with whom he comes in contact. The impact of these "outside" forces on the individual is called *socialization*. In earlier societies, this process of socialization was guided along prearranged lines, which changed little over the years for a boy or a girl of a given social class. A person's behavior was fixed according to his social class, and he was strongly discouraged from mixing socially with people of other classes. Within his class, there were strict, highly detailed, traditional rules of conduct.

"The book I banned twenty years ago is now required high school reading."

Today, however, everything is in flux, and this makes the task of self-definition very difficult. More people are more aware than in earlier generations that it is *they themselves* who must make the decisions as to what constitutes the best conduct.

It would be a mistake to assume that the development of the self-concept begins and ends in the years of adolescence. Very young children are also going through this psychological growth, as are adults, whether they admit it or not. It is during adolescence, however, that a person begins to recognize in himself the potential of assuming responsibility for his own behavior and choosing his own path through life. He begins to respond to the needs, as well as the demands, of other people around him, and likewise he becomes self-consciously aware of how he relates to and gets along with these people.

Many adolescents believe that they can hurriedly figure out who they are, and that once they have reached such a self-image, they have no need to explore and develop their personalities further. The fact is, however, that ideally this self-concept should be subject to continued examination and revision throughout life, as the person undergoes more and more experience, and sees his capabilities, potentialities, feelings, needs, and desires more clearly as they actually are.

Thus, adolescence is a time of testing, of proving one's worth, of intensive learning, of frequent change, and of preparation for the years of adulthood.

Influence of the Family

The family is a major influence in the development of a person's sense of identity. In infancy, it is mainly the parents who transmit and interpret the meaning of the culture for the child. They set up most of the basic conditions in which the child begins the long road to finding out who he is. The parents do this by their continued evaluation of the child's development, and by their conscious and unconscious rewards and punishments which direct the course of his behavior and, consequently, the line of development his personality will take.

With the approach of adolescence, however, the role of the family changes. The adolescent begins to feel the need for greater independence. More and more he relies on himself and on people outside his family to define his experiences and interpret his behavior, his evaluations, and his judgments.

One almost inevitable result of this movement toward self-sufficiency is a certain amount of conflict between the adolescent and his parents. Often the parents still view him as a child and are reluctant to recognize his new status. The adolescent, for his part, is frequently unwilling to accept passively his parents' decisions on what he should or should not do and their judgments on the suitability of his behavior.

While adults recognize realistically that there are many things their children cannot understand because they are not old enough to have had a wide range of experience, they often fail to show awareness of the fact that, in all probability, the world appears much different to their children than it did to them when they were teen-agers. And the differences may be not merely in appearance (in subjective impressions) but in actual institutional arrangements. For example, a father may say to his 15-year-old son, "When I was your age, I was working at a full-time job." There is an implication here that there is something commendable in going to work at such an early age, and also that the son should be extremely grateful that he is not required to do so. But the son probably finds this quite meaningless because he knows that today, by both law and custom, 15-year-olds are required to go to school. Also, with rare exceptions, there are no full-time jobs in the economy for boys and girls of this age. So the father's stricture is probably dismissed (with a good deal of justification) as so much "hot air," inapplicable to present-day conditions.

It is possible, however, to exaggerate and distort the "generation gap" between parents and adolescents. Sympathetic and intelligent parents may have a realistic awareness of what their children are experiencing, and therefore will be in a position to give them sound advice and other forms of help in their character development. The family today, as in generations past, continues to provide support for the growing adolescent.

Peer Influence

Another important force in the self-development of adolescents is the pressure of the *peer group* — that is, boys and girls of roughly the same age with whom a person associates on a basis of "social equality."

A teen-ager is keenly aware of what these "other kids" are doing and what "they" are likely to say about what he is doing. His desire for love and friendship, coupled with a fear of rejection, strongly inclines him to imitate his peers in dress and speech, in music and dancing, in dating and courtship. Consequently, this world of peers is a powerful influence in shaping his values, his attitudes, and his behavior.

Even more important, the peer group provides the adolescent with a social situation in which he can learn, through active participation, some of the basic social processes in our culture. He can confront more or less directly problems, ideas, and experiences that he might find it very difficult even to discuss with his parents or other adults. He can try out his capacity for influencing and leading others.

In his family he is probably "just a kid." In his peer group he has the potentiality to demonstrate that he is fully equal to the others,

and he may even have the heady experience of having his leadership accepted by others.

Sociologists who have studied peer groups have found criticism within the group to be swift, and frequently blunt and to the point. This definiteness can prove to be an advantage to an adolescent, who is striving to achieve a realistic awareness of himself. And along with it comes a demand for unswerving loyalty, which is enforced by the threat of rejection. In return for obedience to the social rules of the peer group or "clique," the adolescent is rewarded with a certain amount of acceptance and trust which gives him a strong feeling of security.

It should be noted that the "unwritten rules" of such groups are not always beneficial to the development of the individual. In addition, there is always the danger that a young person may seek to shift the weight of responsibility for his actions from his own shoulders with the familiar assertion, "Everybody (in my group) is doing it."

The pressure toward conformity can be seen in widely shared standards and tastes in regard to dress, music, dancing, speech, and the like. Few adolescents show much tendency to "rebel" against these standards, although they may react strongly against their parents' demands. This· is because disapproval or ridicule from peers is a potent weapon against those who fear rejection, and because the possibility of high status is a glittering lure for those who enjoy praise and admiration.

Thus, within the peer group, the adolescent has a chance to acquire the skills of cooperation, to exert influence, to compete — in short, to learn the social interactions that are expected of an adult. In fact, the basic structure of adolescent peer groups differs very little from that of all sorts of groups which operate today in the adult world.

Of course, as you no doubt know from your own experience, not all young people become associated with cliques. Some youngsters seem unwilling to accept the standards of conformity imposed by the group, and they either stay out entirely or become only marginal members. There is some reason to believe that young people with an artistic, creative, or intellectual bent are more likely to take the role of "outsiders." Of course, not all "outsiders" accept this role voluntarily. They may be excluded for many reasons — they may be poor, but going to a school in a well-to-do community; they may be black, but living in a predominantly white neighborhood; they may belong to a religious minority. Peer groups, whether adolescent or adult, have the capacity to show a good deal of insensitive cruelty to those who do not "fit in."

The 1970's: A Difficult Time

Young people in the 1970's face a particularly difficult adolescence. Engaged in their own personal transition, they must also cope with a *world in transition!*

This generation of teen-agers is perhaps the first in modern history to show a keen and generally shared awareness of world problems and conflicts. Young people today see that their development is being influenced not only by their immediate environment of peers and adults, but also by broader social forces, issues, and challenges. They are beginning to realize that people from all walks of life, throughout the nation and the world, are not only important but essential to their self-development and well-being. They observe that many of the basic values circulating through the adult world are being questioned as never before. They must seek to answer a question that probably never occurred with such force in previous generations: "What kind of world do I want to live in?"

The boys and girls of this generation have grown up in a climate of rapid social change, and they are possibly better equipped than are their parents to accept and adapt themselves to a world in abrupt transition. Indeed, there are those observers who say that the young people are perhaps the only ones in our society who can see and appreciate what is actually happening. At the other extreme, there are those who assert that today's young people have been spoiled by too much "coddling" and by "permissiveness"; that their values are warped; and that, in spite of superficial sophistication, they really don't know "what life is all about."

But whether they see today's young people with admiration or with sharp disapproval, few would deny that they face a multitude of problems almost unrecognizable in earlier generations. Let us consider a few of them:

Changes in Technology

Throughout history, changes in technology — the application of scientific knowledge to the industrial arts in all fields — have had far-reaching effects on man's way of living.

As the pace of technological change speeds up, so does the need for social adjustment. It has been estimated that the last 50 years have seen more technological innovations than the previous 500; and the last 5, more than the preceding 50. Think of the vast number of technological developments that have done so much to transform our society since World War II. For instance, consider the effects of the massive use of television, computers, copying machines, transistors, *the 70's*

**END OF THE
"YOUTH REVOLT"?**

Love a

Guru

SEX IS NO BIG DEAL ANYMORE'

The Rise of a New Opposition

Too Much With Too Little and Too Little With Too Much

WITH THE END OF THE MODERN AGE – WHAT REMAINS?

'My Life Is My Own'

women's lib

**"JESUS CHRIST
SUPERSTAR
IS A TRIUMPH!"**

get more out of life

The Reality of God

WHO AM I?

DISCONTENT FOUND
HIGH ON CAMPUSES

Carnegie Report Warns of a
Repeat of '70 Turmoil

What If Everything Isn't Enough?

Too Much With Too Little and Too Little With Too Much

**ANSWERS
ARE NOT
ENOUGH.**

Televi$ion

**Magic
IS THE
science
OF THE
future!**

Do It!

supersonic jet aircraft, and antibiotic drugs. Or think of the changes wrought by video tape, laser beams, atomic power, artificial satellites and space exploration.

In industry, business, and even agriculture, we see an increasing use of *automation* — which may be defined as the application of mechanical and electronic devices, rather than the use of human labor, to control and regulate other machines. The overall effect of automation is to make possible "more and more complex sequences of operations with less and less human assistance." In recent years, automation has become essential to the operation of factories, government agencies, banks and insurance companies, telephone systems, health services, and most other phases of our economy.

Although the introduction of a new labor-saving device in a place of employment often leads to the elimination of many jobs, and sometimes makes a good part of a young person's training irrelevant, it is by no means clear that the overall effect of automation has been or will be to reduce the total number of job openings. In fact, in some areas, it creates important new employment opportunities. However, these positions generally demand some type of specialized training, with the result that large numbers of unskilled and semi-skilled workers may be "left out in the cold." The problem here is that many people whose skills have been largely outmoded by technological changes may have a very difficult time learning a new and marketable skill.

This situation certainly creates perplexing problems for young people. It is frustrating to attempt to plan ahead when technological change may eliminate some jobs and open up other jobs only a few years from now. It is much more difficult now than formerly for a young person to get a rather menial job of some kind (such as office boy), "learn the business," and move up on the basis of on-the-job experience alone.

For the boy or girl who hopes to "get ahead" in modern business and industry, formal training or schooling is usually the first requirement, and this is likely to be more specialized, more demanding, and more expensive than comparable training only a generation ago. The paradox here is that a young person must be wary of overspecializing his education too much, since he is then limited in the types of jobs he can handle — but that if he does not become proficient in some *specific* skill area, he may find it very difficult to apply an overly general education to many technical jobs.

The result is that an adolescent who hopes to equip himself with adequate job skills must spend a great deal more time in getting formal education than did the typical boy or girl a generation ago. Thus, "adolescence is prolonged." In some cases, the young person may find himself economically dependent on his parents until he is well into his twenties.

Competition

Competition is woven into the very fabric of American life, and there is no place where this is more evident than in the schools. Adolescents in school feel a great deal of pressure to "do well" or to "win" — whether in schoolwork, sports, or social life. Parents often add to this pressure by "pushing" their children to earn higher grades, to "make" a school athletic team, or to demonstrate popularity among their peers.

Why do parents behave in this way? In the majority of cases, no doubt, they are convinced that they are acting in the best interests of their children. They accept the idea that success in adult life (however "success" may be defined) is determined by success in school. Specifically, they emphasize that high grades and an outstanding record in athletics will help the adolescent a few years later when he is attempting to get into a "good" college, so that he can get a "good" (high-salaried) job.

But adolescents sometimes feel that they are being exploited by their parents. It is often charged that many parents put pressure on their children to excel primarily because it will make *them* (the parents) feel successful and important. Also, a parent may sometimes project his own (often repressed) ambitions and dreams onto a child. For example, consider a man who as a boy had dreams of becoming an all-American college football hero. He never came close to achieving his goal — indeed, he never went to college. Now, however, he has a teen-age son. His fantasies of athletic "glory" are transferred to his son, whom he constantly urges to go out for the school football team, despite the son's lack of interest in the idea. The father is "bitterly disappointed" when his son fails to make the team. Is he disappointed for his son's sake or for his own sake? Or are both feelings intertwined?

Because of the emphasis on competition and "doing well," Americans characteristically show a great fear of failure and humiliation, even at an early age. In junior high school, and indeed even in elementary school, many boys and girls are likely to worry about grades, believing that this may affect their chances of being admitted to college some years hence.

Emphasis on competition, hard work, and self-reliance, is a tradition handed down to us from the early days of our history, when pioneers had to depend on their own courage, strength, and skill to survive in the wilderness. But are these values of "rugged individual-ism" just as relevant in today's highly interdependent society?

It should be pointed out, too, that along with these individualistic values in the frontier society went a vigorous spirit of neighborliness and community cooperation. People had to be ready and willing to help each other if they were to survive under often harsh conditions. But do we have such a cooperative spirit in general acceptance to modify the prevailing competitiveness of our present-day society?

In any event, young people sometimes feel that they are being driven too hard to compete, and they tend to resent this, both because they fear failure and because they so see no real need for being sub-jected to this kind of pressure.

Affluence

Adolescents in the 1970's have grown up in a culture which places great emphasis on affluence — on money and the things money can buy.

This is not to say that all Americans enjoy affluence. Indeed, there are millions of families living below what government officials have defined as the "poverty line." But Americans, rich, poor, and "in between," tend to attach great, and perhaps undue, importance to material wealth; they tend to judge people in large part on the basis of such things as homes, clothing, cars, jewelry, etc. Many people who

One characteristic of an affluent society is intensive development of com-mercial forms of entertainment. Young people play an important part in supporting such entertainment and in setting its standards.

desire even more material wealth are preoccupied with status — that is, admiration in the eyes of others.

Young people are an essential part of our affluent, commodity-centered, and waste-producing economy. As a group, they have tremendous buying power. This becomes evident if you think of the extent of advertising and merchandising in general which is directed at youth. The values and tastes of adolescents set the pace in many industries connected with clothing, popular music and other forms of entertainment, many food products, soft drinks, cosmetics, and many other items and services, running into billions of dollars per year.

Reforming the "System" and Reforming the Individual

We have emphasized the extraordinary pace of technological innovation in our society, but this climate of change goes far beyond technology.

Institutions, social movements, ideas, attitudes, tastes, standards appear to be transformed far more rapidly and on a much greater scale than in earlier generations. Drastic change seems to affect almost every aspect of our "American way of life." On the national, and also on the international, level there are repeated shocks that upset any assumptions we might have about a stable and ordered world.

To be sure, many of these changes may turn out in time to be less profound and less lasting than they seem at first. Nonetheless, the effect on many young people is to leave them with a distressing sense of uncertainty and instability.

Many teen-agers express the opinion that "if we can't depend on the future, then we should live for today." This reasoning may be all right, as long as today's living patterns are *good ones*. However, if the life style is marked by excessive self-indulgence — such as a tendency to ignore or delay essential work in favor of immediate pleasure — one can depend on the future to provide the penalties for neglect.

Perhaps some of the unconventional or "off-beat" behavior of adolescents may be traced to a culture which in many instances does not appear to provide a stable, meaningful way of life. Thus, any momentary experiences that seem pleasurable or rewarding are often highly prized. But are all these pleasures really "pleasurable" and rewarding? Also, doesn't the individual in *any* culture carry a responsibility for working out a way of life that meets his long-term needs (not just a momentary gratification)? Social problems and conflicts didn't begin in the 1970's.

On the other hand, since the culture in all of its aspects is presumably designed for the people, why can't our social institutions be adapted to respond to the urgent needs that come with rapid change? And if institutions can't be adapted in this way, shouldn't they be greatly modified, or even scrapped entirely? This is the background, or at least the justification, offered, for much of the "social radicalism" that dominates the opinions and behavior of many young people today.

There is no doubt that many of our institutions are inadequate and need reform. It may be, however, that there is sometimes too much emphasis on reforming the "system," and not enough on the obligation of the individual to reform and improve *himself* before, in effect, he tries to remake and redirect other people.

The Television Generation

Television and radio must certainly appear on any list of influences affecting the life pattern of the present generation of adolescents.

All adolescents today were born well after television had become a .tremendously powerful force, pervading our economy, our political life, our standards of popular taste, our everyday living habits, and (some would maintain) our basic perception of "reality."

The TV programs watched by so many millions every day have been the subject of many harsh evaluations. Some critics have condemned television as a "vast wasteland" which is culturally debasing. Other commentators point out, however, that there are interludes of worthwhile material. Specifically, they note that educational stations have introduced a new dimension of non-commercial programming. Traditionally, the commercial stations defend their material by claiming they reflect popular taste — that they "give people what they want."

At any rate, no one would question that TV and radio are exceedingly popular in our culture, and that young people in particular are vulnerable to the influences, conscious and unconscious, of what they see and hear on their home screens. The exact nature of these influences is hard to pin down, but most discerning observers would agree in mentioning the acceptance of violence as a means of solving problems, the glorification of youth and sexual attractiveness, and the emphasis on wealth, luxuries, and conspicuous consumption. There have always been great inequalities in our society, but people seeing the "high living" so amply displayed on TV are likely to be less willing to accept poverty, or even a modest standard of living, and more insistent on "getting their share" of the fruits of an affluent society.

How much harm is done by these influences is an open question. On the other hand, it should be noted that television networks have

"Don't you understand? This is *life,* this is what is happening! We *can't* switch to another channel."

done useful work in exploring and publicizing some of the most pressing problems of our society — racial discrimination, the persistence of poverty, drug abuse, the pollution of the environment, urban decay, the neglect of older people, mistreatment of children, etc. In this sense, the impact of television on young people and on the population in general can be considered a good one.

Some social scientists believe that the daily lives of millions are directly affected not only by the content of TV broadcasts but also by the *form* of the medium. Particularly susceptible to this influence, according to Canadian psychologist Marshal McLuhan, are the members of the current generation of adolescents who have been exposed to television from their earliest days. McLuhan, who originated the slogan "The Medium is the Message," asserts that television, regardless of what it may be "saying" or showing, involves the viewer with an impact, immediacy, and totality which other media, such as the printed word, cannot match.

Television offers an instantaneous, "total," and involving image, requiring little or no effort on the part of the viewer. The printed word is slower, more fragmented, "linear," and it requires at least some determination and effort on the part of the reader. Moreover, reading is an individualized activity, whereas a television program may reach tens of millions of people at the same time in exactly the same form. The sense of community or one-ness which some feel we are moving toward because of television is expressed by McLuhan's vivid phrase, "the global village."

Because of this tremendous psychological impact, McLuhan suggests that television alters our way of perceiving "reality" and therefore our way of thinking. The first television generation, now in its twenties, was also the first in modern times to dissent on a mass scale. It is to be expected, in McLuhan's view, that present-day adolescents should be more involved and more aware of world conditions, and less willing to participate in the standardized, though fragmented, culture of their elders.

In any case, few would disagree that in the 1970's adolescents have been and are being profoundly affected by television, and that it makes the movement toward adulthood significantly different than that of earlier generations.

Institutional Regimentation

We have already noted that modern technology calls for workers with more formalized education than was the case in earlier generations. Thus, a principal function of the schools is to supply people equipped with the desired work skills, or who have the background to acquire the desired skills readily.

Another phenomenon of American life is a high level of mobility. People move about in huge numbers from one city, suburb, region to another — probably at a greater rate than in any other country in the world — which leads to a need for standardization in education. Although we do not have a national school system (like that of Japan or France), the thousands of local school systems in the country tend to have a similar grade structure, to follow much the same curricula, and to use the same textbooks and other materials.

Despite the fact that there are widespread disparities in quality from school to school, a grade-school pupil in all probability could move from Seattle, Washington, to Rochester, New York, and then to Miami, Florida, without finding a substantial difference in how the schools are set up, what materials he is given to study, and what he is required to learn.

How well a child does in the educational system now plays a major part in shaping his future. Success in junior high school determines placement in high school, which in turn is often extremely important in determining whether he continues on to college. Likewise, graduation from college is considered essential if a young person wishes to enter one of the professions or to get a better paying job that may set him on the track to executive status.

Most larger employers, including government agencies, are organized hierarchically. A young person enters at a certain level and

"Excuse me, sir. I am prepared to make you a rather attractive offer for your square."

Drawing by Weber; © 1971 The New Yorker Magazine, Inc.

seeks to move upward, into successively higher (and fewer) slots, each with a corresponding increase in pay, privileges and status. (This hierarchical structure is seen in its clearest form in the armed forces.) The level the individual attains in this structure determines his socio-economic class.

Thus, we see that most young Americans today begin an "institutional life" at age six or so, when they enter school, and continue it through their years of schooling and employment. At every stage, they are expected to meet definite requirements (often set by their superiors in the hierarchy) which are applied to them and everyone else of the same status. If they hope to move on to the next level, they must satisfy these requirements. It is usually during adolescence that the individual becomes keenly aware that he is involved in this institutional structure (some would say, this "rat race"), and it is at this time, too, that he must take some crucial steps that may affect his entire future.

Institutions are essential to our society, but they tend to be regimented, inflexible, and impersonal. Because they deal with large numbers of people, most of whom must be treated in much the same way, individuality may be crushed in the process; individual effort and qualities may be overtly or tacitly resisted or discouraged.

The individual in an institutionalized situation (such as a student in a big-city high school, an insurance company clerk, or an army recruit) often feels like a mere pawn, controlled by others whom he knows only from afar, if at all. In effect, he is being "manipulated" like a "thing," and he is powerless to do much about it. There is much talk of *cooperation* in large organizations, but what is not so often expressed openly is that cooperation is motivated in large part by *fear*. In general, people can be manipulated effectively only through their own fears. For example, many organizations back up their demands on the individual by threats (which may or may not be stated openly) that failure to comply will result in various penalties — loss of economic security, decline in social status, and even legal prosecution and punishment.

If a spirit of cooperation is marred by an atmosphere of fear, then rules, standards, procedures often seem dehumanizing. Institutional life is especially difficult for the adolescent, who is becoming aware that he must establish his individual worth and begin to move toward his self-realization.

Political Protest

"The revolution is in the high schools!"

With this pronouncement, Students for a Democratic Society (SDS) indicated a few years ago that it intended to focus on the high schools, as well as the colleges, in promoting a program of radical revolutionary activity. Although the SDS is now defunct, other similar organizations have taken over its program — to convince large numbers of high school students that our political, economic, and social system is no good and must be completely overthrown, by militant action, if necessary.

How much effect specific political organizations, such as SDS, have had in directly influencing high school students is open to question. There is little doubt, however, that much of the politically-related dissent and protest in American high schools today is connected to the issues discussed above and in the following pages. These have forced our young people to search more vigorously, and perhaps frantically, for the answers to questions which may be summed up as *Who am I? . . . Who are you?*

The inherent frustration of youth, aggravated by social institutions and trends which are considered unsatisfactory, has led to a wave of political protest in American high schools. For example, throughout the country, high school students have cooperated with college students in demonstrating against extension and continuation of the war in Southeast Asia, as well as against the military draft. The protest has taken mainly peaceful forms—mass meetings, speeches, marches, distribution of literature—but there has also been some violence.

The phasing out of American participation in the Vietnam fighting and the suspension of the draft in 1973 met some of the immediate demands of the protesters but did relatively little to change the critical and skeptical attitude toward many other phases of our society. Many young people continue to make it amply clear that they are not satisfied with the "way the establishment is running things." With Vietnam and compulsory military service no longer a focal point of discontent, they emphasize other alleged abuses, such as the network of scandals and official misconduct in high places symbolized by the word "Watergate." Such dissatisfaction is not new. Each younger generation since the dawn of history has probably complained about the "mess" their elders have made. What *is* startling is the intensity and seriousness of the criticism (and also the clarity of the resentment), and the strength of the determination to do something to clear up the "mess."

Racism

Racism is certainly one of the focal points of criticism leveled by young people at our society. Unfortunately, it cannot be denied that racism has been characteristic of American life throughout our history.

Our nation was formed with acceptance and legalization of black slavery, and on the basis of expropriation of Indian lands. The racial problems derived from these origins have not yet been overcome. It is

Militant protests by racial minority groups have become a familiar sight on high school and college campuses in recent years.

true that significant progress has been made in recent years, but it is also true that racist abuses remain embodied in our social framework.

Many high school students are deeply concerned over such injustice, since it is something that they can observe directly in the course of their daily living. At the other extreme, efforts to remedy age-old inequities often cause severe difficulties for young people. In recently integrated schools, racial tension is often high, and it is not uncommon today for big-city high schools to be patrolled by security guards. The violence or threat of violence which leads to such measures is not exclusively racial in origin, but racial troubles do play a part in most cases.

The racist issue is particularly important for adolescents of all races, involving, as it does, their personal feelings and fears about themselves and their peers. Often, it provides an opportunity for individual action. Young people can observe in their social activities the results of a problem which the larger society has failed to solve.

Ecology

Ecology is the study of the environment. Because of a variety of forces — including industrialization, urbanization, population growth, an economy which is partly dependent on "planned obsolescence" (deliberate waste), and simple neglect — we are faced today with a massive problem of the pollution and spoilage of all phases of our environment. Pollution represents a major threat to our health, our generally abundant standard of living, and our need to have order, cleanliness, and beauty in our daily lives.

Young people, with many years of life ahead of them, are particularly concerned about ecological abuses. They are aware that, unless large-scale reforms are introduced soon, conditions which are bad today will be all but intolerable by the time their children are growing up. Thus, we find that many students are now playing an important part in various ecology groups both inside and outside schools. Young people are conspicuous in innumerable activities of this nature — cleaning up a city street, rescuing and washing birds covered with oil from offshore oil spillages, planting trees and shrubbery, removing debris from a stream and its banks, monitoring the quality of the air, and the like.

Obviously the ecological havoc provides young people with yet another demonstration of shortsightedness, inefficiency, and outright selfishness on the part of "the older generation."

It remains to be seen, however, whether the young people who voice such bitter complaints will have the strength of character to carry over the necessary changes into their own daily lives. It is one thing to get emotionally indignant over the ecological sins of the past. It is quite another to be willing to do all that will be necessary for reforms in the future. These requirements may include restrictions on the production and use of many commodities, sacrifice of the use of private automobiles in favor of public transportation, huge expenditures of public funds (and therefore higher taxes), and possibly even limitations on the size of families.

Women's Liberation

"Women's Lib" is a movement devoted to exposing and correcting what its advocates consider the systematic oppression, degradation, and exploitation of women in our society.

In a sense, this represents an extension and continuation of the "Women's Rights" movement of earlier generations, but it goes much further in its criticism of our social structure and in its program for reform. The "Lib" not only wants women to have absolute equality in all legal and institutional affairs (including employment and politics), but demands a change in traditional *ways of thinking* that have cast women in the role of inferior creatures, who are too often seen as "objects of sexual exploitation."

Whether or not large numbers of women in the United States accept the premises and the program of this movement is not really known. However, there is considerable indication that "Women's Lib" has had a measurable impact on the adolescent generation, boys included. It may be assumed that this will affect their attitudes when they grow to adulthood and begin to have more influence on the basic social patterns of our culture. (Women's Liberation is discussed at length in Chapter 17.)

Educational Reform

In the current uproar over the abuses and inadequacies of our society, the educational institutions themselves are inevitable targets. In fact, educational reform is one of the major concerns of students at the high school and college levels.

Many complain that courses are boring and "irrelevant," and they protest a lack of freedom in choosing areas of study. They say that current curricula are not helping to prepare them for the kind of adult life they want to lead. Regimentation, rigidly structured classes, authoritarian teachers and administrators, and "dehumanization" also seem to be common complaints.

One practical result of this protest is that in more and more institutions — high schools as well as colleges — students are being consulted more seriously and systematically than ever before. The advice, information, and even the "demands" they present may play an important part in shaping changes in the educational program and in the entire administrative structure of the schools.

Drugs

Another problem facing adolescents in the 1970's is illegal use of drugs. There has been a veritable epidemic of drug use, involving mainly marijuana ("pot," "grass"), hashish ("hash"), amphetamines ("speed," "pep pills," "uppers"), barbiturates (sleeping pills, "downers") and LSD ("acid"). In some cases there is evidence of widespread use of "hard" drugs, above all heroin.

Some of the drugs are more dangerous than others, but there is ample evidence that excessive use of any of them can produce undesirable effects on the developing body, mind, and personality of the young person. Some drugs, particularly heroin and barbiturates, are *physically addictive,* meaning that once a person is "hooked," he must have the drug regularly if he is to avoid severe withdrawal symptoms, which can sometimes result in death. All drugs may lead to *psychological dependence,* meaning that they give some form of "satisfaction" and provide emotional support that the person who takes them is unable or unwilling to do without.

Perhaps it is the very illegality of these drugs that attracts some young people to them. When boys and girls are in revolt against the "Establishment" and the conventional standards, they may be inclined to look favorably on anything that is forbidden by the law and condemned by "respectable" society. But the drug world should not be regarded as a valid symbol for non-conformism.* (Drugs are discussed in greater detail on pages 242-253.)

Sexual Permissiveness

There is much talk today of a "sexual revolution." Many observers who have studied this question carefully doubt that there has

---

* Young people are sometimes impressed by the fact that pop singers and other performers whom they admire greatly are reputed to be drug users. "If those wonderful people can do it, why can't I?" But drug use in recent years has brought the lives of some highly successful performers to an early end. Jimi Hendrix, for example, freely admitted using all kinds of drugs. In his album, *Cry of Love,* released after his death in 1970, Hendrix indicates his despair over drugs. If you listen closely, you will hear an anti-drug message throughout the album.

been a change in behavior sufficiently significant and widespread to be called a "revolution."

There is, however, a good deal of evidence that among some groups, at least, the attitude toward sexual activity outside the marriage bond has become more lenient or permissive than it was in previous generations.

This inevitably has had an effect on sexual activity among adolescents, for they are at a stage of life when the sexual drive is particularly difficult to deal with, and when (in contrast to earlier generations) marriage is usually not feasible. Such increase in sexual activity has led to a rise in unwanted pregnancies, in venereal disease, and in emotional problems related to early sexual experimentation. It should be noted that the sense of guilt and confusion resulting from early sex experience often adds to the anxieties and misunderstandings so common during adolescence. (See Chapter 23 for a discussion of this topic.)

Issues and Challenges

Conflicts . . . challenges . . . issues . . . problems — these are the terms we have used repeatedly in discussing the situation of adolescent Americans in the 1970's. For clarity, we have "fragmented" our discussion, considering each change or source of difficulty by itself, but of course they are all operating simultaneously, contributing to the general atmosphere of tensions and uncertainty.

In Part II of "The Adolescent in the 1970's," we shall consider how teen-agers are reacting to demands made on them. Before we turn to this, let us briefly summarize the general social environment of our times from the adolescent point of view:

First of all, each young person is engaged in his own process of self-development and self-definition. As always, this includes an awareness of the society within which he lives. The difference, as compared with earlier generations, is that the boys and girls of the 1970's, with the aid of instantaneous communication, are far more directly and keenly aware of social problems and issues than were their parents before them.

Adolescents react to the forces of their culture, but they are also the products of that culture. We have identified some of the forces that characterize and shape our cultural environment: *mass communication media, institutional life, affluence, high-powered technology, rapid change, an insistent demand for far-reaching reforms on many levels.* You may be able to think of others.

NOTE: Questions and activities for this chapter will be found on pages 295-296.

THE ADOLESCENT IN THE 1970'S

CULTURE AND COUNTER-CULTURE

PART II

●●●●●●●●●●●●●●●●●●●●●●●●●●●

"At this breaking point between two radically different and closely related groups [the younger and older generations] both are inevitably very lonely as we face each other, knowing that they will never experience what we have experienced, and that we can never experience what they have experienced."

— MARGARET MEAD

A Difficult Adjustment

What adolescents today are trying to do, in the broadest terms, is to work out a way of life that responds to the social forces to which they are exposed, and that also meets their own needs.

This is indeed a difficult thing to do. The situation is extremely complex, and even if satisfactory "solutions" were readily apparent, the adolescent is not usually in a position of power to put them into effect. (This holds true for the most part in spite of certain changes that have taken place in recent years, such as the 18-year-old vote and increased representation of students in school and college administrations.)

We have already noted some of the ways in which young people react to the forces and demands which impinge upon them. These include: a break with parental direction and authority; greater reliance on the peer culture for emotional security and for defining experiences; and conformity to the standards and style of the peer group.

Apathy

One response to seemingly overwhelming problems is *apathy,* a behavior pattern that is now typical of many adolescents, as well as adults. Apathy manifests itself as a *lack of concern* for what is hap-

283

pening to other people, to society as a whole, and even to oneself. If nothing can be done about a problem, why worry about it? Why even show interest in it? Or some individuals may claim that their own personal difficulties are so immediate and demanding that they "can't be concerned" about social issues (that is, about other people). This is the attitude that some young people profess in regard to such matters as war and peace, race relations, poverty, drug abuse, and other pressing social problems.

The psychological basis for this attitude is often the avoidance of feelings of guilt by suppressing any sense of personal responsibility to other people. In some cases, however, apathy may be due to ignorance of the seriousness of a problem. Some young people who have appeared apathetic will respond positively when they become convinced that they have a personal stake in such causes as combating environmental pollution or improving race relations. Often the decisive factor in overcoming apathy is a demonstration that there is something the *individual can do* on his own responsibility to influence the course of events.

Frequently, apathy extends to the interests which are considered "normal" for adolescents, such as schoolwork, and sometimes sports, dating, friendships, and other typical activities and relationships. Continued apathy about such matters and withdrawal from personal responsibilities are clearly leading along the path of self-defeat. Such behavior is usually the result of emotional or possibly physical problems, and often professional aid should be sought.

Activism

This is the type of adolescent response to the contemporary social scene that usually receives the most public attention. Ideally, activism suggests a sharp awareness of a problem, and a directed, vigorous, and sustained effort to do something about it. The individual may be working more or less on his own or as part of an organized group.

In the public mind, activism is associated mainly with "radical" or "left-wing" groups. But this is really an oversimplification. There are certainly "conservative" or "right-wing" activists. And there are expressions of activism which have no specific political coloration, such as volunteer work in hospitals and mental institutions, and tutoring services for underprivileged children.

In recent years "black activism" has been particularly important in the United States. In the schools, this takes the form of calling for courses in black studies, the hiring of more black teachers and administrators, programs of remedial or compensatory education where

needed, and more scholarships for black students who wish to continue their education beyond high school or junior college. On the broader national scene, "black activism" seeks to eliminate all the remaining aspects of racial injustice, discrimination, and inequality in American life. The campaign is pursued on many levels, in both government and private sectors. Many young people, including whites, are strongly dedicated to this cause and find great personal satisfaction in it.

Another popular form of adolescent activism relates to the schools themselves. Some young people are working for "reform" of their educational institutions by sweeping revision of the curriculum and by introduction of various experimental programs. A relatively small number of students, dissatisfied with the education they are getting, have set up "free" schools and universities not under the control of the regular educational authorities. Another manifestation of this same attitude is the publication by students of "underground newspapers," not officially recognized by the school authorities. The ideas expressed in these papers are often radical or "far-out," and they may be presented in a style that many adults consider outrageous.

A word of warning is necessary at this point: Some activism is not motivated by healthy impulses but rather is a reaction to strongly repressed unconscious conflicts. Of course, we should not be too quick to accuse apparently altruistic people of such a weakness. On the other hand, we should be aware that when people undertake to correct an "evil," they may be reacting impulsively to their own inner problems. The danger in this situation is that it becomes difficult to tell what is truly an evil, and what is a delusion, or at least a misinterpretation, on the part of the would-be reformer. Adolescents are particularly susceptible to this danger, since they are confronting powerful emotional tensions of which they are just becoming aware, and which often they have not yet learned to work out in the actual "give and take" of living.

In this connection, it should be understood that people are sometimes inclined to demand "privileges" which in the long run may not turn out to be as beneficial as they had originally believed. For example, a law to insure women "complete equality" in employment may in practice deprive many women workers of special forms of protection which they have been given by the industrial codes of various states. This is not to say, however, that there is not a long list of substantial social grievances which can only be corrected through active work.

Violence

An extreme reaction to a person's social environment is physical violence.* In general, this cannot be considered a form of activism, as we have defined it, even when it is advocated by "activist" or militant groups. Violence is almost always a response to frustration resulting from a social situation which the individual finds "intolerable." He then "justifies" the resort to violence by arguing that all other means of bringing about necessary changes have proved futile.

When adolescents feel great anger or a sense of extreme urgency about some matter, they may become involved in violence. This is usually an *almost* involuntary act of desperation, resulting from a temporary but intense emotion, rather than a deliberate, calculated effort to hurt other people or to destroy property. For example, a boy subjected to an insult in a racially tense school may lash out with a violence that surprises even himself, and which may then spread to others, who are caught up in a flash fire of strong passions.

However, even such an emotionalized situation does not excuse violence. It is within the power of nearly everyone to place controls on himself so that he will not respond automatically to momentary rages and desires.

Spur-of-the-moment violence is not far removed from much "planned" violence in its psychological basis. However, a very different type of phenomenon is represented by young people who use

---

* For a detailed examination of violence, see Chapter 19, "Why Do Men Kill?"

violence as professional criminals — who form gangs for stealing, mugging, and controlling "turf" or "territory" by force. The boys who behave in this way are frequently suffering from severe emotional disorders. (The fact that these disorders can often be traced back to severe social disorganization makes them no less damaging to the boys and to other people involved.)

Withdrawal

Withdrawal takes many forms among young people, but its distinguishing characteristic is an unwillingness to face reality and a refusal to undertake some definite course of action designed to solve a problem or overcome a difficulty.

There are, of course, different degrees of withdrawal, and not all of them are necessarily irrational or ineffective. There *are* situations in life, especially for young people, when the best thing to do, in all probability, is to sit quietly "on the sidelines" and wait for things to improve or to work themselves out in some way. After a time, there may be a better opportunity for effective action.

On the other hand, withdrawal is unhealthy and dangerous when the young person shows a pattern of inertness or inactivity for a long period of time, or when he simply ignores or denies the existence of a problem. For example, a boy may have failing grades in school. This, in itself, is no great tragedy. It can happen to anyone under certain circumstances. If the boy makes a reasonable effort to improve his grades, little harm has been done. The experience may even be beneficial to him. But there is clear evidence of emotional trouble if the boy shows no concern about the failure (particularly if it is repeated), if he rejects every effort to help him, or if he simply refuses to acknowledge that any problem exists.

Apathy is sometimes considered a mild form of withdrawal. Long-continued drug use is certainly another form. When a young person habitually seeks the consolation of drugs — whether it be the abnormal stimulation of amphetamines, the hallucinatory "trip" of LSD, or the drunkenness of alcohol — he is, in effect, retreating from himself and his problems. Lacking the courage, or strength or know-how to face certain facts, he pretends, with the help of drugs, that the facts don't exist.

When a young person drops out of school, or quits a job without having any other job in prospect, he is sometimes considered to be exhibiting a withdrawal response. The individual has discontinued one form of activity (school or job) without having anything to substitute for it. On the other hand, there probably are situations where "withdrawal" in this sense is justified. The young person, it may be, is not just "copping out," but is looking for another way of life that will suit him better, though his search may be troubled and confused.

Alienation

Alienation is a much-discussed term used to describe the feelings and attitudes of a person who has become estranged from his cultural environment. He believes that the society in which he is living has little or no meaning for him, and that there is virtually nothing he can do to find a secure and satisfying place within it. He is, in brief, an alien or stranger in his own land.

Adolescence is, almost by definition, an alienated stage of life. The individual is changing so rapidly that "he is not sure who he is." He is seeking his identity and, in the course of this sometimes painful process, he may become estranged from his family, his friends, or even his culture. In most cases, however, the symptoms of such adolescent alienation are relatively mild and show definite signs of correcting themselves as important life decisions are made and positive steps are taken.

But alienation is properly considered to be extreme and dangerous when it persists over long periods of time, and the young person appears unable to adapt himself to the conditions of his life. Of course, it sometimes happens that there is a change in the individual's convictions that causes him to become alienated, perhaps reluctantly, from his family, his old friends, and the culture in general. Such convictions are worthy of respect when they are sincerely held and are the result of serious, careful consideration. Nonetheless, there is a danger involved in this pattern — that the young person will become alienated in an extreme sense *from himself,* thus leading to severe psychic disorders.

Adolescents who display an unhealthy type of extreme alienation vary widely in their reactions. But these reactions, whatever their special characteristics, never seem to fit the situation. This is true of those young people to whom "nothing matters," and also of those to whom "things matter too much." Alienated behavior may be similar to apathy or withdrawal — or at the other extreme, it may show up in the form of an intensity of emotion that most people would consider abnormal.

The usual difficulties inherent in adolescence become exaggerated as the alienated youngster finds himself cut off emotionally from his family and his peers and unable to find a satisfactory social setting for himself.

Traditionalism and Anti-Traditionalism

There are, of course, still a great many young people whose way of life is "traditional" in the sense that it conforms closely to activities and interests of earlier generations. In spite of the social changes all around them, these boys and girls continue to engage in sports, dating, parties, high school clubs, hobbies, and so forth, much as their parents and grandparents did.

No young person who chooses this traditional style of life need apologize for it. In spite of all the trouble in the world, it is still important to have fun. Moreover, being active in sports and in social activities is not equivalent to being "empty-headed." Those who go in for this kind of thing may be just as aware of social problems and, in their own way, just as involved in serious activities as their less traditional classmates.

On the other hand, the "traditionalists" would do well to refrain from condemning and deriding those of their contemporaries whose tastes and interests differ somewhat from their own.

Each adolescent peer group sets its own standards of "normality" and tends to regard those outside the immediate group as "not with it" or "out of it." But in these days of diversity and rapid change, both "traditionalists" and "anti-traditionalists" should show a reasonable amount of respect for each other's life style. It is impossible to say that one is "better" than the other. They are simply different people seeking satisfaction and adjustment in different ways.

The Counter-Culture

We all know that there are many young people today who refuse to follow what is generally considered a "normal" life pattern. They

The big hassle over "long hair" for boys has died down considerably in the last few years. Perhaps other aspects of the counter-culture life style will come to be more widely tolerated — and even accepted as "conventional."

drop out of the educational system; or, if they have been graduated, they regard their certificates and degrees as meaningless.

These young people either do not enter the job market at all, or they decline to compete for high-wage employment and take low-paid work. Many of the more idealistic ones seek jobs with well-defined "social service" functions and are not concerned with making money or "getting ahead"—of someone else. (With the suspension of the draft, young men no longer have to cope with the problem of military service.)

They dress unconventionally, frequently preferring hand-me-down clothing that is rough and shabby. Even the girls make it a point to minimize efforts at self-adornment. In general, they scoff at the American obsession with "consumerism," although there are those who seem to have something of an obsession of their own in regard to high-quality stereo equipment and the latest in psychedelic records. Many also consume quantities of costly drugs.

Some live together in communes. Many undertake hitch-hiking trips across the land. Some work at various handicrafts. And there are those who have no compunctions about panhandling (begging), or even about stealing (from "establishment" types).

This unconventional or "bohemian" life style has been called the *counter-culture*. The phenomenon of the counter-culture represents probably the most complex of all reactions to contemporary social forces. It contains elements of some of the other specific responses we have discussed above, but it is far more comprehensive — more of a total way of life and a system of values than a specific adaptation or mannerism.

The counter-culture, in other words, describes a distinctive sub-culture, comprised primarily of young people, that exists within the larger culture. Members of the counter-culture believe in *withdrawal* to some degree from the dominant culture, although they are also frequently engaged in *activist* protest in an attempt to reform existing institutions or practices. In the ranks of the counter-culture are many young people *alienated* from the majority culture.

Counter-culture people typically differ from the rest of the population in their living habits, which include among other things their speech, dress, hair style, music, sexual patterns, and attitudes toward work and money. Another feature is the use of drugs, particularly marijuana, hashish, and LSD, although drug use is by no means universal, and is certainly not limited to the counter-culture. In fact, many counter-culture people have become disillusioned with drugs and advocate getting away from them.

Keenly aware of their lack of communication with "straight" society, these people seek each other's company. Sometimes, as noted, they form communes, or work together in political organizations, or simply live in close proximity in urban and rural communities, often around college campuses where they can find kindred souls.

The counter-culture, by its own definition, is opposed to the traditional American way of life. Because some of its members are known to use illegal drugs, because they flaunt their lack of respect for traditional authority and symbols of authority, because they reject the values and standards of the adult generation, many people see the counter-culture as an enemy of society and therefore as a threat to their own well-being.

Consequently, the people of this subculture are often faced with harassment in the form of police raids (usually "drug busts"), suppression of their newspapers, violence in public places directed against them during "confrontations," and a general disregard of their constitutional guarantees (sometimes backed up by an attitude that they are somehow not "real" citizens of the United States).

Rock music festivals, which are tremendously popular with the adherents of the counter-culture as well as with young people in general, have been prohibited or at least strongly discouraged in many parts of the country. Defenders of these festivals claim that in general they have been orderly and peaceful, and that such violence as has occurred has often been fomented by "outside" elements, including the police.

Rock festivals are by no means purely an American phenomenon. The "Isle of Wight Pop Festival" (in Great Britain) draws an audience of many thousands, almost all of them young people, coming from many different countries.

Still, it is not hard to see why the adult generation finds it difficult to come to terms with such phenomena as rock festivals. The large crowds *are* difficult to handle, and some people attending *are* given to drug use, profanity, nudity, and other forms of behavior which shock the sensibilities of many of the older generation. Violence *has* occurred on occasions. The music itself is an unsettling factor. To begin with, this kind of music rarely appeals to older people. The lyrics, insofar as older people can decipher them, refer at times to anti-establishment politics, drug use, and sexual "freedom" in a favorable context.

Rock festivals are significant to the extent that they highlight the deepseated opposition between the majority culture, dominated by older adults, and the counter-culture, dominated by young adults and teen-agers.

Divisions Within the Counter-Culture

There is a temptation to speak misleadingly of the counter-culture as though it were a highly unified organization. Actually, it is not in any real sense an "organization," and there are many schisms or divisions within the movement which cannot be overlooked.

The clearest opposition is between the *activist-militants* and the *hippies* (or *street people,* as they are sometimes called), although it is frequently very hard to say who is a "real" militant and who is a "real" hippie. Many people appear to fit both categories, and there are certainly "anti-establishment" types who fit into neither.

The activist-militants face the dilemma of whether or not to fight the system on its own terms. Their most realistic members realize that they cannot hope to gain their ends unless they adopt some of the values and the style of the "straight" society, including discipline, restraint, subordination to leaders, postponement of immediate satisfactions, and appeal to large cross sections of the population. Often these values are strongly at odds with individual inclinations. Thus, activist groups, particularly the more militant ones, face a continuing struggle to keep their own members in line.

The activists usually advocate exhausting all possible non-violent remedies before resorting to violence. Nonetheless, their efforts do sometimes have unforeseen violent results when individuals show impatience with "gradualism" and "persuasion." Also, the bitter hostility and resistance of the larger society may well contribute to explosive situations.

As for the hippies, it is quite hard to define who they are. Originally, they were the "flower children," who preached peace, tranquility, and love. Many young people are still firm believers in such an outlook, but others have come to the conviction that these virtues must be accompanied by hard, sustained work of some kind. Frequently, the lives of many hippies, contrary to popular belief, do have a strong sense of direction, order, and purpose, but they refuse to follow a fixed cultural formula imposed from the outside. In many cases, it is unclear whether they have "dropped out" entirely, or are working within the system according to their own convictions.

Very often hippies are criticized for excessive self-indulgence, but it is not certain that this is any longer true, if it ever was. Young people throughout history have always been prone to a degree of self-indulgence, whenever they "can get away with it." The behavior of the hippies in this respect may not be very different, except in specific form, from that of other young people of today or of earlier generations — or of many older people, for that matter.

The Generation Gap

Margaret Mead, a leading anthropologist and social scientist, has suggested that people born since the close of World War II (1945) have been living in a different world, in terms of experience, than those born earlier. The post-World War II generation has grown up in a social atmosphere compounded of fear of nuclear destruction, dynamic social change, "far-out" technology, environmental deterioration, television, urbanization and suburbanization, population pressure, and other forces already identified in this book.

According to Dr. Mead, this is the background for the much-discussed *generation gap*. As she puts it, "At this breaking point between two radically different and closely related groups, both are inevitably very lonely as we face each other, knowing that they will never experience what we have experienced, and that we can never experience what they have experienced."

"As far as I'm concerned, all this flapdoodle about the environment is just a trick to take our minds off the Commies."

Drawing by Donald Reilly; © 1970 The New Yorker Magazine, Inc.

Where Do We Go from Here?

The extreme form that the counter-culture has taken and the extremism of many of the reactions to it are important signs of the profound changes our society is undergoing. There is ample historical evidence that internal violence and wars often accompany periods of great social change. Our society may be groping toward a new way of handling its problems — toward a greatly modified index of human values by which we may judge both the benefits and the evils that modern technology can bring us. Another way of saying this is that we may be in the process of *reordering our values and priorities*. This process is not an easy one in any case, and the youthful members of the counter-culture do not make it easier by an attitude which sometimes seems dogmatic and provocative. The life style of their elders, with its standardized, fragmented, and "anxious" outlook, is loudly rejected as being unreal, inappropriate, and undesirable.

But cultural change in the real world is usually a process of compromise and fusion. Dr. Mead has suggested that we may be moving toward a future culture in which the old will allow the young to discover new ways of life, and the young will allow the old to give them skills, guidance, and perspective, when needed. *Can the two generations and the two cultures work together in some effective way to help solve our social problems and create an improved quality of life?* The answer to this momentous question will take shape during your lifetime.

Challenge and Change

The adolescent in all times and places is in a period of transition when he must establish a self-concept, apart from his family and usually with "a little help from his friends." This is always difficult, but the adolescent in the 1970's faces the additional challenge of growing up in a society in transition. This is a time when social problems are becoming more urgent, when traditional values are under attack, when authority is being questioned as rarely before in our history. In this trying situation, young people are more involved in society than ever before. They are earnestly seeking answers to the questions and problems that beleaguer us. But the situation is extremely complicated and the difficulties are massive. What can and should be done is far from obvious, and ideas based on sweeping generalizations and simplistic slogans may have little worth in the real world.

The responses of young people to this state of affairs range across the philosophical and political spectrum — from withdrawal to activism, from apathy to violence, from sacrifice and self-denial to uninhibited self-indulgence.

Adolescence in our times is marked by unanswered questions, confusion and contradiction, fear and frustration, and above all challenges and change. It is not far-fetched to say that the way young people (in the United States and other countries) respond to this confused and trying situation will have profound effects on the future of our society.

THINGS TO DISCUSS :: THINGS TO DO :: THINGS TO READ

1. Very often, in discussions of the dominant culture and counter-culture in the United States, reference is made to the "American way of life." What does this phrase mean to you? What does it appear to mean to many older people who use it in criticizing the counter-culture? Can you see any way of bridging this gap in interpretation?

2. Analyze a peer group of which you have some direct, first-hand knowledge. Describe how it controls the behavior of its members. What services does the group perform for these young people?

3. Select several popular television shows of different types — drama, news, documentary, quiz, comedy-variety, etc. How does each of these reflect important currents and problems in our society? In what ways do you think the ideas and feelings of the people who watch these shows may be influenced? Are you aware of any such influence that has been exerted on *you*?

4. What is meant by "militancy" as applied to contemporary social problems and activities in the United States? What advantages and/or disadvantages do you see in such militancy? Discuss fully.

5. "The ills of our society are exceedingly complex and deep-rooted. There is little that one person, especially a young person, can do to affect them. Therefore, the best thing to do is simply to accept prevailing conditions and institutions and try to function successfully and decently as an individual."

   What do you think of this diagnosis? If you think that there is something wrong with it, try to pin down exactly where it is fallacious and inadequate.

6. Collect some "underground" newspapers and magazines and some "establishment" newspapers and magazines. Write an essay analyzing the differences and similarities. Some points to consider might be content, style of communication, what these publications seem to be trying to accomplish.

7. Young people often claim to be rebelling against the "system" and the "establishment." What is the "system"? Who are the "establishment"? Are these terms mere "vogue words," or do they have meanings which can help young people orient themselves in our society?

8. At any given time, there are usually one or two movies that are extremely popular with young people. Select such a picture that has this status now, and try to get everyone in the class to see it. Then discuss it. Why is it so popular? What does it have to say? Is it likely to become a "classic" — a film that retains its popularity and prestige year after year? What are the elements that make it so popular and enduring?

READINGS

Growing Up Absurd, by Paul Goodman (Random House, 1960). This is an entertaining, useful book. It provides a profound insight into personality and society.

The Vanishing Adolescent, by Edgar Z. Friedenberg (Beacon, 1959). This book provides an interesting perspective on adolescence in relation to our culture. Note that it appeared in 1959. Does it still apply to today's world?

The Making of the Counter-Culture, by Theodore Roszak (Doubleday, 1969). Roszak first made the word "counter-culture" popular. The book contains many important, if controversial, ideas.

Youth, Marriage, and the Seductive Society, by Frank D. Cox (Revised edition: William C. Brown, 1968). Cox gives an excellent analysis of how the "seductive society" operates on human development.

Summerhill, by A. S. Neill (Hart Publishing Company, 1960). The first statement on "free schools." Now considered a classic.

The Psychology of Changing Life Styles

> *"Behold, here I am."*
> —*ABRAHAM (in* Genesis, 22-1)

A Time of Troubles

We live in troubled times, with strong tides sweeping over the familiar institutional forms of our society. At any given time, the headlines scream of profoundly unsettling developments—Watergate . . . the energy crisis . . . threats to the environment . . . armed conflict in many regions, . . . inflation . . . crime . . . and a host of others.

The reactions to these disruptions are as diverse as American society itself. At one extreme are the optimists who say, "However damaging these events may be, they do not destroy my faith in America as a country and a civilization. We are facing reality and benefiting from our mistakes. What is good will survive and grow stronger. As time goes on, people will stop deceiving and hurting each other." At the other extreme is the counsel of despair: "Our society is based on irrationality and lies. The world is in worse shape than ever, and is bound to get still worse."

Many of us, probably, would express opinions somewhere in between these extremes. But few of us would deny that some of the old certainties are crumbling, and that there is a greater need than ever before to think our way through to new values, or to a reaffirmation of old values, that will be personally meaningful and socially responsible.

From the 1960's to the 1970's

Whatever the evaluation, the fact remains that our society is changing rapidly, and that these changes rarely conform to anyone's predetermined ideas of what is rational or desirable. Young people in the

1970's reflect this sense of uncertainty and ambiguity. The 1960's began with a burning conviction that things were wrong in many respects but that they could be put right by relatively simple "reforms." Out of this attitude came the philosophy and program of the counter-culture, shared to a greater or lesser degree by a vast number of the most able, intelligent, and socially conscious young people. But the decade ended in confusion, and the 1970's have not produced a movement as coherent and dynamic as the counter-culture once appeared to be.

The idealism of the 1960's, to be sure, has not simply disappeared. There is still a strong sense of devotion to various "causes"—civil rights, environmentalism, Women's Lib, justice for migratory farm workers, consumerism, a many-sided program for economic reform. But there is probably less conviction now than there was a decade or so ago that all of this can and will add up to a constructive reshaping of our society. Young people today are not so much proclaiming their counter-culture as groping for a life style that will be satisfying and in accord with reality. They are involved in a search for answers that will give their lives meaning and direction. In a sense, this is the job of *every* new generation, but it is particularly difficult and urgent today because we are apparently living in a transitional period when major social changes (however dimly perceived at present) are taking form.

This attitude of dissatisfaction, of quest for values, of willingness to learn from experience rather than from rigid dogmas, shows itself in many different aspects of present-day life.

Getting "Into" Something Socially Useful

Many young people today are intent on doing something socially useful *right now*—not many years from now, when (as they see it) they will be old, tired, and complacent. It has become quite fashionable to get "into" something, including such fields as psychology, the health professions, and child development work. This usually calls for a period of preparation and formal study, so that the individual will have not merely the qualifications but the formal credentials to engage in the activity. In this sense, the scornful rejection of the "establishment," more typical of the 1960's, has had to be modified.

But entering a field of professional service does not imply uncritical acceptance of the established ways of doing things. Many young people think of themselves as catalysts—agents for necessary change. Thus, in the field of education, they may become active in "alternative" or "free" schools, which focus more on the child's individual self-expression and creativity. Not all experiments in this area have been dazzlingly successful, but they have had some impact on public school systems. In the health professions, the young newcomers may "carry the torch" for innovations that will make quality medical care available to everyone, without regard to economic status.

A New Attitude Toward Death

The search for new values shows itself strongly in a changed attitude toward death. Death, like sex, was once a subject which in polite society was not discussed at all, or was handled only with flabby euphemisms. Now, among many young people, there is a tendency to regard death more frankly and openly as an inevitable part of the human condition. The question is being asked whether there is not a "right to die" when, because of age and/or hopeless and agonizing illness, life has ceased to have any meaning. There are, of course, basic moral and legal questions involved in such a question, but it is striking that the issue is now being seriously raised by young people at the very threshold of life.

Love and Sexuality

The plurality of values being generated by youth is probably most obvious and most highly publicized in the areas of love and sexuality. We shall discuss this in some detail in Chapter 23. At this stage, it should be emphasized that there is little basis for the doleful and familiar complaint that young people today have "no sense of morality." Surveys indicate that the high school and college students of this generation *do* accept the basic values of loyalty, integrity, sincerity, and honesty in relation to the individuals with whom they form love relations. There is strong emphasis on fidelity, but the tendency among young people is to see this as a personal commitment, rather than a societal obligation imposed from the outside. Such a relationship, it is maintained, is more truly moral than a pattern of behavior based on fear and unthinking conformity.

A 1973 poll of 26,000 high school student leaders by "Who's Who Among American High School Students" revealed that about 80% favored traditional marriage, and 68% said they would raise their children more or less as their parents had raised them. All such figures are somewhat questionable in the sense that many young people polled may be inclined to give the answers that they think are "expected." Nonetheless, such figures may be "trying to tell us" that attitudes have changed somewhat since the 1960's.

A New Attitude Toward Marriage

Marriage is, if anything, more popular than ever, and the rate of marriages (per 1000 people in the 18-30 age group) is expected to go up in the years ahead. But the institution is changing noticeably. There is increasingly a tendency to regard marriage as a genuine partnership between equals. We hear more and more of couples composing their own marriage vows and drawing up comprehensive contracts for sharing responsibilities (earning money, controlling the budget, taking care of children, etc.). Such contracts may be limited to the *avant garde*, but the spirit behind them is widely diffused. (See Chapter 17 on Women's Lib.)

The rise in the marriage rate is paralleled by a rise in the divorce rate. There is reason to believe that young people today are particularly insistent on the "freedom" to terminate marriages when they are no longer satisfying. Census Bureau statistics show that people who marry young (men under 22, women under 20) are twice as likely to be divorced as somewhat older couples. Does this mean that people are marrying more irresponsibly today, or that they are simply behaving in a more forthright fashion when the relationship goes sour? This is a question on which you will have to form your own judgment.

In the event of divorce, there is a negative attitude toward the traditional alimony arrangements, which have been based on the idea that a woman cannot earn her own living and needs a "handout" from her former husband, unless and until she remarries. In the years ahead, accepted practices in this area will probably change to conform to economic realities.

Even more than in the 1960's, young people today are keenly aware of population pressures in relation to a limited land area and dwindling natural resources. Thus, the old ideal of the "big family" is generally rejected. Some couples, indeed are questioning whether they should bring *any* more children into this world.

Formerly in the case of divorce, the children of the couple almost always went to the mother. Today, fathers are questioning this practice, and courts are increasingly awarding child custody to the father.

Another significant change in which young people have taken the lead is the growing tendency for young couples, and even single individuals—to adopt children of other races. This was all but unheard of a few years ago. This single development reveals new attitudes toward race relations, toward marriage, and toward the family structure.

Getting Help from Peers

Young people today often feel a need for advice and counseling to help them cope with personal problems. There's nothing new in that. Obtaining outside psychological support, at least occasionally, is a constant of human experience, and it's by no means limited to those in the lower age brackets.

What *is* somewhat new in recent years is that many young people are not inclined to rely too heavily on the "wisdom" of their elders. This has led to the development of "hot lines," street clinics, peer counseling groups, and other improvisations through which advice can flow from those who have had useful experience to others in the same age group.

There is in some quarters an apparent reluctance to go to professional sources for treatment for mental, spiritual, and even physical problems. Young people who are having trouble with their sex lives, for example, are more likely in many cases to attempt to "talk it out" in their own group than to consult a professional counselor of some kind, such as a physician or psychologist. Admittedly, this may sometimes lead to serious mistakes, or at the very least to neglect of danger signs. But it may also serve as a challenge to the adult professionals to develop a more sympathetic and responsible approach to their young patients.

Work and Money

Many young people are now following the lead of the generation of the 1960's in taking a more critical attitude toward the question of working and making money. They are asking, in effect: "Can I fulfill myself most effectively by doing what I really *want* to do, or by working at a career that will yield me a maximum income?" And once the question is presented in these terms, the probability is that there will be at least a partial rejection of purely monetary values and motivations.

Such a rejection can be recognized in the many boys and girls of middle class background who have given up the possibility of relatively lucrative careers to work in hospitals, day care centers, settlement houses, neighborhood recreational programs, and the like. Young lawyers may spurn jobs in established law firms to serve in organizations concerned with civil rights, ecology, and the legal defense of the poor.

On another level, we have witnessed in recent years many young workers revolting against the "tyranny of the assembly line." They have demanded a "humanization" of their jobs in automobile factories, for example, even though the jobs pay relatively high wages. Major manufacturing companies and labor unions have had to make concessions to this new attitude. Older people (workers and union officials, as well as businessmen) sometimes ask dolefully: "What do these kids expect? At their age, all I wanted was a steady job at a decent wage." To which the "kids" are likely to answer, in effect: "We want more out of life than tending machines to make other machines."

It is, of course, possible to exaggerate this anti-materialistic spirit. A great many young people are still very much "career-minded," and they certainly should not be criticized indiscriminately for such an attitude. Making a good living is still, as it has always been, one of the major problems (and satisfactions) of life, and no one appreciates this more keenly than boys and girls who have grown up in dire poverty. In a sense, the sweeping rejection of material values is a "luxury" available primarily to young people who have always enjoyed a high level of material well-being.

Concern for the Environment and Nature

Many young people have been directing their energies into *Public Interest Research Groups* (PIRG). These agencies, pioneered in large part by Ralph Nader and his associates, are concerned mainly with consumer and environmental interests. Staffed largely by college students and recent college graduates working for nominal pay, the PIRG have been remarkably effective in combating pollution, destruction of beauties of nature, and exploitation of ordinary.consumers. They have fought the "environmental battle" in many different locales—the Everglades, the Alaskan tundra, the High Sierras, and the Lake Michigan dunes—to mention only a few.

Another aspect of this renewed concern with nature is the "back to the land" movement. A considerable number of young people have devoted themselves to farming, homesteading, practicing handicrafts, and in general leading an "organic" existence close to the soil.

Many others are intensely interested in this movement and content themselves, at least for the time being, with studying such fantastically successful manuals as the *Whole Earth Catalog, Woodstock Crafts,* and *Mother Earth News.* They may also affect "rustic" clothing and devote themselves to "folk" and "country" music.

Is this a genuine commitment to a new way of life, or it is an "artsy-craftsy" affectation that cannot possibly survive on a large scale in our industrial society? One answer may be that even if there is no sound economic basis for subsistence farming, the *impulse* among so many young people to engage in this life style is of great significance.

The Search for Heightened Consciousness

Many young people today, like their forerunners of the 1960's, are intent on breaking out of the humdrum realities and inadequacies of everyday living. They are searching for *heightened consciousness* and are exploring a variety of "movements" concerned with psychological and spiritual growth.

There are still some who regard drugs (including alcohol) as a suitable means to this desirable end. However, although firm data are lacking, there is some reason to believe that the acceptance, to say nothing of the glorification, of drugs, is past its peak. In particular, the fantasy of "instant enlightenment" by means of the LSD trip has been discredited and generally abandoned by young people.

On a far more positive and constructive level, the search for a higher level of consciousness and a more intense, purposeful, rewarding life style has expressed itself in participation in various movements and organizations. All of these movements have in common an attempt to break down the psychic barriers that prevent us from living spontaneously and fully, and from relating openly to other people.

Many young people in the United States in the 1970's have been strongly attracted by religious movements originating in India. Among these are the *Divine Light Mission* led by Guru Maharaj Ji, the *transcendental meditation* taught by Maharishi Mahesh Yogi, the *Hare Krishna* movement, *Zen Buddhism,* and *Yoga.* In general, they espouse the techniques of meditation, as described in Chapter 12. The idea is that we can revitalize our lives by using such techniques to become aware of the basic reality and energy of the universe.

Within the Christian tradition, there has developed a program of revitalization known commonly as the *Jesus Movement.* The proponents, mainly young people, emphasize personal acceptance of Christ as the only way to salvation and a higher level of consciousness and joy. They make use of highly emotional literature, revival meetings, public testimony, active evangelism in schools and colleges. Also they have experimented with communal living. Their long-term impact on young people and American society in general remains to be determined.

A somwhat similar movement has been launched within Judaism. This is called *Hineni* ("Here I am"). It emphasizes pride in Jewish heritage and use of traditional Jewish values to deal with the frustrations and neuroses typical of modern life.

It should be mentioned, finally, that many young people especially those from underprivileged minority groups, are seeking personal fulfillment in programs designed to cope directly with the social problems of American life. They are serving, as already mentioned, as housing and welfare consultants, advocates for the poor and handicapped, workers in drug rehabilitation programs, and leaders and participants in many other forms of community action.

The Crisis of the 1970's

These examples represent only a small part of the extremely diversified, constantly changing, and highly confusing picture that faces young people today as they seek to develop a life style that makes sense to them in the context of the 1970's.

Will the 1970's avoid the massive failures and costly conflicts of the previous decade? Will young people be more successful in modifying their ideas and behavior to develop a life style that comes closer to their needs, and the needs of society in general?

The answers to these questions are being determined now.

16

ENCOUNTER GROUPS

● ●

"Lose your mind and come to your senses."
— FREDERICK S. PERLS

▶ A fat housewife and a Catholic priest stand on chairs and strike each other with pillows.

▶ A man assumes that he is his own right hand and proceeds to hold an argument with his left hand. Then he reverses roles.

▶ A group of adults dance in "ring-around-the-rosy" fashion, singing of a man in the middle, "He's not crippled! He's not dead!"

▶ A group of adult strangers, men and women, jump into a swimming pool together. All are nude.

Freak-out? Orgy? No — these people are just participating in a relatively new type of planned psychological experience called *encounter groups.*

The people who take part in such groups are usually "normal" and reasonably successful in their careers and their man-woman relationships. But they do have problems, and they are interested in growing to their full human potential. They use a variety of expressions to describe the goals at which they are aiming — *self-actualization, self-development, self-realization, autonomy, productiveness,* or simply *joy.*

The term "encounter group" serves as a rather broad label for different kinds of activities and organizations intended to yield the psychological benefits suggested above. As we shall see in the following pages, these activities show many variations, but they have a good deal in common which identifies them as belonging to the same overall movement. The movement goes by a variety of names, in addition to "encounter groups." You may have seen or heard "sensitivity training," "human potential movements," "human relations laboratories," and "T-groups."

Group Therapies

The encounter group movement was derived from techniques of *group therapy,* that in turn grew out of the psychoanalytic methods pioneered by Freud. The group therapies include *group psychotherapy,* the *psychodrama* of J. L. Moreno, and the *Gestalt therapy* of the late Frederick S. Perls.

The classic method of psychoanalysis calls for a doctor working with a single patient at a time. This one-to-one approach is necessarily expensive and therefore, it is said, "elitist" — designed for a favored few. In the 1930's, psychologists suggested that it would be possible to help a great many more people, and in some cases at least to bring them greater benefits, by organizing *groups* of troubled men and women and allowing them to interact with each other. Different methods were developed for this purpose.

Group psychotherapy is a controlled situation led by a trained psychotherapist, who guides a number of people in discussions that are designed to lead to greater self-understanding and a resolution of their problems. Kurt Lewin, a prominent social psychologist, studied interaction in such therapeutic groups. It was this experience that inspired the original T-groups, conducted mainly for businessmen.

J. L. Moreno, who coined the term "group psychotherapy" in 1931, became interested particularly in the possibilities of dramatic (play-acting) techniques in revealing and relieving psychological tensions. In *psychodrama,* the members of a group are encouraged to act out their feelings toward important figures in their lives — mother, father, husband, wife, etc. A dramatic situation of some kind is devised — for example, a family crisis — and a "central character" is chosen to activate the drama, with the help of the other members of the group. Again, this technique has been borrowed by some encounter groups.

In *Gestalt psychotherapy,* a member of a group acts out his conflicts by assuming the roles of his conflicting parts. The aim is to bring these parts together — to integrate them into a unified whole (or

Gestalt*). Perls, who developed this technique, used dreams as a means of enabling the person to discover the conflict for himself. The patient relates a dream to the group as though it were happening at that moment (in the "here and now"). Instead of saying, "I was in a windswept house," the patient may be directed to say, "*I am* a windswept house." Later, the patient may take on the roles of the staircase, the furniture, or anything else in the dream which seems significant because of the force of the symbolism.

The dream symbols are believed to express relationships inside the personality of the subject. Usually, what this amounts to, Perls taught, is an energy-wasting struggle between "Topdog" and "Underdog." In this relationship, "Topdog" is impossibly demanding; "Underdog" is intolerably sneaky. Perls believed that many people suffer the "curse of perfectionism," and can never let themselves be happy since anything they may do is unable to satisfy their unrealistic standards. This "curse," he thought is a major block, preventing the development of the personality into an integrated whole.

Some Historical Background

In 1947, the National Training Laboratories, conducted the first "national training lab" in Bethel, Maine. This was an experiment to develop better teaching and training in human relations. It was attended by 67 persons, mainly business executives, whose aim was to find techniques for developing greater openness and harmony among people working together. The result, it was hoped, would be higher levels of cooperation and efficiency. T-groups such as this (the *T* is for "training") rely primarily on verbal communication to break down the barriers between people. In a group situation, the pressure is on each individual to be completely frank about his own feelings and sensitive to the feelings of others.

Meeting in this way, with no specific agenda, no stated purpose, and no rules of order, the businessmen found it far easier to reveal their true feelings to each other than in the "defensive" situations of everyday life. Some conflicts developed. The sessions revealed the (normally) concealed attitudes of aggressiveness, defensiveness, confidence, fear, etc. With polite evasions stripped away, the participants became more keenly aware of who really trusted whom. In general, the participants left with the assurance that a greater feeling of hon-

---

* The German word *Gestalt* means "unified whole" or "configuration." The general idea it suggests is that "the whole is greater than the sum of its parts."

esty and trust had come out of the meetings. As word of this innovation spread, similar T-groups were formed by the National Training Laboratories for other organizations.

These activities, however, were confined pretty much to the worlds of business and education. The next step was to adapt the techniques for use in a broader arena.

This was developed under the leadership of a new thrust in psychology called the *Human Potential Movement*. The psychologists involved in this used the term *encounter group* to describe the kind of "coming together" of men and women which they felt would be emotionally beneficial. At its best, the encounter group differs from the T-group in its emphasis on the release of deeper feelings among the participants. There is a more ambitious goal — not merely to resolve conflicts that may hamper business efficiency but to give each individual the psychological freedom and health he needs to develop his fullest potential. Much use is made not only of verbal communication but of physical techniques and the acting out of emotions. These can be very effective in releasing the hidden feelings that govern so much of our behavior.

Experience has shown, however, that there are also dangers involved in having the individual let down his defenses and reveal himself so completely to a group of strangers. When the participant is a person seriously disturbed by emotional problems, he may find that "bringing everything out into the open" involves greater strains than he can withstand. (This is discussed further on pages 316-317.)

The Esalen Institute

The Esalen Institute was established in 1962 in Big Sur, California, by Michael Murphy and Richard Price. It quickly became a center for the Human Potential Movement, with such well-known psychologists as Perls, Abraham Maslow, and Carl Rogers running workshops and laboratories that set up the early encounter groups.

The interests of these men interacted creatively in the Esalen environment. Maslow was concerned particularly with the possibilities for growth in human beings. Rogers is the inventor of "non-directive" therapy, in which feedback is emphasized. (See below.) Perls' *Gestalt* theory emphasizes the importance of awareness of the "here and now" as a way of bringing feelings to the surface.

Most encounter groups today seek to combine such special emphases. They use the method of feedback to bring about an awareness of the "here and now," which may lead to a growth of human potential.

A group encounter session isn't always emotionally charged and "dramatic." A quiet discussion may help to prepare the way for better understanding and fuller expression of feelings.

Feedback

> O wad some Pow'r the giftie gie us
> To see ourselves as others see us!
> It would frae mony a blunder free us
> And foolish notion.
>
> — ROBERT BURNS

What is *feedback*? In its simplest form, it is an exchange of information. But it can also be an exchange of feelings: "I look at you, you look at me, I smile at you, you talk to me — and we're on our way." In everyday life almost all of us have the habit of holding back our feelings, or of expressing them guardedly and indirectly. In encounter groups, participants are encouraged to express their feelings openly. If conventional language is not satisfying, a person may weep, shout, make faces, lie on the floor, and even shriek or curse. Each such expression stimulates the next person, enabling him to "feed back" his own emotional reactions.

For many people, words seem to get in the way of an honest, uninhibited expression of feeling. Accordingly, encounter groups frequently emphasize non-verbal techniques. Following are some of the games which are used to express feelings and maximize feedback through physical actions:

Break-in. Often when a group begins to function, it becomes obvious that some members are "in," and others are "out." The "out" people then have a painful feeling of rejection, and any attempt to set matters right by means of words will probably lead to denial, distortion, and even anger.

To cope with this situation, the *break-in* game is used. The "in" people form a tight circle, interlocking their arms. The "outsiders" then try to break into the circle, in whatever way they can. They may crawl between someone's legs, separate two pairs of arms, try to make a breach by tickling, or power into the circle like a fullback going through the line. The experience helps to neutralize self-conscious feelings of separation between the "in-group" and the "out-group." Moreover, the methods which different individuals choose to "break in" are very revealing and often lead to a discussion. The discussion itself helps to bring the group members together.

A variation of this game when circumstances are somewhat different is called *breakout*.

Push. The physical act of pushing is sometimes helpful in competitive situations when feelings among the participants are unclear, or when it seems desirable to increase involvement. Two participants stand facing each other and place their hands together, palm to palm. They begin pushing against each other, each trying to make the other give ground. They stop whenever they want to. This is a good way of discharging tension. After a "push" session, people often feel more comfortable with each other.

Milling. It is often important to know the "structure" of a group — how the people feel about each other, who is "in" and who is "out," who (if anyone) feels alienated. Only with such awareness can the needs of the various participants be understood and met. Talking about this is likely not to be productive because the individuals may not be willing to admit their feelings, or may not even be aware of them.

Milling is designed to clarify these issues. The group leader stands apart and tells the participants to walk toward him, one at a time. Then they are to continue walking in any direction they wish and to stop wherever they feel most comfortable. Before long the whole group is "milling about." Some may come to a halt but others continue moving. At a given signal, everyone sits down where he or she is.

A discussion follows. Typical questions are: "Why did you (or didn't you) keep walking?" "Why did you (or didn't you) stop next to me?" "Why did some people huddle together, while others went off by themselves?" The answers to these questions (or even the questions themselves without the answers) give some idea of how the people in the group relate to each other, and help it to function more effectively.

Falling. Another method of physically expressing feelings in an encounter group is called *falling*. It is used when one or more of the group members seem to be distrustful of the others — to lack confidence in their intentions, or capabilities, or both.

The group members stand forming a tight circle. A "distrustful" member stands in the middle and, without bending his knees, simply falls backward, so that someone has to catch and support him. He is supposed to continue this until everyone in the group has had a chance to prevent him from falling. It may often happen, however, that, deliberately or unconsciously, he overlooks one of the people in the circle.

This exercise, like the others, is performed in silence, but discussion follows. The "distrustful" person may then become aware for the first time that he did not give everyone in the group a chance to catch him, and the significance of this is explored. The experience of falling — being momentarily in danger, and then being "saved" each time by a different member of the group — usually helps to evoke more positive feelings (confidence and gratitude) in the subject. He becomes more open in his own expression of feelings and more receptive to the feelings of others.

In all of these exercises, *emotion is converted directly into physical action.* The whole body, or a part of the body, is used to reveal and clarify internal feelings. Moving toward or away from a person, of course, indicates different attitudes toward him. So do hitting and caressing, as well as the other actions described above. The group members may thus find out about their own and each other's attitudes and feelings, which are often hidden under layers of conventional words.

Body Language — Non-Verbal Communication

The emphasis which encounter groups give to body movements as a means of expressing and releasing feelings has led to a new theory of communication called "body language." In brief, this is an attempt to explain how people unconsciously convey their emotions and indicate the personal relations they wish to establish by the way they hold their bodies.

For example, a girl at a party sits with her legs crossed when talking to a particular boy. According to the theory of body language, this means that she is afraid of him and is signaling to him that she is inaccessible.

How would you interpret the facial expressions and the body language of the young people in this photograph?

A boy and a girl at a party are sitting so that each has a leg crossed toward the other. The message they are conveying to others is in effect, "Do not disturb!"

Here are some other "translations" according to the theory of body language:

If you stand far away from someone while talking to him, this means that you have a high degree of respect for him, or feel that you don't know him very well.

If you stand close to someone while talking, it means that you like him or feel that you know each other intimately.

If you hold a glass or a pipe in front of you in the midst of a crowd, you are supposedly trying to ward off or to minimize contact with others.

(It should be emphasized that all these interpretations represent only a tentative *theory,* about which many psychologists may have serious doubts.)

As we have noted, non-verbal techniques of communication are widely used in encounter groups. The theory behind this is that it is often possible to achieve greater honesty and authenticity through body movements and attitudes than through language. The body movements, it is said, become "uninhibited" much more readily than does verbal communication.

This is why group members who "get stuck" at the verbal level are encouraged to express their feelings about each other physically. Instead of saying "I hate you" (an emotion which is often felt but rarely verbalized in public), a group member can convey the same idea by hitting the other person with a pillow. When violent feelings are "vented" in this way, they often have a better chance to give way to feelings of friendship, or at least acceptance. But if the feelings are kept back, or expressed only partially and unsatisfyingly in words, it is probable that they will remain beneath the surface.

Awareness

How aware are you? Not of world events, not of social problems, not of music or art . . . but of *you*! Of *here*! Of *now*!

What gets in the way of a high degree of awareness? Maybe you waste your time in unproductive thought. Many psychologists are convinced that a mind which "jabbers" away at itself, never giving itself a moment of relaxation or stability, is immature. If you use up energy lavishly trying to anticipate the *future*, or feeling guilty or regretful about the *past*, you can't concentrate adequately on the *present*. This doesn't mean you should never reflect on the past, or should never consider the future. But it is possible to get so entangled in what *has* happened, or *may* happen, that you don't allow yourself to have a present — or a future either.

If you are absorbed unduly in analysis of things and situations far removed from you — in time and space — you will not be acutely conscious of what is around you here and now. To people entrapped in this psychological pattern, Frederick S. Perls recommended, "Lose your mind and come to your senses."

Perls gives a rather gentle example of how it is possible to do this in an exercise called "Here and There."*

> Shuttle between *here* and *there*. . . . Close your eyes and go away in your imagination, from here to any place you like. Now the next step is to come back to the *here* experience, the here and now. . . . And now compare the two situations. Most likely the *there* situation was preferable to the *here* situation. . . . And now close your eyes again. Go away again, wherever you'd like to go. And notice any change. Now again come back to the here and now, and again compare the two situations. Has any change taken place? Continue to do this until you really feel comfortable in the present situation, until you come to your senses and you begin to see and hear and be here in this world.

---

* Frederick S. Perls, *Gestalt Therapy Verbatim* (Real People Press, 1969).

"CAT STRETCH"   LOTUS POSITION   "SHOULDER SQUEEZE"

Yoga

There are many exercises and disciplines used in encounter groups to bring the individual closer to his own senses and thus make him more sensitive to himself and to other people. The ancient Oriental traditions of *Yoga* and *Tai Chi* have long been used for these purposes.

Hatha Yoga was developed in India as a means of disciplining the body, thus making it possible to go on and *relax the mind*. There is a widespread tendency to abuse the body and to be highly insensitive to it, while at the same time we complain of aches, pains, fatigue, and other symptoms that keep us out of sorts and prevent us from living a more complete life. A deadened, painful, tired, or unresponsive body cannot experience itself with full awareness. The Hatha Yoga discipline, enthusiasts claim, helps to restore circulation to parts of the body that are often neglected. Some Yoga exercises used in encounter groups are as follows:

▶ *"Cat Stretch"*: Kneel on the hands and knees, palms forward. *Inhale,* and slowly lower the chest, trying to rest the front of the neck on the floor. Hold for 5 to 10 seconds. *Exhale,* and return to the kneeling position, humping back like an angry cat, sucking the stomach up toward the spine. Repeat twice. This makes the back both stronger and more supple. Very often, the back is a prime source of stiffness and general discomfort throughout the body.

▶ *"The Pulley"*: *Inhale* deeply and extend the arms straight out in front, at shoulder level. Clench the fists slowly toward the chest as though pulling with utmost strength on a heavy weight. *Exhale* quickly, and drop the arms to the sides. This exercise develops lung power, squeezing the retained air deep into lung areas rarely used.

▶ *"Shoulder Squeeze"*: In a sitting or standing position, hold the arms out to the sides at shoulder level. Then draw the shoulder blades in together, as though trying to hold a coin between them. Hold tightly, then release. Do not move the arms, except as the motion of the shoulders requires. This will tone up the muscles of the neck, upper back, shoulders, and chest.

During all such exercises, Yoga specialists emphasize, you should allow the mind to clear itself of all "chattering." Concentrate solely on being aware of the motions of the body and the rhythm of your breathing (which is of great importance in all types of Yoga). Such "sensory awareness" is also the goal of another somewhat similar discipline called *"Tai Chi."*

Tai Chi

The basic principles of *Tai Chi,* which is practiced in some encounter groups, are: harmony, circular movement, and looseness.

The "ball-holding position" is a typical exercise. Take a sideward step, and put all your weight on the foot moved to the side. The opposite hand is raised to the level of the armpit, palm down. The other hand circles down to the waist, palm up. The hands curve naturally to fit the top and bottom of an imaginary ball. Then, sink the shoulders, drop the elbows to the sides, and curve the fingers naturally. Bend the knees slightly. The bending of the knees is harmonious with the dropping of both arms.

Role Reversal and Alter Ego

The aim of the encounter group is to serve as a "coming together" of people who, it is hoped, will experience an increased awareness of themselves, and thus acquire a greater capacity to relate to each other. Most of the exercises described under "Feedback," such as *falling,* provide new ways for people to communicate when the old familiar ways are "tired" and "used up." Most of the exercises described under "Awareness" are designed to provide new ways for people to become aware of their own bodies — the feelings in them, and the feelings that they express to others. One aspect of this is increased sensory awareness: seeing more sharply, hearing more clearly, even smelling more acutely.

The increased awareness makes for better feedback to others. And the feedback in turn contributes to greater awareness in these other people. In this way, there is a sort of chain reaction that enables the participants in a good encounter group to express parts of

Role playing helps group members gain a better understanding of their own (and other people's) emotions.

their personality which they are usually too shy, too frightened, or too self-conscious to bring out into the open, or even to recognize.

For example, in the setting of an encounter group, an individual may go on a "guided daydream." The leader suggests an image to the group, and one member is chosen to create a story around the image. The leader may suggest, for example, that you have arrived at the rim of a peaceful, sun-lit valley, surrounded by green hills. You walk down a narrow path into the valley, and you proceed to tell what you observe and how you feel about it. The fantasizer in this free-wheeling situation may experience a wide range of emotions and emotional expressions — fear, elation, laughter, depression, crying, jealousy, relaxation, relief — depending on his personality and also on the skill of the leader.

Frequently, the loss of a significant person early in life has a far-reaching effect on a child. This can later have serious consequences for his adult relationships with others. When such a situation shows itself in an encounter group, and interferes with the immediate functioning of the individual, the group may use two methods borrowed from psychodrama to overcome the emotional block: *alter ego* and *role reversal*.

The troubled group member (the subject) chooses someone from the group who, he feels, can play the role of the "lost" person. Then the group members begin to talk as though the "lost" person is dead but the subject is somehow able to communicate with him. Usually, the subject begins by telling the "lost" person how he feels about him.

After a while, the subject is asked if the role player is portraying the "lost" person satisfactorily. If his judgment is unfavorable, the two *reverse roles;* the subject now plays the "lost" person, while the other member takes on the role of the subject. This role reversal is repeated as many times as may be needed to help the subject feel that he is getting to the roots of his emotional difficulties.

Also, other group members are asked to play *alter ego* — to stand behind one of the players and say things which they think the player is feeling but for some reason not expressing. Often this combination of role reversal and alter ego brings out important but hidden elements in the situation and allows the subject to explore feelings he may not have been aware that he was harboring. The action ends by having the main players, and perhaps the entire group, enact a realistic solution based on all the revealed elements and emotions in the situation.

Growth as an Outcome of Encounter Group Experience

When a person learns something new about himself he has a feeling of fulfillment and *growth.* This is probably the main benefit that most people derive from encounter groups. Whether they truly grow after an encounter group experience depends on how well they can apply what they have learned. Often, when the person moves outside the special group setting, the expanded self-awareness may seem to fade away. It is difficult in the daily routine of the "real world" to hold on to the more positive attitudes and the changed behavior.

However, it appears that there are at least some cases where there is a lasting carry-over as a result of the group experience. The individual may not be "transformed," but he does feel better about himself and relates more effectively to other people.

Dangers of Encounter Groups

When a person participates in a group activity which brings out long-hidden emotions, he is exposing a very vulnerable part of his psyche. The experience can be valuable, as explained above, but it can also be disturbing and even shocking. For this reason, it is essential to have someone in charge of the group who is adequately trained and fully qualified to protect the members against excessive emotional stress. He must be able to recognize when the situation has gone "too far" for a given individual, and must know how to withdraw that individual before he sustains serious psychological and even physical harm. Some members of a group may be insensitive and over-exuberant, and they must be held in check. This is particularly true when the group is employing such methods as role reversal and alter ego, as well as physically strenuous body techniques.

It is difficult to generalize about the qualifications of the people who are now running encounter groups. Some of them, undoubtedly, are responsible people with professional training in psychology and/or psychiatry. Others quite clearly are not, and there have been reports of unfortunate incidents as a result of this. Accordingly, anyone contemplating attendance at an encounter group or sensitivity training laboratory should check as carefully as possible to determine if the organization in question is run by professionally qualified people.

It is generally agreed that there are some people for whom the encounter group experience is not advisable. Certainly, no one with a history of serious emotional disturbance or illness should be exposed to such activities. A responsible group will attempt to keep out such people by carefully screening applications for attendance. These individuals (for example, individuals who may be on the verge of breakdown or even suicide) need much more personalized and carefully controlled forms of therapy. Inevitably, however, some emotionally disturbed men and women do attend encounter groups, and their reactions may go out of control and become dangerous. An outburst of irrational behavior, moreover, may have bad effects on the other people attending the session.

The American Group Psychotherapy Association is much concerned that people attending encounter groups "may be drawn into an experience that has deep psychological import they had not anticipated." The Association report cites a number of instances in which psychotic episodes and even attempts at suicide have resulted from this kind of experience.

The emphasis on spontaneity and openness in these groups is helpful to many people, but it may also have the disadvantage of creating the impression that all problems can be solved merely by expressing them "honestly." Certainly, such expression is a necessary first step, but if the problem is a serious one it still has to be *worked out*. To achieve this under Freudian psychoanalysis may take five years or more of treatment. Other therapeutic methods are shorter, but they all call for a careful, systematic approach. The generalized and "spontaneous" methods of the encounter group cannot be expected to work effectively for everyone.

Perls himself warned against encounter therapy becoming a "faddism." He wrote, "We are entering the phase of the turner-onners: turn on to instant cure, instant joy, instant sensory-awareness. We are entering the phase of the quacks and the con-men, who think if you get some breakthrough, you are cured — disregarding any growth requirements, disregarding any of the real potential, the inborn genius in all of you."*

The danger of faddism is that too often people are woefully ill-prepared for what they are getting into — they may approach the exploration of their inner being as if it were a sort of game. There is reason to think that this may be true of some encounter group participants.

Feeling and Thinking

The basic goal of the encounter group movement is said to be *fully developed personal functioning and feeling* — to *be*. The special techniques we have described are designed to increase relaxation, honesty, awareness and sensitivity.

Increased intensity of feeling and heightened awareness of the present have proved to be valuable to the life experience of many people. It may be questioned, however, whether exclusive emphasis on "immediate experience" is the ideal prescription for a sound, healthy, well-balanced personality. It is said that thought or intellectualization without feeling is sterile, but it is just as true that feeling without thought is undirected and dangerous. If a person is to grow, he must give due consideration to *all* his faculties, and certainly these must include the uniquely human faculty for rational thought.†

There is reason to believe that some individuals connected with encounter groups tend to regard greater intensity of feeling as an end in itself. The search for "pure experience," in the here and now, without the governing influence of the rational, responsible mind, may degenerate into a preoccupation with mere "thrills." Although the history of encounter groups is still very brief, some people seem to have

---

* Frederick S. Perls, *op. cit.*

† Encounter group enthusiasts sometimes respond to this implied criticism by saying that they are aiming for an "integration" of experience, so that there will be no distinction between "rational thought" and "awareness of the here and now." It is not always clear, however, how this is to be achieved in practice.

become almost "addicts," requiring an intake of more and more potent group experiences to meet their emotional needs. Such "compulsive groupists," by dabbling in matters that involve their innermost needs and impulses, may be headed for trouble.

To *grow* means in essence to become a better human being. Not all of us can or should seek such improvement in exactly the same way. Some people undoubtedly need more emotional release and more capacity to relate spontaneously and naturally to others. But this is not to say that the rational faculty should be suppressed. This faculty, too, needs to grow, mature, and develop, so that it plays its part in a balanced, harmonious, smoothly-running personality.

THINGS TO DISCUSS :: THINGS TO DO :: THINGS TO READ

1. Supporters of the encounter group concept often insist on a distinction between "rational" (more accurately "rationalistic") thought and "awareness of the here and now." Try to explain as specifically as possible what is meant by this distinction. If possible, give examples from your own experience, or from the experience of people you know.

2. Do you agree that many people find it difficult to become aware of the "here and now"? If so, how do you explain this?

3. A major advantage claimed for encounter group therapy is that it produces immediately noticeable results, whereas traditional forms of psychotherapy may require years. Can you see any possible danger or other disadvantage which may be inherent in these high-speed methods of "forcing the unconscious"?

4. What qualities or qualifications do you think the leader of an encounter group should have? What is the first responsibility of such a leader to every member of the group? Why does this responsibility take precedence even over guiding the members to greater self-awareness and responsibility?

5. Describe the technique of a "guided daydream." What similarities and differences do you see between this technique and psychoanalytic dream interpretation?

6. Encounter groups have been dismissed in some quarters as "just a fad" and as "gratification for egotists and sensation seekers." Others regard these groups as a significant new therapeutic technique for the modern world that can vastly benefit large numbers of people. Where do *you* think the truth lies? Be prepared to defend your view.

READINGS

Write to the Esalen Institute, Big Sur, California 93920, for available catalogues of courses, tapes, and records. Perhaps you can select some materials, to be ordered for use in class.

Gestalt Therapy Verbatim, by Frederick S. Perls (Real People Press, 1969). Don't let that tongue-twisting title put you off. The book is dynamite — funny, interesting, unusual, perceptive.

Joy, by William C. Schutz (Grove Press, 1967). A fascinating study.

A Catalog of the Ways People Grow, by Severin Peterson (Ballantine Books, 1971). This is an important book because it gives a good synopsis of methods people use throughout the world to achieve psychic growth. The methods surveyed include encounter groups, humanistic psychology, Zen, Shamanism, Yoga, analytic psychology, and many more.

On the Liberation of Women (and Men)

17

●●●●●●●●●●●●●●●●●●●●●●●●●

"The liberation of women is germane to the agony of our whole nation: Until we free ourselves and men from the obsolete sex roles that imprison us both, the hostility between the sexes will continue to inflame the violence we're perpetrating in the world."

—BETTY FRIEDAN

What Is the Issue?

You may be wondering what a chapter on "Women's Liberation" is doing in a psychology text. Wouldn't this fit more appropriately into a survey of political, social, and/or economic problems?

The answer is that there certainly are political, social, and economic problems involved in any movement to "liberate" women, but there is also a strong *psychological component*. And this component is in a sense, prior to and more basic than any specific issue of institutional change.

The arguments and proposals made by proponents of the movement known familiarly as "Women's Lib" have a strong emotional effect on most people. Very few of us (males or females) are simply indifferent to them. Reactions are likely to be strong and definite and, in many cases, are distinctly unsympathetic. You have probably heard statements such as the following about the leaders and spokeswomen of the Lib movement:

"They're women trying to be men."
"They want to take over from men."
"They haven't been able to get men of their own, and they're expressing their frustration in this way."
"They're a bunch of nuts."

What these charges boil down to is that the women leading the Lib movement (and their male supporters as well) don't know, or can't accept, *what it means to be a woman,* and consequently *what it means to be a man.*

And here we come to grips with key questions which are definitely psychological in nature. What *does* it mean to be a woman? What *does* it mean to be a man? We have seen repeatedly that it is impossible to get very far in the study of psychology without confronting these twin concepts of masculinity and femininity. They are deeply embedded in the human personality, including of course the unconscious. They express themselves in every aspect of human behavior, both "normal" and "abnormal." And they are especially crucial where psychology impinges on other areas of knowledge, such as biology, sociology, and philosophy.

"The Natural Inferiority of Women"

Why is there any need at all for a Women's Liberation movement? After all, there was a feminist ("Women's Rights") movement in the 19th century and the early decades of the 20th century that brought about many important reforms, including the passage of the Nineteenth Amendment. Thus, women today have the same voting rights and other political rights as men. They control nominally a large part of all the property in the nation. They have access to higher education, including professional training. What do they want to be liberated *from*?

The answer given by the Women's Lib adherents is that in our society (and in many other societies throughout the world) most people accept the following fundamental premise: *Women are inferior to men.* This concept of natural inferiority, it is said, carries over into every area of life and has resulted in a generally degraded and deprived condition for women, regardless of what the letter of the law may say.

Are You Satisfied With Your Sex?

If you were about to have a child and could decide beforehand whether it was to be a boy or a girl, which would you choose?

When a group of college students was asked this question, they voted overwhelmingly in favor of a boy. Specifically, 66% of the girls and 92% of the boys preferred sons. Although it may be understandable that a man would want a son, why did two-thirds of the women show the same preference? A woman presumably is not looking for someone to take over the family business, or to serve as a pal on fishing trips, or to join her in male camaraderie. And if she has enjoyed being a woman, why wouldn't she prefer a daughter as an extension of her own personality?

In studies cited by Kate Millet (one of the most cogent of the writers presenting the Women's Lib point of view) half of the women

"Attention, male chauvinist pigs . . . ."

in one sampling and a fourth of the women in another said that they would have preferred to be born males. In a study of fourth-grade pupils, there were ten times as many girls who wanted to be boys as boys who wanted to be girls.

A reasonable explanation of the results of such studies (and there have been many others along the same lines) is that in our society *a much greater value is placed on being a man than on being a woman.*

Hierarchy and Patriarchy

Most large social organizations follow the pattern of a hierarchy. We may visualize this in the form of a pyramid. The pyramid is broadest at its base. Most of the people in the "social pyramid" occupy the lowest positions, in terms of authority, prestige, and rewards. As we move upward in the organizational structure, there are at each level fewer and fewer people, but they are exercising greater and greater authority. At the very apex of the pyramid (or hierarchy) is the person — or the very few people — in the position of supreme authority.

A military organization is the classic example of a hierarchy. However, we can also recognize the same basic structure in social groups such as corporations, universities, municipal bodies, religious organizations and governments.

The proponents of Women's Lib emphasize that in our society a hierarchy is almost by definition also a *patriarchy*. A *patriarch* is the top male leader of a social grouping, such as a family, tribe, or clan. His authority is frequently considered to be paternal or "fatherly," in that he is responsible for the welfare of others. Because of the very substantial concentration of power in the hands of males, many consider present-day American society to be essentially a patriarchy. As we move higher and higher in the social pyramid, there is less and less chance of finding a position occupied by a woman. Even in countries with a queen as the nominal head of state, the actual power is controlled almost exclusively by men.

Kate Millet points out that this fact (of male dominance) "is evident at once if one recalls that the military, industry, science, political office, and finance — in short, every avenue of power within the society, including the coercive force of the police — is entirely in male hands."*

Here are a few typical statistics that bear out this generalization:

▶ In 1970, there were about 2,900,000 civilian employees of the Federal (United States) government. Of these, roughly one-third were women. Federal agencies are no longer allowed to have "man only" or "woman only" job categories (except for a few special cases). In other words, all jobs must be open equally to members of both sexes. However, figures indicate that women are concentrated mainly in the lowest grades of the Civil Service — that is, in the jobs paying the lowest salaries. In the six lowest grades, nearly half of all employees are women. Their numbers thin out with every rise in grade, until at the highest level (jobs paying in excess of $21,000 per year), a mere 1.7% are women.

▶ In the early 1970's major professions in the United States showed these proportions of women among their practitioners:

Physicians (M.D.'s)	9.0%
Lawyers, Judges	4.8%
Engineers	1.6%
Dentists	3.4%
Psychologists	38.2%

---

* Kate Millet, *Sexual Politics* (Doubleday, 1970).

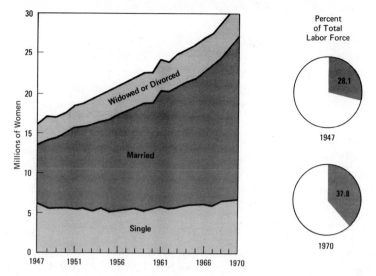

Women in the American labor force, as reported by the U. S. Bureau of Labor Statistics.

▶ A recent survey of large corporations with home offices in New York City identified 9738 executive positions paying more than $10,000 per year. Of these, only slightly more than 2% were held by women. And these women held mainly "specialized" jobs of somewhat limited responsibility, designated by such titles as "home economist," "stylist," "consultant for women's activities," etc.

▶ In the 93rd U.S. Congress (which convened in 1973), not one of the 100 members of the Senate was a woman, while the House of Representatives had 14 women members out of 435.

▶ Among college students in the United States, males outnumber females by roughly two to one.

Millet also points out that today "women's distance from the higher technology" is so great that it is doubtful that women alone could handle the technical work involved in such sophisticated operations as large-scale building construction, or the preparation and launching of a space probe.

Influence of the Past

This subordinate and relatively powerless position of women reflects a situation that has existed for untold centuries in the Western world. Until recently, women had in effect no social, legal, or political status of their own; they existed, in this sense, only as a reflection of their husbands or other male relatives. It was assumed that their proper function in life (their *only* significant function) was to bear children and maintain a household. This applied both to a peasant woman and to the wife of a nobleman or millionaire. In spite of vast differences in standard of living, the poorest and the richest woman were alike in their status of complete subordination to men. Prior to the 20th century, they could not vote or hold public office. They could not hold property in their own names (as long as the husband was alive), or even control money which they might have earned or inherited. They could not bring court suits in their own names, nor could they be sued as individuals. They were effectively cut off from higher education, and indeed in many cases from secondary education.

You may say that all this is a far cry from the position of women in the United States today. After all, women *do* have the full right to vote, on the same basis as men, and in many elections there are actually slightly more women voters than men. There are no legal bars to prevent women from holding any public office. In most states, their rights to hold and bequeath property, to borrow money, to engage in business, etc. are essentially equal to those of men. The Civil Rights Act of 1964 forbids discrimination against women in private jobs, and some states have enacted similar laws. Businesses and even universities receiving contracts from the Federal government are not allowed to discriminate in employment on the basis of sex. Federal, state, and local civil service jobs are usually open to men and women applicants on a basis of equality.

The "suffragettes" of an earlier day campaigning for the right to vote were subjected to criticism, ridicule, and not infrequently physical violence and legal penalties. This photograph was taken in 1912. The 19th Amendment, guaranteeing women the vote in all elections, went into effect in 1920.

These changes, even the most ardent feminists will admit, represent significant progress. But they maintain that the progress made is not enough because the ideas, the standards of propriety, the prejudices inherited from the past still dominate our thinking. And it is the influence of these (largely unconscious) points of view that accounts for the generally inferior position of women in our society, as reflected in the data given above.

In other words, say the Women's Lib people, our society is still *patriarchal*. What really counts, in the great majority of cases, is not the woman herself but her status as a *wife*. As one woman put it, "From the earliest years we are taught that our lives will be determined not by ourselves but by the men we marry." Theoretically, the option is open not to marry, but by and large young women are under great pressure — from their parents, their peers, and virtually everyone else in their lives — to "find a husband and settle down." The single woman after a certain age is subject to many social handicaps, including a fair amount of ridicule. Only a rather extraordinary person will voluntarily choose to cope with such a disadvantage.

Along with this emphasis on "getting married," girls in many segments of our society are systematically pushed into taking a submissive, passive, and "feminine" role. This shows itself even with young children. Parents are likely to scold a young daughter for acting like a "tomboy" (that is, rather aggressively), while a son is told not to be a "sissy" and to "stand up for his rights like a man." All of this may seem quite harmless and even "natural," but the Women's Lib proponents regard it as a process of conditioning that paves the way for the inferior position of women in adult society.

The same tendency is evident in the content of books and other materials that children read. One recent study* showed that there are "five times as many boys, men, or male animals pictured (in children's books) as there are females." There is also a significant difference in the activities assigned to the sexes in such literature. In one book with a section entitled *Things to Do,* the pictures show that "males dig, build, break, push and pull, and do fifteen other active things, including eat. The only two things that females do are watch and sit." In many books, females are shown mainly in the kitchen.

Economic Inequities

Even those who reject many of the concepts and demands of the Women's Liberation movement may agree that in the economic

---

* From an article entitled "The Second Sex, Junior Division," by Elizabeth Fisher, The New York *Times,* 1970.

sphere, American woman today are subject to systematized and flagrant economic injustices.

To appreciate the importance of this, we must pin down a few basic statistics. Women today represent more than one-third of the total work force of the United States. More than one working woman in eight is the sole support of her family, and in a vast number of other cases, the woman's earnings are absolutely essential to the support of the family at a decent level.

Thus, women represent an important segment of the economic life of the United States, not merely as homemakers and consumers but as workers. How are they being treated? Women's Lib says they are being systematically exploited. Figures such as the following are cited to support this claim:

▶ The average earnings of white women are 40% less than those of white men. The average earnings of black women are 50% less than those of black men.

▶ Of women workers with college degrees in the late 1960's, nearly one-fifth were in job categories such as clerks, secretaries, factory workers, and cooks. These women, it is maintained, have had to take relatively menial jobs because they were not given a chance to use their training and abilities on the same basis as men.

▶ Recent U. S. Department of Labor Statistics showed that of roughly 2 million domestic workers in this country, 98% were female. Of these "maids," a quarter of a million headed families; 64% were black; 40% were over 55 years of age (median age, 46). Perhaps the most startling figure, however, was that 4.2% of these women had attended college (and even graduate school)!

▶ Census Bureau figures for 1970 indicated that families (of all races) headed by women accounted for 14% of the population. But they accounted for 44% of all families living below the "poverty level" (by the government's definition). In the recession year of 1970, marked by widespread unemployment, about 1.2 million families were added to the "poverty level" sector of the population, and about half of these represented families headed by women.

There are many "excuses" offered for this economically underprivileged position of women. One is that the earnings of women serve merely to supplement those of their husbands. But this doesn't allow for the vast number of women who head families, or who are living alone, entirely dependent on their own earnings. The "excuse" also assumes (and this arouses the feminists more than anything else) that the working married woman is a sort of appendage to her husband, and that she doesn't really count in her own right.

Another "excuse" is that many women must take maternity leaves, and that this makes it impractical for the employer to give them the more responsible, better-paying jobs. Women's Lib spokesmen assert that this attitude is an antiquated expression of "male chauvinism," devoid of the most elementary sense of social responsibility. Note this passage from a book* highly regarded by the Women's Lib movement:

> The point is that while we consider it "only natural" for employers to consider the possibility that a woman worker might have a baby, many foreign countries, including Sweden and the Soviet Union, won't let an employer fire a woman for pregnancy, or even turn her down for a job solely because she is pregnant. These countries make employers take women back after they have had their babies, just as we make employers take men back after military service. Some 70 countries recognize a social obligation to help a woman worker financially when she loses income due to maternity, but we expect the individuals involved to assume all the costs of childbirth and child care.

Moreover, a recent report of the Bureau of Labor Statistics concluded that absenteeism and turn-over rates depend much more on the nature of the job than on the sex of the jobholder. And this, of course, brings us back to the nature of the jobs available to most women workers. In spite of improvements in recent years, many employers, large and small, still tend to regard women as a sort of "reserve labor pool," to be drawn on in periods of peak labor demand, and to be discharged or "furloughed," without regard to ability, seniority, or need, when business falls off. (In this respect, the status of women workers resembles that of many black workers of both sexes.)

With the acceptance of this attitude (however much it may be rationalized) by many employers, it is not surprising that women are often shunted off to jobs that men don't want to do. Basically, these jobs are parallel to the kinds of work done by a housewife. Women workers serve their bosses directly (personally) as secretaries, typists, receptionists. They handle food as cooks and waitresses. They make life easier for more affluent housewives by working as maids (domestics). In factories, they do "detail" work at which they are supposed to be "better than men." These jobs are mostly tedious and low-paid, and they offer little in the way of valuable experience and ad-

---

* Caroline Bird and Sara Welles Briller, *Born Female* (McKay, 1968)

vancement. If the wage scale for any job of this type should show substantial improvement, there is a good chance that men workers will appear on the scene and will ultimately take over.

"Equal Pay for Equal Work"

This represents one of the basic, minimal demands of the feminist movement since long before the advent of Women's Lib. And indeed it is hard to see how any reasonable person could quarrel with the principle that workers should be compensated for what they *do*, without regard to sex. The principle of equal pay for equal work has been written into many laws, including amendments to the national Fair Labor Standards Act; it is supported by labor unions and embodied in union contracts; it is part of civil service regulations; it has the endorsement of innumerable employers.

And yet, with all this support, there is reason to believe that *in practice*, a great many women workers in our economy do not get "equal pay." The old ideas that a woman is inferior to a man as a worker, and that in most cases she really doesn't need as much money to meet her requirements, are still so strong that they have survived all efforts to root them out.

A story involving incidents of which the author has personal knowledge will illustrate how this sometimes works. A young man

In every employment category, American women's earnings are substantially less than those of men doing comparable work. The figures shown here are annual averages, compiled by the Women's Bureau of the U. S. Labor Department on the basis of the latest available reports.

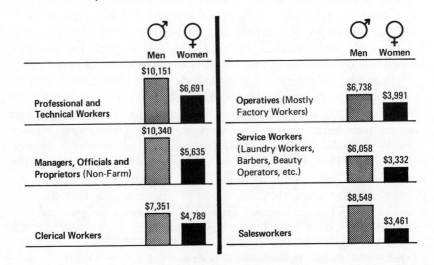

	Men	Women
Professional and Technical Workers	$10,151	$6,691
Managers, Officials and Proprietors (Non-Farm)	$10,340	$5,635
Clerical Workers	$7,351	$4,789

	Men	Women
Operatives (Mostly Factory Workers)	$6,738	$3,991
Service Workers (Laundry Workers, Barbers, Beauty Operators, etc.)	$6,058	$3,332
Salesworkers	$8,549	$3,461

and a young woman recently graduated together from a large Eastern university. They had similar academic backgrounds, except that she was an honors graduate, and he was not. On the same day, they applied at a large corporation for the position of computer programmer trainee. The firm in question was an "Equal Opportunities Employer," which means that it pledged itself not to discriminate in employment on the basis of race, religion, national origin, or *sex*. The young people saw different interviewers. Each of them was offered a job, but *the starting salary for the young woman was $2000 a year less than for her male classmate!*

In many cases, the "equal pay" principle is evaded by having a woman do the same job as a man, but with a job title calling for a lower status. In one firm, for example, men and women worked side by side processing employment applications. But the men were called "interviewers," while the women were merely "clerks." And of course the "clerks" were paid less than the "interviewers."

In recent years, gains have been made in counteracting this kind of "sexist" discrimination. We have mentioned the protection of the rights of women workers by some labor unions, civil service systems, private employers, and Federal and state laws. Why then do average earnings for women workers continue to be so much lower than for men? Because, say Women's Lib adherents, ancient prejudices and fixed attitudes tend to prevent women from qualifying themselves for higher-paying jobs. And even when they do have the qualifications, it is harder for them to win promotions or to gain acceptance for supervisory, executive, or professional positions.

Why Are There So Few Women Doctors?

For example, we have noted that only 9% of the physicians in the United States are women. In other countries, the proportion of women doctors is much higher — *e.g.,* about 40% in Denmark, and 70% in the Soviet Union. Is this because American women do not have the ability to get through a pre-med course and medical school? Is it because they have less willingness and/or less capacity to perform the functions of a doctor and help suffering humanity? There is overwhelming evidence that the answer to all such questions is *no.*

The true explanation lies in our society's attitudes toward masculinity and femininity. It has been assumed for untold generations, and is still assumed to a large extent, that the "learned professions" are the proper province of men. The vast majority of girls from their earliest years are effectively discouraged from thinking of themselves as candidates for these fields of work. It is quite all right for a girl to go into nursing, but to think of becoming a doctor is presumptuous, unrealistic, and somehow "unwomanly." It is difficult enough to become a doctor in any case, but with these added psychological obstacles, it takes a really remarkable young woman to persevere until she becomes an M.D. And even then she must face the prejudices which so many people (including women!) still harbor against "lady doctors."

There is an unexamined assumption widely held that women simply are not suited for many types of work, especially those which involve relatively large responsibilities and pay correspondingly high salaries. And yet during World War II, when manpower was extremely scarce, women stepped into a great variety of jobs previously held only by men and performed them with a high measure of success. This applied even to "heavy" factory jobs, formerly considered exclusively masculine in character. To a very considerable extent in the early 1940's, women became the "economic muscle" of this country, at a time when its industry was being pushed to the utmost to help win the greatest war in history. When the war emergency ended, and the men returned home, women were "eased out" of most of the better paying jobs they had performed so well, although there was *some* permanent beneficial effect on the employment of women in industry and business.

The entry of women into high-level scientific jobs in American industry is basically a development of the period since World War II. We are just beginning to overcome the age-old prejudice that women are "naturally" not suited for such work.

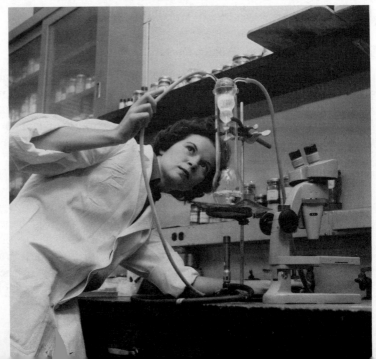

Women Supervising Men?

Above all, there is in our society a strong disinclination to place women in a supervisory position over men. It may be all right for a woman to supervise a large group of girl typists, but there would be something "wrong" in having her in charge of the same number of male clerks.

During World War II, a woman employed by a large advertising agency assumed more and more responsibility until she was actually supervising a large staff of layout artists. After she had been doing this for some time, she asked for the title (and the salary) of "Director" of the department. Her boss just laughed and said, "We can't have a lady pitcher on the ball team." He meant of course that the morale of the "team" would be undermined if a mere woman played the key position. The fact that she was actually doing this job was less important than the open acknowledgment that she was in charge of the men workers.

This attitude, so typical of our social structure, has certain psychological roots, which we shall now examine.

The "Zap-Gap Theory"

> What are little boys made of?
> Snakes and snails and puppy dogs' tails.
> What are little girls made of?
> Sugar and spice and everything nice.

This familiar bit of doggerel actually sums up, in symbolic form, a point of view on masculinity and femininity, and on reality in general, which is held consciously by some people, and unconsciously by a great many others.

The basic underlying idea is that the universe embodies two basic principles — *active* and *passive*. One has no meaning without the other. In Chinese tradition, as we have noted in Chapter 9, this is represented by *yang,* the male, positive principle, and *yin,* the female, negative principle. The dynamic balance between these two principles is said to underly the entire physical universe.

American students have renamed this the *"zap-gap theory"* of the universe. There can't be a *"zap"* without a *"gap,"* and vice versa. And there can't be a world without both of them.

In a social organization, the *zap* or active principle is represented by the men; and the *gap* or passive principle, by the women. Thus, men and women play contrasting but complementary roles. Men are

The prevailing concepts of the "proper" roles for men and women are in-stilled at an early age through communication media, such as children's books. Boys characteristically *do* things. Girls *look on* and then *enjoy* what has been accomplished.

active; women are passive. Men protect; women give nourishment. Men provide the food; women prepare it. Men think rationally; women are emotionally directed. Men are practical; women are senti-mental.

It doesn't take too much imagination to extend this concept to the reproductive roles of the male and female. Again, the male repre-sents the active, aggressive principle, while the female is the passive recipient. The very word *aggressiveness* conveys the image of a self-assertive, forward thrust and is popularly considered to be a mascu-line trait. Thus, by extension, violence is also regarded as masculine. The male is sometimes said to "violate" the female. And, as Freud pointed out, dream images of guns and swords symbolize the male sex organ. Both in mythology and in the unconscious mind, the idea of sexual penetration is equated with "mastery" of another person by means of superior physical strength.

However, it is only when man is in the barbaric or savage stage, or on the unconscious level of his mind, that he gives full expression to these aggressive, sadistic impulses. Murder, rape, and other forms of aggression are condemned as immoral. In a civilized society, the male has the strength to impose his will on others, but he resists using it arbitrarily and against the will of these others. In fact, civilized man is supposed to use his strength *positively,* in the interests of his family and his neighbors, as well as himself.

In popular mythology, then, it is men who have the capacity or the power to inflict violence on others. Women, while capable of "viciousness," are supposed to be far less inclined toward physical violence and less well equipped for it. In this view, they are, as Freud put it, "naturally passive."

The world is a violent place. Man cannot survive without some measure of violence directed against other living things. And it is the masculine role to be ready to exercise this power of life and death. We can see this most clearly in a primitive hunting society, typical of prehistoric times. The people live basically on meat. The males must go out to track down and kill the game, while the women remain at home to care for the children and perform household tasks. As the hunters grow more and more skilled in the use of weapons, it naturally becomes their duty to defend the tribal group against outside attacks. Thus, the male serves as the hunter and warrior, which means that he is the food-provider and the protector of the social group. These responsibilities have led to the image of man as the "hero."

Thus, the ideas of "aggressiveness" and "passivity" connected with roles during the reproductive act are reinforced by roles assumed in the primitive social organization. Out of these basic experiences of life have been derived the mythical types of persons who are thought to embody "pure masculinity" or "pure femininity."

These primitive cultural stereotypes have come down to us to the present day, and on a largely unconscious level they continue to influence the ideas and the behavior of vast numbers of people. Of course in the modern world, they are not the only determinants of what is to be considered authentic "masculinity" and "femininity." The growing child comes in actual contact with many "real" authority

The concept of the male as a hunter and warrior goes back to prehistoric times.

figures — with individual men and women, who help to shape his views and standards. These include parents, older brothers and sisters, other relatives, teachers, religious counselors, etc. To what extent these influences will modify the primitive stereotypes of "masculine" and "feminine" depends on individual circumstances.

The "Hero" Image

The concept of masculinity is closely intertwined with the idea of "heroism." Traditionally, we assume that to be a male means to take chances, to assume risks for the sake of a greater gain, to place oneself in peril because the welfare of the group may require it. We respect a man who has the daring and the "guts" to make and to carry out a decision of "life-or-death" importance. We are far less likely to expect such "heroism" of a woman.

We can see this pattern clearly in the behavior of adolescent boys. Traditionally, they are ready to accept a "dare" and to put themselves into what may appear to be a position of danger — for example, by climbing a tree, or venturing into unknown territory, or issuing or accepting a challenge to fight. By overriding his fear in this way, the boy proves to others (and to himself) that he is able to "act like a man." Above all, he must demonstrate that he is not a coward or "sissy."

The boy or adult male who meets these standards of "heroic" behavior is likely to be rewarded with the acceptance, approval, and even admiration of the people in his social group. This, naturally, is what he desires. But he may be influenced by such considerations to such a degree that he will act "heroically" — take extreme risks not needed for his own well-being — even when no one is observing him. In this case, he has unconsciously transferred the theoretical "onlookers" to a controlling position in his mind. He is measuring his own worth according to what he presumes that "they" will think and say.

Girls may also assume the risks of violent and daring conduct, but they are usually under far less pressure to do so. Their peers, parents, and society in general do not really expect them to be strong and brave in the face of immediate danger. If they scream and run away, they are acting "just like girls" — which in their case is likely to be considered "cute," rather than discreditable. Growing girls are exposed to other anxiety-producing pressures from the group, but accepting risks "heroically" is not one of them.

Thus, a female child in a society begins to get the idea that it is her role in life to serve a man passively, in return for the protection and security he will provide. Women cannot adequately support and defend themselves.

This means that women are discouraged from assuming full responsibility for themselves and for others. Of course, they do have specific "responsibilities" — many tasks which they are required to perform for all the members of the family group — but not the right to make the really important choices or decisions. The fate of the entire family is traditionally supposed to be in the hands of the father, the patriarch. In a really threatening situation, the woman is expected to defer to the man's judgment. There are exceptions, such as a woman left alone with her children, or a woman whose husband is physically or psychologically incapable of playing the masculine role. But in general, a woman is not supposed to act heroically or "responsibly" when a man is at hand to assume this function.

Symbols for Manhood

This ideal or archetype of heroism is certainly a difficult burden for most males to carry. They may be able to measure up to heroic standards on some occasions, but there will inevitably be many other times when they are inclined to fall short. This often leads to a nagging sense of inadequacy or insecurity. "Do I have what it takes to be a real man? Am I behaving the way a hero (or a two-fisted he man, or a regular guy) would behave in this situation?"

Thus, it is not surprising that throughout human history men have gone to extremes to convince themselves and others of their true masculinity (heroism). One way to do this is to obtain and display the outward signs or symbols of heroism. One word for such a symbol is *glory*. Another word is *prestige*. It means simply that a man has done things — or is believed to have done things — which mark him out as one of the select few whom other people admire. His record of achievement is worn like a badge to announce to the world that he is indeed a hero — a "real man."

Here we recognize one strong psychological basis for competition between men. They are eager to outdo each other because any achievement which brings substantial recognition is unconsciously associated with glory, which in turn is associated with heroism and masculinity. Of course, it is more satisfying if the "achievement" in question is something truly outstanding — a victory on the battlefield, or a feat of exploration, or even a scientific discovery. But most men have few opportunities for action on this level, and they may have to fall back on something as prosaic as bringing home enough money to support their family, or keeping intruders out of the home. If the act helps to establish the individual as a "real man," it serves its purpose in this sense.

Another symbol of heroism is *power* — meaning basically the ability to control the fate of others. This is unconsciously — if not always actually in fact — linked to the potential for violence. In the modern world the most familiar and accessible road to power is the accumulation of wealth. The desire to prove one's manhood is certainly one common reason for wanting to become rich. Note that we almost always think of the rise "from rags to riches" in terms of a man. A woman is assumed to be rich when she shares the affluence of her parents or husband.

Still another important symbol for masculinity is *virility,* meaning sexual attractiveness and potency. The "Don Juan" or "lady killer" type may be criticized, but he is also likely to be the object of a certain amount of envy or admiration as a "real man."

Thus we see how our cultural traditions associate such aspects of personality as responsibility, authority, achievement, power, and potency with specifically male attributes and behavior. The female in most cases is seen as representing a contrast to these characteristics. Clearly, these ideas have had a far-reaching impact on the role of women in our society. Freud, however, assumed that women are *"naturally* passive" — that the passive and irresponsible role they assume in most cases is *natural* for them. This is the main reason that Freud is scornfully rejected as a "male chauvinist" by feminist leaders today.

Images of Masculinity

In the popular traditions of our society, going back many centuries, there are various "types" of heroes (or anti-heroes) that represent the masculine image. Among those that you will recognize are the following:

▶ *The Barbarian.* He is violent, brutal, lustful, greedy. He is also slothful and self-indulgent, concerned only with using his power to satisfy his own desires. Although he is condemned as morally contemptible, there is evidence that many men are deeply attracted by this image and, to a degree, seek to emulate it.

▶ *The "Lady Killer."* This is the sexual adventurer, the man who has his way with many women. In more modern parlance, he is the "playboy type." Again, there is "official" condemnation, but also a good deal of covert admiration and envy on the part of many men.

▶ *The Warrior.* In American tradition, he is symbolized not only by the soldier but also by the "crime fighter" and by the frontiersman opposing Indians, outlaws, and other "bad guys." The tremendous popularity of the cowboy* myth, not only in the United States but throughout the world, testifies to the appeal of this masculine type. The image is particularly appealing because the whole point is that the hero is using his strength, skill, and courage in a "good" cause. Thus, he can be as violent as he pleases without forfeiting the approval of society.

▶ *The Stern, Virile Father.* He keeps his family together by strict discipline, but he also provides for it by hard work and selfless devotion. He may or may not also be a warrior.

Other familiar masculine images which combine various qualities of the types indicated above are the shrewd businessman, the soldier-of-fortune, the explorer and discoverer, the hard, conscientious worker, and the "hustler" or unscrupulous but charming rogue. In general, any life style that suggests adventure, excitement, daring, and initiative is considered masculine.

The importance of these myths is that *they influence the way men behave.* Men strive constantly to conform to the images which, they have been taught, represent "true masculinity." We see this re-

---

* We must distinguish here between the myth and reality. In cold fact, the American cowboy was a rural laborer, doing hard and often dangerous work for poor wages.

flected in the personalities and the life styles of the men who become popular "culture heroes," such as stars of television, moving pictures and pop music. Whether these personalities are real or the product of "public relations" experts really makes very little difference. In either case, they express the popular concept of masculinity to which many people aspire.

Images of Femininity

Women, according to the popular mythology of our society, have a "mysterious" power of their own. They are able to make themselves felt in a male-dominated world by subtly influencing the decisions of men.

This skill of exerting power at second hand is characteristic of people who are cut off from direct access to power. A "typical" woman, instead of immediately speaking her mind in a situation that involves men, will probably make her point in a roundabout way. If she is good at this — and many women are — the man in question may not even know that he is being influenced, and his masculine self-image will not be threatened.

There are several images or stereotypes of femininity that have become predominant in Western culture:

▶ *The Loving Mother.* The ideal mother is the ultimate source of unselfish love, ever ready to feed, console, comfort, and reassure. She is hard-working, patient, and uncomplaining. With a measure of despair, and a measure of hope, she tolerates the aggressiveness of her menfolk, whom she is always ready to serve. One of her main duties in the family is to temper the masculinity of her young sons with elements of gentleness, kindness, and sympathy before they are introduced to weapons.

▶ *The Temptress.* In this image, the woman is sensual and allur-
ing. She appeals to men to exercise their sexual powers on her
body, and she demands in return not only sexual but also emotional satisfaction. In the West, she is commonly associated with
"sin." Frequently, she is pictured as self-seeking, devious, "bitchy."
She uses men's sexual desires against them, causing misery to wives
and mothers.

▶ *The Helpless Little Girl.* She is scatterbrained but cute. Although an adult woman, she has an "innocent" quality. She is always ready to admire men for the wonderful manly things they do,
and is delighted when they notice her. Men enjoy being of assistance
to her because it underlines their masculine superiority.

Men like women to show qualities associated with all three of
these stereotypes — a fact which must cause immeasurable psychic
stress in women. The most successful women performers in the mass
entertaining media are usually those who are adept at conveying an
illusion composed of all three feminine images. They are at the same
time "sex symbols," givers of sincere, unselfish love, and delightfully
helpless bits of feminine fluff.

Typical feminine traits, according to the conventions of our society, include patience, gentleness, humility, kindness, consideration
for others, and sweet innocence. These are all expressed in willing,
indeed eager, acceptance of male domination, which suggests a desire
to occupy an inferior status.

Symbols of Femininity

Since the typical woman is cut off from the kinds of accomplishment and the symbols of success that confer status and prestige on
men, she is left with her "uniquely feminine qualities" to express herself as a person. What this amounts to in most cases is that she must
make a "career" of using her physical appeal and her "personality" to
please men.

First and foremost, the women in our society are supposed to
look "pretty" — sexually desirable. This calls for a vast amount of
concentration on the "right" clothes, cosmetics, and hair styling.
Facilities for weight reducing and "body conditioning" have become
a sizable industry. The underlying purpose of this elaborate ritual,
however it may be rationalized, is to catch the attention of *men,* to
arouse the interests and desires of *men,* to improve the female's standing with *men.*

A more insidious practice is the stylization of *personality*. Young women in particular are taught that it is their destiny to make themselves pleasing to men by skillful flattery, by "cute" mannerisms, often by an affectation of "feminine helplessness." This is so familiar to us that it may seem "natural," but the fact is that by continually orienting their thinking to conform to male preferences and emotional needs, women are impairing their ability *to think and act productively for themselves*. This is one of the main points made by the theoreticians of Women's Lib — and it appears to be a good one.

The overriding consideration, of course, is that the young woman must "catch a husband," and not just any husband but one who represents a "good match" for her in age, appearance, education, social background, income potential, etc. Since in many areas and communities, there are more "marriageable" females than males, women are sometimes prodded into fierce competition to be "popular with men." Men, in turn, may use this as a weapon in pressuring women to submit sexually. Women's Lib proponents see in this a well-defined pattern of *sexual exploitation,* which they consider to be one of the most immoral and degrading aspects of man-woman relations in our society.

When a woman does get married, she is in a position to achieve the supreme symbol of femininity — giving birth to children. Then, say the feminists, she is supposed to live through her husband and children. If they are "successful," she shares in the credit; if they do not gain the approval and admiration of the community, she is a "failure." In other words, she is not judged as an individual human being but merely as a reflection of her husband and the other members of her family.

Once Again: "The Natural Inferiority of Women"

Perhaps you will feel inclined to dismiss these stereotypes of images of masculinity and femininity as "sweeping generalizations." And of course they are. They certainly do not tell the whole story about the actual nature, behavior, and potentialities of men and women. But that is just the point. These oversimplified, over-generalized representations of the male and female characters have come to be accepted by vast numbers of people, usually on an unconscious level. And it is not merely what men believe about women, and vice versa, but what each group believes *about itself*. This inevitably has a far-reaching impact on the behavior of these people, and indeed of all of us, in regard to some of the most fundamental relationships of life.

One basic evaluation that emerges from the conventional images of masculinity and femininity is simply this: *In most of the significant activities and responsibilities of life, women are held to be inferior.* Many explanations have been offered to support this idea of the "natural inferiority of women." None is conclusive or convincing. There is no valid reason for assuming that half of the human race is inferior to the other half, particularly in mental ability, because of their respective roles in the reproductive process. And as Freud pointed out, women also have powerful aggressive and sexual impulses, although society usually demands that they be more strongly repressed or concealed by women than by men.

In any event, science can provide no biological evidence to support the idea of the "natural inferiority of women." Man's greater muscular strength is offset by certain physical advantages of women, such as greater resistance to some diseases. The feminists claim, then, that the predominance of males in such areas as business, government, science, the arts, and scholarship *is due to social rather than biological factors.* Women, it is argued, have been systematically deceived over the years into accepting a position of institutionalized inferiority. They must now make a self-conscious, organized, uncompromising effort, with the help of enlightened men, to *liberate* themselves from this degraded status. This is the essence of the philosophy and program of the Women's Liberation movement.

The Bisexual Nature of Human Beings

All human beings have bisexual impulses and feelings. No one is purely masculine or purely feminine.

The majority of psychologists would agree that this is true. But it goes strongly against the grain of most people in our present-day society to admit it. Why? Basically because of our unconscious acceptance of the accepted stereotypes of masculinity and femininity. We have come to accept a cultural fantasy, a time-honored but unexamined mythology, to the effect that each sex has its own essential characteristics which stand in contrast to those of the other sex. Thus, we engage in all kinds of involved, symbolic behavior to advertise and establish our "sexual identity." We are often at great pains to deny any tendencies or feelings in ourselves which, we have been taught, "belong" to the other sex. In effect, we expend enormous amounts of precious energy to repress and disguise essential aspects of our own personality.

Undoubtedly one reason for this mode of behavior in many cases is the fear, conscious or unconscious, of being accused or suspected of homosexual tendencies. Or the individual may fear "latent homosexuality" in himself, or herself, and may react by strongly repressing all aspects of personality which do not seem sufficiently masculine or feminine. The significant point is that people in such a case are reacting not to their own needs, impulses, and aspirations but rather to a conventional set of stereotypes which, in a highly questionable way, presume to define authentic masculinity and femininity. (See Chapter 23 for a discussion of homosexuality.)

In any case, it is foolish and naive to assume uncritically that any particular trait, impulse, feeling, or mode of behavior can be validly classified as "masculine" or "feminine." It is much more useful to look at any bothersome emotion or behavior pattern and to try to decide what value it has *for you*. Does it help you to grow as a happy, well-adjusted, self-actualized, responsible person? If it does, the fact that a popular mythology questions its sexual orientation should be a matter of indifference.

The insight that neither sex "owns" any particular aspect of personality is a strong argument against patriarchy or male supremacy. This does not mean, as is sometimes charged, that men and women will move toward the same "neuter sex" (or "unisex"). It does not mean that they will cease to love one another, complement one another, come together in marital unions, and conceive, raise, and love children together. All these things will continue, although perhaps not in exactly the same social forms that we know today.

What this point of view *does* mean is that men should feel free to choose friends of their own sex without self-consciousness and without worry about "snickering." And the same, of course, applies to women. It also means that men should feel free to work in positions of subordination to well-qualified women, without fear that they are being degraded or sacrificing their manliness. And also that women should feel free to occupy such positions, without apprehension that their womanliness may thereby be called into question.

The Vested Interest of Men in "Male Supremacy"

It is clear that the inferior position of women in our society has in effect created a vested interest for a great many men. This is seen in its most obvious form in the economic field. If women are, by and large, considered inherently unqualified for the most desirable positions, there is that much less competition for men seeking such positions. Similarly in our political and government life, men have pretty much of a clear field in regard to positions of responsibility and power.

From their earliest beginnings, American moving pictures have fostered the "idealized" image of woman as a helpless but adorable little girl, whose highest destiny it is to be loved, protected, and guided by a masterful male. (Lillian Gish and Robert Harron in *Hearts of the World,* made in 1918.)

But there is a more subtle aspect to this vested interest — the *psychological satisfaction* that many men obtain from being in a dominant or superior position. In our society, it is every male's birthright to play the role of protector of the "weaker sex." No matter how modest his education, intelligence, or accomplishment, he may very well assume that his judgment is superior to that of the women in his family, so that he probably takes it upon himself to make important decisions for the family group. Then there is the matter of sexual exploitation, which has traditionally been regarded as a male privilege. In other words, the woman exists specifically to give sexual satisfaction to the man, but not vice versa.

These and other similar factors feed the self-esteem of many men. By the same token, the men regard any changes that may raise the status of women to a position of equality as a threat to their self-concept as superior beings.

But we have seen that the ideas and stereotypes on which this assumption of superiority is based are not realistic. To insist on retaining outworn myths and to try to build good social relationships on them must be considered a form of neurotic behavior.

To be sure, there are women who would like to reverse roles. In other words, they want not merely equality but a position of dominance. There are mothers, for example, who are intent on controlling every aspect of family life, including a tyrannical domination of their husbands. But it is probably true that the majority of feminists today, and their male supporters, see their movement as a struggle to prevent unfair or irrational domination by *either* sex. In this sense, they are working for people of *both* sexes. They feel that love, friendship, child-raising, work relationships, and all the other important areas of life will be more satisfying and rewarding if men and women are truly on an equal footing. This does not mean that their roles will be identical or exactly interchangeable. Such a condition will probably never prevail in our society, or in any other society. But the old "master-servant" or "adult-child" relationship is being challenged today as never before.

Mature and intelligent people can achieve such a relationship in their personal lives even in a generally male-oriented social environment. For example, the world-famous psychologist Erik H. Erikson received much of his early professional training from a woman, Anna Freud (the daughter of Sigmund Freud). A lesser man might have resented being placed in such a position of subordination to a woman teacher. Erikson, however, testifies that he accepted her on the basis of her professional abilities, and that he enjoyed and benefited greatly from her instruction.

Masculinity and femininity are part of the essential biological nature of mankind. But as one young woman put it recently, "The concepts of masculinity and femininity must change. We need more of an open acceptance between people."

THINGS TO DISCUSS :: THINGS TO DO :: THINGS TO READ

1. A key concept used in this chapter is *sex role stereotype*. Explain carefully what is meant by this term. Give specific examples of such stereotypes for both sexes. Do you think that such stereotypes are harmful? Why? If we were to get rid of such stereotypes, would other stereotypes replace them? In other words, is there a *need* for some stereotypes to define the respective roles of the sexes in our society? Explain.

2. Sigmund Freud was undoubtedly one of the most original, creative, and perceptive thinkers of modern times. His ideas and discoveries inaugurated a new era in the history of psychology. Yet, in regard to the role of women in our society, his ideas have been criticized as conservative, rigid, old-fashioned, unimaginative. Women's Lib proponents condemn him as a "male chauvinist." How do you explain this apparent contradiction in Freud's thinking?

3. Shirley Chisholm, a black Congresswoman from New York City, has said she felt that being a woman had been a greater "handicap" to her in her career than being black. "It will take years to discover and eliminate the racist attitudes they (whites) actually have. But how much harder it will be to eliminate the prejudice against women! I'm sure it will be a longer struggle."

   What is your reaction to Mrs. Chisholm's comment? Does it surprise you that she feels this way? Do you agree that it will probably take longer to eliminate sex prejudices than race prejudices? Explain your answers.

4. Is it possible that there is some relationship between *sex prejudice* and *race prejudice*? Explain.

5. "I myself would say it is much more creative to rear and shape the personality of a fine, live child than it is to work in an office, or even to carve a statue."
   — BENJAMIN SPOCK

   ". . . It is the function of advanced groups like the professional femininists to articulate what is only implicit in the behavior of a much larger group. That is the inner logic of their downgrading of woman's biological role, their angry deprecation of motherhood, their insistence on every mother's 'right' to park her baby in a day-care center and hurry off to work, even when financial circumstances do not require her to do so." — WILLIAM V. SHANNON

   Above are two comments on the status and responsibility of women in our society. How would an advocate of Women's Lib be likely to react to each of these statements? What criticisms do you think could be made? How do you feel about these issues?

6. Make a list of words that include the root *man,* even though they refer to both sexes — for example, *human, chairman, ombudsman, workman.* Can you think of any other features of our language which show a similar "sexist" bias or emphasis? Should we change the language to accommodate feminist demands for equality?

7. Choose several members of the class, including some boys, to attend a meeting of a Women's Liberation group in your area. The members of the group should then report to their class.

READINGS

Born Female: The High Cost of Keeping Women Down, by Caroline Bird, with Sara Welles Briller (David McKay, 1968). This is probably one of the best surveys of the problem as it exists in the United States today.

The Feminine Mystique, by Betty Friedan (W. W. Norton, 1963). Written by the founder of the National Organization of Women (NOW), this book provides a cogent, insightful statement of the "case" for Women's Liberation.

Sexual Politics, by Kate Millet (Doubleday, 1970). This book, like Friedan's, has been one of the major forces in animating and directing the Women's Lib movement.

The Female Eunuch, by Germaine Greer (McGraw Hill, 1971). Written by a highly controversial "radical," the book is a scathing indictment of current sex-role attitudes.

The October, 1971 issue of *Saturday Review* features important articles on the theme of educating women.

The Dynamics of Hate

An Analysis of Prejudice

● ●

"When we let freedom ring, when we let it ring from every village and every hamlet, from every state and every city, we will be able to speed up that day when all of God's children, black men and white men, Jews and Gentiles, Protestants and Catholics, will be able to join hands and sing in the words of the old Negro spiritual, 'Free at last! Free at last! Thank God Almighty, we are free at last!'"

— *MARTIN LUTHER KING, Jr.*

How Does Hatred Feel?

Following is a talk given by a black Chicago youth about the effects of prejudice on his life*:

You ain't going to like what I got to say, but that doesn't bother me. The only reason I'm here is because the Reverend asked me and I owe him some favors. As for me, I'm fed up to here with white-black talk. The more we talk, the poorer we get, the richer you get, and the better you feel. Well, I ain't here to make you feel better.

I'm seventeen — my name is Floyd — I got twelve brothers and sisters — and a jail record. I got it when I first started as block leader for my gang two years ago. A landlord waited until a mother of ten

---

* From *Am I a Racist?*, compiled by Robert Heyer (Paulist Press, 1969). This quotation originally appeared in an article by Dolores Curran in the magazine *Ave Maria*, July 20, 1968.

kids was in the hospital, and he dumped her furniture and kids out in the snow. We picked them up and hauled them up the eight floors to her flat. Our gang stayed there with the kids and dared the guy to dump them again. He didn't, but he called the cops and told them I'd threatened him, so I was charged with "intent to do bodily harm."

I didn't have no lawyer and I didn't give a damn besides, so I was convicted and got a suspended jail sentence and a police record. Ever since, the police pick me up any time they feel like it and give me a going over — "cause you got a jail record, hood," they say.

I used to go to school, but I don't bother with that any more. Last year the Rangers controlled the turf where our high school was and didn't let us in for school. They kept about 900 of us out of school for a year, but the school people didn't care because it wasn't so much trouble for them if we weren't there. The cops said it was just two bunches of niggers fighting it out, so they didn't do nothing. My mother said we were going to school, and she walked with us one day and almost got killed herself, so she let us stay out after that. Rather have dumb kids than dead ones, she said.

My old lady, she's okay, but she doesn't know what it's like — I mean, she still thinks that if you're real good and study hard and be nice to The Man, that he'll notice you ain't got nothing someday and give you a nickel. Me? I got different thoughts. I figure that if The Man was so all-Jesus good, he wouldn't turn off our heat in winter and pay off the cops to forget we reported it or dump us when we get behind in the rent a week. I figure The Man has had lots of time to be nice, and we ain't seen much of it.

We live in a four-room flat, a real dump on the tenth floor, and pay $115 a month. My mother gets welfare and works cleaning when she can and ain't pregnant. Last year we couldn't pay for a couple of months, and the landlord says get moving so my aunt and her seven kids moved in to help pay the rent. Now we got so many kids running around — hell, I don't even know who lives there. Two of my brothers are gone most of the time — to the streets or jail — so it leaves about twenty of us in the flat.

Yeah, I want a job, but a real job, not one of them poverty things where you don't do nothing. No one's paying me $1.25 an hour to cool me off in the summer so I forget what a slum I am and smile at Whitey and say thanks. Yeah, that's what I am — a slum. You talk about moving the slum and clearing the slum and building new buildings to get rid of the slum — well, the slum ain't buildings. The slum is me and people like me that you ain't going to let out no matter how smart or educated we get. Man, you've named us the slum so don't gripe if we act like the slum.

I got me a friend who took one of them poverty jobs, and you know what he did all summer? They gave him a rag and told him to polish the slide and stuff in a schoolyard. They just laughed about it. "Now as long as you stay in that schoolyard polishing and off the streets, you'll get your buck and a quarter." Funny thing was, he didn't get paid until it was snowing, and by then he was ready to riot for his money.

Do I think riots is any good? Well, let me tell you, they don't hurt any. Only thing is that the next riot ain't going to be in our neighborhood. If we burn, we burn Whitey, not ourselves. We'll start with Marshall Field's. Why Marshall Field's? Because it's white, man, all white. They don't want us in there except to sweep their floors and haul their garbage. . . .

Sure, there are some things I'd like to do. I'd like to fly planes or even fix planes, but that's far out. I can't even get into service with my jail record, and that's the only way someone like me is going to learn to fly. I got a friend whose brother got back from Vietnam, and he don't sit still for nobody. He says he learned to shoot over there, and ain't anybody going to make him Ralph-Bunche-it here. Ralph-Bunche-it? Well, that's like when somebody keeps saying, "Look, you can do it if Ralph Bunche did it." My friend's brother says that when he wants to move to the South Side, ain't no bunch of Polacks going to stop him.

Sure, I carry a gun — got to. The Rangers would take over our block if we didn't protect it. They'd even knife our mothers. The cops don't care. They only care when Whitey gets mixed up in it. My

brother got rolled and cut up one night and my mother called the cops four times. They never did come. I got my gun for three bucks from an older guy but I know where you can get one now for two. Night before the riot, some Jews were selling them right out on the corner for two bucks.

Would more poverty laws help us? We don't want any more laws. We're sick of hearing about laws. Laws ain't for us. Our Uncle Toms bought the War on Poverty, didn't they? Are we any better off? We get laws and laws and more laws, and things get worse and dirtier and hungrier. The cops get meaner and crookeder, and The Man talks about Ralph Bunche.

Well, The Man is going to get his. Life can't get any worse for us, see? Can the Church help us? Holy Jesus, that's a laugh. All those prayers and gospel hymns about sitting back and letting Whitey show us how to be Christian. "Blessed are the meek so they will get heaven." I ain't waiting for heaven, and neither are any other black guys any longer. We want a little piece of this life. And there ain't no church trying to get us any. Father Groppi?* I don't know what his angle is, but any time a white man lines up with black men, he wants something from them. I don't know much about him and his gang, but I know one thing. We don't want anything to do with a white man — preacher or anyone else — in our gang.

What's my future? Haw. Who cares? You don't and I don't either. I think the only one who'd rather see me alive than dead is my mother. No one else gives a damn, including me. So I got nothing to lose if I set the match.

What do you mean, I must want something out of life? What I want don't make any difference. I'm black. I'm a slum. I got a police record. I won't get a good job — ever. If I get married. I won't be able to feed my kids. I'll run out on them, so welfare can feed them. Then they won't have a father, either. You guys hold all the strings so you tell me — what's so goddam great about living?

To Be Prejudiced Means to "Pre-judge"

The young man quoted above is prejudiced — against whites ("Whitey"), Poles ("Polacks"), Jews, and policemen, among others. Some of the specific things he says are certainly open to question. There is no record of 900 students being "kept out" of a Chicago high school by gang action. The statement about guns being sold "right out on the corner for two bucks" may have some basis in fact, but one

---

* Father Groppi is a white Catholic priest who has been active in the struggle for social justice in Chicago and other Middle Western cities.

would probably be well-advised not to take it too literally. As for the identification of the people selling the guns, it should be borne in mind that in some ghetto areas, *any* white persons who sell things are commonly referred to as "Jews."

And yet there is no doubt that much of what Floyd says is the cold truth — and that *all* of it is an expression of his experience and of his convictions of the truth.

Why does Floyd hate people? Why has he suffered through a life of misery? What makes him describe himself as "a slum"?

A large part of the answer is that he has been tortured by abuse and hatred all his life, as he so well describes. But not all cases of hatred can be so easily traced to flagrant social mistreatment.

Why do some whites hate blacks? Why do some blacks hate whites? Why do some people (both white and black) hate Jews? Why do "hard hats" hate "hippies"? Why did the Nazis murder more than 10 million Jews, Slavs, Gypsies, and members of other "racially inferior" groups? *Why, in short, do men hate each other?*

If one individual does harm to another, we can probably understand the injured person's hatred, if not condone it. But how is it that a man can hate strangers who have personally never injured him? How is it that whole groups or classifications of people can be prejudiced against other groups?

The word *prejudice* comes from the word "pre-judge." To prejudge means to judge something or someone before sufficient knowledge is at hand to justify an opinion. If one man pre-judges another, he anticipates his behavior without knowing or understanding the man as a unique human being. And almost invariably this kind of prejudgment is unfavorable. The individual or group being judged is found to be "evil," or "inferior," or even rejected by God.

Is this kind of thinking logical? No. It is *irrational* — and *irrationality* is the main feature of prejudice. Being irrational, the motivation comes from the unconscious, and therefore is impulsive and frequently obsessive.

In short, the irrationality of prejudice lies in the fact that it originates from unconscious fears and is a mechanical, over-generalized reaction that prevents an individual from seeing what is real.

The Scope of the Problem — Black Americans

If a person is consistently and harshly rejected, particularly during his childhood, he will very likely feel unsure of himself. Frequently when he becomes an adult, his personality will be dominated by feelings of insecurity — self-doubt.

This rejection does not always come primarily from an unsatisfactory home life and insecure parents. It may come from the whole social environment of the individual. Think of the damage that is done when a child goes to school and feels hostility or contempt from teachers and administrators; when he grows older and finds that no one will hire him except for menial jobs; when he is excluded from unions that control the best-paying jobs; when he is unable to find housing in a decent neighborhood and must pay outrageous rents for substandard quarters.

There are more than 25 million people in the United States today who, to a greater or lesser degree, have experienced or are experiencing this and similar situations. They are the Americans whom we designate as "Negroes," "blacks," or "Afro-Americans." They are almost all the descendants of Africans who were brought to this country as slaves (and also of white slaveholders). As a people, they remained in the degraded status of slavery for centuries. This institution was justified on the grounds that while black men belonged to the human race, they were in all essential respects an inferior breed, properly subject to the domination of white men. The deep, irrational prejudices which developed under the slavery system have still not been overcome in this country, in spite of almost universal agreement among scientists that all the ideas of racial "superiority" and "inferiority" are utter delusions, derived from historical misconceptions, fallacious reasoning, and profound psychological maladjustments. Prejudice con-

These graphs show the disadvantaged position of non-whites (mainly blacks) in the United States in regard to employment, education, and income. (Figures for 1969.)

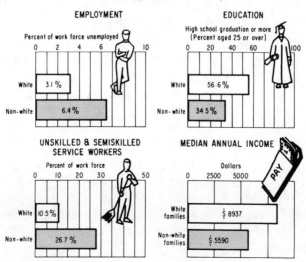

tinues, and it is the primary reason for the generally underprivileged position of the black man in our society.

How seriously underprivileged is the black American as compared with the rest of the population? Part of the answer is given in the graphs on page 353. They show a pattern of deprivation reflected in higher unemployment, less desirable jobs, less education, lower earnings, and a shorter life span. There are many other significant facts that fit into the same bleak picture. We will cite only a few of them.

▶ Blacks by and large are still *segregated*. The vast racial ghettos in our large cities have not even begun to be dispersed. In some cases they are actually worse than they were a decade or two ago. "Urban renewal" has resulted in the destruction of more low-income housing than it has replaced. The government's program of guaranteeing mortgage loans for housing construction has been applied primarily in suburban areas from which black families are largely barred — by social and economic barriers, if not by law.

▶ The educational desegregation mandated by the Supreme Court's 1954 decision has not been carried out "with all deliberate speed." In 1970, government figures indicated that 61% of the black public school students in the United States were attending racially segregated institutions. ("Segregated" in this sense means that the enrollment of the school consists of from 95% to 100% black or other minority-group students.) This was true in all sections of the country — not merely in the eleven states that are usually identified as "the South." Even more to the point is the fact that these predominantly segregated schools, for a variety of reasons, offer an inferior educational program.

▶ In black families, 12% of mothers with children aged 6 to 17 find it necessary to work to make ends meet. Between the childbearing ages of 25 to 34, 57% of black women work, as compared with 41% of white women. Moreover, the black women work predominantly at menial, low-paid jobs. Their average annual earnings in 1968 were only about $2900, while white women averaged about $4500. This is obviously a disadvantage for family stability.

▶ About 24 million Americans (more than one in ten) are now living below the poverty line as defined by U. S. government standards. It is not true that most of these are black; the great majority (probably as many as two-thirds) are white. But the proportion of blacks in the poverty sector is at least twice as great as the proportion of whites.

Has There Been Improvement in Recent Years?

The answer to this is *Yes*.

There has been substantial progress (although not as much as some whites like to believe) in employment and in economic status generally. Large numbers of blacks have in effect joined the middle class. More and more blacks are receiving the benefits of higher education and attaining executive and professional status.

There has been progress in government and politics. In most areas, blacks are now free to vote on the same basis as anyone else. In the Southern states, recent voting-rights legislation has been highly effective in eliminating barriers that kept blacks from the polls. Black Americans in general now have voting strength in proportion to their numbers, and more and more blacks are being elected and appointed to public office — national, state, and local.

Many thousands of black people are now successful in various professions and other occupations and have moved into the upper brackets economically. Yet even those who have "made it" are often subject to harassment and humiliation resulting from prejudice. Whitney M. Young, Jr., the late Executive Director of the National Urban League (one of the leading black organizations), has written of a black doctor of his acquaintance who was constantly "being stopped by policemen who see a black man behind the wheel of a late-model car with MD plates and assume it's stolen." Black professionals, Young continued, "often find that when they walk into a luxury apartment building, the doorman looks them up and down as if Jack the Ripper were coming to violate every tenant in the place. Similarly, while police brutality exists, many more blacks feel the weight of what we might call police *humiliation* — an overbearing manner, a refusal to show the least politeness, an attitude of fear mixed with hostility. . . . "*

It is only fair to point out that there has been some improvement in this area in recent years. Many police forces, especially in our largest cities, are emphasizing the importance of good intergroup relations and are training policemen to relate more positively and rationally to people of all racial and ethnic backgrounds. There are more black policemen, and some of them are attaining high rank. But it would be naive to assume that the problem has been effectively solved. The police simply reflect the prejudices that exist in the community as a whole, but because they serve in an exceptionally sensitive capacity, their behavior is particularly obvious and important to black people.

---

* Whitney M. Young, Jr., *Beyond Racism* (McGraw-Hill, 1969).

Today, in black communities throughout the country, there is evidence of increased self-consciousness and racial pride.

Prejudice Breeds Prejudice

This is the heart of the matter. Many of the black people whose lives have been scarred by the contempt, hatred, or indifference of the majority react with symptoms of hostility directed against "Whitey." This is particularly true of disadvantaged young men, like Floyd, whose eloquent testimony was quoted at the beginning of this chapter. The frustration generated in this way may lead to various forms of antisocial behavior, including crime.

In some cases, hatred is directed against a particular group within the "white world" — the Poles, the Italians, the Jews, the police, government officials, landlords, shopkeepers, etc. Such hatred may be understandable, but in its own way it is just as bad as the prejudices that generated it in the first place. For example, there has been some limited evidence of "black anti-Semitism" — based on a compulsive and fanatical stereotype of "the Jew." To the extent that it exists, it is just as twisted, just as irrational, and just as harmful as prejudice against blacks.

Residential Segregation

In fact, one of the most depressing aspects of the problem is the strong antagonism existing between different ethnic and racial groups. In some major American cities, for example, there is intense anti-black feeling among white groups who represent immigrants (largely from Central Europe) and the first-generation, or even the second-generation, children of the immigrants. These people tend to be fearful of blacks and therefore prejudiced.

Typically, most poor immigrant families upon their arrival in the United States have been forced to live in older, rundown sections, close to, or actually in, predominantly black neighborhoods. Their black neighbors often resented their presence, feeling that these recently arrived whites would get privileges and advantages long denied to non-white groups. The frustration and hostility of black children were sometimes focused on the nearest symbol of "white oppression" — resulting in violence between juvenile gangs.

In recent years, the black population of our great cities has shown sharp increases. The old, limited ghetto areas could not possibly contain these numbers, and the black families have "spread out," looking desperately for decent housing. In many cases, this has brought them into older "inner city" neighborhoods, inhabited largely by white working-class and lower-middle-class families of a definite ethnic character. Under such conditions, a pattern of resentment, hostility, and sometimes violence is likely to develop.

Faced with such a "threat," the white property-owners (immigrants or children of immigrants) sometimes panic. They are more interested in getting their families out of what they consider deteriorat-

ing and violence-ridden neighborhoods than they are in cooperating with their black neighbors to improve conditions. They may try by a variety of devices to keep their communities "lily-white." If this does not succeed, they will probably make every effort to move away from the inner city to the suburbs. Once they have acquired a home in suburbia — a long, hard struggle for many — they want above all to insure peace and quiet, to "protect their investment," and to maintain their hard-earned status of "respectability." Unfortunately, they may be convinced by this time that one way to gain such objectives is to keep black people from moving into the suburban community. It makes little difference how affluent, well-behaved, and well-educated a black family may be. To white people who have gone through a difficult experience in the inner city (or even to the children of such people), the mere presence of a black face may suggest poverty, squalor, and crime.

Thus we see a new pattern of residential segregation taking shape in American life at the very time that strenuous efforts are being made to break down the barriers of segregation and prejudice. The residential segregation, in turn, makes it all the more difficult to bring about genuine integration in the public schools.

Prejudice Against Other Minority Groups

American society has traditionally been marked by prejudices against minority groups other than blacks — Spanish-Americans (mainly Mexicans and Puerto Ricans), Indians, Jews, Catholics, Orientals, and persons of particular ethnic backgrounds. Some of these prejudices which were significant in earlier generations have now been reasonably well overcome — for example, anti-Catholic feeling.

How did this improvement in prevailing attitudes toward Catholics come about? In part, it is probably due to education — to a long period of indoctrination which effectively convinced the great majority of Americans that each man's religion is entirely his own affair, and also that the centuries-old "accusations" directed against Catholics were ridiculous fabrications. But there has been another factor in the situation which is worth noting. Most of the Catholics who came to this country throughout the 19th and early 20th centuries were poor people of "foreign" (that is, non-British) extraction. They were forced to do menial jobs; they lived in the slums; they spoke English badly, if at all. These conditions, combined with a traditional distrust of Catholicism by the Protestant majority, led to a stereotype of Catholics as poor, uneducated, foreign, un-American, and generally inferior. (If you think this is an exaggeration, look up the history of

This old print depicts a riot staged by the anti-Catholic "Know-Nothing" (or "Native American") Party in Philadelphia in 1844. The "native" mob, shown wearing beaver hats, fought with the state militia. Twenty-four persons were killed in these riots, and two famous old Catholic churches were burned.

the Know-Nothing Party, which flourished in this country during the 1840's and 1850's.)

As time went on, however, the new generations of American-born Catholics entered the "mainstream" of American life. Economically, educationally, socially, politically, and in every other way they were about the same as other elements of the white population. As individuals they could not be readily distinguished. Also, in many areas they constituted a very large part of the total population. Thus, the psychological basis for the prejudice against Catholics (as a poor, "foreign" minority) simply did not exist any more. A few fanatics, perhaps, clung to their fears and hatred, but for most Americans, extreme anti-Catholic prejudice simply ceased to make any sense.

In terms of this brief analysis, can you see why it is so *much more difficult* to counteract and eliminate anti-black prejudices?

The prejudices directed against each of the other groups noted above have their own chain of causation and their own special characteristics. They are marked by certain unconscious psychological forces which we shall now consider.

"The Dictatorship of the *They*"

An overriding consideration in the behavior of many, if not most, people is a fear of reprimand and rejection by members of the social group they rely on for love and affection.

This leads to a mode of behavior that one philosopher has called "the dictatorship of the *they.*" Who are *they*? The people on whose opinions the individual is dependent. Before he decides to take, or not to take, a certain course of action, he asks the often unconscious questions: "What will *they* think of me? Will *they* approve or disapprove? Will I be loved and admired, or scorned and rejected by *them*? The fear of such rejection is so strong in many people that they will go to great pains to avoid offending the members of their social group.

An experiment which illustrates this fear of rejection was held in a Northern city in the 1940's. At this time, very few of the "better" downtown stores employed minority group sales clerks. Nonetheless, a number of black sales people were given jobs in one store and were allowed to wait on some white customers. Everything went smoothly. Then the white customers who had made purchases were accosted on the street by an "inquiring reporter" and were asked if they would be willing to be waited on by black clerks. *Most of the customers actually lied and said they would refuse!*

Why did these people lie? After acting without conspicuous prejudice in the store, why did they actually claim that they would allow their behavior to be controlled by prejudice? The answer is, in all probability, that they associated an anti-black prejudice with the standards and the acceptance of their social group. They were afraid that if they admitted a relationship (even a customer-clerk relationship) with a black person, they would be exposed to criticism. By whom? By *them* — the leaders and pace setters of their social group.

R. D. Laing, a British psychiatrist, has noted that many people are afraid above all of creating a "scandal" by inappropriate conduct, and he has suggested the interesting idea of a *scandal network* that dominates the standards and behavior of such people*:

> The members of a scandal network may be unified by ideas to which no one will admit in his own person. Each person is thinking of what he thinks the other one thinks. Each person does not mind a colored lodger, but each person's neighbor does. Each person, however, is a neighbor of his neighbor.

Projection

People who are overly dependent on their group as a mainstay of "identity" and "reality" are those who fear themselves the most. Their fear is shown by their compulsive efforts to obtain support and approval from others.

---

* R. D. Laing, *The Politics of Experience* (Pantheon Books, 1967).

Such people are often unwilling to acknowledge their inner fears. They realize that such an acknowledgment would make them appear weak, irrational, lacking in confidence. Still, some way must be found to deal with the fears and relieve the tension. This is done frequently by *externalizing* the fears — by *projecting* them onto someone else.

The idea of *projection* is fundamental to any study of the mind. In essence it means that unacceptable emotions (desires, fears, hatreds) are shifted to other people. The individual, refusing to recognize that the "dirty," discreditable thoughts are his own, decides that they actually belong to someone else. And, of course, the "someone else" must be despised and perhaps punished in some way for having such thoughts.

For example, consider a nervous speaker in front of an audience. The speaker, in effect, is afraid of failure, but he doesn't want to admit this, even to himself. So he projects his emotion onto the audience and blames those people, whom he may not even know as individuals, for being critical and hostile. He doesn't try to observe the audience carefully to see what the mood is. (The mood may actually be friendly.) He turns his fear outward, and from that point on he is convinced that his evaluation is right. He refuses to look at the individual faces in the audience. All he sees is a hostile blur. If he now does badly as a speaker, he is not to blame. Who can do well with a critical, unfriendly audience?

There are two basic points to be noted. First, the person who does the "projecting" has irrational fears. "The other guy hates me, and he wants to hurt me (rape me, kill me, cheat me, slander me, etc.)." Second, since the projector shifts these fears to the other person, he is unable to see the real individual before him. He reacts not to an actual human being but to an imaginary structure built largely by his own emotions.

In some societies, whites often project their fears onto blacks. Because of the history of blacks in this country, many whites have come to accept (often unconsciously) such stereotypes as that blacks have emerged from "darkest Africa,"* and that they have a background of "savage" customs and mysterious sexual activities. One of the familiar white fantasies is that black men have great sexual prowess, and that their one all-consuming interest in life is to rape white women. Another common charge is that they are "dirty" — an unconscious association with sexuality.

---

* The vast majority of present-day black Americans are the descendants of people who were brought here prior to the illegalization of the African slave trade in 1808. Thus, they are among the "oldest American stock."

Until very recently, the vast majority of Americans (including most Afro-Americans) were unaware of the great civilizations of Black Africa. There was all but complete acceptance of the myth of African backwardness and savagery. We are just beginning to appreciate such works of art as the bronze sculptured heads produced in the Ife kingdom (modern Nigeria) in the 12th century A.D. (The heads shown here are casts of the original bronzes.) Does this have any implication for the self-image of American blacks and for their place in our pluralistic society?

Antisemitism in the United States has never had the violent, institutionalized character that it had in some European countries, but it does exist. It seems to rest on fantasies that Jews are particularly grasping, unscrupulous, and ruthless, especially in money matters. They not only want to rob "Gentiles" of their wealth, but they have the same obsession with seducing "Christian women."

Anti-black and anti-Jewish prejudices are vastly different in their historical origins, but they show a remarkably similar psychological pattern. In both cases, the emotional energy comes from *fears and lusts with which the unconscious is most preoccupied.* And in both cases, these repressed fears and lusts are projected onto an out-group. The more clearly the out-group is distinguished from the dominant population, the easier this act of projection is. Thus, blacks serve the purpose very well because of their skin color; Jews, because of their distinctive cultural tradition and identity.

The prejudices built up in this way do not depend on any personal relationships. People who have had few if any contacts with Jews may have all sorts of preconceptions about them. The important thing is not actual experience but the will to believe, or perhaps more accurately the *need* to believe.

The situation becomes even more confused by guilt feelings within the individual who projects his feelings in this way. He feels a need to be punished for these unacceptable emotions. All too often, the guilt also becomes projected onto the members of the out-group. They must be punished for the transgressions of which the hater is unhappily aware.

Karl Menninger, the noted American psychiatrist, has suggested that this psychological pattern may explain why society's treatment of convicted criminals is so ineffective and contradictory. As Menninger sees it, people who are frustrated within the confines of their own group unconsciously *need* criminals and other "public enemies" to do the things that their unconscious emotions are urging them to do. Then they have the added satisfaction of seeing punishment dealt out to the unconscious self, as projected onto the criminal.

Blinded by Prejudice

A person blinded by prejudices usually becomes highly defensive about his irrational assumptions. It is almost always quite futile to argue with him because he will take refuge in obvious rationalizations and will typically find some way of holding to his preconceptions. If the argument against his beliefs becomes too pressing, he will show anger and hostility.

The late Gordon W. Allport, one of America's leading social scientists, presents a good example of this process (slightly modified here)*:

MR. SQUINT: The trouble with the Jews is that they only take care of their own group.

MR. EYE: But the record of the Community Chest shows that they give more generously, in proportion to their numbers, to the general charities of the community, than do non-Jews.

MR. SQUINT: That shows they are always trying to buy favor and intrude into Christian affairs. They think of nothing but money; that's why there are so many Jewish bankers.

MR. EYE: But a recent study shows that the percentage of Jews in the banking business is extremely small—far smaller than the percentage of non-Jews.

MR. SQUINT: That's just it—they don't go in for respectable business; they are only in the movie business or running night clubs.

The rationalizers are not bothered by any need for consistency. Again Allport gives us an example.

In Rhodesia, a white truck driver passed a group of idle natives and muttered "They're lazy brutes." A few hours later he saw natives heaving 200-pound sacks of grain onto a truck, singing in rhythm to their work. "Savages," he grumbled. "What do you expect?"

The rationalizing process often involves focusing on a "kernel of truth" in an accusation about other people's behavior, and emphasiz-

---

* Gordon W. Allport's book *The Nature of Prejudice* (Addison-Wesley Publishing Co., 1954) is a brilliant survey of this social problem.

ing this to the exclusion of any other factors. This is typical of propaganda generally. Good propaganda is rarely 100% false. It is more effective to find some facts that can be sustained, and then to use these as a basis for a "superstructure" of fantasizing, hatred, and out-and-out lies. Adolf Hitler was a genius at this sort of thing.

The fact is that there *are* shortcomings, abuses, weaknesses, undesirable features in all groups of people and in all social organizations. But the ugly aspects of our own social environment are so familiar that there is a strong tendency to overlook them. In effect, we take them for granted. However, when we shift our attention to another social group or another environment, we become much more sensitized to ugliness. Every imperfection stands out clearly and may be used as the basis for severe criticism. And this prepossession with what is ugly in the out-group may also blind us to what is good and beautiful. These are tendencies which we all have, but they are particularly pronounced and unrelieved in people who show strong patterns of prejudice.

The Authoritarian Personality

There is an impressive amount of evidence that people who are recognizably prejudiced against "outsiders" are also generally intolerant of differences, diversity, and innovation in their own day-to-day affairs. Some psychologists express this by saying that prejudiced people tend toward an "authoritarian personality."

Studies cited by Allport* show that such people seem to think in extreme terms. Things are either good or bad, right or wrong, permissible or forbidden, with little or nothing uncertain or "in between." He quotes the social scientist Else Frankel-Brunswick, one of the pioneers in such studies. She observed a group of children showing strong patterns of prejudice regarding racial and ethnic questions. The children tended strongly to endorse the following beliefs. (Note that not one of them has anything to do with racial or ethnic matters as such.)

▶ There is always one right way to do anything.

▶ If a person does not watch out, somebody will make a sucker out of him.

▶ It would be better if teachers were more strict.

▶ Only people who are like myself have a right to be happy.

---

* Gordon W. Allport, *op. cit.*

▶ Girls should learn only things that are useful around the house.

▶ There will always be war; it is part of human nature.

▶ The position of the stars at the time of your birth tells your character and personality.

Allport's own research with adults indicates that highly prejudiced people are more likely than other people to believe statements such as the following:

▶ The world is a hazardous place in which men are basically evil and dangerous.

▶ We do not have enough discipline in our American way of life.

▶ On the whole, I am more afraid of swindlers than I am of gangsters.

Looking over these statements, we can see that most of them are obviously based on fear. The world appears to be highly threatening to these people, and this reflects a fundamental insecurity in their self-image. It is illuminating that the adults questioned feared swindlers more than they did gangsters. Gangsters extort by means of threats of doing physical harm; but swindlers or "con-men" humiliate by gaining a person's confidence, and then rejecting him as a "sucker." When the need to avoid being rejected and humiliated is stronger than the need to avoid physical violence, a person is displaying serious feelings of insecurity and self-doubt.

These feelings almost always arise from deeply buried conflicts involving parents. Allport cites another study of a group of anti-semitic college girls which showed that "they appeared on the surface to be charming, happy, well-adjusted, and entirely normal girls." He adds that "they were polite, moral, and seemed devoted to parents and friends." But deeper probing, through the use of specialized tests, interviews, and case histories, revealed that "underneath the conventional exterior there lurked intense anxiety, much buried hatred toward parents, destructive and cruel impulses." These girls all asserted that they liked their parents. They seemed extremely reluctant to express any criticism of them.* On the other hand, another group of college girls not recognizably prejudiced were much more openly critical of their parents, while still emphasizing their good points.

---

* We would say that the attitudes of these girls toward their parents were *ambivalent*. This suggests a contradictory or two-sided emotion. The girls at the same time felt resentment toward their parents and were not willing to concede any imperfections in them.

The authoritarian personality frequently must tolerate or excuse "lapses" in his own group, for fear of being rejected. The frustration built up in this way is released by being extremely severe toward people excluded from his circle.

It is well-known, for example, that the Nazis made a great show of observing "German morality" in their dealings with each other. Any violations of the "code" were carefully covered up. "Loyalty" to superiors, up to and including Hitler, became an obsession. But in their dealings with "non-Aryans" (outsiders), the Nazis showed a disregard of all moral standards to a degree unparalleled in modern history.

The Need for Order and Uniformity

A fanatical adherence to an exact ordering of every detail of life is the hallmark of many authoritarian personalities. Such people are eager to become integrated into systems that are designed to take all the weight of life's responsibilities from their shoulders. If no such system is available (such as a military command organization), they will seek desperately for some other protective structure. If necessary, they will have to invent one. Their greatest anxiety is that anything they do on their own responsibility will bring rejection and reprimand.

People with this type of character tend to be bigots. They need scapegoats, but the scapegoats must be clearly outside their own group, for they rely on the group as a system for controlling their forbidden impulses and for providing a measure of love and admiration. But since these impulses must be expressed in some form, they use the scapegoats as "projection screens" on which they depict their own lusts and fears, and on which they pour out the hatred that has arisen because of this frustration.

An experiment by J. Fisher, cited by Allport, supports this concept: Two groups of volunteers, identified as having "high prejudice" and "low prejudice," respectively, were shown a simple drawing, which had uneven ("off-center") proportions. Members of the two groups were told to draw the figure from memory immediately after seeing it. In both groups, about 40% of the members compensated for the unevenness of the figure by "balancing it out." Four weeks later the two groups were again asked to draw the figure (not having seen it meanwhile). This time, 62% of the high-prejudiced group "balanced it out," while only 34% of the low-prejudice group did so. The significance of this is the strong impulse of prejudiced people to try to impose *uniformity* on a situation, uniformity being interpreted as "order" and therefore desirable.

The Need for a "Strong" Leader

Another most striking feature of the authoritarian personality is a readiness to line up willingly and enthusiastically behind a "strong" (ruthless and dictatorial) leader. To a compulsively "orderly" person, the all-powerful leader appears to symbolize the desire for total control of his environment — thus freeing him of any responsibility — and also the expression of the primitive instincts of the unconscious, which can then finally be released aggressively toward "the enemy."

It is no accident that, historically, "strong" leaders are most likely to rise to power when conditions are undergoing marked change. In such a time of social tensions, the would-be dictator has the best chance to attract the support of large numbers of "normal" people who, in more stable times, would not appear to be overly "dependent" or "authoritarian" or "fanatical." But in a social climate where everything seems to be shifting, these people feel themselves seriously threatened, to the degree where their whole concept of "reality" is falling apart. They fiercely desire to maintain their self-image, as based on the group, and they will do anything to preserve "order and stability." Accordingly, they line up behind the political figure who presents himself as a "stern father," and they may well give him the votes, the financing, and the manpower resources he needs to "take over."

Hitler's assumption of power in Germany in the 1930's is the classic example of this. He started shortly after World War I with not much more than a handful of followers (fanatical Nazis) and gradually won over large elements of the middle class, who felt that the very framework of German society was disintegrating. Once in power, of course, Hitler and the Nazis gave vent to their own self-destructive impulses and instead of "order" brought violence and destruction, culminating in Germany's defeat in the most destructive war in history.

Prejudice Toward the Hippies

The "anatomy of prejudice" goes beyond social, ethnic, and religious minorities. It may extend to groups of no specific racial, ethnic, or economic character whose life-style is recognizably opposed to that of the majority. The one group we all will think of readily in this connection is the so-called *hippies*. (They have already been discussed in Chapters 14 and 15.)

The most conspicuous aspect of the hippies, and the one which has probably excited the most attention, is simply their appearance — long hair worn by men, beards, unconventional clothing, strange jewelry, and all the other outward marks of the "freak." Their music and their "psychedelic" art are also familiar badges.

But beyond the clothing, the hair, and the music, the significant thing about the hippies is *their rejection of many of the assumptions which most Americans accept regarding the "good life."* This is why we have referred to these young people in earlier chapters as the members of the "counter-culture." They do not believe in the accumulation of consumer goods (paid for "on time"), the concentration on "getting ahead," and what they consider the "cult of patriotism." They emphasize the value of imagination, of a poetic vision of life, of more intense, more direct, more "ecstatic" experience — sometimes to be achieved with the aid of drugs.

What concerns us here is how the great majority of "straight" Americans have reacted to this startling new minority. In general, there has been sharp disapproval, but the intensity of this disapproval and the way in which it is expressed differ widely, depending on personalities and attitudes. It is probably true that those who are most prejudiced in racial and ethnic matters are most likely to be vehement, bitter, and rigid in their opposition to the hippies. Those who feel a sense of kinship with people of all extractions and who have no ritualized ideas about "in-groups" and "out-groups" are far more likely to regard the hippies with a measure of tolerance, a live-and-let-live attitude. They do not necessarily approve of the hippies; they may be amused by them; they may seriously question some of their ideas and habits; but they do not *hate*. Note that there is no specifically racial issue involved here. The great majority of the hippies appear to be white, middle class young Americans.

It goes without saying that the type of authoritarian personality we have discussed above will almost invariably be repelled and infuriated by the hippies. His whole life style tends toward *submission* to recognized authority; and the hippies' whole life style emphasizes *rejection* of authority.

Toward Better Intergroup Relations — What Can We Do?

Changing the United States to make it a genuinely pluralistic society, without racism and other forms of prejudice, is a formidable task. Some progress has been made in recent years, but a great deal more remains to be done. This will be one of the great challenges and opportunities facing the next generation of Americans, and it will call for social action on a vast scale.

But one thing all of us can start to do now, as individuals, is to assess *our own* attitudes and to try to overcome prejudice in *ourselves,* no matter what "majority" or "minority" we may belong to. A useful guide for this purpose has been developed by Bertram M. Lee and Warren H. Schmidt.* They are concerned specifically with black-white relations, but the approach they suggest is useful for developing healthy relations between all the diverse racial, ethnic, and cultural groups making up American society.

Lee and Schmidt introduce their discussion as follows:

> The development of authentic relationships between black people and white people is of critical importance in building a healthy society in America. Both races must come to know that "authentic" means much more than the easy acceptance and overlooking of racial differences — it means full acceptance *and* recognition of differences. It means the appreciation and valuing of these differences, seeing them as a source of mutual enrichment and learning. We believe that a step in this direction is to increase the individual's awareness of his own assumptions and his sensitivity to behaviors in the other that reveal his assumptions.

The writers list a number of *assumptions* and a number of *forms of behavior* which are both positive and negative in fostering authentic relations between the races. These lists are given below (slightly modi-

---

* Bertram M. Lee and Warren H. Schmidt in the *Training News,* published by the National Training Institute for Applied Behavioral Science (Vol. 13, No. 4).

fied). You will do well to go over them carefully. Whether you are black, white, or of some other racial background, try to score yourself as accurately and objectively as possible. Where do you fall short? What can you do to improve yourself?

Assumptions which BLOCK authentic relations
Assumptions whites make:
Color is unimportant in interpersonal relations.
Blacks will always welcome and appreciate inclusion in white society.
Open recognition of color may embarrass blacks.
Blacks are trying to use whites.
Blacks can be stereotyped.
White society is superior to black society.
"Liberal" whites are free of racism.
All blacks are alike in their attitudes and behavior.
Blacks are oversensitive.
Blacks must be controlled.

Assumptions blacks make:
All whites are alike.
There are no "soul brothers" among whites.
Honkies have all the power.
Whites are always trying to use blacks.
All whites are racists.
Whites are not really trying to understand the situation of the blacks.
Whitey's got to deal on black terms.
Silence is the sign of hostility.
Whites cannot and will not change except by force.
The only way to gain attention is through confrontation.
All whites are deceptive.
All whites will let you down in the "crunch."

Assumptions which AID authentic relations (for blacks and whites)
People count as individuals.
Blacks are human — with individual feelings, aspirations, and attitudes.
Whites are human beings — and, whether they should or not, they have their own hang-ups.
Blacks are angry.
Whites cannot fully understand what it means to be black.
Interdependence is needed between blacks and whites.
Whiteness or blackness is a real difference but not the basis on which to determine behavior.

Openness is healthy.
Most blacks can handle whites' authentic behavior and feelings.
Blacks want a responsible society.
Blacks are capable of managerial maturity.
Negotiation and collaboration are possible strategies.
Some whites can help and "do their own thing."
Some whites have "soul."
I may be part of the problem.

Behaviors which BLOCK authentic relations
Behaviors of whites:

Interruptions.
Condescending behavior.
Avoidance of contact (eye-to-eye and physical).
Verbal focus on black behavior rather than on white behavior.
Insisting on playing games according to white rules.
Showing annoyance at black behavior which differs from their own.
Expressions of too-easy acceptance and friendship.
Talking *about*, rather than *to*, blacks who are present.

Behaviors of blacks:

Confrontation too early and too harshly.
Rejection of honest expressions of acceptance and friendship.
Pushing whites into such a defensive posture that learning and re-examination is impossible.
Failure to keep a commitment and then offering no explanation.
"In-group" joking, laughing at whites — in black culture language.
Giving answers blacks think whites want to hear.
Using confrontation as the primary relationship style.
Isolationism.

Behaviors which AID authentic relations
Behaviors of whites:

Directness and openness in expressing feelings.
Assisting other whites to understand and confront feelings.
Supporting self-initiated moves of black people.
Listening without interrupting.
Demonstration of interest in learning about black perceptions, culture, etc.
Staying with and working through difficult confrontations.
Taking a risk (*e.g.*, being first to confront the differences).
Assuming responsibility for examining own motives and attitudes.

Behaviors of blacks:

Showing interest in understanding whites' point of view.
Acknowledging that there are some committed whites.
Acting as if "we have some power" — and don't need to prove it.
Allowing whites to experience unaware areas of racism.
Openness.
Expression of real feelings.
Dealing with whites where they are.
Meeting whites half-way.
Treating whites on one-to-one basis.
Telling it like it is.
Realistic goal sharing.
Showing pride in their heritage.

THINGS TO DISCUSS :: THINGS TO DO :: THINGS TO READ

1. In 1960, Adolf Eichmann, a former officer in the Nazi *Gestapo,* was tried in Israel for having played a major role in the arrest, deportation, and killing of millions of European Jews during World War II. He was found guilty and hanged.

   In his defense, Eichmann asserted that he had "nothing against the Jews," individually or as a group, and that he often found his duties as a mass exterminator extremely disagreeable. However, he had been "morally obligated," under his oath as a German officer, to carry out these "duties" to the best of his ability, and he claimed that his "conscience was entirely clear."

   Analyze Eichmann's personality in terms of the ideas presented in this chapter. Have there been any events in more recent history which suggest a similar point of view and pattern of behavior?

2. We have emphasized repeatedly that *all thoughts are normal,* including amoral thoughts that spring from the unconscious. Is it possible that an individual would be less likely to be highly prejudiced if he were able to accept and tolerate even his own unpleasant thoughts?

3. Two qualities or characteristics which may exist in any social group are *uniformity* and *order.* How would you distinguish between the two? Can there be order without uniformity? Uniformity without order? Which of these attributes (either, both, neither) would you consider characteristic of a healthy, growing social organism?

4. In this chapter we have not directly discussed what it takes, psychologically, to be a *demagogue* — a political leader who seeks to gain power by exploiting and manipulating the baser emotions and fears of his public. What psychological characteristics do you think might drive men to be demagogues?

5. How do you explain the fact that working class whites often appear to show a stronger pattern of prejudice and greater antipathy toward minority groups than do whites in the upper-income levels? Does this necessarily show that the upper-income whites are more "enlightened" or "fair-minded"?

6. Does prejudice exist to a significant extent in your neighborhood? Plan and carry out a project that would enhance the well-being of at least one person who is a victim of societal hate or discrimination. Try to do this in such a way as not to expose yourself to the charge of "paternalism."

7. Run an experiment with the "Assumptions" listed at the end of this chapter. Each class member should score the person sitting behind him. For instance, under the "Assumption" reading "Color is unimportant in interpersonal relations," write *True* if in your opinion the class member does feel that way, and *False* if he does not. (If you are not sure, but if you suspect strongly that the individual accepts this attitude, write *True*.) Do not sign your name or write the name of the person you are evaluating. Then run the same evaluation on yourself. (Again, don't sign it.) Have the instructor or a student committee compile the results and read them in class. Then discuss those results.

8. If you are white, list all the "standard" reasons why you wouldn't want your brother, sister, or best friend to marry a person of another race. If you're black, or a member of another minority, do the same. Examine each "reason" carefully, and try to determine if it actually makes any sense in the light of what we know about psychology, biology, sociology, etc. (It may be that the very idea of drawing up such a list makes you uneasy — perhaps so much so that you will be extremely reluctant, if not flatly unwilling, to do so. If you feel this way, can you suggest why it is that you are upset by such a purely theoretical activity?)

READINGS

Manchild in the Promised Land, by Claude Brown (Macmillan, 1965). This is a fast-reading, compelling autobiography about "growing up black" in Harlem.

The Autobiography of Malcolm X (Grove Press, 1964). This is another stunning and highly influential book. It tells of a man's struggle from poverty, drug use, and imprisonment to a position of leadership and respect in the black community.

Soul on Ice, by Eldridge Cleaver (Dell, 1968). Cleaver is a talented writer and fiery critic of American society who also rose from poverty and jail to a position of political influence.

Am I A Racist? compiled by Robert Heyer and Fortune Monte (Paulist Press, 1969). This is a small, but valuable and provocative collection of essays, poems, interviews.

One Generation After, by Elie Wiesel (Random House, 1970). The author is haunted by his conclusion that the terrifying events leading to the mass murder of Jews during World War II have not really changed down to the present day. A poetic and moving novel.

Down These Mean Streets, by Piri Thomas (New American Library, 1969). A stirring account, based on first-hand experience, of a Puerto Rican "growing up absurd" in a New York City ghetto.

When Trees Were Green, by Owen Dodson (Farrar, Straus and Girous, 1951; original title: *Boy at the Window*). Probably the best of the "growing up black" novels.

Why does man
KILL?

●●●●●●●●●●●●●●●●●●●●●●●●●●●●●

"I spend a hell of a lot of time killing animals and fish, so I won't kill myself. When a man is in rebellion against death, as I am in rebellion against death, he gets pleasure out of taking to himself one of the god-like attributes, that of giving it."

— *ERNEST HEMINGWAY*

The Nature of the Problem

The problem is revealed by events such as the following:

▶ More than six million people are exterminated in Nazi Germany's efficient "death factories," otherwise called concentration camps.

▶ Atomic bombs are dropped on the Japanese cities of Hiroshima and Nagasaki, resulting in a death toll in the hundreds of thousands.

▶ A juvenile gang in New York City beats and stabs to death a 15-year-old boy disabled by polio.

▶ A man concealed in an upper story of a Dallas warehouse skillfully aims a rifle and assassinates the President of the United States.

▶ In a northern New York town, a man ends an argument over a football game by fatally shooting his brother.

▶ A man climbs to the top of a tower on the University of Texas campus in Austin and begins firing with a rifle at everyone he can see. He hits 45 people, of whom 14 die.

▶ Holdup men gun down a bank teller who does not follow their orders.

▶ Investigating a report of a fight, a Chicago policeman walks into an empty apartment and has his head blown off by a bomb planted in a suitcase.

▶ In a small New York town, a ten-month-old baby dies after being severely beaten by her mother.

▶ Members of a motorcycle gang hired to "keep order" at a Los Angeles rock concert beat a black man to death.

▶ In Vietnam thousands of innocent villagers fall victim to deadly weapons used by both sides in a savage conflict that has raged with little interruption since the close of World War II.

▶ "In the last 50 years, we human beings have slaughtered by our own hands coming on for 100 million of our species," as British psychiatrist R. D. Laing put it.

This grim list could be continued almost indefinitely. It represents only a tiny part of the vast number of killings that have taken place in the recent history of the human race.

But even in this limited sampling, we can identify some of the rationalizations, justifications, and "mitigating circumstances" involved. For instance, in some cases, the killings were undertaken "legally" — in response to government orders and with the belief that some "national policy" was being furthered. In other cases, murder was motivated by an individual's momentary rage or passion. In a number of cases, there was a conviction, however distorted, that killing a particular person would contribute to some political or "ideological" cause. Additionally, many killings have resulted from attempts to seize money or other valuables controlled by someone else. And, most baffling and chilling, we find that some of the killings *apparently* had no motivation at all — and that the killer did not even know who his victims were.

This shocking information leads us to the question: *Why does man kill?* This is a question with which students of human behavior have been wrestling since the dawn of history, and even today we are far from the complete answer. In a vast number of instances we cannot be sure why one man will kill another, and it is exceedingly difficult to predict who will kill and who will not.

However, there has been extensive scientific investigation in this area, and we shall consider some of the significant facts and influential ideas that have been developed.

Man Is Set Apart from Other Life-forms

Man is set apart from other life-forms by his use of language, by his ability to think on an abstract or generalized level, and by his creation and use of tools. In the long process of his historical development, man has learned to depend, to some extent, on his ability to act and to make decisions on the basis of forethought, as opposed to acting on the basis of his reactive instincts.

It should be emphasized that on the physiological level man has much in common with other life-forms. Moreover, he does show certain kinds of instinctive behavior that have been essential for his survival in the past. This is apparently still true today, even though man has learned to use his intelligence to organize and control phases of his environment. Many of the instincts that direct our behavior are analogous to those shown by other life-forms.

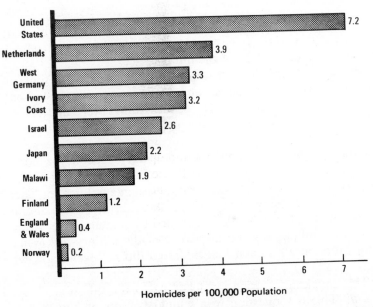

Homicides per 100,000 Population

The United States has the unhappy distinction of having one of the highest homicide rates in the world. This graph gives the figures for a number of representative nations in 1969. (Source: Interpol and FBI.)

Is There a Killer Instinct?

Although there is some doubt as to whether man has an inherent "killer instinct," it is clear that he is born with instincts which con-

The mystique of "man the hunter" is probably as popular and as firmly established in the United States as in any other country in the world. This has expressed itself throughout our history in extraordinarily widespread distribution and use of firearms. This print shows railroad personnel and passengers shooting buffalo on the line of the Kansas-Pacific Railroad (1871).

tribute to *aggression,* a characteristic which sometimes leads to killing of other men.

At first glance, aggression would appear to be simply an aid to the survival of an animal and the species. In other words, it may be interpreted as a means of motivating the animal to satisfy appetites for food, sexual intercourse, and possibly the care of offspring.

In large part, these are the main purposes which aggression does seem to serve. Often, however, it appears to work against the best interests of the animal and the species, particularly when animals kill members of their own species.

According to Charles Darwin's theory of natural selection, aggression plays an important part in the survival and development of many animal species. For instance, when two animals fight over a female, the stronger usually prevails, and it is the stronger which mates with the female. The offspring of this mating will tend to inherit the traits of superior strength (or other advantages). Additionally, the stronger or dominant animal will presumably be better equipped to protect the female and her young from predators.

There is speculation that hunting animals — and men do hunt — are born with instinctual apparatus that might be called by some a "killer instinct." According to such thinking, this instinct or group of instincts makes it certain that the predator will be sufficiently aggressive at the time of the kill to leave little room for successful retaliation ("overkill"). Also, the inborn drive may help to keep the animal in proper shape for hunting — ready to attack at any time. Still another effect is that it may motivate the animal to eat when it is not hungry — an important aid to survival, for the predator may sometimes have to go without food for a long time.

In some animals, it is believed that there is a *blood lust,* whereby the smell and taste of the warm blood of the victim heightens the excitement of the killer, imparting a pleasure which reinforces the desire to kill again. This presumably increases his drive as a hunter and enhances his success in staying alive. There is some speculation that man shares this blood lust, but it is not really known if this is the case.

In other animals it is believed that there is a surplus of energy which leads to the repetition of instinctive hunting patterns, even when the animal is not hungry. Thus, the renowned Austrian zoologist Konrad Lorenz comments that it is "a mistake to suppose that an instinctive movement whose species-preserving function serves for example, nutrition, must necessarily be caused by hunger." He adds, "We know that our own dogs go through the motions of smelling, seeking, chasing, biting, and shaking to death with equal enthusiasm whether they are hungry or not, and every dog owner knows that a dog which is a passionate hunter cannot be cured of its passion by abundant feeding."*

Aggression Against Members of the Same Species

These hunting instincts, however, do not account for aggression which results in the death of members of the animal's *own species.* There are a number of animals which do kill members of their own species. In most cases, however, this type of killing is comparatively rare and appears to be directed at intruders of the same species from outside the immediate group (family, clan, tribe, pack, etc.). For example, rats in a given area will attack and kill strange rats, which apparently have a different scent. Such aggression does serve a useful purpose: it helps to keep the group sufficiently "spaced out," so that territories and their populations will be reasonably well adjusted to the food supply and other local conditions. In general, this type of aggression is not considered unfavorable to species survival.

However, man not only kills strangers; he frequently murders intimate friends and close relations. In fact, man appears to be the most wanton and unreasonable killer on the planet. To explain this, Freud postulated a "death instinct" in man.

---

* Konrad Lorenz, *On Aggression* (Harcourt, Brace & World, 1966)

Freud believed that aggressiveness is motivated by a built-in death instinct, but that a contradictory fear of this instinct causes a projection of the aggression onto the external world — other people and things. Stated otherwise, Freud believed that a natural desire for one's own death is opposed by the survival-oriented forces in the mind and is redirected against other people. However, in his opinion, the more this projection is restricted (by social pressures), the more the instinct remains directed toward self-destruction.

Freud backed up this notion with speculations on the origins of life, which allowed him to draw "the conclusion that, besides the instinct to preserve living substance and to join it into ever larger units, there must be another, contrary instinct seeking to dissolve those units and bring them back to their primeval, inorganic state."*

Whether or not this is so, experiments have shown that when an electric charge is applied to certain areas of the brain, some animals, such as cats and rats, become intensely aggressive, and this aggression always takes the form of an attack on another animal if one is present or on a substitute, such as a doll. This seems to indicate that aggression is a basic drive, although it is possible that there is more than one basic form of aggression.

Inhibitions Against Killing

Lorenz disagrees with Freud's notion of a "death instinct."

His central point is that aggression does not necessarily aim toward death and destruction, but rather that it is primarily directed toward the maintenance of the animal's own life, and also the life of other animals of the same species. He says, however, that when an animal's natural environment is significantly altered, the balance between its various instincts can be thrown off, and the animal may then act against the best interests of itself and its species.

For instance, we may see fish in an aquarium kill each other when they are fighting to control territory, but in the natural state the defeated fish is usually able to escape. The victor will not pursue the loser outside its own territory because of inhibitory instincts which cut off the aggression. In an aquarium, however, there may not be enough space for two "territories." Thus, the weaker fish is killed.

Another example of animal inhibition against killing its own species can be seen when two wolves from the same pack fight each other for pack status, which means a choice of food and females. The stronger animal in most cases is physically capable of killing the weaker. However, when the weaker wolf is convinced he has no chance

---

* Sigmund Freud, *Civilization and Its Discontents.*

to win, he performs what Lorenz calls a "submission ritual." He turns his head aside, exposing the jugular vein, which could easily be ripped open by the other wolf. This action triggers a built-in inhibition response which cuts off the aggression, and the attack ceases.

Lorenz has observed that many animals armed by nature with deadly weapons, such as fangs and claws, also have some type of automatic aggression shut-off. This is activated by an appropriate submission ritual, which acts as an instinctive safety valve. The submission ritual, of course, varies considerably from species to species.

In answer to Freud, Lorenz says that man's aggressive instinct has got out of hand because he is *not* equipped with natural weapons. Lorenz points out that, physically, man is weak. He is not equipped with stingers, poison secretions, fangs, quills, horns, and other devices that some animals use effectively in combat. Nor is he outstanding in bulk or swiftness of movement, and his sensory organs are certainly not outstanding for their keenness.

Lorenz theorizes that since our earliest ancestors apparently lived mainly by gathering fruits and vegetables, they could survive without the sharp claws, teeth, and other adaptations of hunting and meat-eating animals. By the same token, Lorenz thinks, man's natural weakness and his difficulty in killing his fellow man *made it unnecessary for him to develop strong instinctive inhibitions against killing.*

The invention of *artificial weapons,* however, upset this state of affairs. With a heavy rock, a sharp stick, or a hand ax, primitive men could attack each other, and in the process were more likely to inflict deadly wounds. Moreover, this destructiveness was not cut off in midcourse by an automatic response to an instinctive submission ritual, since such a reaction had not been needed before the use of artificial weapons.

Weapons and tools developed by prehistoric man.

1. Stone ax-hammer, perforated for hafting.
2. Flint ax, partly polished.
3. Flint saw, one edge notched.
4. Flint dagger.
5. Flint knife or sickle blade.
6. Arrow point. Such points were also made in larger sizes and used as spear points.

Even at the earliest stages of development, however, men lived together in social groupings, such as tribes. Obviously, if members of the same tribe were free to direct violence against each other whenever some rivalry or disagreement arose, the group would not be able to function or even to survive. Accordingly, as a matter of necessity, primitive man developed strong cultural taboos or inhibitions against killing members of his own band (which usually consisted of a few closely related families).

Lorenz points out that the *cultural* or *learned* prohibition against killing fellow group members was not nearly as effective as the *natural* or *instinctive* prohibition against this type of killing. But the taboo was still strong enough to allow the development of larger social groupings. As a result, men could increase substantially in numbers.

Frustration and Fear

Aggression is closely tied to fear and frustration.

On the face of it, one might think that aggression is merely the opposite of fear, but many observers are convinced that, in fact, it is either fear or frustration that triggers many types of behavior, including aggressive behavior. Very often an animal or a man is either trying to *get something* (the more difficult this is, the greater the frustration that may arise), and/or trying to *get rid of something* (the more dangerous this is, the greater the fear that ensues). A typical reaction to such a situation is aggression. For instance, a cornered rat will ferociously leap at its attacker, or a starving lion may attack a man, its most feared enemy.

In man, frustration often comes about because of fear*, particularly fear of rejection. Very often these fears and frustrations are unconscious, being repressed by other fears. This can lead to psychic confusion or conflict, which must somehow be dealt with. As this works out, however, the target of the aggression frequently is *not* the thing which originally caused the fear or frustration. Thus, we have such familiar patterns as the businessman who is henpecked at home and "takes it out" on his employees by being a tyrant in the office; or the child who rips apart his toys when he is angry at his parents.

Severe psychic confusion can lead to "senseless" violence. Thus, soldiers who have been through climactic psychic shocks on the battle-

---

* Technically, perhaps, we should use the word *anxiety* here. Freud describes *fear* as a reaction to "a definite object of which to be afraid"; whereas *anxiety* is "a particular stage of expecting the danger or preparing for it, even though it may be an unknown one." However, we use the word *fear* here in a general sense, assuming anxiety to be a type of fear.

field may become so severely confused that they later murder innocent people without understanding why. However, we must bear in mind that many other soldiers who have undergone similar stresses do not commit such murders.

As Lorenz notes, it is possible to control or at least modify instinctive reactions. He writes that "it is an error to assume that . . . hunger, sexuality, flight, and aggression are irresistible tyrants whose commands brook no contradiction."

Love That Kills

Psychologists have long known that there is a powerful relationship between the emotions of love and hate. Both emotions strongly commit one person to involvement with another person. Love directs a person toward *forming a close bond* with another, whereas hate directs him toward *destroying* another. These emotions at first appear to be direct opposites, but in fact a person may feel both in relation to the same person.

There is a proverb which states, "We can only truly hate where we have truly loved." The truth of this becomes clearer if we consider that of the approximately 13,650 murders committed in this country in 1968, about 75% occurred among people who knew each other. Of these, 33% involved people who had close relationships with each other. And in this last category, the largest number of murders occurred between husbands and wives (13% of all murders). From these statistics, we can see that a person is more likely to be killed by a friend or close relative than by a stranger.

The fact that most murders occur among people who have an emotional involvement is not so puzzling when we consider that impulsive violence is often a sudden reaction to a frustration that has been building up for a long time to an intolerable level. Also, we must realize that people are more likely to be keenly frustrated by individuals on whom they depend for love and support.

Animal Sexual Relationships

Some light might be thrown on this problem if we take a look at aggression in animal sexuality.

Among animals there is often a very close similarity between the instinctive, ritualistic behavior performed during aggression and during mating. For example, among a species of fish called cichlids, there is a "ceremony" performed between two mates which appears to have evolved from the aggressive actions of these animals. The female confronts the male with her fins outspread and her colors brightly showing, which is the way these fish challenge one another to a fight. The male becomes infuriated by this display and, showing his fins and colors also, charges directly at the female. Just as it seems that he is about to strike the female, he veers slightly off and continues on to attack a neighboring male, if one is at hand. This ritual of "redirected aggression" is the way in which the two mates acknowledge the bond between them. The ritual allows the fish to come together for mating without any suppression of the aggressive instinct necessary for their survival.

The "bonding ritual" of geese operates on a similar principle. A male and female approach each other with ruffled feathers and necks outstretched and parallel to the ground, which is exactly the position geese assume when they intend to fight. The difference is that instead of squaring off and moving directly at each other, the two turn their heads slightly to one side, each directing the stare past the other. The message in this ritual seems to be, "I am not attacking you; I am attacking another." Lorenz has observed that the longer two geese have been together, the longer and more intense will be their bonding ritual, with the mates furiously ruffling feathers, honking loudly, and doing a kind of dance around each other. Usually this ritual culminates in intercourse.

Aggression Between Human Mates

Although there is no specific, formalized, instinctive "ritual" in man's wooing, there is a significant relationship between aggression and mating in human beings.

When a man and woman are very closely attached to each other, there often develops an unconscious resentment against the demands of the relationship and therefore against the other partner. This does not necessarily mean that the two people are no longer in love, but it does mean that an element of hatred has been added to the relationship.

In line with this, one partner may unconsciously identify his mate with a figure from childhood, such as a mother or father. But the partner chosen for this role may not fulfill it as expected. In this case, the other partner may unconsciously generate activities, including hostile ones, intended to get the mate to respond in ways that are more in keeping with the mother or father image.

Moreover, aggressiveness on the part of the male is often a vital part, at least culturally, of romance. Indeed, the custom of carrying the bride across the threshold has its origin in a medieval European tradition in which the groom pretended to kidnap the bride from her

"Oh, young Lochinvar is come out of the west. . . ." The famous ballad by Sir Walter Scott, based on an old Scottish legend, tells of a daring young knight whose beloved is betrothed to another man. Lochinvar attends the wedding and kidnaps the bride — with her enthusiastic consent. Her father and kinsmen pursue, "but the lost bride of Netherby ne'er did they see." There are similar stories in the folk traditions of many other groups. If you have seen the popular moving picture *The Graduate,* you may notice a similarity there.

family, and the bride pretended to resist. This custom is derived from more remote times, when the male in many cases actually *did* have to kidnap his bride from her family or clan.

The point of this example is that the man was required, either in fact or symbolically, to show courage and physical prowess to prove that he was worthy of "possessing" the woman. There is still an element of this in our present-day courtship and marriage customs. We speak of a young man "winning" a girl as his bride, or of "sweeping her off her feet." Such phrases may well be a carryover, however indirect or metaphorical, from the time when the male was expected to demonstrate aggressive abilities in a physical sense as a condition for taking his mate.

Depression and Aggression

One of the most common psychological ailments of human beings is depression. This can vary from a temporary mood of sadness or discouragement (which we all have at times) to an all-pervading feeling of hopelessness so powerful that suicide and/or murder results. Depression is a form of psychic confusion, which, as we mentioned in Chapter 4, can sometimes trigger an aggressive outlet, even though this aggression is usually irrational.

Characteristically, severely depressed people have a low opinion of themselves, often assuming guilt for misfortunes that are not always their fault. Thus, they doubt their ability to succeed and consequently fear taking on responsibilities or new enterprises. An underlying cause of *chronic* (long-lasting) depression is usually a terrifying fear of rejection. A serious danger in chronic depression is that the unconscious tends to assume that because the person in childhood received little love, or love that was inadequately expressed, he is also *currently unworthy* of love. He may become so convinced that he is unlovable that he is virtually unable to accept love offered by others. This may build up his frustration to an all but intolerable level.

Occasionally, such frustration reaches the point of intensity at which it explodes into violence. Many experts are of the opinion that a large proportion of the murders committed in our society are the acts of severely and chronically depressed people.

The Schizoid Personality

The schizoid personality, like all of us, has a great need for love, but he fears rejection and distrusts people so much that unconsciously he tries to keep all relationships on a superficial level, to minimize the possibility that he will be hurt. So far as possible, he may even withdraw from the ordinary social contacts of everyday life, frequently hiding behind a mask of cold indifference. In order to compensate for his neglected love, he often has a strong urge to dominate others.

Although the schizoid individual does his utmost to convince others of his superiority — that is, to convince them that he doesn't need them or their love — secretly he realizes that he is weak and vulnerable.

A schizoid individual tends to transfer his self-doubt and self-hatred onto others. He is convinced that other people hate him, and he irrationally exaggerates minor or inadvertent hostilities expressed by others into major threats (a characteristic of *paranoia*). He fears the hostility of others more than he fears his own destructive hostility, which he usually keeps strongly repressed. One common symptom of a schizoid personality is a compulsive obsession with "order," in the sense of uniformity and regularity; he tries, rigorously but irrationally, to control every detail of his daily routine.

Charles Whitman, the man who in 1966 shot 45 people from a tower on the campus of the University of Texas in Austin, before he was slain by police, was very likely a schizoid personality. According to follow-up investigations, he had gone through life trying to maintain rigid control over his pent-up hostilities. Being cold and moody, he had few friends, although casual acquaintances remembered him as a "nice, well-mannered young man." Occasionally, however, his self-control would break down, and he would release his hostility by beating his wife. When the psychic pressures born of intense frustration became overwhelming, he plotted in detail his murderous rampage, and the day before he ascended to the tower, he wrote a letter indicating his intent. It is significant that, on this day people who had dealings with him found him relaxed and cheerful — noticeably less tense than he was ordinarily. It was as if he had finally attained a release from the maddening pressure that was driving him berserk. After the slaughter, police recovered a poem written by him which reveals strong schizoid tendencies:

> To maintain sensibility is the greatest effort required—
> To slip would be so easy, it would be accomplished with
> little effort—
> To burden others with your problems—are they prob-
> lems?—
> Is not right—However
> To carry them is akin to carrying a fused bomb—
> I wonder if the fuse can be doused—
> If it is doused what will be gained?
> Will the gain be worth effort put forth?
> But should one who considers himself strong, surrender to
> an enemy he considers so trivial and despicable?

A typical schizoid, such as Whitman, is continually at war with his own hostile emotions — much more so than are people with other forms of emotional disorder.

Psychopaths

Badly depressed people, including schizoids, usually have strong inhibitions against expressing hostility violently, at least up to the point where the inhibition breaks down. In contrast to this, there is another type of personality disorder in which inhibitions against expressing hostility or aggression are reduced abnormally, to the point where they scarcely seem to exist at all. People who habitually show this kind of behavior are called *psychopaths*.

Psychopaths are concerned almost solely with their own desires, and in their efforts to get what they want they show virtually no consideration for the interests and feelings of others. They will not hesitate to resort to violence to achieve their ends when they think it is to their advantage to do so. Their hatred and aggression are directed outward toward others, and they show little or no feelings of remorse for the effects of their action — not being concerned for other human beings. Psychopaths seem to lack a normal awareness of danger, and fear of punishment apparently has little effect on their behavior. Thus they are sometimes identified as "criminally insane."

Psychologists are still uncertain about the causes of psychopathic hostility. It has been suggested that these people have never progressed beyond, or have regressed back to, the emotional level of a baby. Psychopaths usually harbor a strong resentment against people in general and against "society" (which is why they are sometimes called *sociopaths*). They identify "society" with authority figures, such as parents, police, school systems, and even economic institutions.

This resentment may be attributable to severe rejection in childhood, when their parents did not allow them to form strong human relationships. Thus they were deprived of what they badly needed — recognition by others of their essential human worth. Consequently, as adults they see people only as objects to be manipulated and exploited, rather than as individuals with feelings, needs, and worth of their own.

Whatever the root cause, all of the types of disordered personalities we have been discussing have one feature in common: *great difficulty in forming satisfactory relationships with other people.* This is certainly a crippling disability, because healthy, satisfactory relationships with other people are the key to solid character development, through which a person strives to realize his "fullest potential."

A person who is incapable of maintaining good relationships with others is likely to have little respect for life — his own or the lives of others. He finds it exceedingly difficult to direct his aggression toward achieving worthwhile goals. Although it does not necessarily follow that such a person will murder, a murderer often has this disability.

War: Organized Killing

War is the most visible — and violent — symptom of the disorder the people of this planet have inflicted on themselves and have endured since the beginnings of history. War is killing on a massive scale, and if killing is to be massive, it must be "organized." The men who do the killing are organized into *armies,* which are in the service of other organizations, called *nations.* These nations usually claim that they are "defending themselves" which frequently means that they are fighting to gain or hold territory, or to gain other advantages in competition with other nations.

In war, the killer and the victim — whose roles are often interchangeable — do not know each other. Usually the killer's first interest is to avoid being killed and/or to kill, rather than to gain any particular advantage from the victim. This state of mind is accomplished by training the soldier to recognize that the supreme virtue is to obey orders quickly and unreservedly, without time to reflect on the consequences. Thus, he becomes an agent of somebody else's will, relinquishing part of his individuality and the responsibility for his actions.

Another aim of military training is to utilize as much of a soldier's "ordinary" hatred and aggression as possible, and to channel it toward "the enemy," who may often be characterized as inhuman demons deserving nothing but violent death. This kind of indoctrination is often carried out on another level as government *propaganda* aimed at uniting the entire population (military and civilian) against the enemy nation. During a war, especially a war that appears to threaten the very existence of the nation and its institutions, there is a great emphasis on this notion of national unity. "Whatever our differences in the past, we must now work together and fight together to defeat the enemy." On this basis, disagreement with the policies of the government, or refusal to accept its version of events, may be condemned as "disloyal" and "playing into the hands of the enemy." Often, the propaganda is so designed that any hatred, aggression, and dissatisfaction that may inwardly threaten the society and its leadership are directed outward onto the enemy.*

Another important factor that contributes to overcoming any moral or cultural unwillingness to kill is the increasing *depersonalization* of killing in war. As man increased the range of his weapons, the less the killer was forced to confront his victims face to face. This, according to Lorenz's theory, tended to weaken or nullify the cultural prohibitions against killing. Specifically, to kill a man with a rock held in the hand is one thing, but to kill him with an arrow from a distance of some yards is quite different, and to kill him with a bullet from a high-powered rifle is still more different. The end result, of course, is the same for the victim, but the emotional involvement of the killer may be reduced by distance.

In our own times, a plane may bomb a village so far below that even the buildings cannot be seen, much less the people in them. This impersonal killing frequently "allows" the killers to be much less aware of any immediate emotional involvement or personal responsi-

---

* We are not asserting here that all wars are necessarily irrational and unjustified, or that all accusations against enemy nations are fabricated propaganda. During World War II, for example, charges were made that the Nazis had been guilty of atrocities, and these charges turned out to be not only justified, but understated. What concerns us here, however, is the fact that *any* nation at war tries to develop a psychological pattern that makes its people more willing and more able to engage in mass killing.

"The Bomb" has become the universal symbol of impersonal mass destruction, made possible by modern science and technology.

bility. The men in the plane may be able to see the explosions, but they do not directly witness people being blown to pieces as a result of their acts.

The ultimate extension of such "anonymous" killing would be the activation of the current systems of intercontinental ballistic missiles, armed with hydrogen bombs. If these weapons are ever used to their full capacity, technicians will sit at consoles and simply push buttons, launching rockets that will then rain inconceivable death and destruction on "targets" consisting of millions of persons living perhaps halfway around the world.

The whole operation is on so vast and impersonal a scale that many of the people involved prefer to think of themselves as "workers" or "technicians," rather than as potential killers. It is a familiar fact that each of us can respond emotionally to the death of one person close at hand, but there is usually little direct reaction when we read of the deaths of thousands in an earthquake in South America or a tidal wave in Pakistan. Even more, the deaths of several *millions* would be so vast a catastrophe that it would probably become an abstraction which we are incapable of "feeling." Likewise, if a large group of individuals take part in an activity that brings about one or more deaths, it is difficult for any one of them to feel a sense of responsibility. Each individual's contribution, in his own mind, is simply a tiny part of a complex process, beyond his control, or even his comprehension.

Fortunately, the same intellectual capacity that makes it possible for man to create and use deadly weapons also enables him to develop a strong sense of responsibility for his actions. But these moral prohibitions are not as persuasive to the organism as instincts, and they often break down entirely when the natural aggressive drive is not allowed to work itself out peacefully. This is particularly true in time of war, when hysteria*, which is a form of psychic confusion, is widespread.

The fact that man combines such vast technological ability with the lack of an automatic inhibition against killing members of his own species could lead eventually to the destruction of the human race. In the process, man might conceivably destroy most of the other types of organisms inhabiting this planet.

Controlling Aggressive Impulses

For a happy and successful life, every human being needs the freedom to develop himself to his full capacity. This means, in part, that the individual must learn to work out his aggressive drives by directing them into constructive (or at least harmless) channels.

Ideally, this process would not be distorted by psychological disorders, blocked by rigid social institutions, or misdirected by the misunderstandings and fears that lead to war. When people are unable for any reason to release their aggressive impulses in healthy ways, frustrations and hostilities often develop which may explode as violence, and specifically the ultimate form of violence, murder. A person who finds satisfaction in his relations with others, and in a positive attitude toward life expressed in socially useful work, is not likely to build up the tensions and resentments which provide the fuel for violence.

One troublesome pattern in human relations which often causes violence results from the idea that "the end justifies the means." For example, some people who have great faith in programs of social reform may feel justified in *forcing* others to accept the changes they want. They come to regard these other people as mere instruments or elements in the social reordering, rather than as ends in themselves. Since the other people in question may not take kindly to this attitude, the reformer may well find himself involved in a violent clash. This has been a common situation throughout recorded history.

---

* *Hysteria* is used here in its general sense, rather than in a strictly medical application.

This is not to say that we don't need reformers. We certainly do. But the reformer must first "get himself together," in the sense of building a healthy personality and developing good human relations with others. Otherwise, the "reform" is likely to become distorted into the tyrannies and mass killings that we have observed in dictatorships of the 20th century.

THINGS TO DISCUSS :: THINGS TO DO :: THINGS TO READ

1. As president of the American Psychological Association in 1971, Dr. Kenneth Clark advanced the idea that a drug should be developed which would inhibit aggression. He suggested that such a drug be administered mandatorily to national and world political leaders. Many of his colleagues strongly disagreed, and some suspected that his speech might be at least in part a "put-on." However, the idea had been advanced previously in a book entitled *The Ghost in the Machine* (Macmillan) 1967 by the well-known novelist-historian Arthur Koestler.

    Do you think that Dr. Clark's proposal is (1) practical, (2) moral, (3) warranted by past actions of political leaders?

2. Have you ever noticed that during a moment of extreme anger, your mind is likely to become a blur of emotion? For that moment, your memory is almost blank, your perception of the future is almost non-existent, your perceptions in general are out-of-focus or non-existent. Once the moment of rage subsides, your thinking becomes more normal and more conscious. What implications does this pattern of behavior have for the relationship (in Freud's terms) between the *ego* and the *id*?

3. Has it occurred to you that this description of rage might be applied to other intense emotional feelings, including fear (perhaps to the point of panic), or urgent desire? What role might such "agencies" or "forces" as *ego, id, super-ego,* or *conscious-unconscious* play in how our emotions work? (Remember, there is a wide disagreement among experts on questions such as this. Your theory might be as valid as any expert's, or, possibly, even more insightful.)

4. Alcohol, the world's most abused "mind drug," is implicated in thousands of homicides each year. Such killings are usually spur-of-the-moment affairs. Alcohol, as well as other mind drugs, impairs judgment and unleashes unconscious passions. In fact, most homicides seem to be due to an impairment of judgment on one level or another. What psychological (rather than chemical) factors might impair judgment and allow aggressive impulses to become the deciding force? Can you suggest a good way of developing responsible judgment, so that the rational ego is not suppressed in a moment of rage?

5. The next time you get angry and start making charges or accusations against someone, wait until you've calmed down, and then make written notes of your complaints against the individual or group. Try to consider these charges objectively. Quite possibly you will decide that there is an element of truth in what you said. However, for the sake of the experiment, turn these accusations against yourself. Is there an element of truth in these charges as applied to *you*? In what way are these charges unbalanced or unfair as applied to (*a*) you, (*b*) the original object of your anger?

6. Appoint a committee of ten class members to watch TV for a week during the "prime time" hours. Be sure to cover each channel in your area. Jot down a brief description of each act of violence (excluding news coverage) portrayed on the screen (for example, fist fights, shootings, knife attacks, etc.) Tabulate the results and bring them to class for discussion.

7. Study a single issue of a daily newspaper to see how much attention is devoted to violence, in the form of crimes, war, personal and intergroup conflicts, etc. How much space and emphasis does this kind of activity receive as compared with constructive and peaceful human relations? What conclusions can you draw? If the newspaper puts strong emphasis on violence, then the editors must feel that it appeals strongly to readers. What is the basis for this belief? Do you agree with it?

8. Discuss the current vogue of violence in moving pictures. Mention at least three movies in which violence plays a prominent part. Do you think that the violence in each case is mere exploitation (to "titillate" the customers), or that it has some justification in terms of the theme and purpose of the picture? What about the violence in *Hamlet* or *Macbeth*? What do you think of the theory that observing violence in a dramatic presentation serves a "catharsis" for the viewer, helping him to get rid of his tensions and hostilities harmlessly?

READINGS

Civilization and Its Discontents, by Sigmund Freud (available in several editions). A short but profound discussion of the paradox of man, of great relevance to problems discussed in this chapter.

The Naked and the Dead, by Norman Mailer (Rhinehart & Co., 1948). One of the best novels dealing with World War II. Telling of a relatively small combat operation on a Pacific island, it explores the psychology of the "fighting man" with a realism and impact seldom equalled.

Catch 22, by Joseph Heller (Simon and Schuster, 1961) is another and very different book about World War II which has been described as a "surrealistic tragi-comedy."

INTELLIGENCE

What is It?
Can It Be Tested?

● ●

"When we talk about intelligence, we do not mean the ability to get a good score on a certain kind of test, or even the ability to do well in school; these are at best only indicators of something larger, deeper, and far more important."

— JOHN HOLT

What Is Intelligence?

Any young American in school today scarcely has to be told that intelligence testing is of great importance to him. The classes to which he is assigned, the courses he is allowed to take, his acceptance by a college, the jobs he will get as a civilian or in the armed forces — all of these are determined to a large degree by how well he does on various mental tests.

Strictly speaking, not all of these tests are labeled "intelligence" tests. However, they are all closely related in nature and purpose, regardless of the terms by which they are designated — *achievement, aptitude, classification, qualification,* etc.

We should, of course, attempt to define *intelligence*. The difficulty is that there is no general agreement as to the meaning of the word. And this uncertainty applies not only to those of us who may use the term rather loosely or uncritically in everyday life but even to professionally trained psychologists and philosophers.

The dictionary definition* of intelligence is not too clear: ". . . capacity for reasoning, understanding, and for similar forms of mental activity; aptitude in grasping truths, facts, meanings. . . ."

---

* *Random House Dictionary of the English Language*

393

The reason the definition is not clear is that it embodies words which are themselves the subjects of continuing debate: *capacity* (of a human being), *aptitude, reasoning, understanding, truth, fact,* and *meaning.* A few other related words and phrases which have no settled meaning include: *intellect, intellectual ability, thinking, thinking ability, learning, learning ability, perception, sensitivity of perception, awareness, wisdom, comprehension, knowledge, ideas, experience, creativity,* and *reasoning ability.*

However, the most common practice among scientists today is to equate intelligence with some kind of ability, such as:

▶ The ability to learn.

▶ The ability to profit from experience.

▶ The ability to adapt to or cope with the environment.

▶ The ability to combine ideas into a new (for the individual) idea.

▶ The ability to understand the nature of a problem (to "see" it) and then to solve it.

A well-known educator, John Holt,* writes:

> When we talk about intelligence, we do not mean the ability to get a good score on a certain kind of test, or even the ability to do well in school; these are at best only indicators of something larger, deeper, and far more important. By intelligence we mean a style of life, a way of behaving in various situations, and particularly in new, strange, and perplexing situations. The true test of intelligence is not how much we know how to do, but how we behave when we don't know what to do.

Other experts, however, would consider this too facile or oversimplified. Some feel that it is possible to "pin down" a more precise definition — but it usually turns out that their versions are just as vulnerable to criticism and disagreement as is Holt's.

General Intelligence or Specific Areas of Intelligence?

Currently, there are three major schools of thought on the nature or "whatness" of intelligence. They may be stated briefly as follows:

▶ Intelligence is a general and unified quality or capacity that can be applied in any skill area. This is often what is meant by *general intelligence.*

---

* John Holt, *How Children Fail* (Pitman Publishing Corporation, 1964).

Child prodigies show amazing development of specialized abilities at an early age. Mozart (represented in this picture with his father and sister) began to play the harpsichord when he was three years old, soon moved on to the violin and organ, and completed his first composition before he was seven.

▶ Intelligence is a combination of several broad and somewhat independent abilities.

▶ Intelligence is a collection of separate and largely unrelated abilities. Some of these scientists would go so far as to drop the general term "intelligence" from scientific usage.

Many of the popular mental tests, in fact, are divided into various skill areas, following the lead of L. L. Thurstone, a pioneer in *psychometrics* (mental measurement). Thurstone taught that intelligence consisted of seven primary mental abilities:

▶ *Numerical* — the ability to add, subtract, multiply and divide.

▶ *Verbal relations* — the understanding of ideas in word form.

▶ *Memory* — the ability to recall and recognize past experiences.

▶ *Reasoning* (induction and deduction) — the ability to solve complex problems, to profit from experience, and to plan new activities based on past experience.

▶ *Spatial perception* — the ability to perceive size and spatial relationships correctly.

▶ *Word fluency* — the ability to write and speak with ease.

▶ *Perceptual speed* — the ability to identify stimuli quickly (for example, rapid reading recognition of an entire word, without actually "reading" all the letters).

This listing of individual factors is typical of the psychological school of thought which holds that it is futile to attempt to test for intelligence as a whole, and that we should concentrate rather on individual skills and aptitudes. *Aptitude tests,* in fact, are designed with this end in mind.

Opponents of this view do not deny that intelligence is a complex faculty, and that any person may show greater aptitude in some areas than others. They maintain, however, that ability in one area, such as those listed above, is closely tied in with most, if not all, other aptitudes. In short, as these psychologists see it, there *is* a distinct quality of the mind which can fairly be labeled *general intelligence.*

The controversy over the meaning of intelligence is far from settled, and some experts feel that the riddle will never be solved in any final sense. One writer commented wryly that "Intelligence is whatever intelligence tests test."

The Mental Testing Movement

Naturally enough, if there is uncertainty over what intelligence is, there is bound to be much disagreement over the validity of tests that are designed to test this elusive quality. This is a dispute that has raged throughout most of the 20th century, and as we shall see has become particularly heated in our time.

The first notable figure in the field of intelligence testing was Alfred Binet, a French psychologist. Even his pioneering work was the subject of widespread controversy.

In 1905, Binet was assigned by the French Ministry of Education to determine which children were what we would now call "slow learners," so that they might be given special attention in the schools. Thus, the challenge to Binet was to find a way to distinguish children who were merely academically backward from those who were actually *deficient in mental ability,* before too many years in school had elapsed. The tests Binet devised for this purpose are the direct ancestors of our present-day mental ability tests.

The items Binet included in his tests were selected on the basis of two standards: (1) Children with greater intelligence can reasonably be expected to do better in school than children with less intelligence. (2) Older children tend to have a greater ability to master complex school material than younger children.

Many experts today would question the validity of both these ideas in relation to testing *intelligence,* but Binet tended to use this word rather loosely. Confusion might have been much reduced if he had called his tests by some other name, such as "school-achievement probability" tests.

The *Binet-Simon test* (Simon was a coworker of lesser renown) contributed to the development of the U. S. Army Alpha and Beta classification tests by such psychologists as Walter Bingham. The entry of the United States into World War I in 1917 created a need to test large numbers of men in groups — rather than individually — in order to determine all sorts of abilities, aptitudes and achievement levels in which the armed forces were interested.

Another leader in American psychology, Lewis M. Terman, translated and revised the Binet-Simon test so that it would be particularly suitable for use in American schools. He called this version the *Stanford-Binet test.*

In the years following World War I, large businesses adopted features from the armed forces tests and incorporated them into their hiring procedures. These were then called *personnel tests.* Public schools were pressured by educational reformers into adopting the Stanford-Binet test or one of its variants. With the added push of the massive classification testing by the armed forces during World War II, the mental testing business grew rapidly.

What's the Score?

An *intelligence quotient* (*IQ*), derived from an intelligence test, is meant to be a convenient index of an individual's intelligence, as compared with the intelligence of other people who have been or will be tested. The IQ is found by dividing a person's *mental age* (*MA*) by his real or *chronological age* (*CA*) and multiplying the result by 100. (This multiplication is simply to get rid of decimals or fractions.) Thus:

$$MA \div CA \times 100 = IQ$$

The mental age for use in this equation is arrived at by comparing a person's performance on a test with the average score of large numbers of people of the same age. Suppose, for example, that a 7-year-old child answers successfully all the questions usually answered by 7-year-olds and 8-year-olds, and also some of the questions usually answered by 9-year-olds. His mental age would then be established as somewhat more than 8, and it would be assumed that his intelligence is higher than average.

This means that a child of 6 who tests as well as most children do at 9 would be known to have a mental age of 9. His IQ then would be:

$$9 \div 6 \times 100 = 150$$

This is considered very superior. Of course, when this 6-year-old reaches the age of 9, he will probably be far superior in test performance to the average 9-year-old, whose IQ by definition is close to 100.

Test-makers proceed on the basic assumption that *the mental age for the majority of people is the same as their chronological age.* It follows that IQ scores are most commonly in the vicinity of 100, and that as we move away from this "normal" figure, we find fewer and fewer people. Most people get scores between 90 and 110; very few get scores lower than 70 or higher than 140. If these results are plotted on a line graph, we form what is known in statistics as a *bell curve* (or *normal distribution curve*) — a graph line roughly in the shape of a bell, where the peak represents scores of 100, and each end of the line represents extremely low or extremely high scores. (See the accompanying graph.)

It is assumed that slightly less than 50% of the population have an IQ *above* 100, and slightly less than 50% have an IQ *below* 100. (A relatively small number will be exactly at 100.) In the IQ

Graph showing the presumed distribution of IQ scores in a general population. This shows the normal distribution (bell) curve.

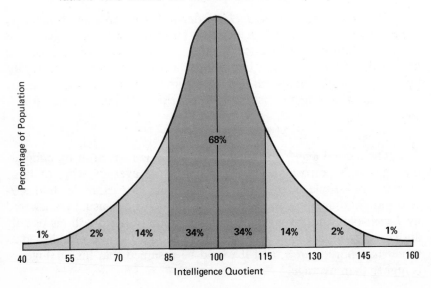

range between 85 and 115, we find 68% of the population; in the range between 115 and 130, 14%; in the range between 130 and 145, 2%; and above 145, only 1%. Turning to the lower end of the scale, we find 14% of the population in the IQ range between 70 and 85; 2% in the range between 55 and 70; and 1% below 55.

Sometimes IQ scores are characterized in the following way:

CLASSIFICATION	IQ
Mentally Retarded	69 and below
Borderline	70 - 79
Dull Normal	80 - 89
Average	90 - 110
Bright Normal	110 - 119
Superior	120 - 129
Very Superior	130 and above

Testing the Intelligence of Adults

Obviously the "mental age-chronological age" method of determining IQ, as described above, would not work with adults. For example, a brilliant man of 60 might answer almost all the questions on a test correctly, but if the mental age indicated by his score were divided by 60, the resulting IQ would be absurdly low. Terman avoided this difficulty by arbitrarily assigning to anyone 15 years or older a mental age of 15. The justification advanced for this is that intelligence potential does not develop past the age of 15, although many psychologists disagree with this judgment. In any case, the Stanford-Binet scales have been proved to be generally unreliable in assessing adult intelligence.

To overcome this difficulty, psychologists have developed what is sometimes known as the *derived intelligence quotient*. This is somewhat similar to the mental age method, except that in place of using mental age as one factor in the equation, the derived IQ is statistically formulated in such a way that the average IQ for any given age group will turn out to be 100. Various individuals will then be scored above or below 100, depending on their performance.

Making the Tests More Difficult

The distribution of scores we have indicated is obviously "built into" the tests. They are designed statistically to yield average scores of 100, with progressively fewer individuals (children or adults) as we move up or down the scale.

However, one of the problems that emerged is that if the tests are made unduly easy, most people will get very high scores on them — that is, will answer a large proportion of the questions correctly. The IQ distribution will still be the same (with the average at 100), but the ratings will be largely meaningless because people of fair intelligence and of very good intelligence will get the same or very nearly the same scores. There will be nothing in the tests to "extend" the brightest individuals.

The obvious solution for the test-makers was to incorporate increasingly difficult questions into the tests. However, the result of this in many cases was that more and more knowledge accumulated in the past was needed just to understand the questions. This raised a substantial doubt as to whether the tests were really measuring intelligence, or rather the individual's background of accumulated knowledge.

Some of the test-makers attempted to justify this procedure by the assertion that it is primarily intelligence that determines whether a child will have gained enough information to be able merely to understand the questions. Thus, the scores, it was held, would still be determined by intelligence. Today, however, it is well known that people from different social environments have inevitably assimilated different *amounts* of some areas of knowledge, and even different *kinds* of knowledge. Thus, the relative ability to understand difficult questions may be influenced not only by intelligence but also by various features of experience. In this way, another serious factor of uncertainty is introduced into "intelligence" testing.

Uses of IQ Tests

Intelligence tests are used widely today throughout American society. Almost everyone who has attended a public or private school in the United States has taken some kind of IQ, or "achievement," or "placement" test.

Elementary schools use such tests to group school children according to their ability to learn. The theory is that in this way the slow learners will be identified and will get the special attention they need, while the fast learners will be challenged and stimulated to develop their abilities to the "fullest potential."

The Stanford-Binet test, the Wechsler Intelligence Scale for Children, and the Peabody Picture Vocabulary test are among the most popularly used IQ tests in American schools. In general, the test-makers and the school officials are convinced that these tests are reasonably good predictors of *how well a child will do in school*. In addi-

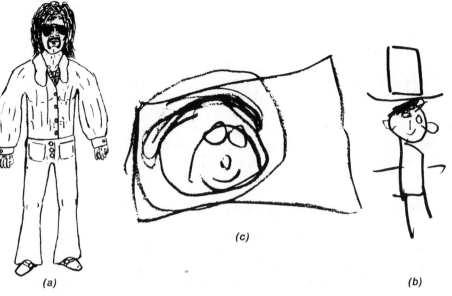

(c)

(a)

(b)

Responding to directions to "draw a man," (a) a bright 14-year old, (b) a mentally retarded 14-year-old, and (c) a schizophrenic 14-year-old of good intelligence produced the pictures shown here.

tion, intelligence tests are used in the diagnosis of special conditions, such as severe confusion or deterioration resulting from brain damage.

These tests are designed to be administered individually (to one student at a time), preferably by a trained test-giver, such as a psychologist. The individual IQ tests are thought to be superior to the group tests, including those designated by such labels as "achievement," "personnel," "aptitude," and "classification" tests. Although achievement tests and the like do not pretend to measure strictly intelligence, the fact is that they are often not markedly different from the standard IQ tests.

Achievement tests are designed to measure the scope of the academic achievement of a student, with the purpose of getting a reasonably accurate idea of his future academic performance capabilities.

Aptitude tests were originally designed to provide an index of a person's potential skills, many of which are academically related. In fact, however, aptitude tests differ very little from achievement tests because experience has indicated that a person must evince some kind of *achievement* in a particular skill area to demonstrate existence of a *potential* in that area.

In the usual school system, it makes little difference in practice whether the mental tests actually measure "true" intelligence or a complex set of other factors as well. The schools in any case use them as a predictor of academic progress and as a basis for making class assignments. Much the same practical purpose goes for adult mental testing. For the most part, adult tests are designed to show how well an individual is likely to fit into a job or a job-training program.

One possible weakness in routine testing of children and adolescents is that although the tests may be to some degree reliable in predicting an individual's performance within a given school or school system, they are based on the assumption that the school is pretty much as it should be. In other words, the school's program and methods are taken for granted. The emphasis then is exclusively on *changing the child to fit the system* — not to any degree on *adapting the system to accommodate the child.*

Effect of Heredity and Environment on Intelligence

One of the most hotly debated issues in American education and society today (as it has been for many years) is the relative importance of heredity and environment in determining intelligence. To put it concretely: To what extent is your intelligence a product of the genes you received from your parents, and to what extent is it the result of all the experiences you have had since you were born? This is sometimes called the "nature vs. nurture" dispute.

Some experts claim that heredity accounts for as much as 80% of intelligence (as measured by IQ tests); others feel that the influence of heredity as such is much less than this. Some observers believe

This boy is being given a test based on his ability to judge relationships among objects of different sizes, shapes, and colors.

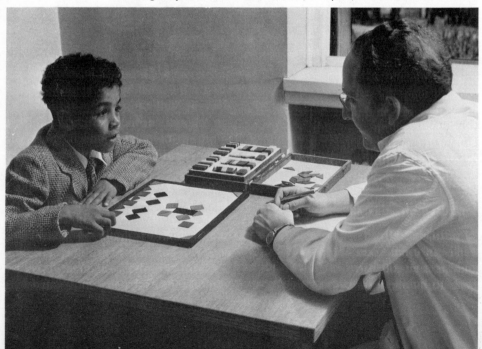

that the wide range of IQ scores found in any population is due primarily to differences in environment. In particular, they maintain that people with "high intelligence" (those who consistently do well in intelligence tests and in intellectual work) are those lucky enough to have been raised in an environment, especially during their early years, which fosters these special capabilities.

However, the views of most psychologists today fall somewhere between these two extremes. They believe that both heredity and environment are strong influences on *intelligence* and the *development of intelligence,* although they are not always clear on the difference between these last two concepts. Some psychologists speculate that the factor which is actually inherited is the upper limit or potentiality of intelligence development. But how close a child comes to attaining this upper limit depends on his environment.

In the words of psychologist Arthur Jensen, "I am afraid there is nothing you can do to create an Einstein without the right kinds of genes." This view, however, has not been proved categorically, although most psychologists accept it in practice. Jensen, like many others, in effect argues against the old notion that the newborn child is like a blank sheet of paper on which virtually anything, including genius, may be written by the environment. Most researchers agree that there are significant individual differences in the makeup of the central nervous system — of which the brain is a part. But whether these differences commonly limit *learning potential* (another description of intelligence) is not known.

One theory holds that a newborn human mind might much more aptly be compared to a lump of clay than to a sheet of blank paper. A lump of clay, of course, is subject to being molded by the forces of the environment. Clays, however, *do* differ in their inherent properties. Some clays, being relatively hard, may not take on new shapes easily, but once molded they may have the advantage of being stronger and longer lasting. Others may be highly malleable but may tend to lose their shapes after a time. Who is to say which set of characteristics is more valuable or desirable?

Sometimes a person will have a difficult time grasping something but will show a very thorough and lasting understanding once he does "get the idea." In fact, his understanding may be much more solid than that of someone else who grasped the subject quickly but perhaps superficially. On the other hand, experiments have shown that people who learn rapidly often appear to be more capable of learning in depth than those who learn less quickly.

There are studies which suggest strongly that the closer the genetic relationships among the members of a group of people, the

Can a child raised in poverty, under severely deprived conditions, be expected to score well on intelligence tests emphasizing verbal abilities and certain specialized types of experience? What relationships do the results of such tests have to "native intelligence"?

more likely it is that their IQ scores will be closely comparable. For instance, one study showed that identical twins (who have exactly the same genetic makeup) tend to have somewhat similar IQ scores, whether they have been reared together or apart. Even here, however, environment has been shown to have a direct influence, since IQ scores are *less* similar when twins are reared apart than when they are raised together.

Such studies are interesting and valuable, but there have been relatively few of them, and they can hardly be considered conclusive evidence proving that there is a definite correlation between intelligence and heredity.

Other studies indicating the heritability of intelligence are largely based on experiments with animals, particularly with rats. Obviously the results of such research must be viewed with caution, since what is true for rats may not be true for humans. This applies particularly to intelligence, since any notion of human intelligence cannot be easily separated, if at all, from language.

In one experiment spanning eleven years, it was demonstrated that rats can be bred to run mazes faster than their ancestors, much as cows have been bred to produce more milk. If we take the fastest maze-runners and mate them, their offspring will presumably stand a greater chance to run the mazes faster than other rats of the same age. The experiment showed that when this *selective breeding* is carried out over enough generations, the descendants *are* more likely to be much faster at running mazes than other rats.

Later investigations, however, showed that when experiment conditions (the environment) were slightly altered, the "dull" rats learned as fast as, or faster than, the "bright" rats. In any case, an ability to run mazes is not necessarily an indication of intelligence.

An Unsettled Issue

Until scientists agree on a clear definition of intelligence — what it is, and how it works — it is unlikely that the "nature vs. nurture" controversy will be solved satisfactorily.

This is not just a theoretical issue. It raises many practical problems, some of which are related to the nature and purposes of our educational system. If we don't know to what degree mental ability is inherited, and to what degree it is due to environmental influences, we can't be sure whether it is possible to help some children develop their intelligence considerably by "improving" the environment, including the school environment. If heredity is really dominant, all attempts at such improvement will be of limited effectiveness. If environment is dominant, then for all practical purposes there is no limit as to what can be accomplished.

Do Mental Tests Have a "Cultural Bias"?

One of the most severe and most frequently voiced criticisms of intelligence tests, particularly the ones now in common use, is that they have a *built-in cultural bias*. The critics claim that the test-makers, and even the test-givers, are unwittingly discriminating against minority groups in our society. The assertion is made that there are powerful cultural barriers of which many people — teachers and school administrators included — are in fact unaware, even though they may believe otherwise.

There are differing opinions as to what a *culture* or a *cultural group* is. It is clear, however, that under the conditions of American life today, there are various groups within the overall population that show marked and well-defined differences, particularly in language, in the use of leisure time, in relations between parents and children, and in the entire life style. All of these factors have far-reaching effects on children.

One important problem is that in order to do well on a test designed to measure intelligence, the test-taker must already have at hand the appropriate "general knowledge," which in itself is not a test of intelligence. But what does "general knowledge" mean? If you think back to the IQ tests you have taken, you will realize that a significant part of this "general knowledge" has to do with language ability — in particular, reading skill.

However, one of the most striking differences between cultural groups lies precisely in the way they use language. Most of the tests are drawn up by middle-class, white psychologists, who have spent a good part of their lives studying writings by middle-class, white authors. In general, the middle-class, white culture, being socially dominant, makes use of what is called Standard (American) English. Some minority groups (racial, ethnic, and cultural) tend to speak in *dialects*, or variants of the standard language, which are just as meaningful and just as "correct" to them as academic English is to people in the academic world.

But what is sometimes overlooked is that there is no sound basis for regarding a dialect as "improper," or "wrong," or "inferior." We all know that languages are constantly changing. Words take on new meanings; new words are invented; expressions which were once considered "sub-standard," or even "vulgar," become fully permissible; grammatical distinctions tend to die out.* Thus, the idea that there is one fixed form of the English language which is "authorized" and is inherently "superior" to all others is linguistically naive and historically unjustified.

A child who has been exposed to a certain type of English at home until his sixth year may well be confused when he goes to school and encounters what is almost a different language — Standard English. The child is further bewildered when he returns home each day and must resume the use of his original language patterns. Such a child will almost inevitably have a hard time learning from primary readers adjusted to Standard English. The effects may be so damaging that his reading skills will be severely retarded, and he may be "turned off" from reading altogether. Obviously, such a child is bound to have a hard time with any of the common intelligence tests, so strongly oriented toward reading skills.

In line with this, there is a popular tendency to label minority group children as "*culturally* disadvantaged." True, many members of minority groups are *economically* disadvantaged, but there is an almost unconscious tendency to extend this fact to imply that their entire culture is thereby inferior in worth to others. It is hard to find any rational justification for this. As a matter of fact, children who are sometimes called "culturally deprived" may actually only be "culturally somewhere else," in relation to the person making the judgment.

---

* For example, not too many years ago, grammarians considered it highly improper to say "I *will* go there." Only the form *shall* was to be used for the future in the first person. Today, this distinction is regarded as unnecessary and even prissy. Similarly, the expression "It is *me*," once condemned as "ungrammatical," is now accepted by most grammarians as "natural" and "idiomatic."

A mother in a rural village in Burma plays with her children. Can the "brightness" of these children be judged by the same standards developed for children in affluent, urban communities in the United States and Western Europe?

Effects of Unconcious Bias

Psychologist Robert Williams feels that this kind of unconscious bias is strongly evident in mental tests. He points out that the Stanford-Binet test, the Wechsler Intelligence Scale for Children, and the Peabody Picture Vocabulary test were built around studies which *included no black children*. In fact, one of the leading testmakers has specifically warned against using his test for black children, but the warning has been widely disregarded. Williams holds that it is "unfair to assume that the typical black and white cultures are so similar that the same tests can properly be used in psychological testing and placement" for black and white children.

Williams, who holds a doctorate in psychology, and in 1970 served as national chairman of the Association of Black Psychologists, says that he himself was advised not to attempt to go on to college because he had an IQ score of 82. On this basis, he is opposed to the use of the standard tests for black children, believing that the results are being used to label such children as uneducable — a concept which perpetuates inferior education for blacks by placing them in "special" schools and classes.

This same analysis may well be applicable to other cultural minorities, including substantial numbers of "poor whites," such as those in Appalachia and in depressed sections of our large cities.

In any event, many experts are convinced that social prejudice, much of it unconscious, has had negative effects on minority group members — and the black population constitutes the largest single minority group in the United States. These experts maintain, in particular, that the unfavorable social climate severely hampers a child's ability to learn, especially his ability to master the basic academic skills that are a prerequisite for academic (and economic) success in this country.

For example, a child who is not expected to do well — which may be due, in part, to a lack of communication between him and his teachers — is likely to suffer a deficiency in his self-confidence and self-esteem. Childhood feelings of rejection are always a serious threat to normal development. Particularly, in the early years, this influence may greatly diminish a child's enthusiasm or readiness to attack difficult problems. As the child grows older, his mental apparatus for dealing with problems tends to become less and less flexible until he reaches a point where he is obviously a "slow learner." His apparent "lack of mental ability" is reflected by his low IQ score. But the attitudes generated by his low IQ score may well have contributed to his poor performance in the first place.

An Experiment on a "Self-Fulfilling Prophecy"

One study which relates to this point was made by Harvard psychologist Robert Rosenthal and educator Lenore E. Jacobson. In their writings*, they describe an experiment conducted in a California elementary school attended mainly by children from Mexican-American families.

Teachers in this school were told that intelligence tests had shown that 20% of their pupils could be expected to display marked increases in learning ability and academic achievement during the school year. The teachers were given the names of these "gifted" children. Unknown to the teachers, however, the names had been *selected at random.*

Tests administered four months later, and then a year later, showed that the "gifted" children tended to score significantly higher than most of the other pupils. The experiment also showed that the greatest difference came in the first and second grades — at a time when a child's attitude toward school is still forming, and therefore a time when he is most likely to be influenced by his teacher's attitude

---

* Robert Rosenthal and Lenore E. Jacobson, *Pygmalion in the Classroom* (Holt, Rinehart & Winston, 1968).

toward him. Although this study has been severely criticized by some psychologists for using an inadequate research design, the findings are generally acknowledged to be suggestive of what *may* happen, and often *does* happen, in a classroom with a great many minority-group children.

The point is this: An IQ test may become a "self-fulfilling prophecy." It may not merely *measure* what a student is capable of achieving; it may, in part, *determine* what he will achieve.

"Culture-Fair" Intelligence Tests

Special intelligence tests have been designed to be "culture-fair," but there is grave doubt that they actually achieve this end. A study of the simplest such test, the "Draw-a-Man," revealed that different groups from all over the world showed wide variations in average scores. Moreover, these variations appear to be due far more to environmental influences than to heredity. A group of Bedouin Arab children, for example, made an average score of 52 (extremely low). It appears likely that this low rating is related to the cultural and religious prohibition in Arab societies (and in Muslim societies generally) against "graven images." This has been interpreted traditionally to forbid drawing, or even looking at, an artistic representation of a natural form, such as a man. The whole social experience of the Bedouin children reflected this taboo and must have affected their performance on the simple drawing test.

A few representative questions from popular IQ tests will further illustrate the fact that it is extremely difficult for such a test to be "culture-fair."

Symphony is to composer as book is to (1) paper (2) sculptor (3) musician (4) author (5) man

On the face of it, this is a simple logical analogy which children in the age range above 12 years should be able to complete without too much trouble. But consider a child raised in an environment where such words as *symphony* and *composer* are rarely if ever encountered. How can he handle the problem of the logical relationship if he doesn't know what these "strange" words mean in the first place? When this question was given to a cross section of the children in the public schools of a large city, the results showed that 81% of the children from upper-income and middle-income families correctly chose "author" as the answer; only 51% of lower-income children did so. The results are significant — but do they have anything to do with "intelligence"?

Where does rubber come from?

Name four men who have served as President of the United
States since 1900.

Again the questions seem "innocent" enough, but they presup-
pose a background of information that generally comes in grade
school geography and history courses. A child who has had a chaotic
and frustrating experience in grade school is far less likely to have
such information at his finger tips than a child of the same age who
has gone through the early grades in a generally harmonious and
successful way, and who moreover has been exposed to books, newspapers, magazines, informed conversation, and other sources of information at home.

Now let's look at the other side of the coin. How would white,
middle class children be likely to fare if confronted with questions
like these?

What is a "pik" used for ?   (1) basketball defense   (2) Afro
hair style   (3) asking a girl to dance   (4) cleaning teeth
(5) turning barbecued meat   ANSWER: (2)

"Dust" is what you get when   (1) someone fusses with you
(2) someone runs in front of you   (3) a car screeches to
a halt in front of you   (4) there is air pollution over the
ghetto   (5) the eagle flies   ANSWER: (5)

Which word is out of place here?   (1) splib   (2) blood   (3)
gray   (4) spook   (5) black   ANSWER: (3)

These questions were taken from a general intelligence test designed by psychologists Adrian Dove and Allen R. Sullivan as a cultural "counter-balance" for blacks.

IQ and Race

IQ scores of black children throughout the United States average
about 10% less than IQ scores of white children. Similarly, a far higher proportion of blacks than of whites are rejected by the armed forces
for failing mental tests.

This has been interpreted by some to mean that black Americans
tend to be born with less intelligence than whites.

A recent major proponent of the idea of racial differences in intelligence is University of California psychologist Arthur R. Jensen,
who stirred up a national controversy several years ago when he published his conclusions to the effect that the "preponderance of evi-

dence" indicates that black Americans on the whole tend to have a lower level of native intelligence than white Americans. Since Jensen's theory is the most publicized "scientific thinking" to come along on IQ and race in recent years, we shall examine his basic argument with some care.

Jensen's line of reasoning holds that black Americans have suffered from too much inbreeding, which supposedly has contributed to a higher rate of mental retardation. He uses as a basic principle that inbreeding or overly "selective" breeding can bring about genetic deterioration. In support of this idea, he cites studies of isolated rural families that have apparently suffered genetic damage because of long-continued inbreeding.

It is not safe to assume, however, that because this may happen within a single family line, it may also happen with a larger population, such as a tribe or a clan, to say nothing of a sector of a national population comprising many millions. In particular, some scientists suggest that despite Jensen's admission that black geniuses do occur, his reasoning implies that the genes which presumably contribute to higher intelligence will be "bred out" over a period of time if a pattern of inbreeding is maintained. These scientific critics believe that a population as large as a race or a "racial group" (such as the black population of the United States) is not likely to have become limited in its supply of "higher intelligence" genes in as short a period of time as blacks have been in this country. (The period of 300 years is a very short time indeed on the evolutionary time scale.)

In addition, genetically it is very difficult to define clearly what a "race" is, especially in a situation where there has been over the centuries extensive interbreeding between people of different racial and ethnic backgrounds. Jensen concedes that the question of children born of parents of different "races" should be "explored." However, he does not recognize explicitly what his theory actually implies — that the greater the degree of African ancestry in a present-day American, the greater the chance that his intelligence will be low. This would be a very difficult proposition indeed to defend convincingly.

The basic characteristics that mark a person as a member of the so-called "Negroid" race are primarily skin color, followed by hair type and facial features. However, it is often overlooked that people with such "Negroid" characteristics also have a large number of less conspicuous and less easily definable characteristics, inherited at some point in their ancestry from people of *other* "races." On the basis of these standards, many a person generally classified as "black" could with good reason be said to be a member of the "Caucasoid" or "white" race; and many a "white" person could be said to be a member of the "Negroid" or "black" race. Indeed, the entire concept of "race" is so uncertain and so blurred that it provides an extremely unsatisfactory basis for any theory regarding the relative intelligence of various groups in the overall population.

Results of the Armed Forces Qualification Test

A good deal of Jensen's "preponderance of evidence" is based on nationwide results of mental test scores, which must be accepted more or less at their face value if the statistics are to be significant. Many experts feel that Jensen has greatly undervalued the cultural bias built into these tests. (Note our analysis above.)

The most massive and consistent test statistics available to Jensen came from the Armed Forces Qualification Test. However, a report from the office of the U. S. Surgeon General has in effect admitted that these tests are culturally biased by reason of the fact that a man's score depends in substantial part "on the level of his educational attainment, the quality of his education (quality of his school facilities), and on the knowledge he gained from his educational training otherwise, in and outside of school."

Official statistics show sharp differences in draftee performance on the qualification test, not only by "race" but also by state or region. A study of inductees revealed that rejection rates on the basis of mental test scores have been lowest in the Far West and Middle West, and highest in the South. This pattern applies regardless of the "racial mix" of the examinees. Specifically, the study showed that:

▶ Southern whites are behind whites from other parts of the country in mental test performance.

▶ Southern blacks are behind blacks from other parts of the country.

▶ In every state, test performance is higher for whites than for blacks.

Presumably, it was this last item that Jensen used to add weight to his theory of the native mental inferiority of blacks. However, if we accept this reasoning, we should also conclude that Southern whites have a native mental inferiority as compared with Northern whites.

It seems far more reasonable to conclude that what is really showing up in these statistics of test results is (1) differences in the quality of education available in the different regions of the country; and (2) differences in the quality of education generally available to blacks and whites within the *same* regions.

The professional organization known as "Psychologists for Social Action" released a statement specifically to refute Jensen's thesis. Following is an excerpt from this statement*:

The suggestion that there is a scientific basis for drawing conclusions about race differences in intelligence is based on the following premises:

1. That intelligence tests provide a reliable measure of a scientifically understood entity called intelligence.
2. That there has never been a single black child in this country who has not suffered from some form of racial oppression.
3. That there is a body of accurate information based on the administration of intelligence tests to black and white children under comparable circumstances.
4. That intelligence is inherited as a fixed trait.
5. That the science of genetics provides a basis for the definition of intelligence in terms of innate and acquired components.
6. That hunger and malnutrition, prenatally and during early childhood, do not seriously impair and debilitate intellectual performance.

All of the above premises are either obviously false or seriously questioned by many competent scientists working on these problems.

Early Learning

If theories such as those of Jensen were tenable, there would be little purpose in concentrating on development of intellectual potential by seeking to stimulate learning during a child's early years. Many psychologists believe, however, that the *early years are of key importance to mental and intellectual growth.*

In support of this belief, psychologist Benjamin Bloom compiled a mass of statistical data which, according to his analysis, shows that by age four a child has reached half the intelligence he will have at maturity. In other words, the period of the greatest leaps in learning occurs before the age of four.

Various studies have demonstrated that the development of intelligence appears to be related closely to the amount and quality of *parental efforts* to stimulate their children mentally during the early years. For example, one experiment was conducted with mothers who, mainly for economic reasons, had little free time to devote to their

---

* The statement appeared in the December, 1969 issue of *Social Action.*

young children. These mothers were paid to read aloud to their children for 15 minutes a day. By the time these children reached the age of 18 months, they showed substantial gains in language development, as compared with other children from the same neighborhood.

A striking case was reported by a California scientist-father who spent a great deal of time with his first-born son, devising toys and instructive games for him. The boy later scored very high on IQ tests. By the time a second son was born, however, the father was preoccupied with his affairs and found comparatively little time to spend with this child. The boy later scored an IQ within the average range. A third child, a daughter, was given the same treatment as the first, and she later scored a high IQ.

Piaget and Bruner — Environmentalists and Theorists of Early Learning

The examples cited above are, of course, not in themselves conclusive evidence that intelligence is powerfully influenced by environment, but they serve to illustrate the thinking behind the environmentalist-oriented theories of early learning. Two important theories of this type have been developed by Jean Piaget and Jerome Bruner. Piaget, a Swiss psychologist, while basically an environmentalist, is somewhat more conservative than his American colleague, Bruner, but the ideas of the two men do agree in many fundamental respects.

The basic source of disagreement is that Piaget believes that a child's capacity to recognize and understand relationships comes in *definite stages,* and that accordingly he should not be "pushed" into attempting to learn things that he is really not ready to master. Such a premature attempt, as Piaget sees it, may result in emotional problems. Piaget does agree that some types of mental development can be accelerated to some extent, but he departs from Bruner and others in setting rather strict limits on the *degree of acceleration* that can and/ or should be attained. He questions whether maximum acceleration in learning is necessarily a good thing, pointing out that modern societies too often confuse speed and apparent efficiency with quality and ultimate worth.

Piaget believes that all students must go through essentially the same "learning stages" in the same order, without skipping any, regardless of whether an individual is a "fast" or a "slow" learner. However, these stages, he believes, do vary in length from person to person. According to Piaget, any effort to "push" a child through one of these stages too rapidly *for him* will not yield good results.

He believes that during the first two years of life a baby reacts mainly out of inherited instincts and is not capable of handling much in the way of mental relationships. From this, he concludes that attempts at mental stimulation during this earliest stage will be unproductive.

Many scientists are in sharp disagreement with this conclusion, pointing out that it is at this early period that the babies learn to *use* their five senses. For instance, it is at this time that they learn how to see — that is, they develop a skill for picking "things" out of their field of vision. These scientists agree with Bruner, who feels that the ability, for instance, to identify "things" can be accelerated by devising games that encourage the child to grasp relationships.

Bruner and his colleagues point out that their support of early stimulation in helping a child to "get ready" does not mean that he should be forced to learn *against his will.* What is needed, these experts feel, is parents who can give their youngsters a great deal of attention in such a way as to arouse their *desire to manipulate information.* Even Piaget agrees that the more new things a child sees and hears, the more he *wants* to see and hear.

Attempts to Help Pre-School Children

The work of the environmentalist-oriented scientists in the field of early learning, along with tremendous social pressures in the United States, has brought about experimental efforts designed to reach low-income children. This applies particularly to black children from poor families. Such children may suffer serious disadvantages because their early stimulation is not on a par with that of other children.

In the late 1960's, the Federal government initiated the program popularly known as *"Head Start,"* which is closely coordinated with the activities of various state and local agencies, such as school systems. The purpose is to aid pre-school children (as young as three) by giving them a variety of "intellectually stimulating" experiences which they would very probably not be able to get in their home environment. There is a tendency to control these experiences carefully, more or less according to Piaget's "readiness" standards.

Almost all of these programs have reported positive, although by no means "magical," results. These results are admittedly very tentative and are subject to the reservation that project directors in general are probably reluctant to admit failure. However, even if the programs have failed in some cases to provide an improved foundation for later academic achievement by the children being taught, many observers would say that this is due not so much to weaknesses in the scientific theories involved as to *widespread underfinancing and mismanagement.*

One view shared by many psychologists (including this author) is that "compensatory education" efforts, including pre-school programs, that are designed to make up for deficiencies in the child's home environment, have failed precisely because they concentrate on the *pupil's failure to learn* rather than on the *school's failure to teach*. In other words, compensatory programs rest on a series of carefully documented but demonstrably false assumptions.

One such assumption is that the disadvantaged child has a short attention span and poor auditory acuity. The "short attention span" is a child's response to boredom and frustration. Thus, the same child who appears unmanageably hyperactive ("fidgety") in the classroom will stand patiently for hours at a pinball machine, or will discipline himself on a basketball court, perhaps practicing until after dark. Why the difference? Obviously, because the pinball machine and basketball have captured his interest, while the classroom activities have not.

Many school people also assume that the disadvantaged child cannot handle abstractions; the only thing he can learn is specific subject matter "relevant" to his daily life. This explains the wide acceptance of programs emphasizing "black history" and "ghetto life." The new standard elementary readers are relevant, black, and urban — but as boring as ever to the child.

Any program based on a conviction that minority groups cannot deal with abstractions virtually guarantees "stupidity" and low standards of achievement. The new curriculum for the poor emphasizes concrete materials. Yet, especially in language development, there is little evidence that successful learning proceeds as a progression from concrete to abstract concepts.

At any rate, even though the success of various programs is at best unclear, there is considerable, although not absolutely conclusive, evidence that parental relationships in the early years are of extreme importance in forming skills which are later subject to measurement and are called "intelligence." After these years it becomes increasingly difficult to expand the child's learning skills. But in spite of this, Bruner believes that "Any subject can be taught effectively to any child at any stage of development."

Bruner's opinion is not very different from a judgment made by the father of modern intelligence testing, Alfred Binet, who said, "With practice, ambition, and especially method, one can succeed in increasing his (the child's) attention, memory, and judgment; and in literally becoming more intelligent than before."

THINGS TO DISCUSS :: THINGS TO DO :: THINGS TO READ

1. If you were a college admissions officer, how would you go about selecting students who, you feel, would have a good chance of successfully handling college work? How would you go about selecting students who would be likely to make a good contribution to a vital and interesting college community?

2. What part, do you think, *memory* plays in intelligence?

3. What, in your opinion, is the relationship between intelligence and *emotional maturity*?

4. Is *creativity* the same as intelligence? Is it a factor in intelligence? Are all intelligent people creative? Are all creative people intelligent?

5. No doubt you regard some of your friends and acquaintances as being "more intelligent" than others. On what bases or standards do you make such judgments? Can you apply these same standards to yourself?

6. Do you see any connection between native intelligence on the one hand and ethics or morality on the other? Stated more simply, is there any connection between "being smart" and "being good"?

7. How does *intuition* differ from *conscious intellect*? How does it relate to *conscious intellect*, if it does?

8. Is it possible for a person to do anything to develop and possibly expand his own intelligence? If your answer is "Yes," how would you advise going about this?

THINGS TO DISCUSS :: THINGS TO DO :: THINGS TO READ

9. Hans J. Eysenck is a well-known British psychologist who has written many popular books about psychology. One entitled *Know Your Own IQ* (Penguin, 1962) contains several IQ tests (with answers) that you can take yourself.

   Eysenck's work and ideas are controversial, and many psychologists (as we have noted) have grave misgivings about the use of IQ tests as the main indicator of intelligence and as the basis for determining suitability for college or for various types of employment. However, after reading this book and testing yourself, you may have a better basis for forming judgments about yourself.

   Do you believe that Eysenck's tests are mostly "culture-free," in the sense that the term is used in this chapter? Specifically, are they basically unrelated to the quality of education that the individual has had in school and/or at home?

10. Look at a famous painting. Read a poem by a highly regarded poet. Read a short story by a notable writer. Read an essay by a leading philosopher or social scientist. Examine some mechanical or electronic device, and try to figure out how it works.

    All of these things are creations of men's minds. Are they all expressions of intelligence? Of the same kind of intelligence? To the same degree? Explain your answers.

11. Do you think that being good at chess is a sign of high intelligence? Hold a class debate or discussion on this.

READINGS

How Children Learn, by John Holt (Dell, 1970). A short book packed with many interesting ideas on learning and intelligence.

The Relevance of Education, by Jerome S. Bruner (W. W. Norton, 1971). This influential book provides fascinating information and insights obtained from experiments on literacy and thinking patterns with various groups, such as the Wolof tribe in North Africa.

Culture of the School and the Problem of Change, by Seymour Sarason (Allwyn Press, 1971).

Too Many People? 21

The Psychology of Population Pressures

● ●

"It is clear that questions about the quality of human life are inextricably bound to those about the quantities of human beings on earth."

— PAUL EHRLICH

INTERVIEWER: *"Why wouldn't you like to have seven children?"*

GIRL (8 years of age): *"Seven would be too much for me to take care of. . . . They would be running all over the house and I would have to catch them to finish their breakfast. And I don't have a big enough table."*

Too Many Children?

Children are wonderful! Certainly, it can be a rewarding, an enriching, and a beautiful experience to be responsible for a child and to help it grow to healthy maturity.

Then again, parenthood may be frustrating, humiliating, and painful when parents cannot adequately provide basic necessities for growth, which include: love, knowledge, and a decent material standard of living, including above all a good diet.

There are many families, and also many larger social units — classes, economic and regional groupings, whole nations — which do not have enough food to go around. By government standards, there are some 25 million people in the United States who are living below the poverty line, and this means in a high percentage of cases, a substandard diet. Although reliable statistics aren't available, a shocking percentage of these Americans — perhaps half — are hungry much of

419

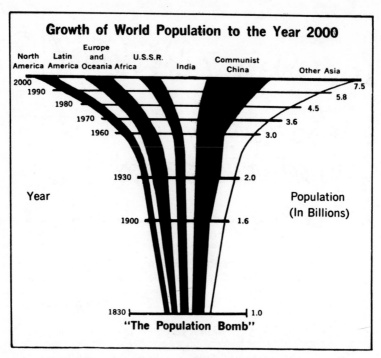

The world's population growth, past and projected.

the time. Many others suffer from forms of bad nutrition that are not easily noticed, even by the sufferers themselves.

But the United States has been called (perhaps not with full accuracy) "the best-fed nation on earth." What about the rest of the world? Of the 3.5 billion people on this planet, possibly half are on substandard diets. Untold millions of children die each year, directly or indirectly as a result of malnutrition. And those who survive may suffer severe damage, not only to their bodies but also to their mental capacity.*

And yet, in a world where so many children (and adults) cannot be fed adequately, the population is increasing at an alarming rate. This *population explosion* has emerged as one of the major problems (in the opinion of some, *the* major problem) of our time. The situation has grave implications, not only for social scientists (such as economists, geographers, and ecologists) but also from the point of view of the psychologist.

---

* See *Disadvantaged Children — Health, Nutrition, and School Failure,* by Herbert G. Birch and Joan Dye Gussow (Harcourt, Brace, 1970). These researchers conclude that "nutritional imbalance of severe degree may produce structural damage in the brain and spinal cord . . . abnormal electrical activity in, and physical damage of, the central nervous system." Moreover, such damage may be done *before* birth as a result of malnutrition of the mother.

How Did the Population Grow?

One week from today, there will be 1,695,000 more people in the world than there are today.

It took hundreds of thousands of years for the world's population to reach half a billion in the year 1650. Then within 200 years, the population doubled, to 1 billion, in 1850. The next doubling process took only 80 years; that is, there were 2 billion people in the world by 1930. From 1930 to 1970 (only 40 years!), population nearly doubled again. By the latter date, there were more than 3.5 billion people living on the earth.

How long will the next doubling take? No one knows for sure, but on the basis of present tendencies, it will require perhaps 30 years, and there may be close to 7 billion people inhabiting our planet by the year 2000. (See the accompanying graph.) Demographers* studying the population explosion emphasize the following facts:

▶ The time for each successive doubling of the earth's population has been steadily shrinking.

▶ Each successive doubling involves a far larger number of people than the previous one. When the earth's population doubled from 1850 to 1930, there were only one billion additional human beings on the earth. But the near doubling from 1930 to 1970 added 1.5 billion people, and the prospective doubling by the year 2000 will add another 3.5 billion. In other words, population tends to increase *geometrically* (2, 4, 8, 16, etc.).

▶ The one thing that does *not* increase is the dimensions of our physical environment. The planet earth, it has been said, is a "closed system." It may be thought of as a sort of "spaceship" of fixed dimensions into which many thousands of additional "passengers" are crowding every day. Today, there is no more air, no more water, no more soil, no more mineral deposits, no more space than there was 1000 years ago or 100,000 years ago. To be sure, our ability to use the resources of nature has increased tremendously, but this does not nullify the fact that the constantly growing human family must depend on a *fixed resource base*. Indeed, it might even be called a *shrinking* resource base because we are rapidly using up available deposits of such materials as coal, petroleum, and iron ore.

---

* The statistical study of human populations is called *demography*. It considers such aspects of population as "size and density, growth, distribution, migration, and vital statistics, and the effects of all these on social and economic conditions." The "effects" in question include psychological as well as physical aspects.

Questions to Be Considered

The population explosion has become a source of deep concern to thinking people in all parts of the world. Specialists in various natural and social sciences are asking questions such as the following:

▶ Will it be possible to feed this vastly expanded population adequately?

▶ Even if (as seems possible) food production can be expanded sufficiently to feed 6 to 7 billion people, can our productive resources furnish enough of all the other "good things" of life to provide a decent standard of living? In other words, what happens to the *quality* of life?

▶ How will our social and political institutions be affected by a vast increase in population density? Will democracy and individual freedom have to be sacrificed to the need for strict discipline and controls when 6 or 7 billion people inhabit this planet?

In recent years, we have become keenly aware of the fact that pollution of the environment (air, water, soil, etc.) represents a major threat to man's continued existence on this planet. We are just beginning to develop programs of *ecological reform* — to remedy some of the damage done in the past and to prevent further damage. But can we expect such programs to be effective if population growth continues at the present rate? Every human being inevitably creates some

The miscellaneous litter that so often defaces the American countryside is one symptom of our increasing population density in some areas.

wastes and some pollution. Indeed, it has been said that population growth is the "ultimate pollutant." Will there be any chance of preserving the environment even reasonably well in a world of 6 to 7 billion people?

Finally, and perhaps of most immediate interest to us, what will be the *psychological effects* of the severe overcrowding unavoidable in a world of 6 to 7 billion people? Imagine a world in which there is no chance to avoid crowds, to get off by yourself, to maintain privacy, to enjoy nature in the wild state! May we expect that this situation will lead to personality disorders whose exact nature we cannot even hope to predict?

In the future, as at present, population density will undoubtedly be far greater in some areas than in others. But even the areas which are more favored in this respect cannot expect to escape the impact of severe overpopulation elsewhere. To quote Paul Ehrlich, to say that India's population problem, for example, does not directly concern the United States is like saying, "There's a leak in your side of the boat."

Causes of the Population Explosion

The population explosion that is already in effect and that threatens us in the future is the result of the achievements of science and technology (1) in overcoming many diseases that cut short human life, and (2) in providing a greater supply of food and other necessities to

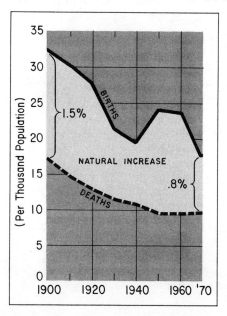

Since 1960, the birth rate in the United States has dropped off sharply, while the death rate has shown little change. The difference between the two (the *natural population increase)* is sufficient to add about 1.6 million persons to our population each year. (This growth is supplemented by immigration.)

sustain a large population. In particular, with vast improvements in medical services and in sanitation, a far greater proportion of all babies born now live to maturity and are able to have children of their own. When George Washington became President, a baby born in the United States had no better than an even chance, on the average, of living to reach age 35. A great many children died during the first few years of their lives. Today, the average life expectancy of a newborn child in the United States is over 70 years.

Throughout the history of the United States, population growth has been due to two factors: (1) the *natural increase* — that is, the excess of births over deaths; and (2) *immigration*. Since the 1920's, immigration has been a relatively minor factor, and our birth rate* is one of the lowest in the world. Thus, the population increase of the United States, in spite of the increasing life span, has been limited as compared with other nations, and the density of population is correspondingly low.

It is in countries that continue to have very high birth rates that the falling death rate results in drastic population increases. This is true particularly of economically underdeveloped countries throughout Latin America, Asia, and parts of Africa. Although these countries for the most part are backward in their industrial and agricultural practices, they have received many of the benefits of modern medicine and sanitation. Thus, their death rates have dropped drastically, largely as a result of decreases in infant and child mortality. At the same time, birth rates have continued to be very high, as compared with those of such economically developed parts of the world as the United States, Western Europe, Japan, and Australia.

This is true, for example, of a country such as India, which now has more than 2½ times the population of the United States in about one-third the land area, and with far less than this proportionately in the way of natural resources. From 1870 to 1920, the population of what is now India rose at an average rate of about one million persons a year. In 1968, the increase in population was more than a million a *month!* The average annual income in India is extremely low, and tens of millions live in conditions of extreme poverty. In such major cities as Calcutta, thousands of inhabitants are literally homeless and live in the streets. Yet even the poorest people receive some of the benefits of public health services provided by the government; improved methods of food distribution prevent actual starvation, which was once wide-

---

* The *birth rate* is expressed as the number of babies born per 1000 population. In the United States in recent years, this has been about 17 (per thousand). In other nations, it is much higher — for example, in India, 41 (per thousand).

Throughout much of the world, as population grows, more and more people migrate from rural areas to metropolitan centers. Many of the migrants then live under conditions of extreme poverty. This situation is prevalent throughout much of Latin America. Here we see a "shantytown" on the outskirts of Caracas (Venezuela) with modern apartment houses in the background.

spread. Thus, population surges upward at a staggering rate, although the government, conscious of the dangers, has launched a large-scale campaign of birth control.

Reasons for Wanting Large Families

The urge to have many children and to rear them successfully to adulthood is a tradition handed down from our prehistoric ancestors. Throughout most of the time that man has lived on earth (estimates vary from 600,000 to 2 million years), the human species was actually struggling against extinction. The population grew very little, if at all, and in many years, when conditions were particularly unfavorable, the death rate might exceed the birth rate.

But we know that this situation has changed radically, particularly within the last few centuries. Advances in medicine and sanitation, as well as other forms of progress (for example, in food production), have greatly reduced the death rate. At the same time, the birth rate (except in a relatively few technologically advanced societies) has not changed much. The result is the population explosion, which has become one of the main concerns of modern society.

Thus, the "primal urge" to have many children no longer has validity in terms of overall social needs. But that doesn't mean that the urge no longer exists. The desire for parenthood remains a powerful psychological fact of life. And more specifically the desire to have a large family continues to dominate the attitudes of many people, perhaps mainly at an unconscious level. The reasons for this are diverse, varying from person to person and from culture to culture. We can, however, recognize a number of basic factors as set forth below. (Of course, it must be recognized that in a great many cases, people have large families not because they want to but simply because there is no method of preventing pregnancies and births which they are able and willing to apply.)

Religious Considerations. First, there is the religious influence. The Biblical injunction to "be fruitful, and multiply" has its parallels in the doctrines of other religious groups. This is often interpreted as an obligation of the individual man and woman, rather than as a broad requirement for the human race as a whole. A consequence of this is the widely held conviction that parents who have many children are virtuous — that they are doing "God's will." This accounts in part for the prohibition of various religious groups (*e.g.,* Roman Catholic, Orthodox Jewish) against birth control and abortion.

Nationalistic Policies. On many occasions, the desire for large families has been spurred by nationalistic considerations. Governments have encouraged married couples to have children, on the theory that this would add to the nation's power, particularly to its military potential. This was true, for example, of Fascist Italy and Nazi Germany in the period before World War II. Communist countries, such as the Soviet Union, still continue to glorify large families and to offer material rewards based on number of children.*

Throughout a large part of its history, the United States was an almost empty continent, in great need of population for economic development. Under such conditions population growth was naturally regarded as a sign of progress. This is why our government long followed a policy of almost unlimited immigration. It is also one reason for the traditional American attitude of regarding large families as a contribution to a larger, stronger, and better nation. It is only within recent years, under the pressure of growing population density and ecological disruptions, that this attitude has begun to change markedly.

---

* However, the efforts of the Soviet government to encourage large families appear to have been of limited effectiveness. The 1970 census showed that only a small minority of families throughout the USSR had more than two or three children.

Economic Considerations. Economic considerations have also been important. In earlier generations, when most people made their living by farming, a large family was a distinct advantage. There was always plenty of work to be done on a farm, by girls as well as boys, and children were pressed into service at a very early age. A farmer with several able-bodied sons had an extremely valuable labor supply until they married and set up households of their own. And even in non-farm families, children could do many types of work. Moreover, having children was regarded as a sort of "insurance policy." The more children, the better the chance that some of them at least would be willing and able to support the parents in old age.

Today, of course, with the great bulk of our population living in an urban environment, these considerations are far less potent. Children, far from being an economic asset, are extremely costly to raise. This is especially true in middle class families, and there is reason to believe that this cost factor is influential in convincing many middle class couples that they should have no more than two or three children. In this way, the parents believe, they can give the children more advantages, and also provide a higher standard of living and a more secure future for themselves. With the protection provided by Social Security and by many private pension and savings plans, there is less necessity for parents to depend on their children for support in old age.

On the other hand, we find that income tax laws still favor large families. Many countries (France, Canada, Great Britain) pay special subsidies to families based on the number of children. And even in the United States, Social Security and welfare payments are scaled to the number of children in the family.

Assertion of Masculinity and Femininity. For many men, having a large family is a way of asserting their masculinity. This is particularly true in "Latin" societies, such as those of Central America and South America. The feeling is that a man who is sufficiently virile to father many children has effectively demonstrated his *machismo* ("maleness") to the world. Another somewhat related consideration is the desire on the part of the father to make sure that he will have children to carry on the "family name." For this reason men who have had only daughters may feel that they should "keep going" until they have a son. If they have one son, they may want others to insure continuity.

Similarly, women may want large families to prove to the world (and to themselves) that they are truly "feminine" and desired by a man. The mother in our society is the very embodiment of "womanliness." This is why the strongest obstacles to introducing a program of birth control among married women in our society are psychological ones. A woman who is "deprived" of having a large number of children may feel, perhaps unconsciously, that she is giving up the one role for which she has been intended by nature, and for which she has been preparing ever since she was born. Note how girls in our society spend much of their childhood playing "house" and simulating motherhood with dolls. The "dating" ritual of adolescence is another phase of this extended preparation for the motherhood role.

In recent years, however, a new feminine consciousness in the form of the Women's Liberation movement ("Women's Lib") has been actively questioning the age-old assumption that women are destined primarily for the purpose of having and rearing children. The proponents of this movement maintain that women throughout the ages have been systematically exploited and underrated. They must now change their social role to one of full equality with men in every area of life — economic, political, intellectual, and familial. This does not mean, as derogators of the movement sometimes unfairly assert, that "Women's Lib" wants to abolish the difference between the sexes, or discredit motherhood, or end the institution of the family. It does indicate an unwillingness to accept uncritically the picture of femininity and motherhood that has been dominant in our society, with rare exceptions, for many centuries. (See Chapter 17.)

One result of "Women's Lib" and of similar reform movements will probably be to accelerate the trend toward smaller families. Many women today, particularly those of good educational background, do not see themselves cast in the role of "breeders" of large families. They probably wish to get married and have children, but only as many as they can care for properly. They see other values in life for themselves beyond the family and the nursery. They are keenly aware of the menace of overpopulation and the ecological problems connected with it. As these attitudes and ideas spread in our society, we may expect that the favorable stereotypes long connected with large families will be modified.

The Population Picture in the United States

Because of our large land area, our relatively low birth rate, and a restrictive immigration policy, the United States has a lower density of population as a whole than most of the other economically advanced countries of the world. For example, the average density of population in this country is 55 per square mile, as compared with corresponding figures of 92 for Great Britain, 416 for India, and 700 for Japan.

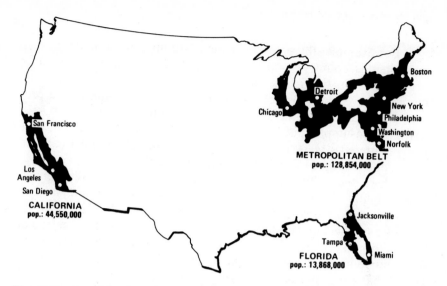

The Urban Land Institute has predicted that on the basis of present trends, by the year 2000 the United States will have a population of about 312 million, of which 60% will be living in three "megalopoli," as shown on this map. The three areas in question constitute only 7.7% of the total land of the continental United States.

However, average figures by themselves can be misleading. A large part of our population is concentrated in a few urban areas, and as the accompanying map shows, this may be expected to be even more true in the future. Even today, the major urban areas are very densely populated indeed, as anyone can testify who has been in the New York City subways, or on the Los Angeles freeways, or in the streets of downtown Chicago during rush hours.

True, we have vast areas of "wide open spaces" in such states as Idaho, Wyoming, Montana, and the Dakotas, but these areas show little if any population growth over the years. Our population is concentrated more and more in the great urban centers, where economic opportunities and other advantages are available.

Thus, we may suffer from the maladies of high population density, even though, on an overall basis, our national area is quite sparsely populated.

Economic Development May Complicate Population Problems

It may be suggested that an economically advanced country, such as the United States can "absorb" a large number of additional people without undue strain. In a sense this is true. But in another sense, the very prosperity and high economic standards of the United States magnify the problems of a growing population.

For example, there are more than 100 million automobiles registered in this country — perhaps half of all the automobiles in the world. In itself, this is fine. It indicates that people are well off, and that they have more of a chance to enjoy life. But think of the problems this massive production and use of automobiles creates — in terms of consumption of limited natural resources, air pollution, traffic jams, cluttered streets, disposal of scrapped and abandoned cars, and use of precious space for highway construction!

These facts illustrate the principle that economic development may actually *aggravate* the problems of overpopulation. As living standards rise, people naturally consume more goods. Thus they use up more of the limited store of natural resources. They create more litter and junk. They generate more wastes to pollute air and water. They move about more and "get in each other's way." It is not suggested that these and other similar problems are insoluble in the long run, but they do exist *now,* and they are the result in large measure of our technological development and economic prosperity.

Throughout the world today, people are demanding higher economic standards. They are unwilling to accept continued poverty, hunger, and squalor. They believe that a better life is attainable by all. (This applies even in the United States, where perhaps 25 million people are living below the poverty line, and there are many others not too far above it.) No one questions that such improvements are urgently needed. But if greatly expanded per-capita consumption of goods is combined with great increases in population, what chance will there be to preserve the environmental balance on which the very existence of the human race (and of all other life) depends?

Psychological Effects of Overcrowding — Noise

Great density of population, whether on a national or a local level, inevitably means overcrowding for many. It has been demonstrated that this has drastic psychological effects on people.

One of the most familiar and most unpleasant conditions resulting from overcrowding (especially in a modern industrial community) is simply excessive noise. No city-dweller in the United States has to be told that we live in a noisy environment. One automobile passing by creates a decibel* level of 70 in the immediate vicinity. The corres-

---

* The *decibel* is the unit used to measure the relative loudness (intensity) of sounds. As a basis of comparison, take the decibel rating of ordinary conversation as 50-60 decibels. It should be noted that the decibel is a logarithm unit. Therefore, a noise level of 100 decibels is 10 times as great as a noise level of 90 decibels, and 100 times as great as a noise level of 80 decibels. One estimate is that the average level of noise in the American urban environment is rising at the rate of about 1 decibel per year.

ponding figure for heavy traffic is 100, and for a jet plane taking off, 150. Within the home, a food blender in operation causes a noise level of 80 decibels in that room.

To appreciate the significance of these figures, we must understand that noise levels as low as 50 decibels are known to delay or interfere with sleep. Even when the person exposed to such a noise does fall asleep, he is likely to feel fatigued and nervous the next morning.

Constant exposure to "noise pollution" makes people tense and often gives them severe headaches. They may become nervous and unstable without knowing why. Working efficiency may suffer. Virtually everyone accomplishes more and works more harmoniously with other people in a room that is quiet or where the sounds are pleasant and unobtrusive.

Recently there has been evidence that prolonged exposure to noise in the 90-decibel range may cause irreversible damage to the nervous system, including impairment of hearing.

Efforts are being made to reduce noise levels in cities. For example, there are ordinances against unnecessary horn blowing or driving a car with a defective muffler. But in a crowded urban environment, it is difficult indeed to find a really quiet place. It is highly probable that many American children today have never "heard silence." Even in moments of quiet, there is still a car moving somewhere in the distance; a voice in the next house or apartment; the faint tones of a neighbor's television or radio; the hum of the electric refrigerator. And people who live near major airports may find that the shattering sounds given out by the huge jets as they take off and land are enough to make their environment all but unbearable, even if they live in expensive homes located in otherwise attractive suburban communities.

Depersonalization in Overcrowded Areas

Under the conditions of modern urban life, many people are almost always "part of a crowd." It is not unusual for a poor family of six, eight, or even more members to live in a few small rooms. And when the parents or the children leave their home, they join another crowd — on the street, at a place of work, at school, in public transportation, etc.

One of the results of this way of life in many cases is to create an effect of *depersonalization*. This means that people lose much of their feeling of individuality. The sense of personal responsibility, individual confidence, and self-respect becomes weakened. The individual by himself appears insignificant or powerless. It is only when he is acting as a member of a group that he takes on dimensions and importance.

Another way of putting this is that people under such conditions tend to assume a *collective orientation*. They think of themselves not as independent, individual agents but as parts of a collectivity — a crowd.

It is easy to see how people with this psychological background can be exploited by a skilled leader or manipulator of crowds. The "leader" in question may be a political demagogue, a pseudo-religious charlatan, or a gang chief of some kind. The specific activity is probably less important to the participants than the sense of being integrated into an undifferentiated mass, and of being directed by a strong personality.

There have been many studies relating population density to delinquency, adult crime, and emotional disturbances. Many middle-aged and older people today talk about how the world used to be "friendlier," and this may not be simply nostalgia or romanticizing the past. There have been authenticated cases in recent years of people being assaulted, robbed, and even killed on the streets of large cities, while other people looked on and refused to take any action — even as much as calling the police. Such an attitude of withdrawal or alienation is caused, at least in part, by the depersonalized quality of the urban environment. We are surrounded by people, but for the very reason that there are so many of them, they cease to have individual significance and value. They are *strangers* in the fullest sense of the term — faceless shadows to whom we do not relate as fellow human beings.

This provides part of the psychological background for crime, and even more for toleration of crime by the law-abiding majority. What happens to someone else may be regrettable, but it is "none of my business." The one explanation offered again and again by people who have witnessed crimes without attempting to intervene in any way is, "I didn't want to get involved." But "getting involved" with other people is an essential part of *living* in a real community and of assuming the responsibilities of a neighbor and a citizen.

Weaknesses in Family Relationships

In large families, particularly those under economic stress, children usually cannot get the same amount of attention from parents as children in small or medium-sized families. This may lead to chronically disturbed behavior, as the child makes exaggerated efforts to attract the attention which he demands as proof of love. Also, a child may not grow as close emotionally to his brothers and sisters if he has, say, six or seven of them, rather than two or three.

On the other hand, it is sometimes said that large families are the happiest, and the children in such families best adjusted. This does not necessarily contradict what we have noted above. It is certainly possible for a large family to be happy and well-adjusted, but it does place extra demands on the parents, and particularly the mother. And when she is handicapped (as is often the case) by poverty, poor housing and lack of educational background, the burden may become all but intolerable.

The problems of excessive competitiveness, leading to over-aggressive and anti-social behavior, arise more frequently in large families than in small or medium-sized ones. Much the same is true of large, crowded communities as compared with places where people do not feel overwhelmed or threatened by the sheer pressure of other people in their immediate environment. A certain amount of competition is valuable — in a family or in a society. But there is a point beyond which it becomes disruptive, to the individual and to the social structure.

Unplanned Children

A great number of children arrive in this world by accident. Surveys have indicated that between one-fifth and one-fourth of all babies born every year in the United States (perhaps 700,000) fall in this category. Many of these births are by unwed and usually adolescent mothers. A high proportion of these children are unwanted and inadequately loved and cared for.

Small children are extremely sensitive. An attitude of resentment against the child, no matter how carefully repressed and concealed it may be (and often it isn't), can have devastating effects on his psychic development — as we have described in other chapters.

Why are so many births unplanned? There are several basic interlocking reasons: (1) ignorance, (2) risk taking, and (3) traditionalist social and religious attitudes against birth control and abortion. We shall discuss these factors in some detail in Chapter 23, "Sex and Morality."

According to authoritative estimates, if only babies who were planned and wanted by their parents were born, the population explosion in the United States would be virtually arrested. Our population would still reach the 300 million figure some time after the year 2000, but it would then probably stay close to that level, instead of plunging toward 400 million.

Population Growth and Poverty

We have already noted that the problem of a high birth rate (while the death rate goes down) is most acute in the economically underdeveloped countries of the world. Thus, population figures continue to show startling increases in Latin America, the Far East, the Middle East, and parts of Africa.

What can be done about this situation? The first point to be noted is that it is not the duty or the privilege of the United States, or of any other "advanced" nation, or even of the UN, to impose a solution "from above." Outside nations or agencies can perhaps be constructive in providing help, when help is desired. But no proposed program of "family planning" (birth control) can be effective in any society unless the people themselves are ready and willing to apply it. Even the government of the Republic of India has experienced great difficulty in introducing birth control measures among its own people, although the population problem there is admittedly desperate.

There is one hopeful sign in the picture. The historical record has demonstrated repeatedly that when a society becomes industrialized, and a large part of its population attains middle class status, the birth rate tends to go down. This has been true, for example, in Great Britain, France, Germany, the United States, and more recently Japan. There is certainly reason to hope that this will also be true some day in countries where the people are now mostly illiterate peasants, living in societies whose popular traditions have changed little over the centuries. But first there will have to be substantial economic development.

We have a somewhat similar problem *within* our own population. The birth rate tends to be higher in the poorer, educationally deprived classes. It is here that large families (five or more children) are most common. And it is here that the efforts to institute family planning have had the least success.

In the United States, discussion of this matter has sometimes involved considerations of race. In general, birth rates in this country are higher among non-whites than among whites. Efforts to curb the birth rate among poor families have been criticized as a campaign to prevent growth of the black population and even to practice "genocide."

This reaction is understandable, particularly when one considers that there have been ill-advised proposals to *require* recipients of relief payments to practice birth-control measures. Nonetheless, a more detached analysis indicates that the problem is essentially economic, rather than racial. Birth rates tend to be high on the average among poverty-level families of *all* racial and ethnic backgrounds, white as well as black, European as well as Latin American. Actually, black middle-class families have one of the *lowest* birth rates of all identifiable groups in the United States.

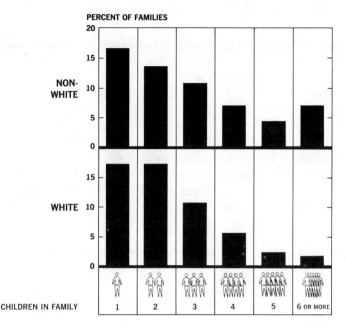

PERCENT OF FAMILIES

NON-WHITE

WHITE

CHILDREN IN FAMILY — 1 — 2 — 3 — 4 — 5 — 6 OR MORE

These graphs show that non-white families in the United States are much more likely to be larger than white families. (Figures for 1970.)

The purpose of holding down the birth rate among poor families (by *voluntary* methods, it should be emphasized again) is not only to help curb general population growth, as important as that is, but also to help give children of such families a better chance to rise from poverty. A poor family — black, white, or Oriental — can certainly use its income more effectively to raise two children than five or six children. The smaller number of children will receive more attention from parents, and the burden on the mother will be less overwhelming. The children will have a better opportunity to grow up without the physical and psychological hardships that so many of them suffer from today. These facts apply regardless of racial or ethnic background.

The problem must be attacked from many different angles. A strong economy that will offer good job opportunities is part of the answer. So is better education and job training. So is the ending of the racial prejudice and discrimination that continue to disgrace our society. So is the accumulation of knowledge and skills that will enable us to detect psychological difficulties at an early age and to do something about them.

In any event, it is certain that we cannot legislate birth control, small families, and population restraints. The purpose of public policy should be to create the conditions that will cause people to *want* to have relatively small families, and that will make available the means to achieve that goal.

There are some signs that significant changes are already taking place. Analysis of the latest Census Bureau data showed a substantial decrease in the birth rate in the United States during the decade of the 1960's. In particular, the birth rate among lower-income women (with a family income of less than $5000 per year) declined so sharply in the late 1960's that they bore a million fewer children than they would have if births had maintained the rate of the early 1960's. During the decade, the birth rate for lower-income women fell by 21%, while the birth rate for all other women went down by 18%. Even with this narrowing of the gap, however, poor women still were having significantly more children than their richer sisters.

THINGS TO DISCUSS :: THINGS TO DO :: THINGS TO READ

1. Hugh O. Englemann, a well-known sociologist, suggests that the key factor to be considered in problems related to population density is not how close together we live but rather *how much we interact*. In general, he says, interaction leads to progress, but *beyond a certain point* it tends to be destructive. When this happens, the family falls apart; the individual loses value; technology breaks down; and totalitarianism rises. Violence increases, and moreover tends to become more and more of the nondirected, purposeless type. People incline to stereotype their experiences and are less likely to perceive and to appreciate unique individuals.

    What do you think of this analysis? What would you say is the "certain point" beyond which the quality of life tends to deteriorate so markedly? Do you think that the symptoms of deterioration are appearing in our society, or in any other society of which you have knowledge? If you feel that the problem is a serious one, is there anything which we can and should do to deal with it?

2. Distinguish between *population growth* and the *rate of population growth*. How is it possible for population to rise while the rate of growth is going down? What implications does this have for population control in a particular country or in the world as a whole?

3. About 1950, the government of the Republic of India began a nationwide campaign to encourage family planning (meaning smaller families). At the time, the population growth rate was about 1.3% per year. In the early 1970's, it was about 2.5%.

    Kingsley Davis has said that economic influences, cultural mores, and the motivation of parents are far more important in determining family size than the availability of contraceptives. Explain how this interpretation may account for what has been happening in India. In the light of this, what kind of program(s) do you think the Indian government should undertake to curb population growth?

4. What evidence is there for the belief that as countries like Pakistan, India, and Brazil become more economically developed, and as standards of living rise, population growth will tend to "taper off"?

5. A special commission on "Population Growth and the American Future" was set up by President Nixon in 1969 to study the nation's population problems. You can address this agency at 726 Jackson Place, N.W., Washington, D. C. 20506 to obtain copies of their latest reports and other literature.

In a report issued in March 1971, the Commission made the following statement:

> ". . . . if families in the United States have only two children on the average and immigration continues at present levels, our population would still grow to 266 million by the end of the century; if they have three children, the population would reach 321 million by then. One hundred years from now, the two-child family would result in a population of 340 million persons; the three-child average would produce nearly a billion."

Discuss the implications of this statement.

6. In 1971, the U. S. Census Bureau released a study made in 1969 entitled "Fertility Variations by Ethnic Origin." Some of the findings were as follows:

(a) White women between the ages of 35 and 44 had borne an average of 2.9 children; for Mexican-American women the average was 4.4; and among black women the average was 3.6.

(b) At the highest income levels the figure is about 2.4 for *all* ethnic and racial groups.

What in your judgment are the implications of these findings?

7. Organizations that are now working to promote population stability are listed below. Perhaps you can write to one or more of them to get a clearer idea of their activities. They will probably be glad to send you literature. And you may find some way in which you personally can be helpful in this work.

(a) *Hugh Moore Fund,* 60 East 42nd St., New York, N. Y. 10017. Distributes literature; supports individuals and organizations active in this field.

(b) *Planned Parenthood-World Population,* 810 Seventh Ave., New York, N. Y. 10019. Conducts clinics; carries on various educational and promotional activities.

(c) *Zero Population Growth,* 367 State St., Los Altos, Calif. 94022. Activist organization which plans political action.

READINGS

Some good books in the area of population problems are listed below. All are available in paperback editions.

Paul Ehrlich, *The Population Bomb* (Sierra Club-Ballantine, 1968).

William and Paul Paddock, *Famine — 1975!* (Little, Brown, 1967).

Arthur Hopcraft, *Born to Hunger* (Houghton, Mifflin, 1968).

Charles and Leslie Westoff, *From Now to Zero — Fertility, Conception, and Abortion in America* (Little, Brown, 1971).

22

The Psychology of Mass Persuasion

-A Look at Advertising and Propaganda

● ●

"Nobody ever went broke underestimating the taste of the American public."

— H. L. MENCKEN

"It's the Real Thing!"

"It's the real thing, in the back of your mind. . . ."

No doubt you've heard this slogan used in television and radio commercials for a soft drink. Millions of dollars have been spent, in all probability, beaming it at the American public. It seems simple and harmless enough — but what does it *mean*?

To begin with, it is not a rational statement, and it isn't supposed to be one. What it seems to be implying is that in this period of stress and change, there is at least one part of "reality" that we can hang on to without uncertainty or guilt. And, by association, it suggests that this can be done pleasantly and inexpensively by buying and consuming a particular soft drink.

This message is typical of much advertising today in that it is directed to the unconscious, emotional side of the consumer — to his fantasies, illusions, and secret desires. For a long time, advertising men have intuitively understood that their special craft lies in reaching the

438

consumer at a deeper level than rational judgment. Increasingly in recent years, advertising agencies have been making use of the science of psychology to help them influence the consumer more effectively and to avoid costly mistakes in merchandising methods.

Motivational Research

Psychologists working in this field are called *motivational researchers*. The term implies that they try to look deep into the motivations that determine how and why consumers spend their money — what they respond to, and what "turns them off." The insights gained in this way can then be used to plan more effective advertising approaches, and to sway the consumer in other ways, for example, by more appealing packaging.

Here are some examples of motivational research in action drawn from recent advertising experience.

Why Do Men Smoke Cigars?

An advertisement was designed which showed a pretty housewife handing out cigars at a party to male guests. It looked good, but when the ad was tested, it proved to be a flop. Men seemed to react very negatively. Puzzled and disappointed, the advertising executives consulted a firm of motivational researchers, and they came up with an explanation based on psychological insights. The interpretation was that men smoke cigars, in good part, to *proclaim their masculinity*. They know that many women don't like the odor of cigars. Thus, smoking cigars, particularly in the home, becomes an act of defiance against feminine domination, which men unconsciously enjoy. For this reason, an advertisement that shows a smiling woman handing out cigars doesn't make any sense psychologically. It actually frustrates, at an unconscious level, one of the main impulses motivating men to smoke cigars.

Baking a Cake and Having a Baby

A bakery goods company had developed a new cake mix which the housewife had only to mix with water and then bake. It seemed to be an excellent product, but it didn't do well when placed on the market. Again, motivational researchers were called in. Their finding was that baking a cake meets several different needs for a typical housewife. First and most obviously, she wants to create something that her family will enjoy eating. But on another level, the very act of making the cake is satisfying to the woman because it gives her a chance to "act out" symbolically the birth of a child. When a woman merely added water to the cake mix, her participation was so limited that she didn't feel she was "creating" anything. The cake mix was then changed so that the user was required to add eggs and milk, as well as water. Sales rose promptly.

Selling Competitive Products

The most typical advertising situation, whether in publications or on radio-television, is that an effort is being made to push the sale of one brand or make of a product in competition with many other brands that are or do essentially the same thing.

Thus, we are assailed with multiple claims for many different soaps that will do the most thorough and "gentle" job of cleaning . . . for gasoline, all of which will deliver maximum mileage . . . for tires, each of which is the safest and most long-lived. How can eighteen brands of cigarettes and twenty brands of beer all have the "best taste," especially when tests have shown that there is little difference between most brands of these products? How can every detergent clean better, and whiter, and brighter, and cheaper than every other detergent? And if each of these products is such a miracle of efficiency and economy, why is it that eventually almost every one of them will be superseded by a "NEW, improved version"?

Competitive claims are even made for products which are in their very nature identical. For example, consider aspirin. This is a name given to a specific chemical compound — acetylsalicylic acid ($C_9H_8O_4$). It is impossible for one specimen of acetylsalicylic acid to be "better" than another. A given substance either has or does not have this formula. Yet we all know that there are various brands of aspirin on the market, packaged differently and selling at different prices. There are also products marketed under different names whose active ingredient is aspirin. Again, the prices vary. Thus, there is a competitive marketing situation, sustained largely by advertising, for a product which is a standardized chemical compound. There is in general no rational basis, except price, for choosing one brand of aspirin over another.

Much the same is true of milk. Unless the milk is flavored or processed in some special way, or the cows have been allowed access to a patch of wild onions, every batch of milk meeting a given set of specifications will taste the same and have the same food values as any other batch. How then is it possible to gain a competitive advantage for one brand? Well, for one thing, you may tell people that your milk comes from "contented cows." We all know that "contented" is a word with strong emotional connotations, and it is particularly well suited for milk — a food associated with children, the security of home, and basic nutritional needs.

Creating a Distinctive "Personality" for Products

Karl Menninger, a noted psychiatrist, once asked the head of a large advertising firm why advertisers couldn't eliminate the exaggerations and just say: "Our brand of this product pleases many people. Naturally we think it is better in some respects than competing brands, and we would like to have you think so too." The advertising man replied: "Every experiment in advertising copy shows that extravagant claims, boasting, promises held out, etc. produce better results than simple, straightforward announcements. Wishful thinking and simple hopefulness influence the actions of human beings far more than rational intelligence. Effective advertising is, therefore, based on emotions and not on intelligence."

Keenly aware of this emotional factor, advertising men expend their efforts on trying to create a distinctive "personality" that will make a particular product stand out from its competitors. And the more alike the competing products actually are, the greater the importance of this emotionally charged "personality" factor. It is crucial, for example, for cigarettes, precisely *because* blindfold tests have shown that most smokers can't tell one brand from another. Yet the advertising appeal is so potent that "brand loyalty" among cigarette smokers is extremely high. The loyalty, of course, is not to the cigarette itself (which is indistinguishable from other cigarettes) but to an idea or "image" that has become attached to a particular brand name.

Changing the "Image" of a Product

Experience may show that the "image" which a particular product has acquired is not advantageous in terms of maximizing sales. In such a case, an effort may be made to give the product a different "personality" that will attract consumers.

Motivational researchers have tried to determine the "hidden meaning" that cigarettes have for typical smokers, and they have discovered that in many cases this form of tobacco is associated with potency and being in the prime of life. Youngsters start smoking in order to look and feel like full-grown men; many older smokers seem to feel, perhaps unconsciously, that cigarettes carry them back to a more youthful stage of life. Both groups are apparently aiming at the "prime years" of vigorous maturity which they have come to associate with the satisfaction of smoking cigarettes.* (This is particularly ironic in view of the connection of cigarettes with lung cancer and other diseases.)

On this basis, it was decided that an advertising campaign that presents a *strong masculine image* for a given cigarette brand would get at the "hidden meaning" of smoking for many consumers, and thus would be bound to boost sales. Such a campaign was launched some years ago for a brand of cigarettes that had been on the market for a long time but was lagging in sales. The new advertisements showed the cigarette being smoked by lean, tough men, particularly cowboys, in rugged, outdoor settings. Distinctive "gimmicks" were added, such as a tattoo shown on the arm of one of the smokers in every ad. Gradually the image of the cigarette was changed from the "sissy" category to "real he-man." And there was a sensational increase in sales which has been sustained over the years.

The Symbolic Value of Advertising

A *symbol* is something which is recognized as representing or standing for something else. An effective symbol can have great emotional force. How symbols work in the human mind has long fascinated psychologists — as well as poets, politicians, teachers, and more recently advertising men.

The cowboy in the cigarette advertising campaign described above is obviously a symbol of masculinity, toughness, and healthful, outdoor living. Note that the use of the symbol for this purpose is far more effective than a direct, literal statement would be. Obviously, it wouldn't do to say in so many words: "Smoke X-cigarettes and you will feel healthier and more sexually potent." Such a claim is too ridiculous to be taken seriously by anyone. But the closeup of the cowboy carries the same message in far more acceptable form. A cowboy already symbolizes fully the idea of masculinity — there is no need to add any words. And the same quality is transferred to the product

---

* For purposes of convenience, we shall limit this analysis of cigarette advertising to appeals which are directed specifically to males.

being advertised, thus appealing strongly to the fantasies of a great many men who may feel — consciously or unconsciously — that they are lacking in some degree of masculinity.

Take another example — a high-priced automobile. In advertisements, it is shown in front of elegant mansions, country clubs, and other locations suggestive of prestige, status, and "class." The people represented are handsome, "distinguished-looking" men in evening clothes, and attractive, beautifully gowned women. Every detail contributes to a complex symbol that spells *success, importance, money*. The suggestion is implanted with great persuasiveness that anyone who wants to announce to the world that he is "successful" can do so by owning and driving this car. He will not only raise his esteem in the eyes of others; he will enhance his *self-esteem*. The car becomes part of his *self-image*.

The use of such symbols in advertising is particularly helpful because they directly involve the person at whom they are directed — the potential purchaser. He is not merely passive in relation to the ad. He brings his own emotions and fantasies to complete the image suggested by the symbol. Virtually all of us, for example, have a vast store of memories, feelings, and other associations about cowboys, accumulated from all sorts of experience — old movies, books and stories, games and daydreams from the early days of childhood. If we are led to connect these recollections and fantasies with a particular product, that product becomes more attractive and distinctive — and under the right conditions, we are likely to buy it.

Effect of Color in Packaging and Advertising

Other types of stimuli in addition to evocative symbols are used in merchandising to influence consumers. One of the most important of these is color.

There is actually an agency called the Color Research Institute that specializes in testing colors as they affect choices made in the market place. Some of its findings are not too surprising. For example, they have found that most of us have a negative reaction to the color black. It has connotations of mourning, darkness, dirt, and other unhappy aspects of life. On the other hand, if the idea of "blackness" is attached to certain products (for example, black lingerie or a black evening gown), the reaction may become decidedly favorable.

Here is another Color Research Institute test whose results are much less predictable. Housewives were given three different boxes filled with detergent and were asked to report after a few weeks of use which had proved to be the best for laundering delicate fabrics. The housewives were told that the three detergents were different, but actually *they were identical, except for the color of the containers.* One

By a variety of psychological appeals — including slogans, packaging, and skillfully planted associations — the cigarette advertisers relentlessly pursue the consumer, especially young people. (This illustration is from a film entitled "Time for Decision," made by the American Cancer Society.)

container was mostly bright yellow; the second was blue with no yellow; and the third was blue with splashes of yellow. The majority of the housewives believed that the detergent in the brilliant yellow box was "too strong;" it even "ruined" the fabrics in some cases. As for the detergent in the blue box, the women complained that it didn't do a good job of cleaning; it left the fabrics "dirty-looking." The detergent in the blue-and-yellow box (identical to the other two samples, remember) received a strongly favorable response!

Getting at Unconscious Motivations

Motivational research has borrowed from psychology an analysis of three different levels of human consciousness which can be reached in designing an advertisement, a container or label, or an entire marketing approach.

The first of these is the *conscious, rational level*. This is where people are aware of their thinking and are able to give reasons for their decisions. Advertisements try to appeal to this type of response by making a factual presentation — by explaining on some objective basis why the product is worth buying. For example, an advertisement may summarize the results of a series of tests made by some outside agency. We are not suggesting that the claims made in such an advertisement are necessarily justified, but at least the approach is evidential and directed to the consumer's power of reason or judgment.

In many cases, however, the fact is that there *is* no reasonable basis for choosing one product over another — or indeed for buying that type of product of all. In such cases, the advertiser must aim at the two deeper layers of human consciousness.

The second level is called the *preconscious* level. (The term "subconscious" is used by some — it means the same thing.) This is the level at which the person is vaguely aware of his feelings, sensations, and attitudes but is not willing to bring them to the surface or to question them consciously. Preconscious fears, prejudices, and assumptions motivate much human behavior.

The third and deepest level is the *unconscious*. This is where we are not at all aware of our true feelings or attitudes. Unconscious motivations are primitive and primary; they include instinctual drives toward sex and aggression.

The two deeper layers of consciousness cannot be appealed to *directly*. An example of this can be seen in marketing campaigns which operate on the basis of fear. Many products are sold largely by playing on the individual's preconscious fear of social embarrassment;

mouthwashes, toothpastes, and deodorants are common examples. A direct approach would be: "Use Puro Soap so that you won't smell bad." But this is too obvious, too crude. It seems to be directed to the type of person who is *likely* to smell bad. How much more subtle and flattering to say: "Aren't you glad you use Puro? Don't you wish everyone did?" This addresses the consumer as someone who is too careful and fastidious to offend other people. So naturally he *already* uses Puro! The slogan plays on the fear of embarrassment indirectly by suggesting that unfortunately there *are* some people so lacking in the finer sensibilities that they neglect to use this soap — and of course they are offending others. The advertisement says in effect, "You're not one of *them,* are you?" The theory is that the typical consumer is likely to stammer, "Of course not!" And at the first opportunity he will run out to buy the magical protective soap.

Sex is another area that is exploited in advertising on the unconscious level, but the approach in this case must be very careful. The use of the "pretty girl" motif to sell everything under the sun, from cosmetics to insurance, is all but universal. On the other hand, any advertisement that is *too* blatant in its appeal to sexual motivations may offend many people and thus may actually do more harm than good.

"Does she . . . or doesn't she?" may not sound too risqué today, but in 1955 it was considered so suggestive that *Life* Magazine refused to run an advertisement for a hair-coloring product that used this slogan. The advertisement that was finally worked out (and used in a national campaign) was a clever compromise between sexual suggestion and "respectability." It was designed to make hair coloring

more acceptable to women who had previously considered it somewhat "cheap" and "flashy" but who nonetheless were eager to enhance their looks and perhaps to have a more active social life. The advertisement, with minor variations, showed a beautiful model with lovely colored hair — and a little girl (obviously her daughter) hanging on her arm. The idea was that the young woman shown, far from being of questionable "respectability," *was married and a mother.* This, by association, made hair coloring more in keeping with the self-image of large numbers of women who previously had been somewhat reluctant to use it. At the same time, the unavowed motivation for changing one's hair color — to feel younger and more sexually attractive — was hinted at by the teasing slogan, "Does she . . . or doesn't she?"

Later ads for the same product put the idea somewhat more directly: "Is it true blondes have more fun?"

Familiarization and Recognition

Although we have focused on appeals to the preconscious and unconscious in TV commercials and in printed advertisements, we should also recognize the fact that many advertising approaches succeed not through subtle suggestion but through sheer brute force of *repetition.*

Much advertising is based on the principle that it is all-important to make the brand name and the appearance of the package, or of the product itself, thoroughly familiar to the consumer. Then, when he goes into a drug store to buy toothpaste, for example, the brand name will "pop into his head." When he walks along the aisle of a supermarket and sees perhaps 20 competing brands of soap, arranged on the shelves, he is much more likely to pick up a "familiar" brand than one whose wrapper he has never seen before.

Psychologists who work in the field of consumer motivation are discovering ways of making the basic tool of repetition more effective. For example, they have found that using the same advertisement in one national magazine, and then in another magazine the following week, is much more effective than repeating the same ad in successive issues of the same magazine. This holds true even though it can be shown that many of the same people look at both magazines. The explanation is that the changed context creates an impression of newness in the minds of many consumers who see both publications. There is a vague sense that something is different and that they are not being asked to look again at "the same old thing." Thus the two advertisements make a greater impression.

Learning theorists have also discovered that loud, blaring commercials may be more effective in getting a message across than those which do not annoy the viewer. Learning, in the sense of influencing the consumer, proceeds better under conditions in which the subject matter is either *highly pleasing* or *highly displeasing* to the learner; results are likely to be much poorer when the learner feels *neutral* about the subject. Thus, annoying commercials are probably here to stay as long as you continue to watch TV.

Merchandising Political Candidates

Many observers of the American scene today are particularly troubled by the use of high-powered merchandising methods in political campaigns. We have seen in recent elections that political candidates may be "packaged" and "sold" to the voters, almost like so many brands of toothpaste or beer. This applies particularly to the use of political advertising on television. Candidates for national, state, and local offices now engage advertising agencies and spend large sums to prepare filmed sequences. These are carefully designed to present a favorable "image" of the candidate, just as though he were a product in a highly competitive market. Instead of longer presentations, which tend to bore many voters, there is now preference given to one-minute "spots" that stress a single theme, such as the candidate's fight against the drug traffic, or his good relations with minority groups, or his personal background. Then time is purchased on TV stations or networks, and the "spots" are shown again and again. Just as with a commercial product or service, the "prime time" is the mid-evening hours, when most people are watching. Also, it is considered advantageous to have the "paid political announcements" appear immediately before or after the most popular entertainment shows.

The appeal in these political announcements is far more to the unconscious emotional background of the voters than it is to any reasoned issue or argument. Nonetheless, there is no question that this type of "TV exposure" is effective in winning elections. This is particularly true for a candidate who begins the campaign as a relative unknown to the voting public.

The danger, of course, lies in the fact that a candidate may win or lose an election on the basis of qualities that have nothing to do with his fitness for the office being sought. What counts, in large part, is how much money he has to spend, how skillful the people are who prepare his materials, and how well he "goes over" on the TV screen (voice, appearance, personality, etc.). To some extent, factors such as these have always been important in American politics, but the

The Kennedy-Nixon television debates during the Presidential campaign of 1960 marked the advent of a new era in American political campaigning. It is generally agreed that Kennedy made a more favorable "impression" during these programs, and that this was a vital factor in his close victory. Many political analysts also believe that the advantage which Kennedy gained on this occasion had relatively little to do with the actual substance of what the two candidates said.

emergence of television as a tremendously powerful medium of mass communication has increased the chances for abuse.

This is why many observers now feel that we would do well to adopt a system similar to that prevailing in Great Britain. There, political candidates receive *free* a certain amount of TV time to appeal to the voters; they may appear individually or in debates with their opponents. *But no television time may be purchased for political purposes.*

Non-Logical Motivations

A famous Italian sociologist named Vilfredo Pareto (1848-1923) developed a theory that human activities and beliefs are basically of a non-logical nature. He carefully examined the key ideas of a number of world leaders of his day, as expressed in important public statements, all of which paid tribute to logic and rational thinking — and then tried to reconcile these ideas with what the men were actually doing. He came to the conclusion that their acts and policies were directed very little by any kind of logical thought processes. Like most other people in less conspicuous positions, they were controlled largely by motivations on an unconscious, emotional level.

Motivational researchers accept as a basic concept the fact that people are directed in this way. Ernest Dichter,* a pioneering motivational researcher writes, "Whatever your attitude toward modern psychology or psychoanalysis, it has been proved beyond any doubt that many of our daily decisions are governed by motivations over which we have no control and of which we are often quite unaware."

Professional "persuaders," such as advertising men and public relations experts, have tried to justify their work on the claim that "persuasion is an inseparable part of a democratic way of life" guaranteed by the Bill of Rights. They even assert that, in a free society, we are all "persuaders," trying to influence each other to our own ends. Thus, it is argued, the fact that some people are more adept or professional at persuasion than others should be no great cause for concern.

Many people *are* concerned, however, because the tools of persuasion have become so much more specialized and effective. Sophisticated applications of psychology and social sciences to the technique of influencing people have already transformed modern advertising, and there is promise of more to come as knowledge increases. The technological resources for spreading the "messages" (particularly television) are far more potent than in earlier generations. Moreover, these resources are being put to work to sell not merely products but also ideas, values, and political programs. Image-building, so successful in "putting over" brands of cigarettes otherwise virtually indistinguishable from competing brands, is now being used with great skill and energy to promote political candidacies. The basic premise of such campaigns (primarily on television) is that what counts is not the candidate himself but the "received image" of him projected on the minds of the viewer.

How Long to 1984?

There is certainly a danger that the methods of *emotional manipulation* we have been describing may be extended into other areas of our daily lives, controlling not only what we buy and how we vote but also our most basic attitudes, values, and desires. Such a nightmare world of ruthless exploitation of persuasion techniques through the mass media of communication was foreseen in George Orwell's novel *1984.*

---

* Ernest Dichter, *The Strategy of Desire* (Doubleday, 1960).

We can guard against this kind of abuse by sensible legislation and regulations, and also by preparing ourselves to recognize manipulative methods, and to reject them when they are obviously being employed for purposes of which we do not approve. Bear in mind that advertising which is designed to influence your decisions by manipulating your secret fears and desires can be successful only when you allow yourself to be controlled by such fears and desires.

There is some consolation in reflecting on the fact that techniques of persuasion may also be employed for purposes which most of us would consider worthy or positive — for example, campaigns to discourage cigarette smoking and to promote ecological reforms, better race relations, cleaning up our urban slums, and highway safety. This is not to say, however, that desirable social ends should be served by methods which are misleading or manipulative. Such causes can be furthered most effectively by appeals based on reason, on established facts, and on accepted human values.

The American Cancer Society uses the techniques of mass persuasion to warn people against the dangers of cigarettes, and in particular to induce young people not to start smoking.

THINGS TO DISCUSS :: THINGS TO DO :: THINGS TO READ

1. The Columbia University Survey of Broadcast Journalism recently referred to TV and radio advertisements as "messages lovingly fashioned to recommend the unnecessary to the unwitting, the superfluous to the superficial." Is this *necessarily* true? Is it *generally* true? Give examples of advertisements you have seen or heard recently that back up your evaluations.

2. "A large part of advertising is designed to exploit the tendency of most people to choose the familiar over the unfamiliar." Show how this will apply, for example, to a person buying aspirin in a drug store or canned soup in a supermarket. What psychological factors may be involved when a consumer shows an almost compulsive tendency to choose the familiar product or package, regardless of other factors?

   Do you think that this same psychological pattern may be involved in political contests? Explain.

3. Here is an experiment to try: Collect magazine or newspaper advertisements for ten different brands of cigarettes. Display these ads to the members of the class (or some other group). Then ask the subjects to rate the brands on a scale of 1 to 10, with 1 being the "most feminine" and 10 the "most masculine." Are there any brands which are consistently ranked high or low on this scale? If so, can you account for the "feminine" or "masculine" image on the basis of advertising?

   After this, ask a different group of subjects to rate the cigarette brands on the same 1-to-10 scale ranging from "weak" to "strong," but this time without reference to the ads. Are the "strong" cigarettes correlated with "masculine" and the "weak" with feminine? Or are there surprises? Discuss your results.

4. Ask a number of people of different ages and backgrounds which television commercial annoys them most, and which they like the most. Do people tend to remember annoying commercials as easily, or more easily, than entertaining ones? Do your data support the idea that a person will remember a commercial well even if he has a strongly unfavorable reaction to it?

READINGS

The Hidden Persuaders, by Vance Packard (David McKay, 1957) is now somewhat dated, but it is still a forceful and informed survey of how advertising and public relations experts think and function.

The Selling of the President — 1968, by Joe McGinnis (Trident, 1969) is one of the most provocative accounts of the use of the "merchandising" type of persuasion in politics. This book gives the inside story of how advertising men created a sequence of television commercials and appearances designed to produce a carefully controlled and directed "image" for a Presidential candidate. It is a fascinating and in some ways frightening book — particularly because we know that such methods are not limited to any particular campaign, candidate, or political party.

23

SEX
AND MORALITY

(WITH A BRIEF COMMENTARY
ON LOVE AND MARRIAGE)

● ●

"I lose my respect for the man who can make the mystery of sex the subject of a coarse jest, yet when you speak earnestly and seriously on the subject, is silent."

— HENRY DAVID THOREAU

The Sexual Revolution

We hear a great deal of talk these days about the "sexual revolution," especially in relation to young people. The changes supposedly involved in this "revolution" are usually not spelled out too clearly, but they appear to include the following: that young people today have much more sexual experience than was true of previous generations; that their attitude toward sex is more "healthy" and "natural" than in the past; that they have fewer sexual "hang-ups" than their elders; and above all that they *know* much more about sex — that they have substituted authentic information for the superstitions, delusions, half-truths, and utter ignorance that used to prevail among adolescents.

On this basis, there is good reason to assert that the much-publicized "sexual revolution" is largely a fraud. Young people today, like a great many older people, are still largely misinformed about sex, although they *do* tend to have sexual experiences earlier and more frequently. More sexual experience however, does not necessarily mean that a young person (or an older one) is more knowledgeable about sex.

As a matter of fact, the evidence now at hand suggests that the earlier boys and girls engage in sexual relations, the less they really know about the "facts of life." A typical finding in one high school

453

attended mainly by children of working class families showed that about 60% of the students acknowledged having had sexual relations. However, half of these sexually active students indicated on a questionnaire that they believed a girl can become pregnant only if she has sex relations during her menstrual period. (This, of course, is the time that she is *least* likely to become pregnant.) Many other equally flagrant misconceptions were widely accepted.

Young people from middle class families tend to have sexual relations at a later age and less frequently than their contemporaries from working class backgrounds, but they are more likely to have "hang-ups" that lead to problems in sexual adequacy when they become adults. This is not because they are less "experienced," but again because they are *ignorant of basic facts and ideas*.

Evidence of Sexual Irresponsibility

The White House Conference on Children, meeting in Washington, D. C. in December, 1970, published a paper entitled "Children and Health." On the basis of this, news stories appeared in newspapers throughout the country. One of them was:

VD RATE UP AMONG TEEN-AGERS

Three health associations have warned of a developing rise in the incidence of infectious syphilis and an epidemic of gonorrhea, which is soaring "clearly out of control" in the United States.

The warning was issued by the American Social Health Association, the American Public Health Association, and the American Venereal Disease Association, on the basis of information obtained from a survey of public health officials throughout the nation.

These authorities estimated that about 2 million cases of infectious venereal disease were treated in the United States in 1969. Statistics indicated that nearly 500,000 cases of gonorrhea and more than 18,000 cases of infectious syphilis were reported, with the actual numbers of cases estimated to be perhaps four times as high.

Here is another news story:

TEEN BIRTHS HIGH IN UNITED STATES

More pregnancies are reported among adolescent girls in the United States than for this age group in any other industrial nation.

This finding appeared in a recent report on "Maternal Nutrition and the Course of Human Pregnancy," prepared by the Committee on Maternal Nutrition of the National Research Council. The report also notes that poor nutrition and the youthfulness of the mother are major causes of low infant birth weight and poor pregnancy outcome.

Robert E. Shank, chairman of the Committee, cited 1965 figures showing 196,000 live births to girls 17 years of age or younger. "Average birth weight of these infants is substantially lower than that of infants born to older mothers," he said. "The proportion of low birth-weight infants is greater, and infant mortality rates are higher."

The evidence nationally is overwhelming that young people may be more sexually "free" but are no more knowledgeable and certainly appear to be no more "responsible" than the youth of earlier generations. The increasing incidence of venereal disease and of unwanted pregnancies, as well of cases of emotional problems related to sexual behavior, is clearly far greater than would be expected on the basis of population growth alone. And all too often there is a totally innocent victim, in the form of an infant who is physically subnormal and likely to be subjected to great handicaps and difficulties (if it survives at all).

The Information Gap

In the United States, the gap between available sex information and its communication to young people has not yet been bridged. Often, parents are unable to convey this information to their children simply, clearly, and without embarrassment — assuming of course that the parents actually know the facts.

The author became acutely aware of this lack of communication between parents and children when he interviewed hundreds of young people and their parents at a child guidance clinic. Most of the parents were well-educated people and said that they had "spoken" to their children about sex. Yet, not one of the children felt that his parents had communicated with him in a really helpful way. Most were embarrassed, disturbed, or bored by what turned out to be a parental "sermon."

Further exploration indicated that many boys felt compelled to pretend that they "knew all about sex." Admission of ignorance would have exposed them to what they regarded as an attack on their masculinity. Girls believed that they were generally prepared for the onset of menstruation, and had been provided with dark hints about the dangers of pregnancy, but they knew little or nothing about the wider implications of their sexuality. There was also a suggestion in many cases that this lack of knowledge was appropriate for girls and a testimony to their "virtue." In general, these young people had learned little beyond the physiology of human reproduction, and their information in this area was in the majority of cases far from complete and reliable.

In short, boys cannot admit that they don't know *everything,* and girls cannot publicly admit that they *are even interested.* What an irony in the midst of a "sexual revolution"!

Areas of Ignorance

During the years that the author served as a counselor and teacher in secondary schools and colleges, he was asked questions relating to sex by a great many students. Among the questions that occurred most often were these:

▶ How many times must a woman have sexual relations before she becomes pregnant?

▶ How can you tell if a girl or boy has a venereal disease?

▶ Is prolonged or excessive masturbation a danger to fertility, potency, or general health?

▶ During what periods of time are girls most likely to become pregnant, or capable of becoming pregnant?

All of these questions, of course, betray an ignorance of fundamental aspects of sex and reproduction in human beings. And even worse than mere ignorance is misinformation. Many young people do come up with "answers" to their questions based on what they hear from their contemporaries, on rumors, on miscellaneous references in books and in the mass media. At best, this kind of information is likely to be fragmentary and misleading. At worst, it leads to flagrantly wrong ideas. And of course the result of this can be misdirected attitudes, leading to inappropriate, self-damaging behavior.

Sex Education in the Schools?

The question then, is: Where are young people supposed to get the straight facts?

One possible answer is: From their parents. But unfortunately many parents are frightened, or at least uneasy, about "sex" in relation to their children. They really don't know how or what to tell their children about this area of life. They may expect the schools to help them out; or perhaps they wish that the entire subject would just "go away."

On the other hand, it is also true that a substantial number of parents are convinced that "sex education" is not a proper responsibility for the schools. They feel that anything so closely tied to moral principles should be left to the home and the church — that it is none of the business of the schools, especially public schools, which by definition are not supposed to present any sectarian religious teachings. Thus, sex education in the schools has become a controversial, and a highly emotional, issue in recent years.

On the other hand, there *is* a broad and solid area of support for sex education in the schools. Survey after survey conducted in schools and colleges reveal that at least 90% of the students, both boys and girls, believe that such courses are needed, and that they personally would like to be enrolled in them. Similarly, an overwhelming majority of the parents interviewed have indicated a strongly favorable attitude toward sex education in the schools.

In addition, an impressive array of national organizations have expressed approval of school programs of sex education. Among them are the American Medical Association, the National School Boards Association, the American Association of School Administrators, and the National Congress of Parents and Teachers. Just as significant is the support given by such broadly representative religious groups as the National Council of Churches, the Synagogue Council of America, and the United States Catholic Council. It is certainly a mistake to suggest that organized religion in this country views sex education in the schools as inappropriate or "immoral."

The mass media continue to play a major part in influencing the attitudes of young people toward romance, sex, and marriage. Is it possible that in the years ahead the schools will become increasingly influential in this area?

Common Questions About Sex

Of the many thousands of questions about sex presented to the author by young people, the following have been among the most common:

1. *Does frequent masturbation at any early age cause any harmful effects in later life?*

Masturbation means using the hands or some device to stimulate one's own sexual organs. No matter how often this is done, it does not cause *physical* harm. On the other hand, the sense of guilt or shame that some people feel about it may be psychologically harmful. Masturbation (for both males and females) may be considered a normal expression of sexuality. However, it ceases to be "normal" when it becomes compulsive (involuntary) and almost mechanical. In this case masturbation may serve as a means of avoiding mature life attachments, responsibilities, and fulfillments.

2. *Can a girl become pregnant when she has sexual intercourse for the first time?*

Yes. The fact is that the "first time" has no significance as far as pregnancy is concerned.

Indeed, during the child-bearing stage of life, there is no absolutely "safe" time for a female to have intercourse without risk of pregnancy. Proper use of contraceptives, however, will greatly reduce the risk. In addition, women whose menstrual periods occur regularly are less likely to become pregnant during that period, and for a few days before and after it.

3. *How can you tell if you have venereal disease (V.D.)?*

The two most common venereal diseases are *syphilis* and *gonorrhea*. They are contracted as a result of having sexual relations or other close physical contacts with an infected person.

The first sign of gonorrhea is usually a burning sensation in the sex organ during urination. This symptom is likely to be noted about two to six days after the individual has had sex relations with an infected person. Soon afterwards, pus is discharged from the sex organ. If the infection is not checked, it will spread to the deeper urinary and genital tissues.

The first sign of syphilis is the appearance of a single sore (chancre) at the site of infection, followed by a generalized body rash and inflammation of the mucous membranes. These symptoms occur from two to six weeks after the infecting contact. While these signs may disappear, they often are followed by fever, headaches, and sore throat.

If left untreated, gonorrhea and syphilis infections, despite eventual disappearance of the external signs, remain active in the body. They may do severe damage, causing insanity, blindness, paralysis, heart disorders, other crippling conditions, and even death. Moreover, the diseases, while not hereditary, may be transmitted by a mother to her fetus (unborn child), or during childbirth to the baby. Gonorrhea at one time caused many cases of blindness in newborn infants.

Venereal diseases are usually curable if they are discovered and treated in their early stages. Treatment now is usually by antibiotic drugs, especially penicillin.

One problem involved in control of venereal disease is that many infected women may not be aware of their condition because their symptoms are commonly not as well-established and as distressing as when they appear in males.

4. *What causes homosexuality? Can it be cured?*

A *homosexual* is a person (man or woman) whose sexual activities involve exclusively or mainly persons of the same sex.

The causes of homosexuality are not fully understood, but they are known to be complex, and they may differ widely from one person to another. Family experiences during early childhood are often at least a contributing factor. Purely physical (glandular) conditions appear to be of minor, if any, importance.

Homosexuals have existed in every culture and society. The ancient Greek culture (known for its intellectual and artistic achievements) found homosexuality acceptable. Our culture frowns on it, although in some quarters a more tolerant attitude seems to have developed in recent years.

It is known that homosexual experiences are fairly common during childhood and adolescence. The fact that a young person has had one or more experiences of this type certainly does not mean that he or she will eventually become an adult homosexual. Many young people who have had more than just a few homosexual experiences have been known to marry successfully and raise families. It is completely untrue that if you have homosexual thoughts or dreams, you must be a homosexual. Many mature people are aware of the fact that they have both homosexual and heterosexual impulses, even though the majority prefer sexual relations with members of the opposite sex. It is said that almost everyone has a "homosexual potential," which may manifest itself under certain conditions, such as prison confinement.

A few male homosexuals are easily recognizable because they make an attempt to look, walk, talk, and generally act like women. On the other hand, some "feminine-looking" men or "masculine-looking" women are thoroughly heterosexual, while a rugged, muscular, "all-American" type of man may be homosexual. Appearance is not the deciding factor.

At least one state (Illinois) has provided by law that homosexual relations between "consenting adults" are not a criminal offense. In the opinion of most students of sexual behavior, this is a far better approach than the traditional criminal prosecution of homosexuals. Such legislation is based on the premise that adult homosexuals who engage only in voluntary relations with other adults are not harming anyone, and that nothing is to be accomplished by treating them as criminals. (Homosexual *aggression,* particularly against minors, would of course remain a crime—but the same is true of acts of heterosexual aggression.)

Can homosexuality be cured? In recent years some encouraging results have been gained with male homosexuals who have wanted to change their sexual behavior. Treatments range from the traditional psychoanalytic method to directed psychotherapy, group therapy, behavior therapy, and any combination of these. Chemical treatment is not regarded as appropriate, since all the evidence indicates that the vast majority of homosexuals are biologically normal. The one characteristic that is considered essential for successful treatment is a strong desire on the part of the patient to change his or her sexual orientation—that is, to become a heterosexual. It is also helpful if the patient begins therapy at a relatively early age.

Less is known about therapy for women homosexuals because relatively few have volunteered for treatment.

5. *How is it that so many parents let their children find out about sex by themselves?*

Some parents are uncomfortable about sex.

Some parents think that sex is "dirty."

Some parents waited too long before they "dared" to talk about sex with their children, and when they finally did, found that their children were unwilling or too embarrassed to listen.

Many (perhaps *most*) parents simply do not know enough about sex to enable them to be comfortable in discussing it with children. Such discussions should have started when you asked your first questions. (When did you ask your "first questions"? Probably when you were about 4, 5 or 6 years old.)

Sex and a Code of Morality

There is ample evidence these days that more young people (teen-agers) are engaging in sexual activity than in previous generations. Does this mean that this form of "sexual freedom" is right? As a people, we Americans tend to be too much influenced by surveys which indicate what "the majority" is doing. You have to form or adopt your own moral standards on the basis of what you believe to be right, and sound, and healthy. Also, of course, you must consider the judgment of people whom you respect, including your parents, teachers, and others, possibly even the author of this book.

In developing your moral standards, you will want to bear in mind this fact: People who have studied the matter carefully over a period of years are in general agreement that sexual intercourse should be undertaken only when there is a deep and lasting relation between two people — not just infatuation or a sense of physical attraction. Intercourse without true affection and respect for the other person is little more than a mechanical act, and it is primarily exploitative. We mean by this that the sex partner is being *used* as a source of momentary physical gratification. The "exploiter" is concerned only about himself and disregards the needs, values, and human dignity of his partner.

This judgment, however, does not negate the fact that a significant number of young people not yet married are now in fact sexually active. Under these conditions, it is certainly advisable that young people have the benefit of authentic information about sex so that they will at least know how to minimize the chances of venereal infection and unwanted pregnancies.

But beyond this there is the more significant area of appreciating sex as an act of love, rather than of self-indulgence or exploitation. It is precisely here that there is a need for a vigorous, sincere, viable *code of morality*. Perhaps one of the best things that will come out of the current changes in moral standards and living patterns is the increasing refusal of "liberated" women to allow men to use (and abuse) their bodies without regard to mutual respect, to say nothing of love.

Love and Sex

We have been using the word "love" quite a few times without attempting to define it in any meaningful way. Yet it is a word that means a great deal to young people, and it is also unfortunately one of the most misused and degraded words in the language.

You can *love* many people in different ways — your parents, your friends, your relatives, your team mates, etc. However being "in love" usually refers to a powerful desire to be with, and to please another person of the opposite sex. When you are in love, you will be eager to win not only the affection but the respect of the other person. You will want him or her to be proud of you, in as many ways as possible.

Young people sometimes say (and believe) that they are in love, but then act in a way that is calculated to undermine the relationship. They may neglect their studies or their work; they may be careless about their appearance; they may be jealous, or irritable, or petty when they are with the other person; they may fail to keep promises or to assume obligations that are natural when people really love each other.

Such a pattern of behavior makes it quite clear that while there may be a strong attraction between the boy and girl, it is far too immature to be considered love. A person who is truly in love will be so intent on making himself the best possible partner for his loved one that he will be inspired to improve his work, to enhance his appearance, and to show the best side of his personality. He expresses his love, in short, by *trying in every way possible to make himself a better person,* so that he will be more worthy of the love that he wants to receive.

Real love must be a shared experience. It sometimes happens that a man falls in love with a woman who does not return his feeling (or vice versa). When this happens to a mature person, he will make a reasonable effort to evoke affection from the other person. If he fails, he will naturally be disappointed, but after a time he will in effect concede that he can't have what he wants, and will seek out another relationship.

In this connection, it is not true that "really" being in love is something that can happen only once in a lifetime. It is possible to be in love many times. Even an intense love affair, when it comes to an end, may be followed by another relationship that is even more deeply rooted and more emotionally and physically satisfying.

Marriage

In our culture, a genuine love relationship between a man and a woman is normally formalized in marriage. Yet marriage as an institution appears to be in trouble. It is estimated conservatively of all the marriages that took place in the United States within the last decade, about half have "gone on the rocks." About 30% have ended in

divorce or separation; 20% are being maintained unhappily and with great difficulty.

We cannot analyze here all the complex factors that cause marriages to fail. However one of the reasons certainly is that too many marriages are contracted impulsively without any real awareness of what is needed for a successful life union between a man and a woman.

Perhaps you feel that you have already found the person you want to marry. Or perhaps you will be contemplating matrimony only a few years from now. No one wants to "scare you off," but everyone who has your best interests at heart wants you to think very carefully and objectively before taking so important a step. Here is some advice that you might try to follow, even if it seems difficult.

DON'T GET MARRIED (at least for the time being) if one or more of the following conditions obtain:

▶ If you frequently have to ask questions like, "Do you love me?" "Do you *really* care about me?"

▶ If when you are together, you spend most of your time disagreeing and quarreling (even if you miss each other when you are not together).

▶ If you don't really know each other *as persons,* even though you have spent a great deal of time together.

▶ If you are both still very young (roughly, under 20). The majority of "young" marriages end in divorce or separation. Obviously, we don't mean that under-20 people in love should *never* get married. However, it is usually wise to wait until some career decision has been made, and both partners have had a few more years of experience in the "outside world" of work or college.

▶ If you don't get along with either your father or mother, and your prospective mate is "just like" that troublesome parent. Or if you are really marrying someone to "mother" or "father" you. Marriages of this type rarely work out.

▶ If you find that your decision to get married has been influenced in large measure by your prospective father-in-law or mother-in-law. Don't laugh! Not a few young people are led into matrimony by the warm acceptance, the flattery, the moral support, or even the cooking of a potential in-law.

"In a moment, I will pronounce you man and wife, but first I want to thank you for not regarding marriage as obsolete."

Copyright © 1971 Saturday Review, Inc. Cartoon by Herbert Goldberg.

▶ If you keep having thoughts like, "Maybe things will be better after we're married." It rarely happens!

▶ If your prospective mate has behavior traits that you "can't stand" (such as nonstop talking), but that you don't want to risk mentioning for fear of giving offense.

▶ If after marriage you plan to drop your present circle of friends and get by without much social life, except perhaps some new couples that you may meet. This is sometimes unavoidable — for example, if you must move to a new city — but experience has shown that couples who don't keep at least some of their old friends do tend to get bored with each other. For reasons that are not always clear, males need their male friends, and females their female friends. After marriage, both have a tendency to drop single friends of the opposite sex.

And that perhaps is enough in the way of DONT's.

DO MARRY if you believe firmly that you are in love (not just infatuated); if you really know your prospective mate (as a person, not just as an attractive specimen of the opposite sex); if you are old enough to be making realistic plans to be self-supporting; if you are prepared not only to enjoy the pleasure of marriage but also to accept its responsibilities, its strains, and even its boring routines.

Happy marriages may be getting rarer, but if you can achieve one, it will be a rich, rewarding, and mutually fulfilling experience.

THINGS TO DISCUSS :: THINGS TO DO :: THINGS TO READ

1. Does your school have a good sex education program? If not, do you think it should have one? Perhaps a suitable innovation would be an honest human reproduction sequence in the biology curriculum. Consider strategy issues. (Do you have to start with your parents?) Prepare yourself by learning more about the issues. For example, the July 1969 issue of *Psychology Today* was devoted to human sexuality.

2. A good basic "starter" in sex education is a publication entitled *Preparation for Marriage*. This is available at a charge of 50 cents from the American Medical Association, 535 North Dearborn St., Chicago, Ill. 60610; or from the National Education Association, 1201 Sixteenth St., N.W., Washington, D. C. 20005.

3. Following are some good sources of information in this area:

Family Life Division
United States Catholic
   Conference
1312 Massachusetts Avenue, N.W.
Washington, D. C. 20005

National Council of Churches
Commission on Marriage and
   Family
475 Riverside Drive
New York, N. Y. 10017

Synagogue Council of America
Committee on Family
235 Fifth Avenue
New York, N. Y. 10016

Sex Information and Education
   Council of the U. S.
1855 Broadway
New York, N. Y. 10023

American Association of Sex
   Educators and Counselors
815 15th St., N.W.
Washington, D. C. 20005

Child Study Association of America
9 East 89th St.
New York, N. Y. 10028

Family Planning and Population
   Information Center
760 Ostrom Ave.
Syracuse, N. Y. 13210

Write these agencies for literature. You will not necessarily agree with everything they have to say. (Indeed, they may not agree fully among themselves.) But the ideas and points of view they present are certainly worth considering.

4. What do you understand by a "code of morality"? Can you imagine any organized society operating without some accepted standards of sexual behavior? Explain. Do you agree with the judgment that we are now experiencing a drastic and lasting modification of traditional standards of sex morality?

5. It has been suggested that we no longer have a consensus as to what constitutes "morality" in our pluralistic society. Is it possible to live in a society with many moralities, or is there, in fact, only one "higher" morality?

6. Your parents may appreciate a good introductory discussion entitled *What to Tell Your Children About Sex* (published by the Child Study Association of America, 9 East 89 St., New York, N.Y. 10028). As a matter of fact, you may enjoy looking into this yourself.

A Parents'
and Teachers'
Guide
to What Goes On
in the Mind of a Child

WARNING TO STUDENTS

This chapter is written for your parents and teachers.
You can read it, too — especially if you plan to be a parent or teacher — but it is hoped that you will not use this material as a weapon against your parents or teachers, but rather to help them if they have problems.

I have been talking to teachers for many years, and almost invariably after a talk, at least one teacher would get up and say, "It's all very well for you to talk so glibly and give us all this good advice, but *you* don't have to teach a class."

For a long time, I didn't pay too much attention to this implied criticism. I wasn't interested in telling anyone how to teach a class. I was interested in psychology and psychological difficulties — in dealing with disciplinary problems, with the exceptional child, with the disadvantaged child. I finally sensed, however, that unless and until I went into a secondary school and tried to teach a class, I somehow had not fulfilled my obligations.

I recently taught for a year in a high school in a well-to-do suburb, where about 80% of the students go on to college, and the other 20% seem to get lost. I thought that we could offer a useful program for this "lost" 20% group of seniors. Most of them were unable to read above a grade-five level. They were mainly troublemakers — 17- and 18-year-old seniors who would be allowed to graduate because teachers had received the signal: "Let these guys through." It was agreed that I might offer them an enrichment course, an "Introduction to Psychology," in which we would talk about sex, the unconscious, hypnosis, and other intriguing subjects.

I soon found, however, that with all my realistic plans and good intentions, I couldn't get the boys and girls to listen to me. On the first day, I was greeted with, "Hi, Doc. I'm the class nut. Analyze me!" Another student said, "Hi, Doc. I run this class. Nobody teaches me anything without my permission." He was six feet three inches tall, and a star basketball player. Somewhat to my relief, he then said, "I'm going to have a little snooze, so you just go ahead." Soon he was snoring. I finally said, "Jimmy, how would you like me to analyze you?" He woke up fast. Yes, he was interested, and so were the other members of the class, who cheered him on.

Improvising, I said, "Jimmy, you have difficulty with your masculinity. You're trying to prove yourself all the time." After a moment he said, "You come to the bathroom and I'll prove it." I said, "I'm not interested in your anatomy but in your feelings."

Considering this statement, he replied, "Doc, in this class I'm the leader and speak for the feelings of everyone in it. We are the generation nobody cares about. But I will never let anybody forget us. I'll cause so much trouble that no one will be able to." The class was astonished. The whole atmosphere changed, but they all knew what he meant.

Subsequent sessions revealed that this "dumb" class included many bright young people who had the capacity to do college work. However, I discovered that these boys and girls wouldn't or couldn't pay attention to any teacher because *they equated learning with submission*. They felt that if they ever allowed anyone to teach them, they would be humiliated or even destroyed — their personalities would be degraded in the process. They were, naturally, quite unable to risk this, and consequently said "No" to anyone who approached them in the teacher-student relationship. This, in essence, was why these teen-agers couldn't learn.

Some children will equate education with submission as long as much of their education consists in denying the *impulse life* of the individual. Very often, we parents and teachers operate against the impulse life of children by acting as though their spontaneous thoughts, fantasies, and feelings are not acceptable or do not exist.

Let me cite some examples. Consider a four-year-old who has a nightmare and is very upset. His mother rushes into the bedroom and says, "You shouldn't be frightened. There's nothing to worry about." But the child *is* frightened and worried. He doesn't want to be told that he's "silly." He wants to be reassured in terms that will mean something to him. How much better, then, for the mother to say in effect: "Yes, it is very frightening to have a bad dream, but now it's over, and you're perfectly safe in your own home and your own bed. So go back to sleep, and you'll be all right. But I'll be right here to help you if you need me."

Another example: Two brothers fight constantly. Their mother is continually saying to them, "You shouldn't fight; you're brothers" — as though being brothers precluded any kind of disagreement. But there actually is a hate relationship between the boys. Each one's perception of the other is, "If my mother really loved *me,* she wouldn't have had another child." Recognizing this, the mother might say to each of the boys: "You don't have to like your brother. I hope you will, in time, but right now I can see that you don't feel good about each other. But even so, I don't want you to hit him, and I don't want him to hit you. It upsets me, and it makes it very hard for us to live together in this house, as we have to."

Now let's go back to a school situation. Susan comes home depressed and upset after the first day of school, and her mother says, "What's the matter, honey?" Susan answers, "I don't like my teacher. She's a nut!" The mother replies emphatically, "You mustn't say that!" But the child may be right. There *are* teachers who are emotionally unbalanced, and children are very quick to recognize such symptoms. So the mother might handle this situation by saying, "Oh, that's too bad. It's not nice to have a teacher you don't like. But she's still your teacher, and you may get to like her better in time. Meanwhile, I hope you won't punish yourself *twice* by not doing well in your studies."

We have a myth that only strict teachers are good teachers. Anyone who has spent much time in schools knows that this is wrong. There are wonderful teachers who are highly permissive, and equally good teachers who are strict. The same holds true in parenthood. In many years as a clinical psychologist, I have seen perfectly normal children come out of strict homes, but equally normal children come out of permissive homes. However, children do tend to grow up confused, unhappy, and neurotic when a parent is *insecure* about his or her role and behaves unnaturally toward members of the family.

Some parents have become all but paralyzed by an overabundance of advice. As a result, they are so self-conscious that they cannot respond in a spontaneous way to their own children. They are constantly fearful of "doing the wrong thing."

For example, suppose a 10-year-old girl comes to her mother and says, "All my friends are wearing lipstick and dating. Why can't I?" The mother knows this is absurd, but perhaps she remembers some scraps of "psychological" advice she has heard or read, and she decides to "explore the situation." So she says, "Well, which of your friends are dating?" At this stage, she has just about lost the argument and may be on the verge of making a serious mistake. She could have disposed of the whole thing very easily by saying firmly, "I don't care what your friends are doing. You're ten years old, and you're just too young for that kind of thing. Wait a few years."

The important thing, then, is not strictness or permissiveness as such but rather establishing and maintaining a reasonable, healthy balance between *control* and *acceptance*. Of course, children need to be told in no uncertain terms when their behavior is out of bounds — like the ten-year-old who wants to start dating. But if parents or other adults communicate that what *they* want the child to do at any given time is always right, and that what the *child* wants is uniformly wrong, the child will almost inevitably become hostile. If we try to "legislate" feelings and thoughts, and tell the child that his feelings and thoughts are worthless, he will naturally react angrily.

In contrast, a reasonable degree of acceptance of the child's own thoughts and feelings provides him with a sense of security. Children who are secure will learn in school, even if they do not have exceptionally talented or devoted teachers. (Most teachers are, by definition, "average.") Characteristic of the secure child is his inner striving to become a more complete person. Characteristic of the maladjusted child is his constant struggle against his mother, his father, and other authority figures.

Another example: Peter is an underachiever. He has a very high IQ, but his school work is poor. He is a handsome boy, with blond hair and blue eyes, and he inspires a "rescue fantasy" in his teacher. She calls him aside at the end of the school day and says to him, "Peter, you're such a nice boy, and you have a high IQ. I'm sure you could do your work well if you tried." With these remarks, the teacher has eliminated herself as an educative influence in the boy's life. All too often, he has heard almost precisely the same thing from his father and mother. As a matter of fact, in spite of his good mental capacities, he *cannot* do the work expected of him. He cannot study effectively. He cannot concentrate. It would be far better for the teacher to say, "Peter, it's hard for you to do the work, isn't it?" Then Peter might think, "This teacher understands me a little. Maybe she can help me." And this would represent at least a first step toward Peter's becoming educable.

But the teacher talks, and talks, and talks. She is not aware that perhaps the most frequent problem of a typical underachiever is *a mother who talks too much*. This mother may be a charming and intelligent woman, but to Peter she sounds like this: "Get up, Peter, you'll be late for school! Peter don't forget to brush your teeth! Peter,

I hope you'll be ready for the math test today!" And so forth . . . and so forth. Peter gets the idea that there is *nothing* he can do right on his own. And when he returns home after school, mother is *still* talking. Remember, if a child is insecure and maladjusted, the teacher is only too likely to continue and reinforce the influence (the *disturbing* influence) that his mother and father have had on him. If the child is secure and well-adjusted, he can have some conflict, or some sense of dissatisfaction with his teacher — and still do well in school.

Often our own stereotyped and repressed attitudes tend to prevent us from accepting the feelings and thoughts of children. For example, many parents and teachers are ill-prepared to cope with the ordinary problems of sex in relation to children.

Consider, for example, Ralph, a nine-year-old, who is caught in class drawing a "dirty picture." The teacher gets very excited. She snatches the picture from the boy's hands. (In this country a prosecutor needs "evidence"!) Aside from disturbing Ralph unduly, the teacher has revealed to the class that *she* has a sex problem. She rushes the boy to the principal, who also shows disturbance, indicating that he too feels threatened by the question of sex. And what are the effects of all this furor on poor Ralph? How is he to develop normal, healthy attitudes toward sexuality when all this evidence indicates that the adults on whom he is supposed to model himself are so obviously "uptight" about the subject?

And this brings us directly to a basic truth that lies at the heart of many, many such situations: *There is no such thing as an abnormal or dirty thought.* What a powerful impact it would have on the mental health of our society if only more of us could accept this and could convey it to our children! Thoughts of sex, of death, and of aggression stem primarily from the unconscious, and they become abnormal only as a child feels guilty and becomes preoccupied with them. It is not hard to teach a child the difference between *fantasy* and *behavior*. We can get him to understand that while his *fantasies,* whatever they may be, are normal, his *behavior* must be modified by social custom and by a sensitive appreciation of the rights, worth, and dignity of others.

A good teacher can be the single most helpful and stabilizing influence in a child's life. Some children seen in mental health clinics are manifestly more adequate and mature than their parents. Where did they acquire this ability to deal with life? In nine cases out of ten, it turns out that it was a teacher who had this beneficial effect.

Of course, even resourceful and generally successful teachers cannot always assess in advance the effect they will have on *particular* children. Some time ago, I saw a piece of writing produced by 10-year-old Linda. Her class had been asked to write a composition on

"What I Think of My Teacher," and Linda had chosen to use the theme "My Teacher Is a Witch." I thought I should meet this "witch," and I visited the school. The principal said, "Oh, you're going to meet Miss Roth. She's a lovely young lady, and one of our best and most popular teachers." Scarcely a "witch"! Yet Linda was obviously disturbed about her. Why? It turned out that Miss Roth liked to tell jokes in class. Most of the children enjoyed them, but Linda somehow got the idea that *she* was the butt of the jokes — that everyone was laughing at *her*. Naturally, she was deeply upset. So, even with a fine teacher in a fine school, there may well be children who cannot respond positively if they are emotionally disturbed when they enter the classroom.

The teacher is responsible for developing the kind of classroom atmosphere that supports feelings of personal adequacy in children. Through his relationship with the individual child, the teacher can contribute toward the development of those positive feelings toward self and others that are favorable to learning. Certainly the more positive the child's perception of his teacher's feelings, the higher his achievement is likely to be. It may be hypothesized that the child learns what he perceives he is *able* to learn, and that such self-perception is acquired during the interaction with "significant others," who hold expectations of the child as a learner. Further evidence suggests that teachers, through their role as "significant others," can enhance the self-image of their pupils by creating an atmosphere of greater psychological security.

It is not crucial how teachers deal with students who are reasonably well-adjusted — that is, who already have a good self-image. Such children do not present the critical challenge in our schools today. It is certainly true that they will learn better with a highly sympathetic and inspiring teacher, but it is also true that they will learn in spite of having a teacher of modest qualifications, or even an out-and-out bad teacher. The real challenge is to educate the child who has a conviction of inadequacy, who feels insecure. This does not mean that educators should seek to erase or make over their own personalities in order to meet the needs of poorly motivated children. What it does mean is that teachers must come to a better understanding of themselves and of their own perception of children.

Some years ago, I visited an elementary school located in a predominantly black neighborhood of New York City and observed two first-grade classes. The children were all black and had been assigned at random to the two classes. One of the two teachers was an attractive, warm person and was very cordial to me. She had had 15 years of experience and showed a thoroughly professional attitude toward her job. She said to me, "I feel deeply troubled about these

"Someone told him we're over thirty!"

children. They come to school hungry and poorly dressed. Fully a third of them don't have fathers in their homes. My heart goes out to them — sometimes I just have to take money from my own pocket and give them milk in the morning because I know they haven't had any real breakfast. How can you teach children like these, to whom such terrible things are always happening?" And, as a matter of fact, less than half of her children had made satisfactory reading progress at the end of the first grade.

The teacher of the other first-grade class was a much less amiable woman. She didn't receive me too graciously, and I didn't particularly like her. But she said to me, "I don't care what you or anyone else thinks. I don't care where these children come from, or whether they have two parents at home. I don't care how they're dressed, or what they do when they leave here. *Come what may, every one of my children is going to learn to read!*" And all but a few of them did.

This story shows with almost painful clarity that what counts in an educational situation is not sympathy or good intentions but *one's perception of what can be done.*

However, there are no absolutes in education, or in any other area of life. In every setting, there will probably be a number of children who will be unable to learn satisfactorily with any teacher because of certain psychological or physical problems. If we, as parents and educators, are to have a beneficial impact on children, we must get through to the individual — through to his emotional life — through to his impulse life. And, as we have noted, this means as a practical matter getting through specifically to those children who are not adequately motivated.

The Psychology
of a New Experience

(A Personal Statement)

●●●●●●●●●●●●●●●●●●●●●●●●●

> *"Unexpected travel suggestions are dancing lessons from God."*
>
> — KURT VONNEGUT

This chapter and the one following should be approached not as a body of subject matter to be "covered" but as a personal statement from the author to the student.

If this book has a central theme, it is simply this: *Broaden your world!*

Any issue of a daily newspaper will indicate to you that our world is full of weirdos who claim to have solutions for everyone else's problems. With all these people offering us happiness by means of reading certain books, eating certain foods, believing in certain prophets, adopting certain hair styles, or watching certain stars, it's little wonder that life remains full of uncertainties. I think the message of psychology is that each human being tends to be so mixed up that he must put a lot of energy into just getting himself together. The less "together" he is, the more of his time is spent unproductively in being angry. He is too angry for love or rewarding new experiences. His world contracts, rather than broadens.

Our everyday speech is studded with platitudes, many of which are perfectly true. A few samples: If you want something done, ask a busy person to do it. If you need support, you don't seek it from someone who can't even support himself. People who hate themselves hate a lot of other people in the process.

It took me a long time to discover this. I remember one day of "terrific insight" many years ago — sitting around a swimming pool with a friend. What a time we had! We spent four hours explaining to each other why we hated and despised most of the people at the pool, until it dawned on us that all these people we were putting down were having a good time swimming and enjoying each other's company, while we were building up reasons for not liking them. What a waste of time!

Psychology opens up the world — including our dreams, our fantasies, our wishes — and this melange of experience helps us in the never-ending process of defining ourselves. If this definition excludes fantasies or awareness of the infinite number of possible events, opportunities, and kinds of knowledge, then life becomes limited, and therefore boring and tiring. If our personalities are dominated by self-doubts, fears, and compulsions, we become so busy protecting, hiding, or kidding ourselves that we fail to do the things we can do. And the things we *do* get around to doing tend to be self-destructive or exploitative of others.

These are difficulties and problems that everyone has to face. In addition, if someone has to worry about being poor, or a victim of discrimination, life is really rough. People who have a keen awareness of being victimized are seldom "nice people." But the *victimizers* are probably a lot worse. They may devote a lot of time and energy to projecting themselves as "good citizens," but their whole point of view and life style are opposed to the rationale of a working human community.

I feel that life is complicated and ambiguous. Life is not a meaning but an *opportunity* (at least it should be!) to convert random experiences into a meaningful pattern. But getting your life together doesn't mean that you can't enjoy contradictions, offhand impulses, or unrelated and isolated experiences. Sometimes I meet someone for a moment, and it's "love at first sight," even though I know I may never see that person again. Sometimes I think about being a poet and write a lot of poems, although I know full well that I am not a poet. I sense that writing poetry "for real" is an intensely serious occupation, while I write poems without any really serious intention.

But that doesn't mean that I'm not a photographer. Look at the photographs on the following page. I started out knowing next to nothing about photography, but the idea fascinated me, and I had an impulse to express the fascination by taking fascinating pictures. The result: A new experience!

I remember surviving my high school days by daydreaming a lot. It was the only relief I had from hating everyone. (I was *really* messed up when I was a kid!) But, you know, I feel younger now than I did

in those d 's. I do a lot of things I like, and I am very seldom tired. In those days I hated (not necessarily in the order given) —

> French
> Geometry
> Algebra
> Shakespeare
> Music
> Art
> Literature
> History
> People *and*
> Teachers

So I daydreamed and read a lot of books that had sad endings.

Later, much later, when I was in France, I was angry at myself because I didn't know enough French to be able to communicate, to some degree, in that language. Later, even later than I care to admit, I was tricked into seeing a Shakespearean play, and I loved it. A new experience! Now *I* trick people into having new experiences whenever I can.

When I was teaching in a high school, I "assigned" new experiences. Here is a typical "assignment" from those days:

> You are required, in order to pass this course, to have several new experiences.
>
> Write a brief psychological report on three such experiences which you have actually had. Choose from the following:
>
> 1. Even if you don't like poetry (or perhaps *particularly* if you don't like poetry), read a poem carefully from beginning to end. What is the poet trying to say to you?
> 2. If you think of yourself as a "liberal" in political and social terms read from cover to cover an issue of the *National Review*.
> 3. If you are conservatively inclined, read from cover to cover an issue of the *New Republic* or *The Nation*.
> 4. If the only time you've ever been to an art museum is when someone (a parent? a teacher?) dragged you into one — visit a large art museum. Spend part of your time trying to figure out why people visit art museums _voluntarily_.
> 5. Attend a ballet performance.
> 6. Sit through an entire opera, such as *Aida*. Or, if this is not possible, listen to a recording of the entire opera.

7. Obtain a copy of the Sunday *New York Times,* and spend four hours finding out why it is one of the world's most prestigious newspapers.
8. If your everyday personality inclines to be grumpy, spend a whole day deliberately being nice to people.
9. If you have not been getting along well with your parents recently, try being *really polite* to them for two days. (Politeness is a sort of formula for achieving a little harmonious distance in personal relations. It is not an end in itself but rather a preliminary to getting closer together — or moving still farther apart.)
10. If you have the conviction that people should love you for what you are — rather than for how you dress or act — try dressing and acting conventionally for a week. Note carefully the responses you get from people who, you assumed, were either indifferent or hostile.
11. Go to a local bookstore and ask for a copy of *The Last Whole Earth Catalog.* (If your bookseller doesn't carry it, make it clear to him that you think he should.) Then have a good time going through it.

What is the point of all this? Simply that whatever you may decide to do with your life, the choice should be made on the basis of a *wide range of possible alternatives.* If your experience is narrow, constricting, routinized, you may miss out on some of the very best possibilities open to you. Above all, don't decide in advance on the things you hate and "will always hate."

In short, get out of your rut. Or, better still, try not to get into a rut in the first place.

There are so many things you can try with limited effort and little or no expense. Some of them, at least, are bound to be rewarding to you. Here are some examples:

1. Keep a diary.
2. Remember dreams.
3. Learn a new word each day.
4. Photograph trees.
5. Photograph people.
6. Write one poem.
7. Write two poems.
8. Fly a kite.
9. Say hello to a person you think you should hate.
10. Write a letter to your Congressman (or to your representative in the State Legislature) on something you *really* care about.

11. Choose a foreign country to visit. Learn as much as you can about it. (Later on you can start worrying about how you're going to get there.)

12. Read a short book, such as *Love Story* by Erich Segal. Then try to figure out why so many people (including quite possibly *you*) liked such a "corny" book.

13. If you "owe" a letter to someone, sit down and write it.

14. Write me a letter.

15. See a foreign film.

16. See a Charlie Chaplin film. Can you appreciate why such a film, from the "primitive" days of movie-making, still has many admirers?

A Chaplin classic — scene from *The Gold Rush* (1925).

17. See any film which has been highly praised by a reviewer (or by any other person) whose opinion you respect. Do you agree with the praise?

18. If you have a chance, sample some foreign cuisine that you're not familiar with—Japanese, Polynesian, Mexican, etc. Don't decide in advance that you "don't like the food." Give yourself a chance to enjoy it. Remember—millions of people *do* like it.

19. Attend a religious service of some sect or denomination that you're not too familiar with.

20. Fall in love with someone, and then dream or write about it.

People who are bored are boring. People who are down on themselves get other people down. There is really no need for you to be either bored, boring, or down on yourself. *Live a little!*

Here are some of the things I love in life. (It's a very partial listing in no particular order.)

> The Declaration of Independence.
> Marc Chagall.
> Chocolate cake.
> Some students.
> The Sunday *New York Times.*
> Money that's for spending (*not* saving in the bank for my old age, or for my wife's old age, or for my son to inherit).
> My wife.
> T. S. Eliot.
> Leonard Cohen.
> The New York City Ballet (or any other really first-rate ballet company).
> Mozart.
> What used to be the Beatles. (But since they broke up and began to act like *people,* I have second thoughts. So I really should have written "the old Beatle records.")
> Syracuse (the University, not the climate).
> San Francisco, but Jerusalem even more.
> London.
> A bunch of people who remain unnamed.
> Being funny (sometimes).
> Getting high without drugs.
> Chicago when the wind doesn't blow.
> The Mississippi River and a certain restaurant that overlooks it.
> Hot baths.

How about drawing up a list of your own? But don't regard it as final. The longer you can make the list — the more spontaneously you can extend it — the more new areas you can enter, the more indication you will have that you are growing as a person and building your capacity to enjoy and to contribute to life.

26

DISCOVERING
Who YOU Are

(A How-Not-to-Do-It Guide to What You Really Want to Do)
● ●

This is another "I" chapter. Many of the things I feel are important about life as I approach the end of my fifth decade will be squeezed into the next few pages. I like doing this because I have an audience to influence.

Don't trust anyone who says that he is not trying to influence you. Be especially critical of people who claim that they are fair, objective, perfectly disinterested, and who begin sentences with "To tell the truth. . . ." Never, never trust anyone who says, "You can trust *me*."

Are you a little disturbed now? Why should you be? *I* haven't asked you to trust me. Besides, although I do give advice, I give only advice that people find hard to follow. When is the last time that someone said to you, "Don't worry . . .," and you actually *didn't* worry?

I have too much respect for the complexity of personality to expect that my advice will enable people to overcome their problems easily and painlessly. For example, I offer gems like the following:

▶ For those of you worried about gaining weight: *Don't eat so much.*

▶ For those of you worried about sex: *Think of something else.*

▶ For those of you who feel that life is passing you by: *Try to make the most of it.*

I think that if people can, in fact, follow your advice without much effort or strain, you are insulting them by offering it. The only advice worth giving is advice that is *hard to follow*.

481

Not advice like —

BE GOOD.

PAY ATTENTION.

which is never worthwhile, *BUT*

WAIT....

When you base your behavior on trust (of someone else), you are often in effect trying to avoid responsibility. If you want to do something, do it as a risk, as an unselfish act, as an opportunity — but *not* because someone asked you to trust him. The responsibility for what you do should be yours.

Say (to yourself): "I am telling you (a friend) my innermost secrets because I have a need to tell someone, and because I am willing to risk the possibility that you may betray me. If you do betray me, I will be hurt and disappointed. If you prove to be a good friend, I will be joyful." But please *don't* say (or whimper): "I told you my secrets because I trusted you, and look what you did!" Or, the ultimate immaturity: "Now I can't trust anyone!" *Translation*: I will act as though everyone hates me.

I don't really expect anyone who has been "operating" on trust to follow my advice. We all have a tendency to repeat our "mistakes." (Freud called it a *repetition compulsion*.) The fact that I may say *"Don't"* certainly doesn't mean that you *won't*. Life is complicated. Much of our behavior is influenced by forces which we may not understand or even be aware of. But behavior *can* be changed if we work at it, and if we are willing to pay the price for change.

I repeat: Don't do anything on trust alone. You will continue to trust, but if it doesn't work out, you may remember this advice. Later, after more mistakes, you may be able to change your behavior for the better. The price? The change may make you tense, nervous, generally uncomfortable. It's hard to abandon a familiar pattern. The reason people overeat is that eating relieves tension. If you reduce your accustomed intake, you may become very anxious. The ability to tolerate the anxiety is the price you must pay for the desired weight reduction.

Sometimes, no matter how hard you try, and despite your best intentions, you will find that you can't modify the behavior you find unacceptable. This is because your personality *needs* that behavior. It is serving you as a defense against some worry or fear that you are not yet prepared to live with. For example:

A young man with a speech defect discovers that he does not really want to stop stuttering because he needs the handicap so that people can feel sorry for him. No amount of speech therapy will help him until he can gain some confidence in himself.

A mother overprotects her child because she has never felt secure as a mother, and she has convinced herself that if anything happens to the child, it will be "her fault." Telling her that she is being overprotective will fall on deaf ears until she works out the problem of her own insecurity.

These two examples illustrate conflicts that often require professional care — a trained social worker, a psychologist, a counselor, or a psychiatrist.

So one thing I am saying is that if you can't work out your problems by yourself, or with the help of parents or friends, seek out professional guidance. But (*Warning!*) do not respond to your impulse to trust (or not to trust) the helper. Tell him what is on your mind, but remember that you are assuming risks. There is the risk that —

The helper will not understand.

He won't have the time or the interest to make the necessary effort to help you.

For any one of a number of reasons, he may not be able to help. But it is worthwhile to assume these risks because you don't want to miss out on an opportunity, on the possibility that —

The helper will like you.

He will help you.

He will enable you to change your life for the better.

Now I will devote the rest of this chapter to giving advice to people who can profit from advice that is awfully hard to follow.

Do you find yourself looking for yourself? What does that mean? I'm not even sure that *I* know, but the fact is that many young people come to me and say that they can't "find themselves," or that life has "no meaning" for them. They want to "get it together," and perhaps they try to accomplish this by going on a "trip." Sometimes after the trip, they come to me and confess, "I've never been so lonely and unhappy in my life."

My answer: "Life is not a meaning; it is an *opportunity*. Life is made up of a series of meaningful experiences which are often of brief duration."

People who are "messed up" spend most of their time and energy hurting themselves and others. Their behavior tends to be involuntary, repetitive, and exploitative. For example:

A boy hooked on heroin lies to his parents and friends about how he is going to change. He supports his habit by stealing and by borrowing money which he will never return. He hates himself because he is being hateful — most of all to people who care about him.

A girl spends most of her time thinking about the people who hate her. All of the people who are supposed to be busy hating her scarcely know that she exists.

A boy finds school "irrelevant," the world "meaningless." He spends most of his time sleeping, *not* doing his school work, and quarreling with his mother and brother. He is so busy *not* doing things and fighting that he has no time for friends and pleasure. He is currently angry because his parents are unwilling to reward him for his hostility by giving him a motorcycle (and some "eating money" besides), so that he can travel about the country "finding himself."

A pretty girl is fed up with all the superficialities she finds in life. She says that she wants to be liked and appreciated for "her own sake." She wants to be "appreciated for herself" — not for her looks. So she makes it a point to dress sloppily, to neglect her hair, and even not to wash too often. She has come to be accepted more or less as "one of the boys," but she is secretly unhappy because none of the "boys" wants to take her out.

If you are in a situation that is bad, try to improve it. If you can't, it may be because you are too young, too inexperienced, too weak, too timid. It may also be that the reason is not any shortcoming of yours but simply that the odds against you are too heavy. (This may be true in some families, schools, communities.) Then you'll have to discover strategies of toleration and compromise. But in any case —

DON'T PUNISH YOURSELF!

because of someone else's problem or disaster. Here are some specific instances:

If there's a course in school you particularly dislike, make it a special point to pass it. Why punish yourself twice by having to take it over again?

Complete your school assignments on Saturday, and resolve not to do any work on Sunday. Why did you deceive yourself in the first place by "promising" to work on both days? Why spoil the entire weekend feeling guilty about not getting down to any work at all?

"Before you have your teach-in, think-in, love-in, or whatever, it's garbage out."

Agree to take out the garbage when your mother asks you to. Don't say, "I'll do it later," when you know that at least half the time you forget. Then mother or your unfavorite brother will do it just as you are about to go for it. The hassle afterward is often much worse than any inconvenience you might have suffered by doing the task in the first place.

Don't continue a relationship simply because you don't want to hurt the other person's feelings. This is punishing yourself as well as the other person and gives you a false sense of being "nice."

Sometimes it is possible to change things and feel good about it. One group of high school students persisted in their demands for a change in the school's dress code — and won. Another group brought about the introduction of "Black Studies." Another is still struggling for a more flexible curriculum. The point is not that any one of these innovations is *necessarily* of great value, but rather that the young people involved *thought* the change would be worthwhile, and did something effective to bring it about.

Feeling rotten about yourself, whether expressed in terms of "The world is evil," "School is irrelevant," or "There's nothing we can do about it," is no more than a cop-out. There *are* times, to be sure, when there isn't much you can do about the "outside world" except wait until you have adult status and power. But what you *do* in the meantime determines very largely what will happen in your future. If you are neglecting your schoolwork on the theory that you'll reform when you get to college ("*Then* I'll study"), the chances are that you won't ever get there, or that you won't last very long if you do.

It is not too difficult to know when you are doing the wrong thing. (You really have to be in a bad way *not* to know.) But if you want the reassurance of a checklist here it is. The chances are that if you are not doing what is right for you, symptoms such as the following will appear in your behavior:

> Over-dependency, over-eating, over-sleeping, over-talking.
> Fear of high, low, tight, empty places.
> Anxiety.
> Underachievement.
> Loneliness.
> Accident proneness.
> Tension headaches.
> Sexual hangups.

Some other familiar symptoms of being off the track include boasting (*What a bore!*), not having anything to do (*What a drag!*), and not ever enjoying being alone (*What a pity!*).

We all get depressed at times. Sometimes the feeling of being "down in the dumps" lasts a long time. Professional help may be needed to get a person out of it, but more often than not a welcome event, such as an unexpected invitation or an opportune phone call, will be enough to put him in good spirits.

Let me, however, suggest a strategy that can occasionally be used to good effect to speed up getting back into the swing of things. You are depressed, moody, upset, irritable, mean, or whatever. Drink or eat something sweet. It will give you some added energy and a feeling of well-being. The mood will rarely last more than a few minutes — but even this is enough to enable you to *learn something*. Look up a word in a dictionary; glance at an encyclopedia, almanac, or one of the news weeklies; direct a question about something that interests you to a friend or a member of your family. The next step may be to call someone you like and have a long conversation, or to go out for a walk. Before you know it, the down cycle will be broken. The more you do, the better you feel. This is especially true of people who spend a lot of time thinking about what they'd like to do, or about all the things that make them feel guilty. (These are often people who are obsessively thinking the same thing over and over again.) Bear in mind that even if you have a lot of insight (self-awareness), it is of little practical value unless you can *act on it*.

Another strategy will illustrate a psychologically sound approach that helps to overcome "normal" problems of everyday life. All of us at times find trouble in falling asleep or remaining asleep for an adequate period. Here's a procedure that works (for non-insomniacs).

On an evening that you "just can't fall asleep" — get out of bed, and try *not* to fall asleep. Drink some milk (warm, if you can stand it), and then take a leisurely hot bath (a shower only if a bath is not available). Then read a chapter in an interesting book. Soon you will feel very tired and ready to fall asleep. Even if you sleep solidly for only four hours, you will feel much more rested than if you were to be in bed for eight or nine hours while tossing and turning most of the night.

You don't have to be a big-shot psychologist to appreciate that the process of *not* learning is exhausting. Students who don't learn much at school are "worn out" at the end of the school day. If you want plenty of energy for after-school activities, make sure that your time in the classroom, lab, and library is as profitable as possible.

Are you sleeping more than you know you should — say, twelve hours a day or more? If you actually need this much sleep for physical reasons, you will wake up refreshed. But you may be extending your sleep because you are psychologically afraid to face the next day. The symptom of this is unmistakable: *You'll wake up tired.*

If you have a persistent unpleasant dream or nightmare, your unconscious is giving you a message to the effect that you have an unresolved conflict. When you resolve the conflict, the repetitive dream will disappear.

Real guilt can be distinguished from "fake" guilt by how you handle it. Genuine guilt enables you to organize yourself for some kind of action. It helps you to avoid making the same mistake again, and it has a tendency eventually to make you feel a little better about yourself. Phony guilt encourages a tendency toward self-pity, or a wish for punishment, so that you can feel free to make the same mistake again. Rational guilt, which you should feel after doing something wrong, is healthy. Irrational guilt is an emotion you feel even when you haven't done anything wrong. Perhaps the worst manifestation of this is feeling guilty about thoughts and fantasies. Such guilt always makes you feel rotten about yourself, and it is the energy of the "rottenness" that keeps the guilt alive and you unwell.

What a person *says* is not unimportant, but what counts to a far greater extent is what he *does*. Sometimes even "negative behavior," such as forgetting or mere passivity, may communicate more hostility than a big verbal argument. "I love you" is a beautiful sentiment, but it is worth only as much as its expression in day-to-day behavior.

Are you still looking for yourself or for the meaning in life? I hope so because finding the "meaning in life" is a life-long effort which consists of trying to put together meaningful experiences. "Getting it together" is life itself.

There is no way of completely avoiding tensions, frustrations, and upsets, but when these become the dominant forces in your life, you find yourself saying, "Life has no meaning," or "Everybody hates me." People who are striving to find meaning in a mature way are those whose life is made up of meaningful choices. They always have more to do than there is time to do it in. They have alternatives. They take risks. They can enjoy being alone at times. They know that when it is more important to them to meet the needs of some other person than to satisfy their own needs, they are in love.

If you don't feel that your life pattern has just been described, at least in general terms, work to make it more psychologically healthy.

It's hard work. If you have a genuine problem, the shift from conflict to health rarely occurs spontaneously. The shift usually requires boring, mechanical, and tension-producing work to resolve the conflict. For example:

> If your hangup is studying, and it is important *for you* to do your school work — very seldom will you reach a point where you really feel like doing it. You must do it despite your feeling of not wanting to. Set yourself realistic goals. "I'll study for 30 minutes, then I'll watch TV for 30 minutes, then I'll study for 40 minutes, and then I'll eat a snack", etc. "I'm going to study for four hours straight" usually ends up in not studying at all.

> If your hangup is being afraid of members of the opposite sex, there is no way you are going to feel comfortable with them without having a lot of experience of being comfortable with yourself first, being comfortable with members of your own sex second, and *then* slowly working through your conflicts with the opposite sex. Upon reaching the third stage you can't help but feel uncomfortable and awkward on your first dates. But unless you are willing to *risk rejection,* you won't even reach the stage of your first date. What is not often understood is that risking *rejection* is also risking *acceptance.*

How you feel about something is no substitute for the hard, anxiety-producing, and often mechanical work required for problem-solving. Spontaneity develops after the conflict is resolved. Spontaneity is seldom the medium for conflict resolution.

If you are curious as to how I feel about my own self at this stage of my life, let me borrow the talents of a noted writer to express it:

When I take a long look at my life, as though from outside, it does not appear particularly happy. Yet I am even less justified in calling it unhappy, despite all its mistakes. After all, it is foolish to keep probing for happiness or unhappiness, for it seems to me it would be hard to exchange the unhappiest days of my life for all the happy ones. If what matters in a person's existence is to accept the inevitable consciously, to taste the good and bad to the full and to make for oneself a more individual, unaccidental and inward destiny alongside one's external fate, then my life has been neither empty nor worthless. Even if, as it is decreed by the gods, fate has inexorably trod over my external existence as it does with everyone, my inner life has been of my own making. I deserve its sweetness and bitterness and accept full responsibility for it.

HERMANN HESSE (*Gertrude*)

This last chapter of our book has no assignment, except:

Go find yourself!

But wait! As one final "service," let me list for you some of my favorite novels, all of which have influenced me more than any course I have ever taken in psychology. They are not all "great" books (some of them are), but they all have great potential value in helping you to get a better idea of yourself. I hope you read some or all of them.

J. D. Salinger, *The Catcher in the Rye*
Ken Kesey, *One Flew over the Cuckoo's Nest*
Hermann Hesse, *Siddhartha*
Herman Melville, *Billy Budd*
Hannah Green, *I Never Promised You a Rose Garden*
Ernest Hemingway, *The Sun Also Rises*
Somerset Maugham, *The Razor's Edge*
Iris Murdoch, *The Severed Head*
Chaim Potok, *The Chosen*
Elie Wiesel, *Dawn*
Albert Camus, *The Stranger*
Fyodor Dostoyevsky, *Crime and Punishment*
Gertrude Stein, *Three Lives*
James Baldwin, *Another Country*
Leonard Cohen, *The Favorite Game*
John Barth, *The End of the Road*
Sylvia Plath, *The Bell Jar*

ACKNOWLEDGMENTS FOR ILLUSTRATIONS

Author and Publisher gratefully acknowledge the cooperation of the individuals, publications, and organizations listed below. The numbers refer to the pages on which the illustrations appear.

American Cancer Society, 444, 451.
Courtesy, American Museum of Natural History, 155, 188, 191, 199, 335, 362, 380.
Bell Telephone Company, 332.
The Bettman Archive, 22, 121, 359, 367.
Black Star, 54, 249, 251.
Lester Blumberg, 47, 126, 265, 311.
Boston Museum of Fine Arts, 235.
Buffalo Evening News, 42.
Clark University, 99.
Culver Pictures, Inc., 64, 88 (top), 395.
Edmund Engelman, 88 (bottom).
Sol Gordon, 6, 7, 139, 261, 287, 357, 391, 422, 457, 476.
Mike Greenstein, 23 (left and right).
Inglewood Daily News, 244.
Japanese Information Centre (London), 237.
Library of Congress, 103, 326, 377.
Metropolitan Council on Housing, 404.
Mexican National Tourist Council, 180.
Museum of Modern Art, 15.
National Broadcasting Company, 449.
New York City Board of Education, 416.
New York City Convention and Visitors Bureau, 271.
The New Yorker Magazine, 12, 19, 274, 276, 294.
New York Public Library, 182, 195, 202 (Essex Institute Collection), 218.
New York State Mental Hygiene Department (Julian A. Belin), 11, 28, 60, 66, 82, 308, 315, 402.
Pfizer, Inc., 2
J. B. Rhine (Institute for Parapsychology), 223.
Saturday Review, 36, 214, 263, 323, 464, 456, 485.
Kurt Simpson, frontispiece, 278, 290, 356.
Paul Smith, 285.
Smith, Kline, and French Laboratories, 77.
Syracuse University, 23 (center), 145.
United Artists, 479
United Nations Photos, 92, 407, 425.
University Prints, 104, 113, 115.

U.S. Air Force, 389.
U.S. Department of Health, Education and Welfare, 423, 435.
U.S. State Department, 420.
Wide World Photos, 30, 136, 240, 292, 326, 350.
World Health Organization, 212.

Index